Computers, Teachers, Peers

SCIENCE LEARNING PARTNERS

Computers, Teachers, Peers

SCIENCE LEARNING PARTNERS

Marcia C. Linn
Sherry Hsi

Graduate School of Education
University of California, Berkeley

LAWRENCE ERLBAUM ASSOCIATES, PUBLISHERS
2000   Mahwah, New Jersey   London

Lawrence Erlbaum Associates, Inc., Publishers
10 Industrial Avenue
Mahwah, NJ 07430

Cover design by Kathryn Houghtaling Lacey

Library of Congress Cataloging-in-Publication Data

Linn, Marcia C.
Computers, Teachers, Peers—Science Learning Partners /
Marcia C. Linn and Sherry Hsi.

    p. cm.

Includes bibliographical references and index.
ISBN 0-8058-3343-9 (pbk : alk. paper). 1. Science—Study and
teaching (Middle school)—United States—Case studies. 2.
Science—Study and teaching (Secondary)—United
States—Case studies. 4. Group work in education—United
States—Case Studies. I. Hsi, Sherry. II. Title
  LB1585.3 . L56 2000
  507'.1'2 2 21   99-047810
                                           CIP

Books published by Lawrence Erlbaum Associates are printed on
acid-free paper, and their bindings are chosen for strength and du-
rability.

Printed in the United States of America
10 9 8 7 6 5 4 3 2 1

To Doug Kirkpatrick
who inspires and sustains our work

Contents

Preface

Everyone agrees that science education is in a sorry state. Government officials, industry executives, educators, and policymakers, who might angrily attack each other over a variety of economic, social, or political issues, join forces when it comes to complaining that citizens lack understanding of science.

Suggestions for quick fixes in science education come from every conceivable group and take every imaginable form. We have seen group learning, discovery learning, management by objectives, local (or state) control, quality processes, smaller class size, computers, networks, the World Wide Web, teacher certifications, school uniforms, assessments, integrated science, increased science requirements, new standards, and a myriad of other "solutions" offered for improving science understanding.

Although none of these approaches succeeds by itself, our national fascination with immediate rewards fuels a continuous quest for a simple straightforward solution to a problem that is particularly vexing because it is extremely complex.

The reality is that complex problems demand multifaceted solutions. Fixing science education, like curing cancer, managing energy usage, or creating transportation systems, requires designing multiple approaches, supporting local adaptations, and synthesizing experiences into a coherent framework.

Drawing on our experience over the past 15 years with the Computer as Learning Partner (CLP) project, we offer this volume as a guide. Instead of a quick fix, we advocate a process of continuous improvement for science education in which teachers, scientists, educational researchers, technology specialists, curriculum designers, and students work together as partners to improve learning outcomes.

Computers, Teachers, and Peers—Science Learning Partners offers those who share our passion for improving science education an instructional framework, pragmatic pedagogical principles, stories of classroom successes and failures, case studies of student learners, insights from classroom teachers, and designs for powerful computer learning environments. We invite everyone concerned about science education to draw on these tools and adapt them for their own best use.

In the following discussion, we highlight the content of our chapters and the practical features of this volume. Our partnership is described in the Acknowledgments section. The Introduction discusses the issues we address and defines key terms.

Section I: Student Learning Partners

In section I, we introduce Pat, Chris, Lee, and Sasha, four students who follow different paths through the CLP curriculum from eighth grade through high school. In Chapter 1, we characterize the successes and frustrations these students face as they respond to our instruction and wonder whether these students have a firm foundation for future learning.

Section II: Classroom Learning Partners

In section II, we describe how we designed, tested, and refined the CLP curriculum to promote lifelong science learning. We show why we view computers as learning partners rather than as tools, teachers, or laboratory equipment. Our scaffolded knowledge integration framework is discussed, along with the pragmatic pedagogical principles we have derived from our experience with classroom instructional design. The lessons we have learned are supported with specific classroom studies and examples.

Chapters 2 through 5 organize our pragmatic pedagogical principles around the four tenets of scaffolded knowledge integration, as follows:

Chapter 2: Making science accessible—Connecting to what students want to know

Chapter 3: Making thinking visible—Explaining mistakes, animating science processes, and illustrating connections

Chapter 4: Helping students learn from each other—Building respectful, efficient, and effective collaborations in the classroom
Chapter 5: Promoting lifelong science learning—Supporting project work, reflecting on scientific ideas, and revisiting science questions

Section III: Student Learning Partners Revisited

In section III, we examine science learning from the perspective of the students introduced in the case studies. We describe how Pat, Chris, Lee, and Sasha use the features of CLP instruction in high school and what they think about the experience.

In chapter 6, we compare what Pat, Chris, Lee, and Sasha describe as their learning partners with the evidence from their science class performance. We find that they each depend on slightly different features of the curriculum, justifying the varied activities that our classroom studies led us to include. We also explore how these students integrate what they know by asking them to reflect on the nature of scientific endeavor and to apply scientific ideas to novel problems.

In chapter 7, we analyze the foundation that our four students received in the eighth grade and assess their progress as lifelong science learners.

Section IV: New Design Partnerships

In section IV, we discuss how to use our volume to get a head start on designing effective instruction, with special emphasis on making technology a learning partner. We suggest how classroom teachers can join and form partnerships to improve science education. We also offer support for taking the first steps along this path and conclude with a chapter depicting outcomes and opportunities.

In chapter 8, we focus on technology as a learning partner, suggesting models for continuously incorporating the never-ending stream of advances that extend this important frontier and describing new partnerships for interested readers.

In chapter 9, we discuss finding lifelong teaching partners. We analyze the learning partners used by successful science teachers and suggest paths that help both beginning and experienced teachers become lifelong science learners. New partnerships are encouraged to innovate and report their results to others.

In chapter 10, we reflect on science learning partners, discuss the impact of the CLP curriculum, and identify ways to build a larger and more cohesive community for improving science education.

PRACTICAL FEATURES

Computers, Teachers, and Peers—Science Learning Partners offers readers a set of practical tools for learning and instruction.

We provide *case studies* of students to connect our findings with personal science learning and to make the science learning of students in our curriculum visible. We imagine that each reader will identify with some of the struggles our students faced. We expect that each reader also will find, in the successes of our students, experiences that resonate with their own science learning.

We describe the *design studies* we conducted in science classrooms to support our assertions and to model approaches other partnerships might take. We hope that science teachers everywhere will conduct design studies and use the results to improve student learning.

Our *pragmatic pedagogical principles* synthesize the results of our design studies. Designers who use these principles will have a head start because they will be building on our successes. We encourage designers to test these principles and report their findings.

Our *reflections* offer connections across chapters, especially between the case studies and the design studies.

We provide *points to ponder* to encourage reflection on the ideas in each chapter. Partnership groups or classes might use these points as discussion starters or assignments.

Each chapter features *Ask Mr. K*, an interview with the classroom teacher who was a founding member of our partnership and who continues to be our greatest resource and inspiration. In these interviews, Mr. K, adds insights from his own classroom experience.

The *film* of *Computers, Teachers, Peers—Science Learning Partners* illustrates the pedagogical principles described in this volume. The film shows students working with Mr. K to learn science. It answers four questions: Can we make science accessible? Can we make thinking visible? Can students learn from each other? Can students become lifelong learners? The students engage in activities such as real time data collection, graph interpretation, classroom debate, and critique of Internet evidence while studying heat, temperature, light, and energy conversion. CLP partnership members Marcia C. Linn, Sherry Hsi, Doug Kirkpatrick, Philip Bell, Eileen Lewis, Jim Slotta, and others provide commentary. The film also includes perspectives from former CLP students, parents of CLP students, and teachers using CLP activities in other schools.

To supplement the text, we offer the *CLP CD-ROM* and a *web site* (*www.clp.berkeley.edu*) with our complete curriculum, lesson plans, a Quicktime virtual reality visit to the classroom, copies of assessments, copies of interviews, opportunities to join partnerships, and more.

For readers who wish more information, we cite *related readings*, in-cluding work by authors mentioned in each chapter. Additional writ-ings by those who inspired us appear in the bibliography, on our web site, and on the CLP CD-ROM. An annotated bibliography of papers by members of the partnership also appears at the web site and on the CD-ROM.

Acknowledgments

The Computer as Learning Partner (CLP) collaboration began in 1984 at the University of California and continues today as a partnership of classroom teachers, cognitive researchers, natural scientists, technology experts, and middle school students, all of whom contribute ideas and refinements to the curriculum for a semester-long science course.

The partnership had three founding tenets. We wanted students to achieve deep understanding of science, as reflected in their ability to solve complex and somewhat ambiguous everyday problems. We sought to take advantage of the technological tools that scientists regularly use. Finally, we wanted to create instruction that equitably served boys, girls, and students from all cultural groups.

The CLP members came together with mutual respect, diverse ideas about how to meet the needs of a broad range of students, and a willingness to develop a set of beliefs about instruction, learning, and curriculum design. Members have changed in the course of the project, but the core group has persisted—as has our approach to curriculum design and innovation. Newcomers learn from the group. Graduates have gone on to establish new partnerships while remaining connected to CLP.

"It takes a village" to create an effective science curriculum, and we have been fortunate to have wonderful partners, whom we gratefully acknowledge.

Principal investigator: Marcia C. Linn

Postdoctoral scholars: Helen Clark, Yael Freidler, Sherry Hsi, Eileen Lewis, Rafi Nachmias, Jim Slotta, and Nancy Songer

Middle and high school science teachers: Doug Kirkpatrick, Claire Bove, Phil Dauber, Alicia Ruch-Flynn, Suzanna Gogh, Joy Houk, Colette Koretsky, Doug McKenzie, Lawrence Muilenberg, David Murnane, Staci Richards, and Richard Weinland

Scientists: Alice Agogino, John Clement, John Layman, Fred Reif, David Samuel, Judah Schwartz, and Bob Tinker

Pedagogical researchers: Nick Burbules, BatSheva Eylon, and Ellen Mandinach

Graduate student researchers: Philip Bell, Doug Clark, Helen Clark, Alex Cuthbert, Betsy Davis, Brian Foley, Chris Hoadley, Sherry Hsi, Eileen Lewis, Jacquie Madhok, Derek Newell, Dawn Rickey, Nancy Songer, Joanne Stein, Lydia Tien, Mark Thomas, Rich Weinland, and Erika Whitney

Software designers: Judith Stern, Philip Bell, Diana Beltran, Ben Berman, Brian Foley, and Mark Thomas

The CLP partnership formed when Marcia Linn organized a school-university seminar series that brought university faculty members in natural science, computer technology, mathematics, and education together with science and mathematics teachers in local school districts to discuss issues in education. Doug Kirkpatrick, a middle school science teacher known for his innovative work, was invited. Speaker Bob Tinker, a physicist trained at MIT, described real-time data collection software that students could use to investigate questions about heat and temperature using temperature-sensitive probes that displayed results in real time on a graph. As president of the Technical Education Research Centers, located in Cambridge, Massachusetts, Tinker advocated using this hardware and software in science classes everywhere.

University of California physics Professor Fred Reif, an expert on heat and temperature, served as a discussant for Tinker's talk. Reif's work in statistical mechanics is well known in the physics community. Reif is also known for his work in science education, interviewing undergraduate students and designing instruction to address the confusion and difficulties that students have in understanding science concepts. Reif lauded the software as useful for teaching thermal concepts.

After Tinker's presentation, a group of us started meeting before each seminar to discuss ways to improve middle school science. Kirkpatrick, Reif, and other seminar members participated, as did several graduate students, including Joanne Stein and Nancy Songer. Kirkpatrick was excited about computers and enthusiastic about applying for a Wheels for the Mind grant for Apple II computers from Apple Computer, Inc. At the time, he was using a textbook, *Introductory Physical Science*, for some courses as well as hands-on activities that he had developed during National Science Foundation Summer Institutes at the Lawrence Hall of Science. These summer workshops gathered teachers interested in improving science through innovative technologies.

In 1984, the partnership received a National Science Foundation grant and an equipment grant of 16 Apple II computers from Apple Computer, Inc., and we launched the first version of the CLP project in Kirkpatrick's classroom.

In time to start working in the classroom the following fall, Professor John Layman, a physicist and science educator from the University of Maryland, arrived at the Lawrence Hall of Science for a sabbatical. Layman, who had created and used temperature-sensitive probes for high school and college courses, was very enthusiastic about the prospect of implementing this technology in middle school classrooms using personal computers. Layman's background in physics and teacher preparation made him ideal for the partnership. Rafi Nachmias, who had just finished a PhD at Tel Aviv University—working with David Chen to develop software for science instruction in Israel—became a postdoctoral scholar on the project, bringing with him several programs he had developed for Apple II computers.

Everyone in the group agreed that we wanted students to gain a deep, coherent understanding of heat and temperature. We were inspired by Phil Morrison's dictate that "less is more." We believed this meant spending more time on a few topics, but we were not sure how best to allocate the time. The teachers and researchers provided substantial evidence showing that most middle school students viewed science as a collection of facts to memorize and forget.

Initially, students used Apple II computers to collect and display the results of their experiments. Currently, students use the Internet and networked computers, but they still collect data from experiments using real-time technologies that display results in graphs on their screens.

From the beginning, the CLP project has engaged students in experimentation and reflection. Written reflections, often in response to computer-presented prompts, remain an important component of the curriculum.

To implement real-time data collection and experiments about heat and temperature, the original thermodynamics instruction lasted 12 weeks, or most of a semester. With refinement, the instruction became more efficient. Other topics in energy, such as sound and light, were included in the semester-long course.

From the beginning, we designed assessments along with science curriculum activities. Many changes have been made to these assessments, but students always write a short essay in response to this question: "What is the difference between heat and temperature? Give two different examples that illustrate your answer." Using this question, we can compare any semester to any other semester and look at trends in performance over time.

To foster innovation, we continuously conduct design studies, analyze the results, and redesign the instruction. Our design studies involve careful observation and assessment of student learning in the classroom. The partners then discuss how learning outcomes can be improved. The group agrees on curricular changes and research investigations. Then the group studies these new ideas in the classroom. When the results from these investigations are available, the group reflects on them and makes decisions about changes in the curriculum that seem likely to improve student understanding. The findings from the investigations also lead to refinements in the framework guiding this process. This volume describes the refinement process as well as the pragmatic pedagogical principles we use to guide curriculum improvement.

We appreciate the support and encouragement of our program officers at the National Science Foundation: Ray Hannapel, Barbara Lovitts, Andrew Molnar, Mary Budd Rowe, Nora Sabelli, Gerhard Salinger, and Larry Suter. This volume draws on research supported by the National Science Foundation under grants MDR-8954753, MDR-9155744, and MDR-9453861. Any opinions, findings, and conclusions or recommendations expressed in this publication are those of the authors and do not necessarily reflect the views of the National Science Foundation or other collaborators.

This material was partially prepared while Marcia C. Linn was a Fellow at the Center for Advanced Study in the Behavioral Sciences, with financial support provided by the Spencer Foundation.

This work draws on the research activities of the Computer as Learning Partner and Knowledge Integration Environment projects. We appreciate the contributions of all the group members and consultants: Steve Adams, Flavio Azevedo, Philip Bell, Benjamin Berman, Fred Beshears, Doug Clark, Helen Clark, Alex Cuthbert, Elizabeth Davis, Brian Foley, Christopher Hoadley, Freda Husic, Igal Galill, Doug Kirkpatrick, Eileen Lewis, Jacquie Madhok, Lawrence Muilenburg, Dawn Rickey, Patti Schank, Christina Schwarz, Linda Shear, Jim Slotta, Nancy Songer, Judith Stern, Mariko Suzuki, and Mark Thomas.

We especially acknowledge the students whose dissertation research enhanced our understanding of these issues: Philip Bell, Helen Clark, Betsy Davis, Chris Hoadley, Sherry Hsi, Eileen Lewis, and Nancy Songer.

The software design for the Computer as Learning Partner project was initiated and sustained by the following: Judith Stern designed and refined the Electronic Laboratory Notebook; Brian Foley and Eileen Lewis designed HeatBars; Mark Thomas designed the Thermal Model Kit; Rafi Nachmias designed PolyLine; Sherry Hsi and Chris Hoadley designed the Multimedia Forum Kiosk; and programmers Ben Berman, Diana Beltran, and Fred Beshears contributed to the software.

We appreciate insights and comments from project advisors and critical friends: Alice Agogino, John Bell, Carl Berger, Paul Black, John Bransford, Sean Brophy, Ann Brown, John Bruer, Nick Burbules, David Chen, Micki Chi, Michael Clancy, John Clement, Allan Collins, Lyn Corno, Marty Covington, Lee Cronbach, Andries van Dam, Andy diSessa, Danny Edelson, Bat-Sheva Eylon, Charlie Fisher, Barry Fishman, Bernard Gifford, Bob Glaser, Fred Goldberg, Louis Gomez, David Hammer, Paul Horowitz, Yasmin Kafai, Joe Krajcik, Alan Lesgold, Cathy Lewis, Shirley Malcom, Jim Minstrell, Roy Pea, Peter Pirolli, Buddy Peshkin, Mitch Resnick, Bill Rohwer, Brian Reiser, Bill Sandoval, Marlene Scardamalia, Alan Schoenfeld, Elliot Soloway, Richard Snow, Lawrence Snyder, Sid Strauss, Herbert Thier, Robert Tinker, John Thomas, Ron Thornton, Allen Tucker, Jeffrey Ullman, Susan Williams, Barbara White, Richard White, and Bill Wood.

Special thanks go to students who participated in seminars and reviewed the CLP case studies: Thomas Boegel, Lydia Bonner, Doug Clark, Jennifer Esterly, Melonie Hall, and Ilana Horn.

Special appreciation goes to Lee J. Cronbach, who always found time to offer encouragement, suggest a promising alternative, and point to a related line of work. Cronbach exemplifies our goal of knowledge integration.

We thank Vivian Auslander for helping us to communicate our ideas clearly. We greatly appreciate the support, encouragement, and sage advice of Naomi Silverman, our editor at Lawrence Erlbaum Associates, Inc.

Thanks to all who helped with collection of data, analysis of data, production of reports, and creation of graphics: Joel Boardman, Madeline Bocaya, Marguerita Cervantes, Anna Chang, Dawn Davidson, Darragh Perrow, Tiffany Davis, Rob Fallon, Russell Iwanchuk, Christina Kinnison, Benjamin Liwnicz, Seri Nakazawa, Jean Near, Jennifer Palembas, Erica Peck, Mio Sekine, and Liana Seneriches.

We appreciate the support and encouragement of our families and friends. Special thanks to C. Bruce Tarter and Per Peterson for encouraging us to work on this project. Thanks to Frances Cyrog and George Cyrog for continuous support, encouragement, and enthusiasm for lifelong learning. Thanks also to Daniel, Brian, Matthew, Allison, and Shana for giving us insight into how science understanding grows and develops.

About the Authors

MARCIA C. LINN

In 1983, just before starting the Computer as Learning Partner (CLP) project, I was wrapping up a grant from the National Institute of Education (NIE) to examine the cognitive consequences of using instructional technology for science. I had concluded that current models and practices were unlikely to take advantage of the power of this new tool.

To carry out the NIE research, I had established partnerships involving computer scientists, cognitive researchers, undergraduate and precollege programming instructors, and undergraduate and precollege programming students. At the time, everyone was a novice at teaching programming, and those involved were desperate for better solutions. The benefits of these partnerships were already apparent. One stunning discovery, for example, was that some precollege programming teachers had designed innovative techniques that could improve college teaching and that some college programming instructors had implemented extremely creative ideas that both precollege and college instructors could use to improve their courses. As a model, the partnership approach to curriculum development seemed extremely promising.

As part of the NIE research, I also looked at science curriculum materials, especially those for middle school students, and was struck by their similarity to the college texts I had encountered in my student days, by their complexity, and by their difficulty. In fact, I found it quite difficult to understand the sections on heat and temperature in middle school texts. I wondered how many teachers or students, not to mention research scientists, would have trouble with this material. I wanted to create a curriculum that was accessible to a broader range of students.

On the basis of my NIE experience, I knew I would need to assemble a group of individuals, each of whom would contribute something important to this effort. Clearly, I would need natural scientists and classroom teachers. My interest in computer technology motivated me to look for relevant technology. We would need to work with students and understand their ideas clearly so we would not be lulled into complacency by our own growing expertise in the topics we wanted to teach.

As I began this new undertaking, I was also influenced by my earlier experiences with instruction, student learning, and curriculum change. I had become a lifelong science learner primarily, I think, because of my family. As a result of my work with Jean Piaget in Geneva, I had gained a perspective on student learning that resonated with my own experience as a lifelong science learner. Working closely with Bob Karplus at the Lawrence Hall of Science had shown me how creative new ideas for the curriculum could become a part of an exciting science program that changed students' views of science and imparted deep understanding. These ideas were relatively strange in 1984, but they became the basis for my work with the CLP project.

Family influences

My lifelong interest in science learning certainly stems from my growing up as the oldest child in a family enthusiastic about learning. My father, George Cyrog, believed everyone could learn about all aspects of science and engineering and implemented this in his hobby of collecting rocks and minerals. My mother, Frances Cyrog, developed a philosophy for individualized reading instruction, starting when she taught elementary school and continuing as she became the principal of a local elementary school.

My father communicated his enthusiasm for collecting rocks and minerals, for prospecting in the southwestern desert to locate new sources of petrified wood or green agate, for turning the materials we collected into cabochons, and, eventually, for making jewelry.

Our family made regular trips to the deserts in the western United States to collect rocks and minerals and to prospect for new locations. I walked with my father up dry streams looking for evidence of agate, gold (I always hoped), petrified wood, or obsidian. I frequently read these signs correctly and located rocks I wanted to collect (including "fools gold"). Fortunately, my father willingly collected materials that I thought were interesting. Even today, his house and garage are filled with collected materials he plans to cut or polish. I learned to cut some of the stones I collected and make them into cabochons or paperweights. Along the way. I learned to repair things that broke, to understand how machines work, and to nurture plants in the garden. These experiences convinced me that I could learn new scientific material "just in time."

My mother, Frances Cyrog, shaped my beliefs about learning and instruction. She enthusiastically enacted books for me from the time I could understand any word. Even in high school when I was sick, she often sat by my bed and reread some favorite Jane Austen or Charlotte Bronte novel. She enthusiastically described the advantages of having students select their own books, and she carefully worked out the supports they needed to assist them in selecting books they could understand and help them interpret vocabulary they did not immediately recognize.

I was fortunate to have such wonderful "learning partners." My father was a great guide and tutor, believing I could learn anything and encouraging me to explore rather than telling me the answers. He ensured that I had the tools necessary to explore rocks and minerals and prospect in dry streams, including pickaxes, collecting bags, and maps. My mother inspired a love of books and a disposition to reflect on what I read and what I experienced. Later in life, my own children, Matthew and Allison, taught me that learners follow very different paths in their quest for knowledge.

In retrospect, I interpret my experiences learning about minerals, fixing broken machines, and helping children learn to read as a firm foundation that has allowed me to build new understandings in diverse fields. These experiences also have convinced me that students can learn new, complex ideas if these are relevant to their lives and if they have appropriate support and tutoring along the way.

Piagetian influences

In 1967–1968, I was fortunate to work with Jean Piaget and other researchers at the Institute Jean Jacques Rousseau in Geneva, Switzerland. I spent considerable amounts of time in schools interviewing students and learning to conduct interviews using the Piagetian clinical method. These interviews, and many subsequent ones that I conducted in my own research between 1967 and 1984, formed the basis for my perspective on knowledge integration. In Geneva, listening to researchers probe students' ideas motivated me to listen closely to the ideas that students bring to a learning situation. I learned that their ideas about scientific topics are diverse and often well connected.

On the basis of his research, Piaget concluded that students form a well-integrated, robust understanding from a concrete perspective before they move on to a more abstract or formal perspective. He sought to show that this was a universal phenomenon and even suggested that it was likely to occur at a particular age.

My own research involved interviewing large numbers of students about a much more diverse set of questions, including many problems more naturally occurring and personally relevant than those used in Piagetian research. I noticed that students seemed to develop connections in much narrow contexts than those suggested by Piaget. They might have four or five views of a topic such as light, each connected to a different context, such as dark glasses, lighted theaters, or telescopes. I saw the value of the connections the students achieved, but I recognized the need to help them combine and organize these diverse ideas better.

For example, students often come to class with a repertoire of ideas about heat and temperature. They may believe that inasmuch as metal feels cold to the touch compared with wood, metal is far better at keeping objects cold because it can impart cold. Depending on the instructional approach, this idea might be built on or ridiculed. Instruction could help the student distinguish between how something feels ("It feels cold.") and how something insulates ("Does it keep it cold?").

My approach to extending the perspective of Piaget is to help students develop stronger, more coherent ideas by building on and distinguishing among diverse ideas. Other researchers, also starting with Piaget, have sought to identify a taxonomy of student misconceptions, such as the belief that metals keep things cold. Some of these researchers seek to eradicate such ideas from the student's repertoire of ideas. My research observations and discussions with students support the perspective that a more successful plan is to build on students' ideas and to encourage them to expand on these ideas so that they develop broader, more coherent accounts of situations. In this way, instructors promote predictive and useful ideas.

A common intuitive view of instructional design is that the teacher identifies the material to be learned and pours it into the student, tells it to the student, or otherwise inoculates the student with it via a textbook or a lecture. Providing information this way often will fail because students cannot connect it to their own ideas, or they lack the opportunity to reflect and reorganize their ideas to incorporate the new material.

Interviews with students in Geneva and here in the United States have convinced me that it is advantageous to encourage students to explore many different ideas about any given topic, while helping them combine and restructure these ideas so they can form a coherent and comprehensive perspective on the problem. Supporting this process of making conjectures, gaining new information, and reorganizing ideas is the goal of the CLP approach.

Influence of Bob Karplus at the Lawrence Hall of Science

From 1970 through the mid-1980s, working at Berkeley's Lawrence Hall of Science with Bob Karplus, a physicist interested in elementary science instruction, I observed firsthand how an educator could design curriculum materials that support the process of restructuring students' knowledge by building on their ideas.

Karplus had developed the Science Curriculum Improvement Study over a 10-year period at the Lawrence Hall of Science. By the time I came to the Lawrence Hall of Science, the final trials and refinements were under way. I worked to adapt the materials for special student populations, including students who were deaf and blind, and to design classroom assessment materials that would help teachers pay attention to the ideas held by students.

Karplus had a well-established procedure for creating and refining curriculum materials. The group brainstormed ideas, after which project members who were former classroom teachers tried out these ideas in a variety of situations. Students were interviewed to determine their reactions and understanding of the materials presented. Then the group met again to discuss how successful the materials had been and to devise improvements that would address the ideas expressed by the students. The revised materials then were tested more broadly and put in final form.

Although Science Curriculum Improvement Study activities were used in a large number of schools, a combination of costs and logistics reduced their use over time. A commercial version of the Science Curriculum Improvement Study encountered difficulties, not because the students failed to learn science but because the logistics of teaching science using complex materials in elementary schools across the United States proved to be extremely difficult. Nevertheless, many of the creative activities from the Science Curriculum Improvement Study have been refined, revised, and included in more recent programs, and the process of activity design that Karplus pioneered has been adopted by many other projects. Indeed, Karplus's approach to curriculum development and refinement inspired our design for the CLP curriculum.

SHERRY HSI

I came to the CLP project as a graduate student in 1994. At the time, I was working with an eight-university partnership testing out new approaches for improving instruction in engineering education. This partnership involved engineering faculty, schools of education, and a diversity of students and industry partners.

As a designer of engineering software for undergraduate instruction, I began to look more closely at my own experiences as an engineering student: how I had learned and how teachers had taught. I also wondered why software that had incorporated the most innovative technology, such as interactive multimedia, virtual reality, and the Internet, had not changed students' ideas or improved teaching.

At about that time, I learned about the CLP project through Professor Alice Agogino, my master's thesis advisor in mechanical engineering, who was collaborating with Marcia Linn. My interest in improving learning through better design of learning technologies led me to join the CLP partnership. As an engineer, I had been trained to seek design principles, partnerships, and a framework for studying learning and designing for continuous improvement. Working with the CLP partnership seemed a natural extension of this work.

Meeting Mr. K

For an education researcher, the idea of stepping into a classroom full of adolescents can be overwhelming and intimidating. However, when I first visited teacher Douglas Kirkpatrick in the CLP classroom, I wanted to be in middle school again. Kids were working in pairs, talking in a lively manner to each other, writing, and asking each other questions. On some days, walking into Mr. K's class was like going to a science convention: Students were eager to show their house designs and demonstrate how the cardboard house they had built could reflect light in some rooms and not others. They would support their views with the data they had collected from light probes and recorded in the Electronic Laboratory Notebook. Students often walked around to other stations comparing their designs and asking more questions. Mr. K and the other graduate students often did not answer students' questions, but rather answered them with other questions. Computers were important for supporting students in their science experiments, but not without the help of other students and a teacher who roamed the class looking for opportunities to ask pivotal questions and guide students' reasoning. There was something truly special about this environment that enabled students to be collaborative and autonomous learners.

Considering equity

I also admired how skillfully Mr. K included all students as legitimate members of the classroom learning community. Having grown up in a household in which we spoke three languages and two dialects, I was sensitive to how others perceived my background and language abilities, especially when everyone at school spoke English and had English speaking parents.

I was fortunate to have had many wonderful teachers, especially art, music, and math teachers who provided alternate ways to express ideas, promote peer discussion, and make ideas visible to others in the class. These teachers recognized diversity in student backgrounds and their different starting points in learning. They provided many opportunities for sharing multiple viewpoints, listened carefully to student ideas, and promoted mutual respect between peers in class. These practices, I know from my own experience, are invaluable for meeting the needs of all learners.

Creative use of computers

Mr. K's creative use of computers in the classroom contributed to my view that computers have become useful learning partners as computing technology has become more powerful. When I was in elementary school, our school borrowed a Hewlett-Packard 2000 with huge rolls of yellowed paper as the screen. The teacher would take groups of five students down to the main office where we could play "madlibs," number guessing games, or print out large pictures of cartoon characters formed by printing rows and rows of 1's and 0's. I viewed computers as "fun" typewriters.

In high school, I took a formal computer class in which we could write short programs in Fortran to simulate mathematical functions. My view at the time was that computers were pretty rigid and would not help me solve any problems in which I might be interested. (My interests were art, animals, and music at the time.) Besides, computers were mostly machines for boys who liked to play chess.

It was not until I had a summer job at the Lawrence Hall of Science, where computers were able to support graphics, that I began to consider the computer as a learning tool and learning partner. At Lawrence Hall, I witnessed 4-year-olds creating stories and illustrating them by programming in LOGO. I see the same interest now in my own children, who both learned how to use a computer mouse before they could walk. I hope our readers will be inspired by our experience with CLP and use computer technology to make science teaching exciting and robust.

Introduction

For 15 years the Computer as Learning Partner (CLP) project has studied how students learn science and how to make scientific knowledge accessible—and relevant—to them, not only during the time spent in the middle or high school classroom, but also for the rest of their lives.

This book relates our findings and provides an instructional framework that new partnerships can use to get a head start on curriculum design. We advocate forming partnerships for this endeavor because the problems of science education require expertise from many discipline, and because large-scale efforts in schools, districts, and states are needed to make a serious impact. Our partnership included natural scientists, science educators, cognitive psychologists, technologists, and classroom teachers.

STUDENTS AS LIFELONG SCIENCE LEARNERS

We cannot possibly teach students all the science we want them to know in science courses. Instead, we need to prepare students to continue learning science after they complete their classes. The question is how to set them on a path toward lifelong science learning.

Many middle school science texts, for example, attempt to "cover" everything. They feature more than 40 topics such as mechanics, genetics, plate tectonics, electricity, heat, the periodic table, photosynthesis, light, and the circulatory system—one for each week of the school year. This fleeting coverage of topics means that many students memorize, isolate, and forget the science they encounter. Yet groups setting science education standards have difficulty agreeing that any topic should be dropped.

One major goal of our CLP partnership has been to discover how topics can be taught to foster lifelong learning. How can we enable students to learn additional science topics when the need arises?

As we follow Lee, Chris, Pat, and Sasha, four students who studied the CLP from eighth grade through high school, we see the range of paths that individuals might take as they attempt to understand science. We describe how these students respond to class instruction and use computers, teachers, and peers as learning partners. By the end of the eighth grade, all these students have made progress in understanding science, but have not integrated what they know in some areas. Each student has drawn on some aspects of the CLP curriculum but not others.

After analyzing how the curriculum was designed to meet the varied needs of these students, we revisit them in high school to see whether CLP has provided a firm foundation for each student. Chapters 1, 6, and 7 clarify how middle school students integrate their scientific ideas and illustrate how the various aspects of CLP contribute to the process.

Another question our CLP partnership has addressed is how to make science personally relevant. Today, science students often complain that the science they learn in school plays no role in their lives and report little interest in continuing to learn science. They note that objects in motion may well "remain in motion" at school, but they come to rest at home!

To promote lifelong learning, we must offer students courses that provide scientific ideas they can revisit, reuse, and refine after they finish science classes. They need connections between the problems they face in their lives and the material they study in class. Moreover, they need an understanding of the character of science to guide their future learning. The CLP curriculum responds by providing students with problems that are personally relevant and an approach to learning that they can use throughout their lives.

What do we mean by personally relevant problems? Problems that individuals care about can bring science to life and motivate students to carry out lifelong investigations. For example, determining how to survive in the wilderness, discovering how sunglasses work, or distinguishing among nutritional options engage students in the work of science: considering alternatives, gathering evidence, and identifying research questions.

Ultimately, we hope lifelong learners will identify new problems for themselves and continuously revisit the ideas from their science classes. We refer to students who orchestrate their own science learning as *autonomous learners*. In chapter 5, we describe ways that science courses can encourage students to become autonomous. We show how science courses can include projects that permit students to apply what they learn, identify what they need to know, and find answers to their questions.

KNOWLEDGE INTEGRATION—BUILDING ON WHAT STUDENTS KNOW

Our classroom interviews and observations revealed that middle school students come to class with many disparate and often contradictory ideas that apply to the same scientific problem. For example, whereas scientists agree that temperature is a measure of heat and that heat is the amount of energy that a material could conduct, students have a variety of views. When asked to distinguish heat from temperature, students might have four or more answers, each of which they use some of the time. Thus, they might believe that heat and temperature are interchangeable because we say "turn up the heat" and "turn up the temperature" to mean the same thing. They might believe that "heat" is the higher temperature on a thermometer, or they might remember that they can feel heat in a hot wind, thus concluding that heat is a "substance" and temperature, a "measure." In contrast, they might conclude from television coverage of the "heat index" that heat is a "measure," like temperature.

To help students become lifelong science learners, we can encourage them to integrate what they know rather than to hold disparate views such as these.

What do we mean by *knowledge integration*? The term refers to the process of comparing ideas, distinguishing cases, identifying the links and connections among notions, seeking evidence to resolve uncertainty, and sorting out valid relationships. Students who integrate their ideas seek coherence among diverse perspectives and robust ideas that they can apply widely. Knowledge integration drives scientific research, just as it drives student learning. Our goal in promoting lifelong learning is to help students link and connect ideas continuously.

How can we link knowledge integration to personally relevant problems? We forge this link by identifying pragmatic science principles and pivotal cases that apply to the problems students face and then using these principles and pivotal ideas to help synthesize the ideas that students bring to class.

What do we mean by *pragmatic science principles*? Scientific principles are pragmatic when they synthesize a rich set of practical experiences and can be used to deal with new practical problems. To distinguish between heat and temperature, for example, one pragmatic science principle would state: "When only mass differs, the temperature of the larger mass will change more slowly." Students might confirm this principle by observing that a large tureen of soup stays at a higher temperature longer than a small bowl of soup. They could apply this principle to practical questions such as this: "To keep 10 pizzas hot, should we stack the pizza boxes up or spread them out?" or "Why is it better to put a burned hand in a pot of cold water than to wrap it in a wet cloth?" or "Should we turn on the shower or fill the tub with hot water to warm the bathroom?"

What are *pivotal cases*? When students try to integrate what they know but lack sufficient information, they might flounder or even reach a conclusion that scientists would dispute. How can we support and encourage knowledge integration that leads to more robust, cohesive, and scientifically normative thinking? We can identify cases that, when added to the mix of notions students bring to science class, serve to stimulate the process of sorting out diverse ideas. For example, if students believe that "metals feel cold and can impart cold," we can apply this notion to a broader investigation of insulation and conduction by asking them to investigate how metals feel in a hot car.

Instructional designers at all levels wonder which cases will be pivotal. Good choices help students with their struggle to make sense of science. We also worry about what level of analysis of a scientific problem will be most appropriate. For example, the CLP partnership debated whether to describe heat energy at the molecular level, as was typical of middle school texts, or at the level of heat flow. In chapter 2, we describe how and why we selected heat flow over molecular-kinetic theory.

As Richard Feynman (1995) described in his book *Six Easy Pieces*, instructors have the choice of level of analysis for college-level physics:

> what should we teach first? Should we teach the *correct* but unfamiliar law with its strange and difficult conceptual ideas, for example, the theory of relativity, four-dimensional space–time, and so on? Or should we first teach the simple "constant-mass" law, which is only approximate, but does not involve such difficult ideas? The first is more exciting, more wonderful, and more fun, but the second is easier to get at first, and is a first step to a real understanding of the second idea. This point arises again and again in teaching physics.

Much of our CLP partnership effort was devoted to selecting the pivotal cases, the level of analysis for pragmatic science principles, and the personally relevant problems that enable most students to integrate their knowledge successfully. Our conclusions appear throughout the book.

CURRICULUM DESIGN PARTNERSHIPS FOR LIFELONG LEARNING

Today's science curriculum often is "decreed" by standards committees, textbook adoption committees, or curriculum authors. Yet, no fixed set of instructional materials can succeed with all learners, in all settings, for all time. Furthermore, "decreed" materials often lack connections to the personally relevant problems that interest students and lead to lifelong science learning.

Learners, settings, technologies, and science itself all change regularly. In addition, we continuously gain new understanding of effective pedagogy from classroom research, from teachers, and from students.

Instead of instruction based on a decreed curriculum, we need instruction informed by iterative redesign and continuous improvement. We need design teams that bring together individuals with diverse experience who all can contribute to a flexible, responsive curriculum.

We advocate partnerships composed of experts in the science disciplines, classroom instruction, educational technology, pedagogy, school policy, and related topics who come together to design curriculum materials, develop assessment materials, carry out experiments in diverse classrooms, refine the curriculum based on these experiments, report their findings to others, and continue this process.

In chapters 2 through 5, we describe how our partnership designed, tested, and refined the CLP curriculum over 15 years. To illustrate our thinking processes, we discuss both our failures and our successes, and describe the design studies that helped us to select among alternatives. We synthesize our experiences into what we call the "Scaffolded Knowledge Integration" framework and provide some specific guidance in the form of pragmatic pedagogical principles that synthesize our experiences in ways we hope can be applied readily.

Earlier, we described knowledge integration as the process of linking, connecting, distinguishing, sorting out, reorganizing, and reconsidering scientific ideas to achieve coherence. Scaffolded Knowledge Integration refers to an instructional process that enables individual learners to engage regularly, effectively, and continuously in knowledge integration and lifelong learning.

We chose the term "scaffolded" because successful instruction supports students and enables them to integrate their knowledge, just as scaffolding around a building supports construction workers and enables them to improve the building. Scaffolding enables learners to identify their notions about a scientific topic, consider some experiments, make connections to pivotal ideas, and integrate their perspective into a more robust and coherent view.

What are *pragmatic pedagogical principles*? Pedagogical principles are pragmatic when they synthesize a rich set of practical, instructional experiences and can be used to deal with new practical problems. Our pragmatic pedagogical principles are intended to give a head start to new partnerships designing science materials. For example, one pragmatic principle in chapter 3 states: "Explain scientific processes and demonstrate mistakes." This principle is part of making science thinking visible to students.

Too often, instructors only describe an outcome or a solution without explaining how knowledge was integrated to reach it. In our programming research, we discovered that many instructors only described a brilliant correct solution. In calculus or geometry, frequently only the successful proof is provided. As a result, some students conclude that knowledge integration, the process of sorting out alternatives, indicates a lack of skill in science.

When instructors explain the scientific process and demonstrate (and explicate) mistakes, they model knowledge integration and enable students to recognize this process in their own reasoning. Each of the pragmatic pedagogical principles in this volume offers instructors ways to use their own practical experiences to scaffold knowledge integration.

As a key element in our discussion of scaffolded knowledge integration, we focus attention on the ways that computers can help instructors implement each of our pragmatic pedagogical principles. For example, scientific visualization software can help explain a scientific process and demonstrate mistakes. Our HeatBars visualization, described in chapter 3, helps many students by introducing pivotal cases.

SCIENCE TEACHERS AS LIFELONG DESIGNERS

Just as science curricula must be adaptable and responsive, so science teachers must be lifelong designers of science instruction. In chapter 8, we discuss how teachers establish personal plans for fluency in information technology. We also discuss how teachers can form partnerships for designing science curricula such as CLP, for school technology planning, or for educational innovation.

Pedagogical Content Knowledge

Devising personally relevant problems, pivotal cases, or pragmatic scientific principles that build on student ideas goes far beyond the scope of current university science courses. Even teachers with the most comprehensive science background will encounter many topics, questions, and problems they cannot explain.

As we discuss in chapter 9, science teachers regularly develop *pedagogical content knowledge*. By this, we mean knowledge that helps the instructor understand the ideas students bring to science class. Teachers with pedagogical content knowledge of thermal phenomena will understand when students assert that "metals impart cold." For each science topic, teachers continuously face students with novel ideas. The challenge is to develop responses that keep these students engaged in knowledge integration. As we suggest in chapter 9—and support on our web site—one way for teachers to advance pedagogical content knowledge is to band together in electronic communities with others working on the same topic. We also propose a variety of group and individual resources that teachers can use to integrate their knowledge continually.

Local Adaptations Of Instruction

Science teachers can help students become lifelong science learners by adapting instruction to local conditions. For example, students studying energy might investigate local options for home insulation and examine the role of insulation decisions in energy conservation. Students in environmental science might study local ecosystems such as prairies, rain forests, deserts, or urban parks. Often, teachers create local adaptations that could be used by others but lack ways to report their findings. Sometimes, they may face difficult instructional challenges and wish for support from peers or outside experts. We hope to help teachers form partnerships to address these issues.

In chapters 8 and 9, we describe how technological tools and web resources can support partnerships. By taking advantage of a web site to report experiences and locate information, teachers can overcome isolation and build on the experiences of each other.

The CLP film *Computers, Teachers, Peers—Science Learning Partners* available with this volume, shows how the curriculum works in practice. It captures the rich interactions between Mr. K and his students as they carry out CLP activities in a typical eighth-grade classroom.

Looking ahead, we hope this volume will motivate those concerned about the future of science education to learn from our failures, build on our successes, and join together in similar partnerships to improve science learning, science instruction, and science education research.

I

Student Learning Partners

Science students find ways to make computers, teachers, peers, and other features of instruction their learning partners. In this section we discover how four students in the Computer as Learning Partner (CLP) classroom found learning partners to help them understand heat and temperature in eighth-grade science. Interviews and classroom tests from five points during the semester-long course capture these students' responses to the available learning partners.

These four students exemplify the group of 40 that we studied in eighth grade. They were all involved in a one-semester physical science class taught by Doug Kirkpatrick, known here and to his students as Mr. K.

The students, assigned gender-neutral names, are as follows:

Chris: a science conceptualizer, who likes science, rarely speculates, seeks visualizations of science ideas, and embraces science principles as learning partners when they appear in the curriculum

Pat: a science experimenter, who makes numerous conflicting connections between personal experience, and science activities, and uses all the available learning partners

Sasha, a strategizer about science, who wants to succeed in school, likes to memorize, seeks examples as learning partners, and takes advantage of the social context for learning

Lee: a consumer of science, who makes few connections, relies heavily on authorities as learning partners, and feels uncertain when asked for independent judgments

We use case studies to bring science instruction to life. These case studies demonstrate the diversity of responses to the same curriculum that teachers can expect.

What did students study in CLP?

In the CLP physical science class students used computers every school day to learn about concepts of energy. The curriculum evolved on the basis of classroom research discussed in section II. Every semester, Mr. K taught six classes of approximately 32 students each. The 40 case study students were selected randomly from all 12 classes taught during one school year.

Why gender neutral names?

We selected names for our case study students that could be attributed to either a boy or a girl. We found no overall differences between boys and girls in learning trajectories or preference for learning partners. By choosing gender-neutral names we hope to avoid reinforcing stereotypes about the science learning of boys and girls. We know that, inadvertently, readers will connect a gender to any name we choose, but we hope these names will not dictate well-known stereotypes.

How were interviews conducted?

Students were interviewed by trained graduate students who had classroom teaching experience. The interview questions are interspersed in the chapter and also reproduced on the CD-ROM and our web site. We transcribed the interviews and resolved confusing statements by assuming that participants followed standard grammatical practices. To give readers a more coherent view of the interviews, the Appendix provides condensed versions of the complete interview sequence for two students.

1

How Do Students Respond
to Science Instruction?
Four Case Studies

Art Linkletter in the 1950s capitalized on children's conjectures about the natural world in a program entitled Kids Say The Darndest Things. Visit any middle school science class today, and you will hear surprising statements similar to those aired on this program. Over the 15 years we spent in the CLP classroom, we heard students say that wool sweaters warm cokes up, metal cools drinks, holes in blankets let the heat out, and holes in blankets warm you up. Some students explained that just as humans have the temperature of 98.6°, so do objects such as metal platters or wooden chairs have their own temperature. Students drew on colloquial expressions such as "the baby has a temperature so heat the bottle" to distinguish temperature and heat. Weather reports about the "wind chill factor" and the "heat index" convinced students that objects reach different temperatures in the same room.

These intriguing and creative ideas of children motivated us to study how individuals respond to science instruction. Eileen Lewis, for her dissertation research, designed and carried out interviews of students five times during a one-semester eighth-grade class. We followed up with interviews in the tenth and twelfth grades. A few years later, CLP revised these interviews and gathered the results reported here. We interviewed students before instruction and after each major segment of the CLP curriculum (Fig. 1.1). We compared students' reactions to the curriculum and also described their overall progress.

Every parent knows that students have a range of creative, expedient, and often contradictory ideas about the same topic. Students may

Week #	CLP Activity	Topic	Interview #
0	CLP Pretests		Pretest Interview
1 — 2	Process activities: exploding can, Bernoulli tube, black boxes, mysteries	Observation, inference, modeling, nature of science	
3	Biography of scientist	Introduction to MS Works and MacPaint, science role models	
4	PolyLine	Control variables	
5	Interpret graphs	Computer features	
6	Dinosaur activity, dinosaur debate	Scientific evidence	
7 — 8	Probing your surroundings	Thermal equilibrium, introduction to heat flow,	
9	Heat pulser labs	Intrinsic/extrinsic heat, thermal equilibrium	Interview after thermal equilibrium
10 —11	Introduction to electronic laboratory notebook	Surface area, initial temperature	
1 2	Surface area lab critique	Shared criteria, report sharing	Interview after heating and cooling
1 3	Potatoes and cokes lab	Insulation, conduction, simulation, direction of heat flow	
1 4	HeatBars activity Thermal Model Kit	Conduction, continuum line, inquiry	Interview after insulation and conduction
1 5	Chili lab	Mass, simulation	
1 6	Aliens on tour	Inquiry	
—	CLP posttests		Final interview

FIG. 1.1 Curriculum and interview schedule: The one-semester CLP curriculum addresses energy concepts. Student interviews occur after each major topic.

hold one view of a scientific phenomenon at dinner and another while doing homework. Science teachers report similar variations in student views, often motivated by slight changes in the problem conditions.

In this chapter we describe four case studies of students who follow rather different trajectories as they grapple with ideas about heat and temperature. These students were selected to represent the full range of responses. To get a comprehensive picture of science knowledge development, we asked the students about their views of scientists and their career plans.

Students respond individually and idiosyncratically to science instruction. These case studies underscore the advantages of science instruction that offers a rich variety of experiences. Some students learn best from social interactions. Others prefer independent interactions with either print or interactive materials. Many students report that they need to "see" an idea to understand it. Seeing means different things to different students: It can mean seeing the idea demonstrated in an experiment, or seeing the connections between the elements in the idea, or seeing the idea described by several students. Designing instruction involves creating a mix of learning activities so all students can find what we call "learning partners" that help them gain understanding of science. In this volume, we especially consider how computers, teachers, and peers can serve as learning partners.

Science instruction typically offers a mix of learning partners. Students select among these on the basis of their dispositions, views of the nature of science, understandings of themselves as learners, and motivations to succeed. In CLP, students are offered experiments, peer discussions, class discussions, prototypes (our word for a special type of example discussed in chapter 3), pragmatic science principles, visualizations, everyday problems, simulated online problems, and teacher tutoring as learning partners. These case studies show how diverse students respond to the learning partners in CLP. They help us understand the impact of the CLP curriculum both during eighth grade and later as students reflect back on their middle school experiences after they are in high school.

HEAT AND TEMPERATURE TOPICS

In the use of CLP, student ideas about (a) heat energy and temperature, (b) thermal equilibrium, and (c) insulation and conduction are tracked. To discover how students distinguish heat energy and temperature, students are asked to explain situations such as these: heating 1 L of water versus heating 2 L of water, cooling a large and small milkshake, or spilling a drop of hot chocolate and a cup of hot choco-

Questions
Which will heat up faster, 1 or 2 liters of water? What is the main reason for your answer?
What happens when you spill a drop of hot chocolate on the back of your hand? How about a cup of hot chocolate? Explain the difference.
You and your friend are sharing a milk shake. Because you aren't very hungry, you poor a small amount into another cup. What can you say about the heat energy present in each of your glasses of milk shake? Were the milk shakes the same temperature when they are poured into the glasses?
Which will cool faster? A cup of soup or a bowl of soup? Why?

FIG. 1.2   These questions asked students to explain and distinguish between situations involving heat and temperature.

late on their hand (Fig. 1.2). They also are asked to explain how heat and temperature are related and to give examples. Some typical answers appear in Fig. 1.3.

In the study of thermal equilibrium, (Fig. 1.4), students predict the temperature of a range of objects all in the same room or closed space: objects at room temperature in a house, objects met on arrival at a cold ski cabin in the mountains, objects all placed in an oven, and objects in a hot car trunk. In each case, students are asked to predict the temperature of the objects and discuss how the objects feel when touched. Objects that do not regulate their own temperature all reach the temperature of the room. Thus, in a typical home at 23°C, a table, apple, spoon, metal desk, and wooden floor all reach the same temperature, but a child remains warmer. When touched, the metal desk feels colder than the wooden floor. Students are asked to explain this apparent anomaly. To explain, students need to understand insulation and conduction.

In studying insulation and conduction, a phenomenon closely related to thermal equilibrium, students are asked to select containers or wraps to achieve goals such as keeping a soda cold or a picnic casserole warm. They are asked why a Styrofoam container succeeds in keeping drinks cold or casseroles hot, and whether a wool sweater would be better than aluminum foil for keeping a drink cold.

Students see questions about wool as a conundrum. Many believe that wool warms you up, yet empirical tests reveal that wool is a good insulator and far more effective than aluminum foil in keeping a drink cold. Metals confuse students because students often think they can impart cold because at room temperature they feel cold. In fact, the status of metals as conductors explains why they feel cold: They conduct body heat much faster than wool or wood. The difference in rate of conduction is detected when a student touches metal and wood objects at room temperature. As we shall see, evidence contradicting these expectations sometimes is dismissed by students who believe in the cold-producing quality of metal.

We listened to students making sense of scientific phenomena to understand how they respond to science instruction. Students were asked: "You want to keep a soda cold for your school lunch. What is the best thing to wrap it in?" Here are the responses of students before studying heat and temperature in eighth-grade science:

Questions

In general, are heat energy and temperature the same or different?

A student went to the beach and filled a bucket with ocean water. He measured the temperature of the water in the bucket and found it to be 16°C. He also stuck a thermometer into the ocean directly and found the temperature of the water to be 16°C. He concluded that because these two water sources have the same temperature, they contain the same amount of heat energy. What do you think?

Typical Responses

Temperature can be hot or cold. Heat energy is only hot.

Same. The more heat energy, the higher temperature.

Same. If there is less heat energy there will be less temperature.

The same amount of heat energy. They are both water.

Ocean and bucket are the same. They are both from the same source.

The bucket has more heat energy. It feels warmer than the ocean.

Normative Responses

Heat energy is the amount of heat flowing in an object

Different. Something could have more heat energy, but still be the same temperature.

The ocean has more mass than a bucket of water. The ocean has more heat energy.

FIG. 1.3   Student responses to heat and temperature essay question.

You arrived at a ski cabin in the winter and no heat was left on. The room thermometer reads 5 °C. What can you predict about the temperature of the objects in the cabin? (cast iron stove, small pile of wood, a plate, a chair, a fork) Why? What happens when you touch some of these objects in the room?

a. Predict the temperature of these objects 8 hours after they are placed in the same room:

metal plate   Above room temp.____   Room temp.____   Below room temp.____

plastic spoon   Above room temp.____   Room temp.____   Below room temp.____

cold coke   Above room temp.____   Room temp.____   Below room temp.____

cup of hot chocolate Above room temp.____   Room temp.____   Below room temp.____

wooden table   Above room temp.____   Room temp.____   Below room temp.____

Styrofoam bowl   Above room temp.____   Room temp.____   Below room temp.____

apple   Above room temp.____   Room temp.____   Below room temp.____

b. Choose two objects above and give the main reason for your predictions:

Karen was baking cookies for the ECK Club bake sale, and she accidentally left a metal spoon and a wooden spoon in the oven. The oven was on, but it was set at 40°C (slightly warm). The next day she found the spoons and, being curious, she measured their temperatures.

a. What do you predict their temperatures were?

  temperature of metal spoon _____°C   temperature of wooden spoon _____°C

b. What is the **main reason** for your answers?

If a metal plate and a Styrofoam plate are in the same room, what will happen? (check one)

a.   _____   the metal plate will be warmer.
      _____   the styrofoam plate will be warmer.
      _____   both plates will be equally warm.

b. Give the **main reason** for your answer.

FIG. 1.4   These questions asked students
to explain thermal equilibrium.

Chris: "A cold paper towel covered in foil ... maybe the foil would-
                n't let any of the cold get out and not any of the heat get
                in."

Sasha: "Aluminum foil. I can't think of anything else.... The sun-
                shine reflects on it instead of letting it go inside."

Lee: "Tin foil. I don't know. I guess because my mom puts it in
                tin foil and also I think it keeps it cold.... It wraps all the
                coldness in it, the can."

Pat: "A can holder. Some kind of insulation foam stuff ... keeps
             it cold. Foil. It is a conductor, so it keeps it cold."

These students uncertainly articulated a plethora of ideas about
keeping things cold. Many of the students offered several answers and

Question
a. You want to keep a soda cold for your school lunch. What is the best thing to wrap it in?
b. What is the **main reason** for your answer?
c. What evidence do you have to support your answer?

Typical Responses
Foil. It repels the heat
Foil. It doesn't absorb heat.
Foil, because it keeps it air tight.
Foil cause it's a good conductor and stores. the energy inside the soda.
People use aluminum foil to keep a cold coke cold, and use foil to keep a hot potato warm.
In sixth grade, I remember the teacher saying that wool is better for keeping things cold than foil.
Plastic wrap. It keeps the heat outside.
Plastic wrap. It keeps the coldness in.
I see people doing it.
Tin foil is a good insulator and a poor conductor. I've tried it before. It traps the heat.

Normative Responses
Wool, because is a good insulator.
Because it's a good insulator, like for your house, you have the picnic stuff to keep the cold air in for the summer and warm air in for the winter.

FIG. 1.5   A question about insulation and typical responses.

explanations that appear contradictory to observers. The range of responses from students are summarized in Fig. 1.5.

What about keeping a drink warm? Do students hold similar views? Many distinguish keeping a drink cold from keeping a drink warm. When we asked, "Do containers or wraps that keep hot objects hot also help keep cold objects cold?" the students responded as follows:

Sasha: "Foil will keep a soda cold and a dinner hot.... I guess it keeps the heat inside."

Chris: "I really can't predict.... A cold container could keep something cold; a hot container could keep something hot." ... "It could keep the coldness in, but it could probably keep the heat in."

Lee: "Yes. Because all of the air stays trapped in.... I don't know. Something that, like, doesn't let any air in."

Pat: "Foam cup holder. Keeps in cold. I think it keeps it hot too. Like if you put it in a cup it keeps it hot. It just keeps the temperature in."

These students added new ideas when asked about keeping things hot. They used terms such as "heat," "temperature," "conductor," and "air" loosely. They often thought of wraps and containers as barriers. At times they expected objects actively to heat or cool things.

How do students respond to a conundrum? We asked about wool and its role in keeping things hot or cold:

Lee: "Wool is good for keeping things hot, bad for keeping things cold. Well it kind of, it's making things hot because it's warm and then, but then a lot of air can get into it.... People wear wool in clothes to keep warm."

Pat: "I was thinking that wool keeps people hot. I don't know about wrapping a drink in it ... the fibers. I don't know."

Chris: "It's like my sweater. It keeps you hot, but it doesn't keep you cold. When I go skiing if I'm cold it makes me warmer, but if I'm hot it doesn't really help. It lets the heat in."

Sasha: "It keeps things warm and melts. A soda would probably get warmer a lot faster than one you didn't wrap in wool."

In responding to this question, all the students distinguished between keeping things hot and keeping things cold, and they often expected wool actually to heat things up.

Typical Responses	Normative Responses
It's just because at home we always use like aluminum to keep things hot.	Insulators keep hot and cold in like thermoses.
Aluminum foil is airtight and keeps it (the soda) cold.	Aluminum and other metals are good conductors, so they let heat energy flow through them more easily than would plastic.
Because if they (insulators and conductors) are good conductors, they should be able to do both.	
A good conductor is something that attracts heat or cool energy.	

FIG. 1.6   Typical explanations given about insulation,
conduction, and thermal equilibrium.

Students come to science class with a repertoire of models. Often, these models apply to some situations or problems but not to others. Thus, students may distinguish between keeping things hot and keeping things cold when discussing wool, but not when discussing thermoses.

A range of the ideas about insulation and conduction that students bring to science class appear in Fig. 1.6. Most students express many mutually contradictory ideas and remain uncertain, remarking "I don't know," or expressing alternatives.

As we asked more questions, students added more models to their mix of ideas. We illustrate with thermal equilibrium, in which we asked students to predict the temperature of objects in a room and objects in an oven:

Sasha: [Can something be hotter than the room where it is?] "It seems like it should. If metal is a better conductor than wool. So I don't know." [What is an insulator?] "I don't remember; it was in fifth grade."

Chris: [Predicts metal above room temperature, Styrofoam below room temperature] "Well, I always think that something metal will hold heat better, so it would just get hotter. And when I think of a Styrofoam bowl, it just doesn't get hotter."

Lee: If I have something metal in the sun and I, like, touch it, it's, like, really hot."

Pat: [What temperature would a metal or wooden spoon be in
                an 80°C oven?] "I think the wooden spoon would be a little
                warmer than room temperature, than it was, because
                wood is not that ... it is not a conductor. And the metal
                spoon would be hotter ... because it would attract heat."

These students expected metal and wood to behave differently with regard to room temperature. They distinguished metal from wood on the
basis of insulation, conduction, reflection, attraction, and other factors. Students' experience of touching metal, wood, and Styrofoam
informs their answers. The range of models students offer for thermal
equilibrium appears in Fig. 1.7.

What do students say about heat and temperature? We summarize
the range of student ideas in Fig. 1.8.

Judging by this range of models, how do students respond to the CLP
instruction about heat and temperature? Even in these short comments, we see some variations in the approaches of different students
to knowledge integration. Pat made many connections to personal experience. Sasha tried to recall instructed ideas and frequently acknowl-
edged uncertainty. Chris imagined objects as having properties such as
holding heat, and Lee described actions of objects and people. We selected these students to illustrate approaches to knowledge integration that we observed in interviews and classroom performance. How
did these students' ideas develop?

Typical Responses	Normative Responses
Metals get hotter, but not glass. They'd be as hot as the oven.	Metals feel colder than plastic, but they are at the same temperature.
The soda is still cold and it hasn't let all the cold out. Cup of hot chocolate will be above room temperature. In a cold room, plates would be colder.	All the items would be the same because they can all pick up heat energy like the Coke, or these can lose heat energy like the hot chocolate.
A metal stove lets cold flow through it faster than the wood pile.	When you put something in a warmer or colder area, then it will slowly or faster reach that temperature.
	The objects can't get any hotter than the temperature of the oven.

FIG. 1.7.   Students provided a range of responses on the
thermal equilibrium assessment questions.

Typical Responses
Heat is like if you had a cup of water and you threw in a little bit of salt then the salt would like dissociate and disperse throughout the water until it's evenly distributed.
Metals are good conductors because of the particles inside it.
Foam keeps the cold inside instead of letting it out.
Insulators blocks heat from coming in. Wool lets energy flow in, but not out.
Metal lets heat energy flow through it easily.
Larger substance will cool faster than a smaller substance, but the small one will reach room temperature first.
A larger bowl of oatmeal will let out more air quickly. It has more surface area.
The smaller bowl. It has less heat energy to lose.
Cold energy flows out of cold things. Styrofoam doesn't allow heat energy to flow through it all at.
My hand can feel the coldness flowing. Cold energy and heat energy flow the same.
Normative Responses
Smaller things will cool faster than larger things when they are made from the same stuff.
Heat flows from higher temperatures to lower temperatures.

FIG. 1.8   Typical student ideas about heat flow.

PAT: ADDING MODELS REGULARLY

Pat: "The cold Coke and hot chocolate, it will eventually get the same because the heat or the cold goes out into the air. And the temperature of the air would just make it room temperature. If you just [put] a block of like ice in there; … it is more cold than the air and the room would get cold."

Interviewer: *"So these things [metal and wood block] have been here overnight about 12 hours. Now touch both of them. Does one feel colder than the other?"*

Pat: "Yeah, the metal one.... Well, obviously it is. But I don't know why. Maybe because it is in a draft."

Interviewer: *"Why do you say 'obviously it is'?"*

Pat: "Well because, you just proved it. This one is colder than this one."

Interviewer: *"This one [metal] feels colder than this one [wood], but say we measure their temperatures, put a thermometer here and here and they are both the same. Is that possible?"*

Pat: "Well, yeah. A conductor.... But I don't know how."

Students like Pat both frustrate and help science teachers. They help teachers by describing the reasons behind ideas and by seeking to explain scientific phenomena. For example, Pat accepted the suggestion that the metal block is colder because it feels colder, offering the explanation that "it is in a draft." Yet, when the interviewer suggested that the two blocks might register the same temperature on a thermometer, Pat tried to connect the new information to something relevant, saying, "Well, yeah, a conductor.... " Moreover, Pat tried to acknowledge these seemingly contradictory ideas, remarking, "But I don't know why."

Teachers are frustrated by a student like Pat who holds many contradictory ideas about heat, temperature, insulation, conduction, thermal equilibrium, and related topics. Rather than resolving these apparent inconsistencies the student keeps adding new observations and explanations to the mix of ideas. Where does this all end? Does a student like Pat eventually rely on a coherent set of ideas?

After Thermal Equilibrium Instruction

After several weeks of investigating thermal equilibrium using the CLP curriculum, Pat responded to more questions. Asked about objects in a cold ski cabin or a hot car trunk, Pat used the class thermal equilibrium idea, saying, "They are here for a week: they would heat up or cool down to the room temperature." To explain why objects such as wood and metal that measure the same temperature feel differently, Pat offered many models: "They would still be the same because of the heat energy in your hand.... Because your hand is hot, it [metal] feels cold at first and then your hand warms it up.... " "Because it's a conductor [metal], it's taking the energy from the ... 'cause your hand's hotter." [*Than what?*] "Than the room temperature.... I don't know. "It just feels cold 'cause it's metal." [*Wood?*] "It's not a conductor, so it just, like stays the same. It just is, I guess. [Heat comes] from the sun and air." [*Paper?*] "It has little holes in it, kind of like cloth, and it would let the heat come through."

Pat added new ideas when unable to explain complex phenomena, noting that cloth, paper, and other materials have "holes" and conjecturing that holes let heat in. Pat also asked the interviewer to clarify saying: "Well is it [the metal] hotter than your hand?" Realizing that metal is sometimes warmer and sometimes colder than one's hand helped Pat understand the distinction between how an object feels and its temperature. We refer to these informative examples as *pivotal cases*.

After Rate of Heating and Cooling Instruction

Instruction emphasizing rate of heating and cooling encouraged Pat to focus on materials. Pat embellished the "holes" model while thinking about materials. In thinking about heating, cooling, and thermal equilibrium, Pat continued to distinguish among materials, adding conjectures about materials, such as asbestos introduced in the interview. The idea about holes and fibers remained appealing: "Uhm, I don't know. Maybe there's, like, fibers, and there's, like, little tiny, tiny holes in wood and so maybe the heat energy goes through your hand and it doesn't stay in it or something."

Pat carried this idea about holes forward to explain foil as an insulator. Asked how to keep a frozen candy bar cold for lunch, Pat suggested wrapping it in aluminum foil:

> The metal [would keep it colder] ... because I think the metal would keep the cold in, uhm, better than something like, uhm, a napkin or something, because there's little holes in the fiber and the heat energy would come into the candy bar and then make it heat up. They [metals] hold the temperature in and they don't have little holes in it, and so the heat energy won't go out of, or go in at all.

To explain, Pat added more connections saying, "It's like thermoses are metal on the inside, or they have metal in them." Pat struggled to integrate ideas (like energy goes), experiences (like the way metal feels), properties of materials (like holes), and concepts (like insulation). At the end of this interview, however, Pat held a repertoire of conflicting ideas.

After Insulation and Conduction Instruction

Class experiments, discussions, and activities about insulation and conduction enabled Pat to reflect on why metal and wood feel differently, whether they are in an air-conditioned room or in a hot oven. Pat then offered paragraph-long answers to questions, making visible the process of knowledge integration and the challenges of these questions.

For example, Pat struggled to connect class experiments, comments from Mr. K (the classroom teacher), class concepts (insulation, conduction, heat flow), and class discussion to the novel situation of touching metal and wood heated in a drying oven. Pat reflected on using findings for cold things to explain findings for hot things saying, "Well Mr. K said it was something like if your skin, when you touch it, it's like the heat energy is going between your hand and the object then. Well, actually he said this about a cold thing. I don't know about a hot thing, but I guess it could be mostly the same. But it's like, your hand changes to the temperature really fast so it feels cold at first and then it feels hotter."

When asked about metal and wood objects in the interview room, Pat built on the class discussion and observed that after a short time, the metal no longer feels cold: "If I touch like this side of it, then in like another minute I have to move to this side to see if it was still cold, you know. Because it would feel hot, it wouldn't feel cold that long."

Going back to the oven, Pat applied similar logic to warm wood. Pat expected wood to feel cooler than metal and also expected the sensation to dissipate quickly just like wood: "The wood would just it wouldn't. It would feel warm if you held it, and it would feel warm but not really hot. I mean you could hold it, and it'd be warm, but it wouldn't burn you unless it was in a really hot oven. And then it would feel warm for a minute or two and then it would go back to normal or to your hand."

Pat summarized ideas about the oven, distinguishing the limits of understanding, connecting to class ideas such as the class laboratory experiment on keeping potatoes hot ("the potato thing") and noting information from the teacher: "I think they're the same temperature, but it's just because this one is, the metal is a conductor. I'm not really sure what that means, but that's what he [Mr. K] said. I don't know, but when we did the potato thing [class experiment], the Styrofoam held the heat in more, so the wood probably would too. But I wouldn't really wrap a potato in wood, but I don't know. It doesn't seem like the same thing."

When prompted to design a container to keep something hot, Pat revisited the "holes" idea, incorporating a discussion with Mr. K, the classroom teacher: "Well it's like they're little holes in it so it like traps air, and it's like a blanket and all the little holes, and so it keeps it warm, but before I thought it would let heat energy out, with all the little holes, but I guess not. But Mr. K said the aluminum and the air were the same, if you just didn't wrap it in anything and wrapped it in aluminum, so I think Styrofoam or you could use wool, but I don't know if you would want it with food."

Here Pat could not distinguish the air trapped in the holes from the air surrounding the object. Pat remained perplexed about aluminum and air. Pat reported that heat energy "wants to go out" of aluminum, "to the air," and then tried to explain how this happens inasmuch as aluminum lacks holes: "I know. I don't get it. The heat energy would want to go to the aluminum because it attracts the heat energy. And it would just stay there and not be in whatever you had in there."

These examples illustrate the reason why teachers enjoy students such as Pat. Such students can explain both connections and gaps in science reasoning. They keep wondering about the gaps, welcoming ideas that might fill them, seeking connections among idea, and continuing to add intriguing ideas. These intriguing ideas also can frustrate science teachers.

Mr. K responded to Pat's questions about holes and insulation with a good analogy to thermal blankets. He explained that the holes trap air. Pat added Mr. K's idea, but also decided that aluminum "attracts" heat energy. Pat could not make sense of the air. Mr. K explained that aluminum as a wrap is no better than leaving an object out in the air. Pat could not distinguish between air trapped around the object and air moving about a room.

After Eighth Grade Instruction

At the final eighth-grade interview, Pat continued to express a repertoire of ideas, drawing on class experiments ("the one with Styrofoam was the best"), a variety of concepts ("it's like a barrier so that heat energy won't come in"), class principles ("temperature of the surround"), class discussions, and personal ideas ("air goes into these holes"). Pat was able to apply the repertoire to novel situations, asserting, for example, that "Copper ... well, it doesn't have all these holes."

In the interview, to distinguish heat energy and temperature, Pat connected an impressive array of ideas: " Well, temperature is like the measure of how hot or cold it is. And something could have high temperature but low heat energy because it's small, like a drop doesn't have much heat energy, but it could be really really hot.... The Chili experiment [class experiment on mass and cooling]. One was bigger, one was smaller. They both had the same temperature, and the bigger one had more heat energy because there was more space for it.... Heat energy will flow from the hot thing to the cold thing. But I guess it will still have heat energy in it, so I am not really sure."

Pat reflected on these connections, locating gaps and explaining, "I am not really sure." For Pat, this uncertainty motivated a search for additional information. Pat had elaborated a model of heat transfer that relies on holes to explain why materials differ. Pat projected several different roles for air, including "holes of air," "room temperature of air," and air as the "surround" of objects. Pat answered "I don't know" when these models conflicted.

This conflict led Pat to speculate in a remarkably productive way: "Because the wood has those little holes of air in it. And they just ... it feels different. It's not a conductor [holes].... They keep air ... I'm not really sure. The air does something. Makes it not go in. Makes heat energy not go."

Here, Pat invented a way to connect the situation in which holes filled with air slow heat flow to the situation where air hastens the flow of heat. All during eighth grade, Pat had struggled to combine ideas about heat and temperature while regularly adding new ideas. Here in the final interview, Pat added yet another idea, wondering whether air-filled holes can make "heat energy not go."

Students like Pat followed the *experimenter* pattern. Experimenters continuously experiment with new ideas. They make progress in science while seeking a wide range of connections for their ideas. They have confidence to cross traditional school boundaries and connect science to other topics, to personal experiences, and to interesting observations. Pat's focus on holes illustrates this tendency. Holes are interesting. A hole the size of a door will not insulate, yet holes in thermal blankets or sweaters might.

At the end of eighth grade, Mr. K predicted that Pat would continue to reflect on the ideas from science class. Would Pat settle on a coherent view or continue to hold conflicting ideas? We wondered how Pat would connect the "little holes of air" in high school interviews? We return to Pat in chapters 6 and 7.

LEE: RECALLING AND DISTINGUISHING CLASS IDEAS

Like Pat, Lee started eighth grade with diverse, contradictory ideas saying, "Foil ... wraps all the coldness in it, the can. In a thermos all the air stays trapped in. Wool is making things hot because it's warm. I've tried it [Styrofoam] with cold. Because there's Styrofoam coolers." Lee also responded with "I don't know" when probed for more explanations.

After Thermal Equilibrium Instruction

After several weeks studying thermal equilibrium, Lee distinguished the temperature of objects in a room, a cold ski cabin, and a hot car trunk. In a hot car trunk, Lee said metal would be hotter than wood because "metal gets hotter." For a room, Lee repeated class information, saying, "It would feel colder, but it's the same temperature of the room, but your body temperature's hotter." Lee expressed uncertainty when asked to apply the class model to both wood and metal: "I don't know, because when you touch it, it's harder for this to go to the temperature of your body, and it's easier for wood because it's solid ... because it's ... I don't know. It's going slowly here, it goes—no ... I don't know if it goes slower or quicker."

When the interviewer encouraged Lee to apply this reasoning to the hot car trunk, Lee was equally unsure saying, "I don't know" after each answer.

Lee recalled the primary message from class: Objects come to room temperature unless they have a heat source. However, Lee was uncertain about why things feel warmer or colder than each other. Lee said "I don't know" to signify a lack of ideas rather than use the same expression to indicate indecision among a plethora of ideas as we saw for Pat.

After Rate of Heating and Cooling Instruction

Lee studied rate of heating and cooling, successfully recalling the primary message when asked about large and small beakers of water. Lee remembered that "the bigger one" will have more heat energy because "it's bigger." When asked to comment on objects in a 150°C drying oven, Lee predicted that they would have the same temperature, applying the class model to a new context. Lee was vague about the reason why the metal might feel hotter than the other items, saying, "Probably, well they'll probably all be 150, but when you touch the metal, it'll feel hot ... The heat energy. Something about the heat energy."

Lee had a pattern of describing the results of experiments without understanding the reasons for them. When asked about science learning, Lee revealed good insight into these patterns: "When he's [Mr. K] explaining something and he demonstrates it with different things.... Like when we touched the mouse pad and then we touched the leg to the desk, the mouse pad seemed warmer, but they were both the same temperature, ... but I don't really understand it."

Interestingly, Lee reported liking graphs better than principles and examples in the CLP curriculum saying, "The graph is easier to understand." This was consistent with Lee's propensity to watch rather than make connections. We discuss how the CLP real-time graphs contribute to student understanding in chapter 3.

Before instruction on insulation and conduction, Lee answers "I don't know" to every question. We wondered how Lee would respond to the next interview, after several weeks of instruction on insulation and conduction.

After Insulation and Conduction Instruction

After instruction on insulation and conduction, Lee accurately labeled materials, saying, "Metal is a conductor and wood is a good insulator." Lee reluctantly connected these labels to any sort of explanation, ultimately settling on uncertainty and personal observations: "I don't know ... I don't know. It [conductor] keeps things hot." Lee continued to advocate aluminum foil for keeping a drink cold even while categorizing foil as a conductor.

Lee struggled to sort these ideas out. When asked to design a container to keep things hot or cold, Lee said, "Um, maybe metal ... because, I don't know ... I don't know. I don't know. It just seems better.... If it was outside, the metal would get hotter if the sun was on it, but it would feel hotter than plastic.... Yeah, if metal was on the outside, and you had like cold stuff on the inside, then it would probably melt faster."

Lee connected to an experimental finding, saying "I don't know. On the experiment we did, metal was a good conductor.... The one with the [heat] bars."

Lee struggled to recall class observations or experiments and seemed frustrated when asked to justify choices with explanations. Lee consistently paid attention to vocabulary and observations, but neglected reasons, explanations, or connections. We wondered what this would mean for Lee's final interview.

After Eighth Grade Instruction

After instruction, Lee recalled many isolated terms and results from class, showing progress from pretest to posttest. For example, Lee identified insulators and conductors, recalled results of class experiments (e.g., "we wrapped a Coke in aluminum foil but it didn't keep it any colder than a Coke wrapped in nothing"), recalled class ideas (e.g., "a cup and pot of boiling water" can be the same temperature, but the amount of it can be different, so one holds more heat energy than the other"), and reported comments from the teacher (e.g., "Mr. K said that would happen, ... but I don't know why").

Lee connected these ideas sparingly and instead reverted to personal practices or observations to explain why things work. For example, Lee claimed that foil keeps things hot, saying, "If my mom made, stuffing or something, she'd put ... aluminum foil." This observation allowed Lee to distinguish between materials that keep things hot (aluminum, wool) and those that keep things cold (Styrofoam). To explain how aluminum, wool, and Styrofoam work, Lee often mentioned air, saying that an insulator, "keeps the cold air in," and aluminum "keeps the heat energy in." Lee resisted giving these explanations, constantly adding, "I don't know."

Lee also added experimental results sparingly. For example, Lee added the experimental class result that foil does not keep drinks cold. But at the pretest, Lee relied on parental practices to explain how aluminum keeps things cold, saying, "My mom puts it in foil so I think it keeps it cold." To reconcile contradictions, Lee distinguished the range of applicability of observations. In the final interview, Lee distinguished heating from cooling, asserting that results from the class experiment about keeping drinks cold did not apply to keeping casseroles warm. Rather than making connections across situations that seem similar to scientists, Lee distinguished situations to minimize the need to reinterpret observations.

Lee's strategy yielded modest success in science class. When students distinguish situations rather than integrating ideas, instructors may be misled. Instructors may either assume that students such as Lee are illogical or dismiss one of the answers as invalid.

Students like Lee follow the *consumer* pattern because they "consume" ideas but do not connect one idea to another. They just add all the ideas they encounter in science and recall some but not others. When confronted with a contradiction, these students tend to isolate the various situations (e.g., heating and cooling). They rarely seek connections. We look more closely at this pattern when we revisit Lee in high school.

In Lee's case, we wonder whether the CLP experience provided a firm enough foundation for further reflections. In the high school interviews, we hoped that Lee would have sought more connections among these ideas. We hoped that the CLP experience had encouraged Lee to keep reflecting and perhaps to gather more precise observational information in the future. We worried that this propensity to distinguish situations rather than look for connections would impede science learning.

CHRIS: CONCEPTUALIZING SCIENCE

Chris looked for abstractions and principles to explain the whole range
of science situations, in contrast to Lee who distinguished one situation from another. Chris expected science class to provide syntheses
and principles. Rather than generating intriguing conjectures such as
Pat's ideas about holes, Chris looked for general observations.

Chris started eighth grade with complex observations about containers that might have heaters or coolers or even both. When asked
about unfamiliar topics such as distinguishing heat and temperature,
Chris "guessed" an answer, offered some connections, and appeared to
wait for the interviewer (such as a teacher) to provide an explanation.
Chris reported that objects should have the temperature that they feel
and also concluded that most things will reach room temperature.
Chris kept options open by saying "I would have to test it out" or "I
never tried it." During the first interview, Chris tried to make sense of
the group of questions. By the end of the pretest interview, when asked
to explain whether a hot bath or a warm bath will cool first, Chris answered that warm water will cool to room temperature last. Chris re-
considered this idea in the posttest interview, saying, "I don't know....
Now that I think about it more, maybe it would take the hot water longer.... Hot water would take longer because it's got more heat, and the
warm water is closer to room temperature so it won't take as long....
It'll just get there last ... because it's got more to cool down."

After Thermal Equilibrium Instruction

After instruction in thermal equilibrium, Chris concluded that objects
in a room will all reach the same temperature, remarking: "because it
is in the room and it just gets the temperature of the room." To explain
this view, Chris remarked, "The experiments [changed my mind]."
Chris elaborated: "We took the temperature of different things in the
room, and they are all pretty much the same except living things."

Chris was asked to explain why objects feel differently at room temperature. Chris said, "We learned this. The metal is a better conductor.
Because when you put your hand on it and it is transferring your heat
energy to the metal and it feels colder because your hand can go
through. But with wood, the heat energy doesn't go well through it, so
you just feel more or less warmth of your hand." [Then elaborating]
"Yeah. And it travels through the metal faster so you ... feel it on your
hand. It can't go through wood. It can't move very well, so you feel less

in your hand." Here Chris eagerly incorporated class principles and connected them to novel situations.

Before learning class principles, Chris observed carefully and stuck to agreed-on information. When explaining heat and temperature, Chris mentioned several possible views, saying that large and small milkshakes "have heat energy, but they have more cold energy," whereas a cup of boiling water has more heat energy than a teaspoon of boiling water "because there is more of it." When asked to generalize from the water to the milkshakes to explain whether either of the milkshakes have more heat energy, Chris reported "I don't know," rather than express contradiction. Chris instead responded with established information, asserting that the milkshakes "are the same temperature."

After Rate of Heating and Cooling Instruction

After instruction in rate of heating and cooling, Chris offered many accounts of heat flow, and neglected cold energy or cold flow. Chris said that plastic insulates cold items because it "doesn't let the heat energy come in," and glass conducts because "it doesn't hold any of the heat in. It lets it come out."

Chris distinguished rate of heat flow for metal and wood spoons placed in boiling water or in ice water saying, "In boiling water, the metal would feel hotter.... The heat energy goes up. It won't be as hot as that in the water, but it would still be almost as hot." [Does heat energy go up the wooden spoon?] "It probably won't go up as fast."

Concerning ice water, when the interviewer asked "Where did the heat energy go?" Chris responded, "To the ice." When asked to clarify the role of metal and wood spoons Chris said, "Maybe because the heat didn't go as fast [in wood] ... to the water. I mean it goes slower."

Chris accurately described learning from class explanations and experiments at this point in the interview, saying class helps: "Because Mr. K explains it well. And the experiments prove what he said." [*The principles*?] "Yeah, it is just stating what we concluded from the discussions and the experiments." [*The prototypes*?] "Principles are better because they state it out."

Chris coupled explanations and experiments, expecting science class to offer principles buttressed by evidence. Chris looked for explanations, whereas some students seemed content with just hands-on experiments. When pushed to say what helped the most in learning science, Chris responded, "The experiment and the principle."

After Insulation and Conduction Instruction

After instruction on insulation and conduction, Chris connected rate of heat flow with effectiveness of insulation, saying for example, "Because it is a better insulator, the warm air doesn't go through it as fast as through the metal, and so it is keeping whatever the coldness it has in the wood instead of letting the heat go through ... on the outside."

To explore this relationship, Chris distinguished heat flow at the surface from heat flow at the center of wood placed in an oven. Chris explained that, at first, when wood is placed in an oven, the inside would be "cooler," but the outside would be the temperature of the oven, "because they were in the same surroundings." Here Chris extended a class idea to explain the process of heating up, using the vocabulary of a class principle. When asked about the temperature of the wood after 2 days in the oven, Chris said it "would be the same temperature" as the oven.

Chris also connected the heat flow idea to the way metal and wood feel when touched, saying for wood: "Well, it flows slower, so my hand wouldn't feel it as fast as it did with the metal."

In this interview, as in the first interview, Chris vividly illustrated making connections among ideas. Asked to create a container to keep hot things hot and cold things cold, Chris started by returning to the heat energy and cold energy idea mentioned earlier, saying that an insulator doesn't keep things cold: "Well, it might. Wool just keeps the heat energy in from going outside, but with the cold energy, it might stay cold for a while. It'll keep it warm. But the wool would just keep the heat energy in."

Chris went on to make a series of connections and distinctions about a Styrofoam container, eventually reflecting about putting ice cream in this container: Chris: "It might stay frozen for a while, but I think it might start to melt if there wasn't ice in with it, because there is nothing to keep it cold. [*Will the heat energy from the outside go in?*] "I don't know because if it can't get out of there, it might have trouble going in. So maybe it would stay cold."

Eventually Chris concluded that the container might work for keeping things hot or cold, saying, "Because it doesn't matter which way it goes through the material."

After Eighth Grade Instruction

By the posttest, Chris connected all the principles from class and spontaneously made comprehensive, coherent arguments involving other principles. For example, Chris explained that the ocean would have to be cooler than a bucket of water to have the same amount of heat energy: "The ocean [has more heat energy] ... because there is so much more of it. And if it can't have the same amount of heat energy because then it wouldn't be as hot—I mean hot as the water in the bucket, ... so it needs more heat energy to heat it up. If you just took the ocean at a cold temperature and the water in the bucket at a cold temperature, the one in the bucket will heat up faster."

Here and elsewhere Chris used proportional reasoning to explain heat flow and temperature change. Chris supported responses using class principles, often quoted verbatim, and class experiments. For example, Chris said the HeatBar's lab showed, "that metal conducts heat faster" than wood. Chris also asserted, "Heat flows from hotter objects to cooler objects." Furthermore, Chris said, "Well, if it is hot, the heat energy flows through it to the cooler surround. And if it's cold, then hotter surround will flow through it to whatever you are trying to keep cold."

Chris both identified and resolved uncertainties. When Chris could not explain a connection we hear "I don't know" or "I guessed" rather than a conjecture. In almost every case, Chris came to the next interview with a new model to explain the uncertainty previously expressed. Chris returned to uncertainties displaying a disposition to resolve problems.

In the posttest interview Chris also expressed a repertoire of ideas including some that conflicted with class models. For example, Chris concluded that big ice cubes have more heat energy than small ice cubes when they melt, generalizing the idea that bigger means more and neglecting the direction of heat flow principle. Chris also asserted that heat flows quite slowly in an oven, concluding that a metal and wooden spoon might reach thermal equilibrium only after eight hours.

Teachers enjoy students such as Chris who seek principles or abstractions and apply them widely. A class that offered principles without the experimental proof Chris preferred would probably motivate Chris to seek the proof elsewhere. Chris often said, "I would try it out." Chris's desire for proof might make some teachers uneasy. Chris could easily ask a question beyond the expertise of the teacher. Luckily, Chris would enjoy researching the answer.

Chris looked for coherent connections among ideas and drew on principles learned in other classes, illustrating the process of cumulative learning. We saw this process at work in several interviews in which Chris reasoned about connections and restructured ideas. We expected Chris to continue this process and looked forward to interviewing Chris in high school.

Chris applied class ideas to related situations but rarely added new contexts to discussions with the interviewer. Whereas other students often mentioned home insulation, parental practices, or ski experiences, Chris mentioned a few contexts in the first interview, but sought evidence from class investigations in later interviews. Chris expected science class to provide ideas that apply widely and promoted class ideas over personal observations.

Students like Chris follow the *conceptualizer pattern* because they seek principles that account for a wide range of phenomena. These students often dismiss details and even practical problems, focusing on ideas that apply widely. Conceptualizers learn science the way many scientists recall learning science. As discussed in chapter 2, this approach pays off in many ways, but also can lead to an integrated understanding that does not connect to important, practical problems.

We explore how Chris applied science knowledge to new courses and to complex, everyday problems in high school interviews reported in chapters 6 and 7.

SASHA: GETTING THE RIGHT ANSWERS

Sasha started eighth grade with most of the same ideas as the other students. Sasha, like Chris, resisted speculation, saying, "I can't think of anything else." Unlike Chris, who wanted to try out possibilities and admitted guessing, Sasha tried to recall information from earlier science classes, saying, "I don't remember. It was in fifth grade, … ", "It was in fifth grade, and it was at my old school where we switched around with six different teachers, and each taught a different thing." Sasha preferred right answers to explanations, saying, "I don't know. It's just the different materials," and "No, well, I don't understand why it's like that, but I know that it's like that."

Sasha wanted to answer questions correctly and often directly asked the interviewer for help. For example, Sasha asked "Can you explain to me what heat energy is?"

After Thermal Equilibrium Instruction

After studying thermal equilibrium, Sasha predicted that objects will all come to room temperature and that they will feel differently:

Sasha: "They would all be 5 degrees. They would probably feel different because [of the] different material, but they'd still be 5 degrees."

Sasha predicted which will feel colder, categorizing them as conductors, and resisted further explanation: "The wood would feel colder. Oh—wait a minute. Well, if it was 5 degrees, the stove would feel colder because metal is kind of a better conductor than wood, and the wood would feel like this wood here, I mean. You touch the metal here and the wood here, and they feel different. [*Why?*] I don't know. I am not sure. It holds the cold, and I guess I am not exactly sure. I don't know."

Similarly, Sasha described how metal and wood feel but was not sure why. Sasha, holding pieces of wood and metal said, "My hand is giving out heat energy and it is traveling out into the metal." *Wood?* "It is doing the same thing, but it doesn't really feel like it's heating up. I am not sure why."

To help resolve inconsistencies in explanations, Sasha, asked whether heat energy can be cold too, said, "Well, heat energy doesn't necessarily—it can be cold too, can't it?… Okay, wait a minute. Heat energy from your hand … .I don't know why this—I think it's a little bit of both. But, I mean, some of the cold is going into your hand and some of the heat from your hand is going into it." Sasha added ideas in response to interview questions, but also continued to say, "I don't know." For Sasha, "I don't know" signaled a disinterest in thinking more about the question.

After Rate of Heat Flow Instruction

After studying rate of heat flow, Sasha made accurate predictions about thermal equilibrium and explained that objects feel hotter in an oven when they are conductors. Sasha used the interviewers' question to construct a reason and changed responses in the direction inferred by the interviewers' question:

Sasha: "Uhm, because I guess the heat flows and it doesn't travel out of it as much."

Interviewer: *"Does heat energy flow out of a conductor easily or not?"*

Sasha: "Yeah. I am changing my answer. It flows faster into your hand. They is why it feels hotter."

When discussing insulation and conduction, Sasha also recognized a contradiction but did not resolve it. Sasha said, "The heat energy from the outside doesn't travel very well. The heat energy from the candy bar doesn't go to the outside." [*Is foil a conductor or an insulator?*] "I guess it is a conductor. But it contradicts the last answer. So I am not sure."

In addition, Sasha distinguished how insulators work for hot and cold things, similar to the approach taken by Lee. Sasha said, "Foil. It keeps the cold in. You wouldn't put wool around it because it—I am not sure. Wool keeps hot things hot and foil keeps cold things cold."

In response to other questions, Sasha sometimes relied on class experiments and at other times on experience, giving equal weight to each. For example, about keeping a Coke cold, Sasha said, "Where I know that from is when you have a can of Coke or something in foil to keep it cold for your lunch." About keeping a potato warm, Sasha cited a class experiment saying, "The Styrofoam worked better" than foil.

Sasha reported, "I am getting an A" in class. "I like it because there is no homework, ... but I don't like it because I am not interested in what we are doing.... I like computers.... I'm learning stuff. I know enough, but I'll forget it by next year." In addition, Sasha reported that "The principles help because that is the basic thing they are trying to tell you." Sasha views principles as "telling" rather than "explaining," consistent with making accurate predictions but not offering consistent or frequent explanations.

Sasha offered some explanations to satisfy the interviewer but changed them readily. Sasha took a minimalist stance toward science learning, seeking right answers and sufficient information to earn an "A." Sasha elicited answers from the interviewer when asked to explain scientific ideas.

After Insulation and Conduction Instruction

Sasha continued the pattern of eliciting explanations from the interviewer after studying insulation and conduction. For example, when the interviewer asked about direction of heat flow from one's hand to hot items, Sasha responded "Uhm, this is what I always get confused on. From the hot air temperature to the lower temperature, so I guess it would be from me to the bowl. Right? Or, I don't know." The interviewer prompted Sasha to give appropriate answers. Sasha responded but did not connect the elicited information, instead summarizing with "I don't know." This led the interviewer to remark, "You said it a while ago," and, eventually, to summarize with a more connected explanation than Sasha had given, saying, "Right, so that's why it'd feel different. It's just based on that they're insulators or conductors."

Sasha quickly picked up expected responses and established rapport with the interviewer. Subtle interviewer clues such as repeated questions led Sasha to change answers: "Heat energy would still pass through the Styrofoam or whatever, but it would still be fairly cold depending on how long you leave it there. But if you put it in the metal container, then it would go, the heat. You know what I mean don't you?" The interviewer asked, "*If it was in a metal container, what would happen?*" and Sasha said, The heat energy would go through it faster ... from the cold, whatever you put in it that was cold, what did you say?" [*What direction is heat energy flowing?*]" "From the outside in."

Sasha and the interviewer shared the goal of getting the right answers. Sasha, however, preferred memorizing science over understanding science, whereas the interviewer and classroom teachers pushed for understanding. Sasha, when asked to give reasons said, "It's, I can't give reasons for my answers. That's the way it is; that's kind of the way we learned it. I don't know."

Sasha returned to experience in fifth grade to justify the pattern of responses, saying, "In my fifth-grade class we had this science class that dealt with all this stuff and that was the last time for a long time that I've had this kind of stuff.... I've kind of forgot about it.... I did think that aluminum would keep a Coke cold because I saw everybody do that, but, uhm, I don't really think about it that much."

After Eighth Grade Instruction

On the posttest and final interview Sasha offered a repertoire of explanations for thermal phenomena that earned a high grade. Sasha could distinguish insulators and conductors on the basis of how fast heat flows through them. Sasha said about an insulator: "It stops the heat.... Well, it doesn't stop it, but it slows down the heat flow and the flow of heat energy." When asked about a cold soda wrapped in Styrofoam or wool, Sasha responded: "The cold stays in—wait a minute—the Styrofoam keeps the hot air from going in."

Sasha initially gave a barrier model, "It stops the heat," then changed to a flow model, "It slows down the heat flow," and stuck with it, even on complex questions. Sasha rephrased answers to incorporate class ideas, explaining, "Well, I was thinking that heat energy went from cold to hot, instead of hot to cold. But it's hot to cold."

Sasha responded to interviewer suggestions by adding models. For example, the interviewer suggested that cold energy might exist and Sasha responded, "Yeah. I guess." However, for insulation and conduction, Sasha offered consistent, connected explanations.

Sasha had rich connections between insulation, conduction, and heat flow, but weaker connections to other topics such as thermal equilibrium. Sasha often deferred to a class authority such as a teacher, or peer rather than test ideas against each other, consistent with the pat-

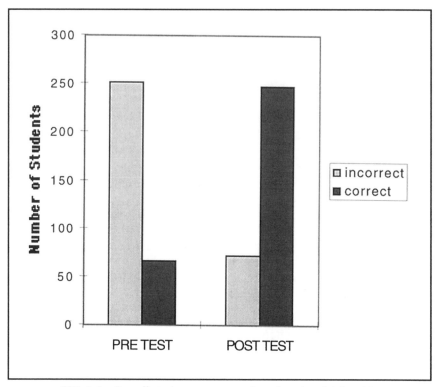

FIG. 1.9   Overall student responses about keeping drink cold.

tern of seeking correct answers. This approach clearly had succeeded for Sasha in the past and also had worked for the CLP class on the topics for which knowledge integration is fragile. For example, Sasha could not explain the connections between rate of heating and cooling and thermal equilibrium but could describe the outcome. When asked whether the metal spoon gets hotter than the oven Sasha said, "Well, they are the same, and I don't know why it wouldn't be hotter, but it doesn't."

Similarly, Sasha gave an answer that sounded reasonable to distinguish heat energy and temperature: "Heat energy is more the amount, temperature is how hot or cold." Sasha's explanation shows that this knowledge is fragile: "I didn't know what to put for that. I know they are different, ... but I forgot what he said, and he said an example too, but I can't remember it."

In fact, Sasha's answer was memorized but not understood. Sasha viewed science learning as giving answers not reasons, saying, "It's not that I don't understand.... I can't give reasons for my answer."

Sasha fit the "good student" model, gathering ideas from class, memorizing, seeking explanations from the teachers and other authorities such as the interviewers, and reporting these ideas on tests. For insulation and conduction, Sasha began to link and connect ideas and give explanations as a result of the CLP curriculum. In distinguishing heat and temperature or linking thermal equilibrium to rate of heat flow, Sasha succeeded without giving reasons, saying "I don't know" when asked to explain. By the end of the semester, Sasha reported, "I am not interested in what we are doing.... I know enough but I will forget it by next year." We wondered whether Sasha's prediction would come true. We wondered how Sasha would interact with subsequent interviewers.

Students like Sasha follow the strategizer pattern because they adopt strategies that lead to school success. Strategizers pay attention to course requirements and try to minimize the effort needed for success. Strategizers often sound like "cognitive economists," thinking about topics only if they contribute to course success. Sasha relied on memorization rather than knowledge integration to meet this goal. Strategizers use the social context of school effectively, determining what the teacher expected and what other students are doing to succeed. Courses that require knowledge integration provide special challenges to strategizers. Would Sasha resort to knowledge integration in high school or find another way to succeed? We discuss Sasha's path in chapters 6 and 7.

REFLECTIONS

Pat, Sasha, Lee, and Chris started eighth grade with similar ideas about thermal phenomena. They all participated in the same instruction and emerged from it with some common predictions about phenomena but considerable variability in their explanations. We distinguish these four patterns of science learning and refer to the students, respectively, as consumers, strategizers, experimenters, and conceptualizers. We wonder whether these patterns will persist or whether students will adopt new patterns for knowledge integration as they mature.

Thermal Equilibrium

All four students completed the CLP curriculum with the view that objects in a room become the temperature of the room. Other CLP students, however, did not endorse this view at the end of the class. For example, another student who, like Sasha, fit the strategizer category, said in the final interview that things will not come to equilibrium.

This student, whom we call Fran, predicted that a wooden and metal spoon in a 40 degree oven would be 45 and 42 degrees, respectively. When asked to explain Fran said, "I think they'd both get above the oven temperature. I think the metal spoon would get way above the temperature. I wasn't sure about how far above, but I just kind of guessed. I knew the wooden spoon would be little bit hotter than the oven" To explain, Fran said, "The metal spoon, it's a good conductor, and heat energy flows through it quickly, so it's able to be hotter than the oven would be."

On the eighth-grade posttest, Fran also predicted that objects in a room would have different temperatures. A cold Coke would be warmer than room temperature; a hot chocolate would be warmer than room temperature; and an apple would be colder than room temperature. Students like Fran who question thermal equilibrium place more emphasis on insulation and conduction than on thermal equilibrium, assuming that objects will not reach thermal equilibrium under all circumstances, especially in hot ovens or refrigerators.

To explain thermal equilibrium the four students give disparate answers and often several answers. They reported uncertainties saying, "I don't know why." They cited authorities saying, "Mr. K said so." They cited class experiments such as Probing your Surroundings. They made analogies from a room to an oven or a car trunk, perhaps based on a prototype, referring to personal experience with objects that feel differently.

Overall, on the pretest, 10% of the students endorsed thermal equilibrium, and on the posttest one half the students predicted that objects would reach thermal equilibrium. Those who did not predict thermal equilibrium often were equally certain of their views. Would the students continue to think about these issues?

Insulation and Conduction

All four students, after studying CLP, concluded that aluminum might be poor for keeping things such as drinks cold for lunch. Lee and Sasha asserted that aluminum might keep things hot. Some CLP students dismissed the class experiment and persisted with a belief in aluminum as good for keeping a drink cold. A student, categorized as a consumer like Lee, said on the posttest interview that aluminum foil can keep drinks cold. This student nicknamed Dale, explained, "If you use aluminum or something, then it go ... uhm it would probably make the—keep the cold thing cold and by the cold energy, it holds the cold energy in the, in the soda or whatever." Dale imputed to aluminum both an active role and a passive role. Dale deemed aluminum capable of keeping things cold.

Other students offered many varied explanations. For example, they assigned aluminum the role of an insulator, cited class experiments, described the results from the HeatBars visualizations, and cited Mr. K. They also stated class principles connected to a class prototype and described personal examples such as, "My mother does it."

Overall, more students believed that aluminum was a conductor, but most had difficulty with materials such as pottery. As Fig. 1.9 shows, most students gained understanding of how to keep a drink cold. Did we provide a foundation for future investigations?

Heat and Temperature

Students mostly started the CLP class with many possible distinctions and similarities between heat and temperature. During the semester they all considered the heat flow model offered in class and a variety of other options. By the end of eighth grade most students held several views with varied amounts of certainty. They often employed several ideas to explain why objects feel different temperatures at thermal equilibrium, why some materials are better insulators, and why heat differs from temperature. Viewing heat as active, insulators as barriers to heat flow, temperature (rather than heat) as flowing, and heat equivalent to temperature remained possibilities for virtually every student. At the same time, some students consistently expressed class ideas in response to class tests. We wondered how students would sort these ideas out as they continued to study science in high school.

Learning Partners

Students in our interviews relied on a wide range of learning partners in the CLP class. They mentioned discussions with Mr. K, class experiments, class principles, class prototypes, everyday examples, class discussions, peer suggestions, the heat flow model, and the class projects. They both scorned and praised constructing graphs, using computers, writing principles, discussing with peers, responding to questions asked by Mr. K, and doing simulated experiments.

All the students reported uncertainty in responding to class experiences. Lee regularly answered, "I don't know." When asked to explain, Lee seemed content to avoid connections in this class and probably in other classes as well. For Lee, "I don't know" meant "I don't have a clue." Lee was not motivated to find connections and seemed to believe that this minimalist approach is sufficient. Pat said, "I don't know" to mean "I can't decide" among the alternatives. Pat made many connections, continuously thinking about the topics in the class but rarely resolving inconsistencies. Sasha said "I don't know" defiantly, resisting entreaties to give explanations. Like Lee, Sasha looked for few connections. Unlike Lee, Sasha put energy into memorizing class ideas. Chris used "I don't know" sparingly. For Chris, "I don't know" meant "I haven't studied that yet." Chris had a clear idea of what constitutes an answer in science class and waited for principles rather than speculating.

Uncertainty motivates many learners to seek further information, reflect, or review to find a resolution. In science, both Chris and Pat responded to uncertainty by reflecting and seeking explanations. In contrast, Lee and Sasha seemed satisfied with their science performance and resisted further thinking. We describe Lee and Sasha as cognitive economists because they allocate cognitive activity to science with caution. They think about science only as much as absolutely necessary.

Lee, Sasha, Pat, and Chris each find a few CLP cases pivotal. By pivotal cases we mean concepts or models that motivate rethinking or reorganizing of scientific views. Each student drew on a somewhat different pivotal case to sort out thermal equilibrium and insulation. For Pat, understanding rate of heat flow proved pivotal. Pat could explain both thermal equilibrium and the reason why metals feel cold at room temperature with this idea. For Chris, measuring the temperatures of objects at room temperature proved pivotal. Chris used this experiment to organize information about how objects feel. For Sasha, the notion that a hand can be colder than objects in a hot car and warmer than objects in a room proved pivotal. Lee used the fact that metal feels hot in a car and cold in a room as pivotal cases to distinguish heating from cooling. For Lee, this meant that metal can heat things that are hot and cool things that are cool. We discuss how we designed CLP to provide pivotal cases for diverse learners in chapter 2.

A combination of pivotal cases and uncertainty about science phenomena can motivate students to integrate their ideas. These students all find pivotal cases in CLP, all express uncertainty, and each rely on distinct curriculum features as learning partners. These features motivate unique patterns of knowledge integration in each student. We describe how CLP features influence knowledge integration in the next section of this volume (chapters 2, 3, 4, and 5).

All CLP students start with similar ideas but take quite different paths. The CLP curriculum supports students who follow a wide range of paths by offering many learning partners. Students who find principles compelling and wish to organize their knowledge around them identify with that feature. Those who like visualizing report that HeatBars and the graph visualizations help them to understand heat and temperature. Individuals who avoid abstractions still find the prototypes and experiments helpful. Students who memorize have rich explanations to remember. All students report difficulty with the heat and temperature concepts and face challenges in integrating their ideas.

Students differ substantially with regard to their propensity, or disposition, to make connections between ideas. Chris and Pat looked for connections. Pat searched for connections constantly in a wide range of ideas. Chris focused on connections emphasized in class, using the CLP principles. Both Sasha and Lee made few connections, behaving like cognitive economists. The CLP curriculum offered something to each of these students. In chapters 6 and 7, we discuss how CLP contributes to high school science learning.

ASK MR. K

How does the CLP course work?

Each year I meet 180 to 190 new kids in each of the two semesters. These students will have completed a full 3 years of science by the time they finish eighth grade. The first year, sixth grade, the focus is on earth and environmental sciences. The seventh grade has a life science emphasis. In one semester of grade 8, the focus is on physical science, and in the other semester, physiology is presented from a medical perspective.

A typical 56-minute period would start with 5 to 10 minutes of review before setting the question for the current investigation. The students would then be doing either real-time or simulated laboratory investigations. Approximately two thirds of the labs are real-time. Frequently, during the period I bring the students back together to focus on an interesting finding or questions from one of the groups.

At the completion of each activity, we take some time to share results and come to some consensus on what appropriate principles apply and how those principles relate to real-life experiences. The opportunity to move from one pair of students to another, becoming the third partner by asking questions and probing understanding, has been one of many positive outcomes of the curriculum for me as a teacher.

What were some course goals you adopted for the CLP course?

I made sure students understood links between different activities and could link one activity to the next. As teachers, we see the connections between different activities in the curriculum because we are so familiar with them. Students do not often make these connections, so we teachers need to make them more visible.

Learning by reflection is another goal. Kids ask me, "Mr. K, is this the right answer." I say, "Let's think about this some more. How does this connect to something you see in everyday life?" I try to get students to reflect on the data they collect and link this to what they did before.

Why does "depth of coverage" make more sense than covering many more topics in science class?

When students look at things in depth, they can begin to reflect, make connections, and understand. When a curriculum just provides snippets of information, and kids end up learning only facts, they resort to memorizing. For me, depth of coverage also means making science important to kids' lives.

I majored in geology back in college. Just recently, a graduate student here developed an activity for kids looking at earthquakes, teaching about P waves and S waves. I admit I had to go back and review those definitions myself! The original activity asks: Which kind of wave is more damaging in an earthquakes? Kids here live in an earthquake center. We often hear about "epicenter" and "Richter scales." Kids also have parents who work in high-rise buildings. It might make more sense instead to ask: Are my parents safe? How did their building fare during the earthquake? When kids start to ask these questions, they then ask: How do I find the epicenter of the earthquake when the station detects a wave? Kids learn how to read and interpret a graph, look at the amplitude, and apply what is relevant to themselves.

The answer to the original question about S and P waves is that S does more damage, but when you stop and think about this, students are not that concerned which kind of wave did the damage, nor likely to remember the answer. I didn't!

To answer the new question, "Are my parents safe in an earthquake?" students read the newspaper, find out about the Richter scale, use graphs of P and S waves versus time, and put together the graphs that scientists use to find the epicenter of the earthquake or the place where their parents' building lies on the map. This they may well remember the next time we have an earthquake.

Some educators believe you can teach the "process of science" without the "content?" What's your opinion on this?

You know, looking back, I adopted the idea of making sure that kids think in depth about a particular content area while also trying to build on student ideas. This did not happen right away. To some extent, before CLP, I tried to teach the process of science more than the content because the movement at the time was to teach inquiry and observation in science. Students could do observations, but they still did not understand the science. It is important to realize that you cannot teach process without content. Lots of teachers I see are still trying but it does not work.

How did you learn to guide student investigations?

I belonged to a group called the Northern California Committee on Problem Solving in Science (NCCOPSIS) that helped improve my teaching. In the late 1960s, early 1970s, educators thought if they could just do some good inquiry, they did not need a curriculum or any context for that inquiry. This group of teachers met regularly. I developed some skills and I thought more deeply about how to teach using the inquiry approach.

Soon afterward I joined this research group at Berkeley. Students doing research would videotape my teaching. It forced me to watch myself teach and see how I was doing. I think it is important to establish trust so you can invite others—researcher, teachers, or visitors—into your classroom or vice versa. This helps open the dialogue about teaching. The observers helped me reflect on my practices.

POINTS TO PONDER

- Interview some students and probe their understanding of a science concept. Identify the ideas and concepts they have.
- Think about some students you know. Describe how these students resemble the students described in this chapter.
- Analyze the questions used for the student interviews. Design additional questions that might have helped clarify knowledge integration.
- Pick one of the students in this chapter. Describe how this student would perform in a course you have taught.
- Analyze the learning patterns in this chapter. Describe a pattern that seems to be missing.
- Describe the learning partners students encounter in a course you have taught.
- Watch the CLP film *Computers, Teachers, Peers—Science Learning Partners*. Write down your impressions and reactions to the film. Comment on how the CLP approach compares to your own.

RELATED READINGS

Bruner, J. S. (1960). *The process of education*. Cambridge, MA: Harvard University Press.

diSessa, A. (1988). Knowledge in pieces. In G. Forman & P. Pufall (Ed.), *Constructivism in the computer age* (pp. 49–70). Hillsdale, NJ: Lawrence Erlbaum Associates.

Erickson, G. L. (1979). Children's conceptions of heat and temperature. *Science Education, 63*(2), 221–230.

Inhelder, B, & Piaget, J. (1958). *The growth of logical thinking from childhood to adolescence; an essay on the construction of formal operational structures*. New York: Basic Books.

Lewis, E. L. (1996). Conceptual change among middle school students studying elementary thermodynamics. *Journal of Science Education and Technology, 5*(1), 3–31.

Wiser, M. (1988). The differentiation of heat and temperature: History of science and novice–expert shift. In S. Strauss (Ed.), *Ontogeny, phylogeny, and historical development*. Norwood, NJ: Ablex Publishing Corporation.

Classroom Learning Partners

The Computer as Learning Partner (CLP) curriculum offers a rich set of learning partners for students. Students including, Pat, Lee, Sasha, and Chris described in chapter 1, find learning partners among the features of CLP during eighth grade that help them integrate their understanding.

The CLP partnership designed this range of classroom learning partners over a 15-year period. Each semester, the partnership implemented a new version of the instruction and carried out design studies to assess progress. *Design studies* are investigations conducted in science classrooms with the goal of gathering valid evidence to inform redesign of the instruction. On the basis of results from the design studies, the partnership then redesigned the instruction to help more students engage in knowledge integration. In the next four chapters we describe this process of iterative refinement and the instructional framework that resulted from it.

Each chapter in this section describes design studies that led to one tenet of our scaffolded knowledge integration framework. In each chapter we synthesize findings from the design studies in three or four pragmatic pedagogical principles about instruction.

Pragmatic pedagogical principles summarize our empirical work in ways that guide practical decision making. They capture the partnership experience in developing the CLP project and they reflect the insights of a partnership of experts in classroom teaching, natural science, pedagogy, technology, and related disciplines. These principles have been tested by teachers, curriculum developers, and others creating new instructional materials.

Chapters 2 through 5 organize our pragmatic pedagogical principles around the four tenets of scaffolded knowledge integration, as follows:

Chapter 2: Making science accessible: Connecting to what students want to know

Encourage students to build on their scientific ideas as they develop more and more powerful and useful pragmatic scientific principles.

Encourage students to investigate personally relevant problems and revisit their science ideas regularly.

Scaffold science activities so students participate in the inquiry process.

Chapter 3: Making thinking visible: Explaining mistakes, animating science processes, and illustrating connections

Model the scientific process of considering alternative explanations and diagnosing mistakes.

Scaffold students to explain their ideas.

Provide multiple, visual representations from varied media.

Chapter 4: Helping students learn from each other: Building respectful, efficient, and effective collaborations in the classroom

Encourage students to listen and learn from each other.

Design social activities to promote productive and respectful interactions.

Scaffold groups to design criteria and standards.

Employ multiple social activity structures.

Chapter 5: Promoting lifelong science learning: Supporting project work, reflecting on scientific ideas, and revisiting science questions

Engage students in reflecting on their own scientific ideas and on their own progress in understanding science.

Engage students as critics of diverse scientific information.

Engage students in varied, sustained science project experiences. Establish a generalizable inquiry process suitable for diverse science projects.

Classroom teachers, software designers, policymakers, textbook authors, and others who use the scaffolded knowledge integration framework and follow the pragmatic pedagogical principles have a head start on promoting knowledge integration. We encourage all instructional designers to join us in helping all students become lifelong science learners.

How did CLP conduct design studies?

Each semester Mr. K taught six classes of about 32 eighth-grade students. The design studies involved comparisons among different versions of the curriculum taught to half of the classes. Student teachers regularly took over several classes. We were able to investigate the impact of these new teachers using the CLP curriculum. We also studied use of the CLP curriculum in other schools.

2

Making Science Accessible to All Students

Learning science for me is most like ... memorizing words and facts, playing around with science experiments, stuff like beakers, plants, bugs or water and total confusion ... because you have to be very into science to know what it is all about.

Memorizing facts is easier than understanding. I don't always understand, and teachers kind of move on and I am a little slower than some people. In science I am not that good at it. But, memorizing facts is easier for me because I can refer back to it in my mind.

Memorizing, well in some ways it's better because usually the facts are all right, but when you learn complicated stuff it just gets you all confused, and you can't think.

It's too complicated for students our age to learn everything about science and remember them.

I am not really into science: it seems too complicated and boring.

Providing accessible ideas to enable knowledge integration contributed to the success of the CLP project as shown in the chapter 1 case studies. We wanted students to integrate all their ideas about heat and temperature rather than isolate science class ideas from everyday experiences or memorize science information. Students who memorize or isolate science ideas often forget. The CLP approach encouraged students to continue the process of linking and connecting ideas throughout their lives.

We designed instruction to help students connect science information to personally relevant problems so they could regularly revisit and improve their understanding. We created instruction to provide a firm foundation for future science learning. We encouraged students to sort out their ideas, identify conundrums, and seek a coherent view of science topics.

Often, students neglect knowledge integration because science ideas do not connect to what they already know. As seen in chapter 1, Pat connected personal experiences to CLP ideas, Lee connected observed practices of parents to CLP ideas, Chris found that CLP principles helped to organize personal experiences, and Sasha linked experimental results with personal practices. How do we create instruction to help students engage in knowledge integration? In this chapter we describe three pragmatic pedagogical principles to guide instructional design and illustrate them with CLP examples. We also warrant these principles with information about the impact of CLP on students.

To make science accessible, our first pragmatic pedagogical principle states: *Encourage students to build on their scientific ideas as they develop more and more powerful and useful pragmatic scientific principles.* To implement this pedagogical principle, instruction must engage, respect, and build on the full range of student ideas in the instructed discipline.

This principle is controversial. Much of science instruction ignores what students already know, offering a coherent but often inaccessible alternative. Some science instruction goes further, aiming to eradicate ideas deemed unhelpful. As we illustrate, our approach assumes that students' ideas grow out of personal experience and have useful aspects that stimulate further thinking. To build on student ideas we seek to identify pivotal cases that, when added to the mix of existing ideas, inspire students to reflect and restructure their views. In addition, as we discuss in chapter 5, building on student ideas sets in motion a lifelong process of knowledge integration that students regularly revisit, improving their views.

This first principle also emphasizes synthesizing science ideas into a few big, coherent, accessible, and useful views. We call these "pragmatic scientific principles," and we make sure they apply to practical experiences. These principles are pragmatic because they summarize scientific ideas and can be used for personally relevant problems.

We find that when students start with pragmatic scientific principles, they can make links and connections and not just memorize. Pragmatic scientific principles allow students to practice using science ideas, preparing them for learning more abstract or mathematical ideas in advanced courses. Identifying big and accessible ideas for each group of learners can be difficult. Ideally, students will embrace the big ideas we introduce and practice applying them in new situations. After some practice, we hope students will spontaneously seek more and more sophisticated big ideas. We think of students as progressively adding more parsimonious and abstract ideas as they integrate their understanding of science.

Instruction that makes science accessible and reusable depends on the problems students will need to solve in the future. In scientific work, theorists, engineers, and citizens encounter quite different problems and need scientific principles suited to these individual problems. Mathematical models of mechanics may help theorists, but not engineers designing airplanes. Qualitative models may help citizens but not theorists. Because all students will need to solve practical, everyday problems such as keeping warm on a cold day or packing a picnic so food does not spoil, we advocate starting with pragmatic scientific principles. We also advocate alerting students to the multiple levels of analysis they will encounter in future classes. Determining the best level of instruction for students in every science class requires research on what students know, creative analysis of student views to identify useful abstractions, and careful analysis of student thinking to devise pragmatic scientific principles. We illustrate this process for thermodynamics here and demonstrate its use with other topics in later chapters.

Our second pragmatic pedagogical principle states: *Encourage students to investigate personally relevant problems, and revisit their science ideas regularly.* Scientific investigation often seems disconnected from student lives because the problems students investigate do not link to personal experience. Students often complain that they never learn anything in science class that they can reuse in their lives. For example, in our early work, students asked why they needed to know about the heating or cooling of water in beakers. Teachers often point out that students do projects mindlessly or "play" instead of "learn" from experiments. We advocate channeling active, hands-on learning so students reuse the results and methods of experimentation in their lives. We also encourage students to compare the methods they use for personal problems to the methods they learn in science, sorting out the most valid approaches. Using personally relevant problems makes experiments accessible to students.

Our third pragmatic pedagogical principle speaks to lifelong learning: *Scaffold science activities so students participate in the inquiry process.* By inquiry we refer to the full range of methods scientists use for gathering evidence and to the reasoning that links evidence to principles. We need to prepare students to revisit science ideas at home, in the workplace, and in future educational settings. To make inquiry accessible, we start by scaffolding or supporting learners while encouraging them to plan their own inquiry autonomously.

We see students, citizens, and scientists as struggling regularly to conduct scientific inquiry. For example, citizens often select home insulation, choose among vitamin supplements, or determine how to vote on a proposed waste facility. Preparing students so they can get valid answers to their scientific problems means helping them learn to gather information, evaluate evidence, select methods for investigation, weigh alternatives, and recognize when they need more information. Both citizens and researchers find this challenging and difficult.

In CLP we prepare students to carry out a research program no matter what they choose as a career. Knowing that scientists have valid methods, and even knowing general descriptions of scientific methods is not sufficient for many problems faced by citizens. The general version of a method such as design experiments that control variables often fails in practice because students may be unaware of the variables. For example, should investigations control the amount of light in the room to research a chemical reaction? Also, students may encounter variables they cannot control such as past smoking behavior or exposure to chicken pox. Students need to establish an inquiry process they can use throughout their lives. We hope students eventually will use this process autonomously as we discuss in chapter 5. To warrant these pragmatic principles, we describe design studies our partnership conducted. To illustrate these principles, we provide evidence from the many versions of the CLP curriculum that this partnership created, tested, and reformulated.

PARTNERSHIP DESIGN STUDIES: EVIDENCE OF SUCCESS

Historically, science curriculum materials in the United States frequently have been designed by natural scientists who tend to learn well from textbooks and require little support and encouragement in their pursuit of scientific understanding. Often, teachers complain that their students cannot understand the materials created by natural scientists and have goals different from those of the designers. At times natural scientists respond by suggesting that teachers need to become more effective in communicating the material. In the CLP partnership we brought these diverse views together to negotiate shared criteria, and design instruction for a broad range of students.

Willing to negotiate a set of beliefs about instruction, learning, and curriculum design, the CLP project partnership came together with mutual respect and diverse ideas about how to meet the needs of a broad range of students. Members changed over the course of the project, but the core group and partnership approach to curriculum design and innovation persisted. Newcomers learned from the group. Graduates went on to establish new partnerships while remaining connected to CLP. "It takes a village" to create an effective science curriculum, and we were fortunate to have wonderful partners.

The partnership jointly carried out the design studies that led to improved instruction. In our partnership, classroom teachers, natural scientists, cognitive researchers, and technology experts brought diverse ideas and commitments to the design task. The partnership process involved negotiating shared criteria for integrating evidence from classroom trials and developing a shared view of the nature of learning and instruction.

The partnership employed shared criteria to evaluate evidence from instructional settings, using the findings to make curricular decisions. For example, we sought continually to improve the proportion of students who could respond correctly to our knowledge integration assessment questions. We shared the view that when a larger proportion of students succeeded, then we had improved instruction. Our assessment questions were designed to measure the integrated understanding we all wanted to impart.

The team assembled in the summer of 1984, although the computers were delivered and installed for the last week of school in the spring of 1984. During the summer, the group designed the order of topic introduction, the activities, and the goals of the curriculum. We negotiated views of heat and temperature, technology, and inquiry.

The CLP partnership started with somewhat disparate views of heat and temperature. Marcia Linn preferred descriptive ideas, whereas Fred Reif, a physicist, held a rich, connected view. We sought depth of understanding, but could not really define it at first. We set an ambitious goal: Our students should be able to write a short essay distinguishing between heat and temperature, and giving examples to explain their answer (Fig. 2.1).

The CLP partnership was both driven and constrained by available technology. We used available computers, software, and equipment. Apple II computers donated by Apple, Inc. served as our first platform.

In general, are heat energy and temperature the same or different? (circle one)

a.   SAME   DIFFERENT

b. What is the main reason for their similarity or difference?

c. Give an example that explains your answer.

FIG. 2.1   Essay written by every CLP student to assess integrated
understanding of thermal concepts.

We used software and temperature sensitive probes donated by the Technical Education Research Centers (TERC). The curriculum materials designed by the TERC emphasized doing the experiments that could be performed with the temperature probes such as measuring cooling curves for various volumes of water, comparing cooling curves for containers with different surface areas, and looking at heating curves for water and other materials. It also was possible to measure phase change using phenodichlorobenzene in a water bath. Soon after we began the experiments, however, phenodichlorobenzene was banned for classroom investigation in California. We never found a suitable replacement and ultimately had to drop phase-change experimentation from the curriculum.

The technology constrained the curriculum in other ways as well. The temperature probes were accurate only within the range of 5° to 110°C, and low temperatures were particularly difficult to measure. In addition, the temperature probes required careful calibration, and two probes often calibrated with the same computer behaved somewhat differently. Finally, the software for displaying data collected in real-time had a number of drawbacks. The most significant drawback of the Apple II software was the impossibility of labeling the actual curves displayed by the computer. Students could title these graphs (e.g., "comparison of a large volume of water and a small volume of water"), but could not indicate which curve represented the large volume of water and which denotes the small volume of water. Without labels, students often assumed that results were compatible with their expectations rather than reporting results accurately (Fig. 2.2).

Members of the CLP partnership held diverse ideas about the science curriculum, but agreed to start with the textbook and the TERC activities. For heat and temperature, textbooks introduced heat in various ways including the molecular kinetic theory (Fig. 2.3). Doug Kirkpatrick reported that students previously had enjoyed measuring changes in temperature and changes in calories. These computational activities had no straightforward links to the TERC experiments about surface area, volume, and starting temperature that were possible using the probes. Nevertheless, the first version of the curriculum combined the TERC activities and the molecular kinetic model. We planned to reflect on what was successful and try to help students connect these various experiences more effectively in the next version. Besides, school was starting!

The CLP partnership started with both diverse and contradictory ideas about making inquiry accessible to students. Rafi Nachmias, a postdoctoral scholar from Israel, advocated teaching a separate scientific reasoning unit addressing topics such as controlling variables. Marcia Linn, on the basis of years spent working with Jean Piaget and interviewing students, believed that students must study inquiry in

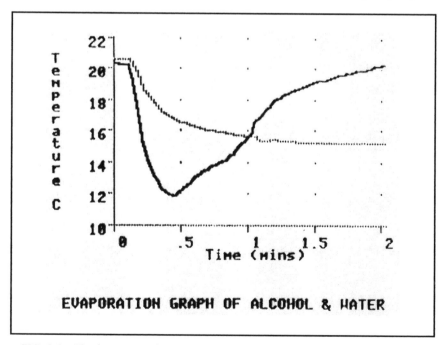

FIG. 2.2   The first CLP software using Apple IIs, which allowed visual display of data collected from temperature probes wired to the computer. Students could add titles to the graphs, but not to the curves.

From Nolan, L. M. and Tucker, W. (1984) Heath Physical Sciences. D. C. Heath and Company, Washington, Mass. [pp. 254 – 256]

"To understand how heat energy can be a form of energy you must keep in mind some facts about the basic particles of matter. Remember that matter is made of atoms and molecules. The kinetic theory states that these particles are always moving and that they often bump into each other."

"The heat energy of a substance is the total kinetic energy of all the molecules or atoms of that substance."

"The temperature of a substance is a measure of the average kinetic energy of the atoms or molecules that make up that substance."

From Hewitt, P. G. (1987) Conceptual physics: A high school physics program (Teacher's ed). Menlo Park, CA: Addison-Wesley Publishing Company, Inc. [p. 304]

"Heat is the internal energy transferred from one body to another by virtue of a temperature difference. The quantity of heat involved in such a transfer is measure by some change such as the change in temperature of a known amount of water that absorbs the heat. When a substance absorbs heat, the temperature change depends on the amount of the substance."

FIG. 2.3   Models of heat and temperature from a middle
and high school textbook.

rich disciplinary contexts where the methods connect to specific questions. She noted that the work of expert scientists includes figuring out the operative variables in new situations. The CLP partnership agreed that students should experience the benefit of sustained reasoning by investigating discipline-specific questions.

Several approaches to scientific inquiry were tried. For example, we decided to introduce both computers and inquiry to the students using software that Nachmias had developed in Israel. This software, PolyLine (Fig. 2.4), allows students to explore many variables that determine the pattern drawn on the screen. The software eventually was translated into English, but students enjoyed using the Hebrew version. Just recently this software was updated again to be compatible with a new operating system.

DESIGN STUDIES: THE FIRST EIGHT VERSIONS OF CLP

For the first 4 years of the CLP, project we taught improved versions of the same curriculum each semester. We regularly reflected on progress and revised our instruction.

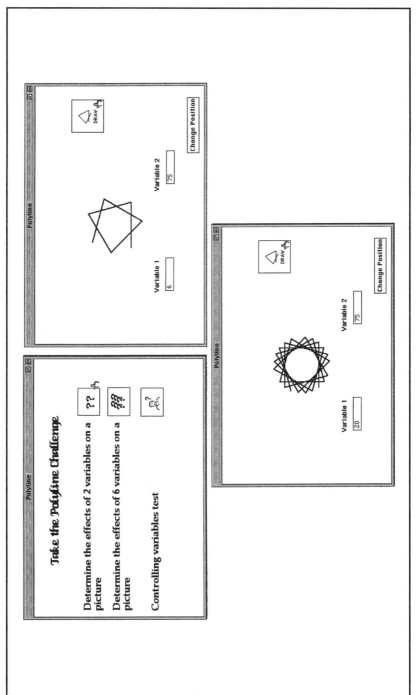

FIG. 2.4   Using PolyLine, students explored the controlling of variables in experimentation.

Our classroom research studies were designed by the CLP partnership. First, we decided to use pretests and posttests to measure progress. Second, to determine whether we had improved the curriculum, we agreed to compare the performance of two groups: students using the current version of the curriculum and students using the previous version. We started by establishing a "baseline." We asked all entering eighth grade students to write the heat and temperature essay (Fig. 2.1). We also used questions from a test developed by the TERC.

At the school, six or seven classes (approximately 180 students) studied CLP each semester. Mr. K, student teachers, and graduate students taught the classes. We compared all classes from one semester to all classes from the next semester. For some comparisons, half of the classes in a single semester used one version of CLP, with the other classes using a different version.

Each new group of students outperformed the previous group on our measures of heat and temperature understanding (Fig. 2.5). As mentioned, our most stringent measure asked students to distinguish between heat and temperature, giving examples to illustrate their view (Fig. 2.6). Successful students described temperature as a measure of the intensity of heat or thermal energy, using an agreed-on scale such as centigrade or Fahrenheit. They described heat as the energy contained in a material or as the energy available, whether or not that energy was described as the kinetic motion of molecules. Examples

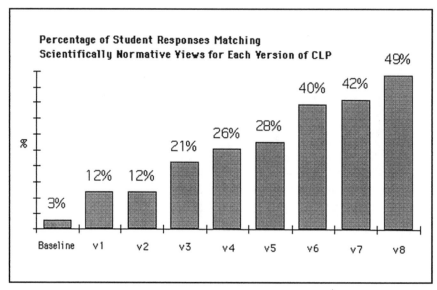

FIG. 2.5   Over the eight versions of CLP, students demonstrated that they could better distinguish between heat energy and temperature.

"Temperature registers everything, but heat is the hot part"

"The difference between heat and temperature is like a baby's bottle is hot with heat and when a baby is sick he has a temperature"

"Different. Heat energy is like if you rub your hands you get heat. If you heat something up, you get a temperaure. Temperature is the heatness."

"Temperature is how hot or cold something is."

"There two different things. One's how hot and one's which way the energy flows."

FIG. 2.6   Student responses to a question asking an explanation for the difference between heat and temperature.

capturing this distinction included the following: A pot of soup and a bowl of soup have the same temperature but the bowl cools faster because it has less heat energy.

We observed a 400% increase in student understanding. The 170 students who studied CLP during the first semester succeeded about 12% of the time, whereas the 172 students who studied CLP during the eighth semester succeeded about 50% of the time. In all cases, the pretest success remained around 5%.

On less demanding outcome measures, such as items designed by TERC that ask students about the role of surface area, the effect of starting temperature on cooling, or the rate of cooling for materials of unequal mass, we succeeded with almost 100% of the students in all versions (Fig. 2.7). Besides these pretests and posttests, we also interviewed students, observed in the classroom, consulted other research groups working on these same topics, and interviewed visitors to the classroom.

During the first eight versions of the curriculum, computers froze, probes failed, new technologies added new problems, student graphs were filled with spikes of uncalibrated input, and students could not interpret their results. Fortunately for us, during the first year John Layman, a visiting professor from the University of Maryland who had previously worked with temperature-sensitive probes, kept the group motivated by constantly reciting far worse experiences than those we encountered.

From the first eight versions of CLP, we learned how to make science accessible to learners. In our design studies, we figured out ways to

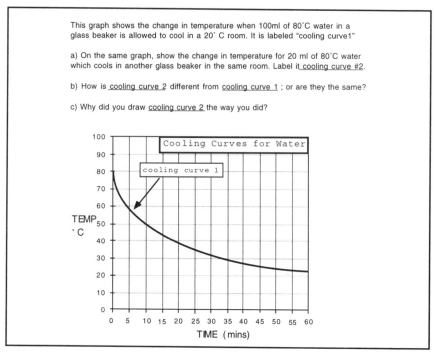

This graph shows the change in temperature when 100ml of 80°C water in a glass beaker is allowed to cool in a 20° C room. It is labeled "cooling curve1"

a) On the same graph, show the change in temperature for 20 ml of 80°C water which cools in another glass beaker in the same room. Label it cooling curve #2.

b) How is cooling curve 2 different from cooling curve 1 ; or are they the same?

c) Why did you draw cooling curve 2 the way you did?

FIG. 2.7   Cooling curve: Students reasoned about heat, volume, and surface area in this assessment item.

build on the ideas students brought to science class, ideas such as "aluminum foil will keep a drink cold for lunch, but wool will warm it up." We also created personally relevant problems students could investigate so that they were able to link and connect ideas. Also, we designed experiences intended to promote lifelong learning. The three pragmatic pedagogical principles for making science accessible grew out of these design studies.

PRAGMATIC PEDAGOGICAL PRINCIPLES

Encourage students to build on their ideas and develop powerful scientific principles

Making science accessible to students means connecting science class experiences to the science ideas they already know. We wish this would happen more often. No wonder adults frequently report they have forgotten any science that they might have learned. We approached this challenge from three perspectives. First, we designed powerful and useful pragmatic scientific principles for students to learn. Second, we sought pivotal cases to make connections come alive between everyday experience and these science principles. Third, we created ways to deliver hands-on experiments that help students build on their ideas.

The first version of CLP relied on textbook principles to help students connect their ideas. Results were disappointing. We learned from the pretest (Fig. 2.1) that few students hold the scientifically normative idea about the difference between heat and temperature. Instead, students assumed that heat and temperature were the same, that heat is "stuff," or that temperature is a measure of heat rather than the kinetic energy of molecules.

Students coming into the program understood many of the variables they could research. Most students had good intuitions about the role of surface area and starting temperature in cooling. Their intuitions about the role of volume were less consistent with normative results. Most students viewed heating and cooling as separate processes.

Before instruction, only three or four students could make any distinction between heat and temperature. After instruction, 10 out of 180 students could explain the difference between heat and temperature. We concluded that the textbook principles had very little, if any, effect on students' understanding of the differences between heat and temperature. At best, the curriculum reinforced ideas about starting temperature and mass that students already understood. Thus, students learned some straightforward definitions, but did not connect them to other information.

How do people link and connect ideas? As the case studies in chapter 1 illustrate, students follow diverse paths as they add science classroom experiences to their own views of scientific phenomena. The ideas they bring to class guide their interpretation of everyday events. Students who believe sweaters warm people expect that wrapping a drink in wool will warm it. We should not have been surprised when students responded to our first version of CLP by isolating ideas about calories and degrees from other knowledge of heat and temperature. No obvious connections existed between these definitions and the many ideas students expressed on the pretest. No wonder three-fourths of our students also asserted that nothing learned in science applies to everyday life:

> Science has almost nothing to do with real life, I mean really it's not like we live in science!

> Most of us don't sit at home doing experiments or science projects all day. There are better things to talk about than science.

Well it doesn't really hurt to know which one is a better conductor, but ... science with bugs and worms, you don't really need to know about their lifestyle.

The CLP partnership reflected on ways we could help students make more connections between the experiments that they were conducting in class and their own ideas. Now, our partnerships have similar discussions. We always hope for even more integrated understanding of the science we teach. This quest for integrated, connected ideas drives our curriculum design process.

Revisiting the curricular goal of integrated understanding the CLP partnership asked, "What does integrated understanding mean?" Textbook writers often accept the calories and degrees answers as sufficient. Does our desire for much deeper and more integrated understanding of heat and temperature ask too much?

To find out whether we were asking too much of students, the CLP partnership decided to interview experts to discover how they connected ideas about heat and temperature from their everyday experiences and their study of molecular kinetic theory. The group agreed to design and carry out interviews with a wide range of "experts," including anybody with advanced training in natural science, from graduate students to university professors.

Marcia Linn became known for trapping physicists and chemists at cocktail parties and asking them to explain why metal desks feel colder than wooden desks, to describe the role of sweaters in keeping people warm, and to recount the advantages of using a wooden spoon rather than a metal spoon for stirring a pot of noodles. Eileen Lewis, a chemist who taught at a local college, joined the project as a graduate student and studied the best wrap for a soda as her first research project. She found that precollege students and typical adults preferred aluminum foil over wool, and that even some experts concurred. Dawn Rickey, a chemistry graduate student, joined the project several years later and conducted more in-depth interviews of experts.

For example, Lewis interviewed an expert we call Robin (Fig. 2.8). This chemist, when asked to explain whether it would be better to use aluminum foil or wool to wrap a drink to keep it cold in a lunch, integrated the question with knowledge of parental practices, rather than with knowledge of chemistry. Robin concluded that aluminum foil would be better than wool because "my mother used aluminum foil to wrap drinks." Robin responded similarly when asked to compare Styrofoam and foil. Despite numerous probes about insulators and conductors and about molecular kinetic theory, Robin stuck with the

Robin's responses to whether aluminum foil or wool would be a better wrapper for keeping a drink cold for lunch:

Robin: Not a clue. It's not something I, it's not an experiment that I would have contemplated doing.

Interviewer (I): Can you make any speculations based on what you know of, I don't know . . . thermal conductivity, insulators, conductors . . .?

Robin: I would guess wool, but I think that's probably wrong.

I: Why do you think it's wrong?

Robin: I don't know. It seems to me it ought to be wrong, but I don't know.

I: So, aluminum foil seems like it ought to be the right answer?

Robin: Yeah. Yeah.... Why? Because my mother takes stuff out of the oven – you put it in the oven with aluminum foil, not in wool, and wool won't burn of course . . . at that temperature. So, aluminum foil ought to be the answer, I would guess.

I: OK, but . . .

Robin: Don't ask me why I say that.

I: But some part of you said that wool . . .

Robin : Yeah.

I: ...should be, but you didn't think it was right.

Robin: That's right.

I: Based on what you know about chemistry and particle motion and so on, can you make a more scientific prediction?

Robin: No, but I would still say, I think probably aluminum, but I can't tell you why.

FIG. 2.8 An expert explains why aluminum is a good wrap to keep a drink cold.

assertion that aluminum foil would be better than wool, continuing to warrant the conclusion with an account of parental practices.

Rickey, interviewing another expert, asked, "Which is safer for stirring boiling noodles, a wooden spoon or a stainless steel spoon?" This expert put forth an idea common among eighth graders: "A wooden spoon because it doesn't absorb the heat as much as the metal spoon. It's like ... the metal one can take the heat up into it." The reader will recall that in the case studies presented earlier some eighth graders espoused the absorption model. As observed in chapter 1, this model can impede knowledge integration.

Taken together, these interviews of experts revealed surprising results. Expert physicists and chemists sometimes sounded very similar to eighth graders when they talked about heat and temperature in everyday contexts. Natural scientists did not always integrate the ideas they had learned from scientific research with their ideas about practical situations, such as deciding how to insulate a picnic lunch or explaining how things feel when touched. They often had considerable difficulty using molecular kinetic theory to explain the practical problems we posed.

Therefore, even for experts, current textbook instruction was hard to connect to complex everyday problems. Abstract and comprehensive understanding of molecular kinetic theory did not help the experts with some personally relevant science problems. How then can we help students make sense of situations they encounter in their everyday lives?

Help came from several engineers. Many of the engineers we interviewed used heat flow rather than molecular kinetic theory to answer the questions we posed. Analysis at the level of heat flow allows engineers to deal with problems that stress the mathematical models of molecular kinetic theory. For example, modeling the heat flow in a spoon in boiling water is mathematically very complex. One engineer that Rickey interviewed, a heat flow expert, also was the parent of a middle school student. Considerable encouragement for using a heat flow model came from this expert. The expert, we call Jules, responded to the spoon question as follows:

A wooden spoon ... that heat conducts much faster up the stainless steel spoon. And so a wood spoon—you could leave it sitting in the pot even—and it won't be hot. But a stainless spoon, you'll rest it against the pot as you turn, and you'll go back to grab it and it's hot....

So how would I explain the concept of conduction? ... If I were talking to ... [an] eighth grader, I would say that you've got a region of hot—high temperature and low temperature. The high temperature is where the spoon's in the water. The low temperature is where the spoon's up in the air. And that high temperature will cause heat to move up the spoon, ... then if he asks any more questions other than the fact that it's the temperature difference that drives the heat through that material, then I'd have to say the way in which it does it is that it makes the molecules move faster, and the really really fast molecules that are at the high temperature bump into the slower molecules that are at lower temperature, makes them move faster, and their temperature goes up, and it keeps propagating along.

These interviews motivated us to use heat flow as a mechanism for helping students to integrate their understanding of heat and temperature.

The textbook-inspired version of CLP established the fact that students do connect ideas in science class and demonstrated how this process works. First, students connect class ideas to each other and isolate them unless other links are clear. Second, ideas that students bring to class remain unchanged unless they get connected to new ideas.

Finally, our interviews with adults and experts demonstrated that even adults fail to make and sustain connections between instructed ideas and intuitive observations. Our first pragmatic principle emphasizes this reality and suggests that we need to design instruction to engage the ideas students bring to class, motivating students to make productive connections among their intuitions and instructed ideas.

Subsequent versions of CLP sought ways to implement this pragmatic pedagogical principle effectively. We noted that insulation, conduction, and thermal equilibrium play a role in many practical heat and temperature problems, and added two activities to the curriculum: Probing Your Surroundings and Insulation in Cups, as shown in Fig. 2.9. These experiments and the heat flow model were responses to our finding from the first version that students learn very little from the traditional curriculum and the TERC experiments.

We implemented the heat flow version of the curriculum with a new cohort of eighth graders at the same school where the first work had been done. Rather than computing calories and degrees, students learned about heat flow primarily from mini-lectures and applied the idea using worksheets. There were similar findings on the pretest, but on the posttest students who no longer had calories and degrees to explain the difference between heat and temperature made an effort to use their findings from insulation and conduction and from experiments about volume to explain the difference. More students were successful, but the numbers were still very small. About one fourth of the students' views matched the scientifically normative view on the heat and temperature essay.

On other indicators students were more successful. For example, on the tea problem, in Fig. 2.10, approximately 60% of the students could construct a heat flow principle and apply a prototype to a new situation. More than 75% could predict the outcome when the principle was applied to a practical situation and explain their reason.

Partnership meetings at this point frequently resulted in heated debates. The natural scientists involved in the project thought that we should find a way to integrate the heat flow and the molecular kinetic theory models to prepare students for subsequent courses in physical science. The classroom teacher was convinced that the heat flow model

Curricular Activity	# of Weeks
Introductory activities	1
Calibration experiment	1
Insulation and conduction experiments – insulation in cups	2
Insulation and conduction simulations	1
Volume – experiments	1
Volume – simulations	0
Temperature difference – experiments	2
Temperature difference – simulations	1
Surface area experiments	1
Surface area simulations	1
Specific heat – demonstrations	1
Adding heat energy experiments – probing your surroundings	2
Calories Experiments and calculations	1
Graph interpretation	1
TOTAL NUMBER OF WEEKS	16

FIG. 2.9   Experiments conducted in one version of the curriculum, which included studying insulation of cups and probing surroundings.

made more sense than molecular kinetic theory. Marcia Linn asserted that she was only just integrating heat flow ideas. Everyone worried about the amount of classroom time spent on heat and temperature. The cognitive researchers wondered whether students could use their ideas about heat and temperature to solve naturally occurring and personally relevant problems, such as the role of aluminum foil in keeping things cold and the role of sweaters in keeping things warm. The experts in technology were frustrated by the interface, the probes, and the reliability of the Apple II computers. They pushed for better technological tools in the classroom.

All members of the partnership agreed, however, that progress had occurred. Approximately one fourth of the students could now give an expert account of the difference between heat and temperature and apply this difference to useful problems. All of the students could explain the impact of volume, surface area, and starting temperature on heating and cooling. Students were making reasonable strides in understanding insulation and conduction as well as thermal equilibrium.

How did science educators, natural scientists, and teachers react to CLP's endorsement of heat flow? We started to describe the results of our investigations at professional meetings. Some of the same issues that the team was raising also were raised by our audiences. Natural scientists criticized the heat flow model and argued that molecular kinetic theory was both more parsimonious and more elegant.

Engineers, when they did attend these meetings, were enthusiastic about the heat flow model.

All of our professional colleagues had ideas about how to express heat flow, and many of them criticized our descriptive approach. We defined pragmatic scientific principles to help students synthesize ideas. These underwent continuous revision and refinement and are still frequently discussed in partnership meetings. We learned that identifying

Two girls ask for hot tea in large cups. One wants a small amount and one wants a large amount.

small amount of hot tea   **large amount of hot tea**

a. Circle **yes** or **no** for each of the following statements.

YES   NO   The small amount of hot tea will completely cool to room temperature first.

YES   NO   The large amount of hot tea will completely cool to room temperature first.

YES   NO   Both amounts of hot tea will completely cool to room temperature at the same rate.

b. Fill in the blanks to make principles that apply to the two hot teas.

When only mass differs, the temperature of the larger mass will change
_____ **the temperature of the smaller mass.**
faster than / slower than / at the same rate as

At first heat energy in the object with larger mass will flow
_____ **the object with smaller mass.**
faster than / slower than / at the same rate as

4 a. Do containers or wraps that help keep hot objects hot also help keep cold objects cold? **(circle one)**

    Yes   **No**   **Cannot predict**

b. What is the **main reason** for your answer?

FIG. 2.10   CLP assessment item asking students to construct principles about heat flow.

an appropriate set of principles for a heat flow model requires substantial negotiation.

Disagreements about which principles are the most appropriate for instruction regularly arose, as discussed in chapter 3. A common debate in our meetings, for example, concerned "cold flow" and "heat flow." Experts agreed that some scientists talk about cold flow. Indeed, Fred Reif, our physics expert whose work in low-temperature physics is well known, said that his colleagues frequently talked about cold flow. Scientists do not, however, talk, as students sometimes do, about heat and cold both flowing and fighting it out when they encounter each other. A long-standing debate between Lewis and Linn concerning ways to build on ideas about cold flow could always enliven partnership meetings.

In summary, our experience in connecting textbook science ideas to student views shows the advantages of reformulating instruction to build on student ideas. The textbook science principles reinforced the well-established practice of isolating school science from everyday experience. By carefully analyzing how experts solve complex and novel problems, we were able to identify a new set of principles that students could connect with their observations of the natural world. The heat flow model promotes knowledge integration by helping students create a robust, coherent understanding of heat and temperature.

Encourage students to investigate personally relevant problems

How can science experiments make science accessible? This second pragmatic principle concerns the activities students conduct in science class. Many educators endorse active, hands-on science as the essential component of effective instruction, yet these experiences may be just as disconnected from students' other ideas as the textbook principles. Students may isolate rather than connect their science activities. Students enthusiastically endorse experiments but may emphasize the excitement more than connecting to other information, saying for example, "I like to experiment much better than memorize. When exploring how a machine works, it would be better to see firsthand how it works than to read in a book."

Making hands-on experiments "authentic" science and essential to education means connecting these experiences to related ideas. For example, Linn remembers a high school physics teacher who ridiculed her inability to construct a pendulum or keep the ripple tank still. Later, she realized she always was asked to help with demonstrations to entertain the class. Many scientists report specializing in theory because of poor experimental skills. After spending hours washing glassware, students select future biology and chemistry classes very carefully. Furthermore, most students recall constructing laboratory reports for experiments they never performed.

Classroom observations during hands-on science raise similar concerns about connecting experimentation to other knowledge. Some students dominate, leaving others to observe or even to do other work. Students may conduct experiments and record results consistent with their beliefs rather than their findings. Anomalies often motivate students to copy results from others rather than resolve the conundrum. Moreover, experiments intended, for example, to use indicators to detect acids and bases can be converted into such activities as mixing vinegar and soda in snap-top vials and determining who can stain the ceiling. Using computers does not change the situation. Some students come in with more experience and confidence about computers than other students. A well-intended computer activity can degenerate into a game of "try to crash the software."

Our first effort to build on student ideas combined real-time data collection experiments, with class discussions in which students linked experiments to everyday life. This decision was based, to a large extent, on the features of the software.

Because the CLP experiments followed the guidelines provided with the real-time data collection software, they addressed laboratory problems. Nevertheless, the team was convinced that experiments in which students could watch data appear on a graph while conducting an experiment would help students connect experimental findings to their entering views. This became an empirical question.

When we discussed these ideas with classroom teachers, many raised a different issue: Would students understand graphing? They pointed out that students would understand graphing better if they had the opportunity to graph their own data point-by-point rather than use real-time data collection. The team argued that when students graph their own data, they make many mistakes and lose track of the point of the experiment. They are so busy writing down numbers that they never actually watch the experiment and end up equating science with recording data. The CLP partnership believed that real-time data collection would help students learn about graphing and enable them to connect laboratory and everyday experience. We were only partly right.

Does real-time data collection teach graphing? Teachers complained that real-time graphing unnecessarily extends the curriculum, because teachers must devote time to two forms of graphing: hand graphing and computer graphing. At one particularly well-remembered meeting, Linn advocated real-time data collection to an audience of more than 300 teachers. The teachers disagreed—loudly.

Linn promised to conduct a more systematic investigation rather than base beliefs about the advantages of real-time data collection on observation and anecdotal evidence.

Nachmias, Layman, Linn, and researchers in other labs across the country set out to determine the impact of real-time data collection on understanding of graphing. We, as others, found that students are much better at interpreting the findings of their experiments when they use real-time data collection than when they construct their own graphs. Student understanding of time-dependent graphs is enhanced even in topics not studied. For example, students were better at interpreting graphs of speed over time after studying cooling over time when they used real-time data collection. No similar benefits arose when students used conventional techniques for graphing their data (Fig. 2.11).

Experiments in many research groups helped to explain this finding. Students come to science class with the idea that a graph is a picture. Animated graphing results help students recognize the connections between a time-dependent process and the resulting graph (see Making Thinking Visible, chapter 4, for more information).

Does real-time data collection teach students to connect laboratory and everyday experience? Despite these successes in graph interpretation, students still isolated their ideas from experiments. Students set

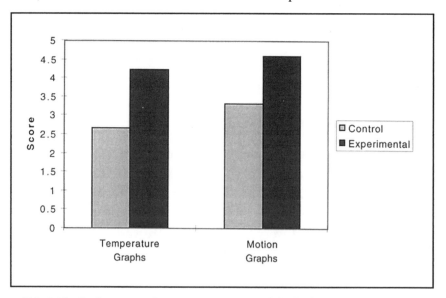

FIG. 2.11   Real-time graphing experience not only helped students learn about heat and temperature graphs, but also improved understanding of graphs depicting motion.

up experiments, recorded their results, and discussed their findings. The class discussions were disappointing because students relied on their original ideas to explain practical problems such as designing a container to keep a drink cold for lunch.

Our observations in CLP classrooms confirmed again that students behave as cognitive economists. They economically resist adding connections unless necessary, seeming to view connections as a costly and rare commodity. Certainly, one reason for this cognitive economy concerns the intellectual energy required to make connections. Links between an experiment, an observation, a vocabulary word, a definition, or an outcome require less intellectual energy than connecting experiments to complex everyday problems or creating a broad comprehensive explanation. Furthermore, when seeking explanations, problems inevitably arise. Does the starting temperature of the objects matter? Why not assume that things near a heat source just always get hotter? Cognitive economists avoid these complicated questions by making simple links. When instruction confronts students with many alternative possibilities and little time to resolve them, cognitive economy makes sense.

How can we help students connect experiments to problems of life importance? Ideas that can be applied to problems such as survival in the wilderness or keeping picnic food safe for consumption need to deal with the complexity of these situations. Individuals who have reasonable explanations for complex problems will be able to respond to many other problems involving similar variables and phenomena. Experiments about surface area, volume, starting temperature, and thermal equilibrium combined with class discussion may not be sufficient, as we found in our classroom research, to connect experiments to students' life experiences.

We wondered how we could help students develop a disposition to build a robust set of connections. We wanted to help students solve personally relevant problems that they might encounter in their lives and to reuse their ideas over time. Why would students ever again think about heat flow, surface area, volume, starting temperature, and thermal equilibrium if their only experiences with these occurred using laboratory equipment in an eighth-grade classroom?

Alternatively, if students have thought about keeping pizzas hot and picnics cold or about wilderness survival, then the chances that they might revisit and rethink their science instruction are enhanced. We conjectured that creating a robust understanding of heat and temperature that extended to problems encountered in students' lives would help cognitive economists develop scientific understanding that improves and grows over time.

Nancy Songer wondered how students connect instructed ideas about heat and temperature to personally relevant problems. She devised an interview to explore applications of heat and temperature ideas and a classroom test asking students to make predictions about a broad range of situations. The jackets problem shown in Fig. 2.12

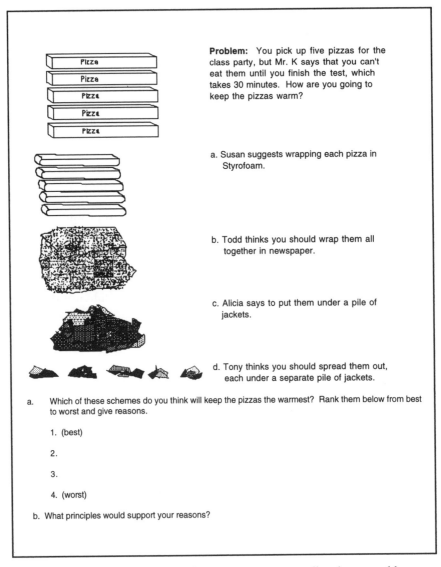

FIG. 2.12   A CLP assessment linking science to personally relevant problems.

shows how students were asked to decide the best way to keep pizza hot for lunch.

Songer found that for many of the problems in the survey, students made accurate predictions but lacked explanations. For example, in the Sam question (Fig. 2.13), students almost universally predicted that using a wooden stick is better than using a metal stick for roasting marshmallows but lacked a rationale. Why might this be? Interviews demonstrated that students could recall relevant experience, but could not connect the experiences to the rate of heat flow in wood and metal.

The interviews that Songer conducted revealed many additional places at which classroom instruction and complex experiences were disconnected. Questions like those in Fig. 2.14 perplexed many students. Because students made valid predictions in some cases, but lacked a way to connect their classroom understanding with complex everyday problems, we added prototypes to the curriculum as described in chapter 3.

The CLP partnership began discussions about personally relevant problems and how they could be incorporated into the curriculum. Many of the variables in personally relevant problems are difficult to study in classrooms for both cost and logistical reasons, but they could be studied in simulations. We proposed adding simulations to investigate complex and ambiguous problems. The National Science Founda-

Sam has two poles of equal length. One is made of wood and one is made of metal. If she holds the ends of both poles and sticks the other ends into the campfire, which pole will heat up first (and burn her hand first!)?

wooden pole

metal pole

The metal pole would get hotter faster and burn her hand first.

FIG. 2.13   Problem in which students had accurate predictions but could not explain their reasons.

Problem: A father and his young daughter were enjoying a football game. Suddenly a large thundercloud rolled in, and it began to rain very hard. The father was prepared for the rain and had brought two small ponchos. The first poncho kept his daughter almost completely dry. The second poncho covered ony the father's legs, or head and shoulders, but not both.

a. Which person was more comfortable?

b. Which was warmer? Why?

c. Can you compare this situation with the experiments you have done in class this semester ?

FIG. 2.14   A CLP complex question asking students to connect class principles to an everyday situation.

tion concurred and funded the project. In addition, Apple Computer, Inc. provided us with Macintosh computers to replace the Apple IIs. Macintoshes could handle the simulations we envisioned and much more.

Judy Stern, a former graduate student, wrote the first Electronic Laboratory Notebook for the Macintosh using Hypercard. The first version is depicted in Fig. 2.15. Stern remained with the project, earning a Master's degree and staying on as a technology expert. Her ability to criticize her own work has benefited the project beyond measure. She developed both the skills necessary to design and implement new interfaces and the understanding necessary to recognize the needs of individuals using technology.

The frustrations of technology occupied the project for approximately a year while we implemented real-time data collection using the new Macintosh computers and designed simulations for investigating personally relevant problems. At one point, students used the Apple II computers for real-time investigations and Macintosh computers for simulated investigations. We were fortunate to have two classrooms for instruction: one, a computer lab, and the other a desk setup, as shown in Fig. 2.16. Soon afterward, however, we were obliged to operate in a single classroom. The classroom became progressively more and more crowded (see Quick Time virtual reality on the CD ROM included with this volume).

Ultimately, we designed and stabilized a curriculum that involved both real-time data collection and simulations. A graphic depiction of the curricular changes are found in Fig. 2.17. The curriculum remained approximately the same length, but, now we were including

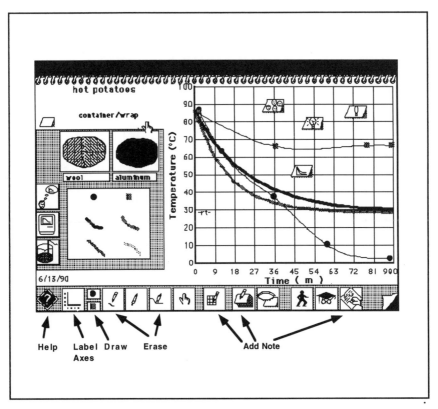

FIG. 2.15   An early version of the Electronic Laboratory Notebook. The post-it–like note icons were designed by students.

both real-time and simulated experiments. Many of the technological problems with the Apple II computers were completely solved using Macintoshes. Students could label their graphs completely, and they could make predictions online rather than on paper. They could compare their online predictions with the outcomes of their experiments. Furthermore, we could store student writing in the Electronic Laboratory Notebook.

Students spent a considerable amount of time writing their comments and reflecting on their experimental outcomes. Indeed, students began to complain that this science course required more writing than their English course.

We tested the curriculum with and without simulations and with simulations of various forms, using this information to reformulate the curriculum. The new curriculum resulted in substantial improvement in student understanding. At this point more than one third of the stu-

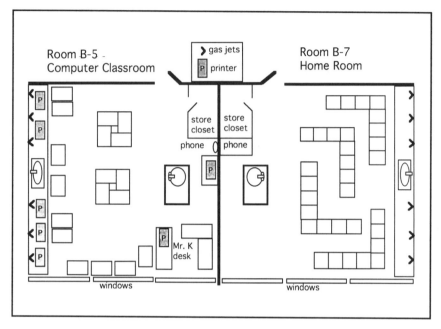

FIG. 2.16   Mr. K would start class in Room B-7, then move students to Room
B-5 for computer activities. Although both classrooms can hold 32 students,
the B-5 classroom allowed the teacher to walk around easily and students to
work in groups at the computer.

dents gave a scientifically sophisticated explanation for the distinction
between heat and temperature and buttressed their explanations with
comprehensive and elaborated examples. Two thirds of the students
gave scientifically acceptable explanations for this distinction, and every student made substantial progress on a variety of issues concerning
heat and temperature.

We concurrently designed assessments and simulated experiments
for personally relevant problems (Fig. 2.18). Overall, our assessments
revealed that adding simulations to the curriculum helped students integrate their understanding and apply their ideas to a broader range of
problems.

We continued to present our results to classroom teachers and science education researchers. Many criticized our simulations, suggesting that students would not view them as realistic and would not use
the evidence from them in their thinking. We conducted experiments
to show the opposite. Students tended to treat simulated findings as
they treated real-time data collection findings. In both cases, they were
skeptical of computers as potentially causing trouble or making mis-

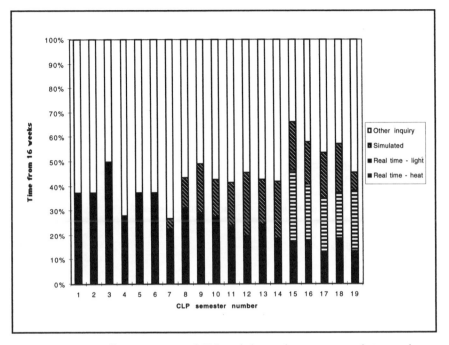

FIG. 2.17   Different versions of CLP and the weeks spent on real-time and
simulated experiments.

takes, but confident when results seemed reasonable. The most sophisticated students pointed out that the curves in the simulations had the
same shape as the curves in the real-time data collection. The less sophisticated students simply said that it was hard to tell the difference
between the two kinds of results.

Responses to our assessments revealed limitations in students' ability to generalize their understanding. We identified several potential
explanations. For example, few students realize that scientists support
their conjectures with evidence from related but not identical investigations and that the progress of scientific work is complex. If students
believe that science consists of "uncovering" facts, they might be less
willing to integrate their ideas and make conjectures than if they realize that science involves this process of integration and conjecturing as
a regular undertaking.

We designed an inventory to measure students' ideas about the nature of science. Sample items appear in Fig. 2.19, and results are discussed in chapter 6. We also decided to spend more time thinking
about ways to help students generalize their understanding of heat and

Three friends were going through a cafeteria line together. One was very hungry and asked for a very, very large bowl of oatmeal. Another was moderately hungry and asked for a large bowl of oatmeal. The third person wasn't very hungry and asked for a small bowl of oatmeal. These bowls of oatmeal are shown below.

VERY, VERY
LARGE Oatmeal   LARGE Oatmeal   SMALL Oatmeal

a. Which oatmeal will cool the fastest so that it could be eaten first?

b. Why do you think so?

c. What evidence do you have for your answer?

d. Write a scientific rule or principle that applies to this situation.

FIG. 2.18   A sample assessment used to see if students applied what they
learned in CLP lab experiments to everyday problems.

temperature to a broader range of problems. Visualizations described in chapter 3 were used to help students generalize their ideas.

In summary, real-time graphing and simulations of personally relevant problems made science ideas more accessible to students. Our redesign of graph instruction also illustrated the benefit of building on student ideas to create more robust understanding. Interestingly, here the expert tool of real-time data collection made graph concepts more accessible. The dynamic character of a graph makes more sense when it occurs in real time. Real-time graphing led us to consider additional ways to make thinking visible, which we discuss in chapter 3. In addition, we noted limitations, especially in ability to sort out personal and science ideas and support conclusions with evidence. We address this in our third pragmatic pedagogical principle and in chapters 4 and 5.

1 a. The science principles in textbooks will always be true.

(circle one)   yes   no

b. Give an example which helps explain your answer:

2 a. Scientists analyzing the same data all reach the same conclusions.

(circle one)   yes   no

b. Give an example which helps explain your answer:

3 a. Which best describes scientific knowledge:

_____   Science knowledge does not change. Scientists do experiments to confirm existing results.

_____   Science knowledge is constantly changing because scientists do new experiments and get new ideas.

_____   Science knowledge is constantly expanding because scientists use the results from experiments to replace or improve current ideas.

b. Give an example which helps explain your answer:

4 a. Name a scientist. This scientist can be either real or imaginary, alive or dead.

_____

What makes that person a scientist?

5 a. The science I learn in school has little or nothing in common with my life outside of school.

(circle one)   Agree   Disagree

b. Give an example which helps explain your answer:

6 a. When understanding new ideas, memorizing facts is better than trying to understand complicated material.

(circle one)   Agree   Disagree

b. Give an example which helps explain your answer:

7 a. Science is too complicated and difficult for ordinary students to understand well.

(circle one)   Agree   Disagree

b. Give an example which helps explain your answer:

FIG. 2.19   Some questions we asked students on the nature of science and their beliefs about science.

Scaffold science activities so students understand the inquiry process

How can instruction concerning heat and temperature help students understand scientific inquiry? Peers and colleagues asked whether our in-depth curriculum helped students understand science inquiry. Could students who participated in a depth curriculum extend their scientific reasoning skills to a broad range of problems involving variables that were not part of the heat and temperature curriculum? We doubted that students could generalize beyond heat and temperature because they could not generalize to personally relevant problems without specific attention to these issues in the curriculum.

Nevertheless, students preparing for future scientific experiences needed ideas that connect to new, personally relevant problems, to media depictions of science, and to related scientific phenomena. How could we make this lifelong process accessible? How could we prepare learners to revisit and refine their ideas throughout their lives? Would pragmatic scientific principles and personally relevant problems help students become lifelong users of the inquiry process? Our first approach was to help students successfully engage in all the aspects of inquiry while studying heat and temperature. We wanted to help students connect class experiments to their personal views and to connect one experiment to another.

Our first effort, initiated by Rafi Nachmias and Yael Friedler, post-doctoral scholars from Israel, investigated both these types of connections with the Apple II computers. In the *observation* condition, students connected experimental events such as "the water is boiling," with graphed phenomena such as "the temperature on the graph is staying the same." In the *prediction* condition, students built on their past experiments to describe what results they expected. Both conditions improved performance. We discuss how this approach also improves knowledge integration by making thinking visible in chapter 3.

We experimented with scaffolds that encouraged students to make connections among their ideas and experiments, using a variety of "notes" accessed by icons designed by the students themselves. Responding to these notes often encouraged students to make connections between experiments and related experiences. Eventually, the notes were converted into prompts as we discuss in chapter 5. In particular, we used the new Macintosh computers to deliver online prompts encouraging students to observe and predict at appropriate times (Fig. 2.20).

As described in the next chapter, we automated the inquiry process of making connections, using a checklist and help facility. This im-

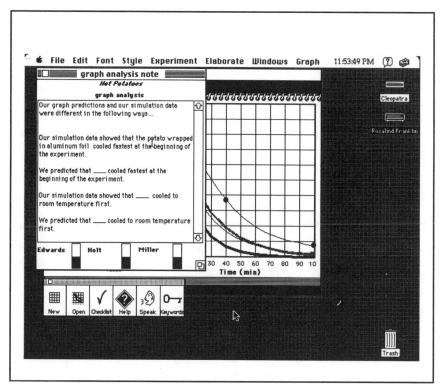

FIG. 2.20   In the CLP Electronic Laboratory Notebook, students made notes to experiments.

proved the efficiency and effectiveness of experimentation, freeing the teacher to concentrate on tutoring rather than guiding students to the next prompt. These scaffolds model inquiry enabling students successfully to make predictions, observe their experiments, explain their findings, reconcile predictions and outcomes, and plan the next study.

Our second approach built on the class discussion idea. Doug Kirkpatrick, the classroom teacher, started by using class discussions to connect laboratory experiments to naturally occurring problems involving heat and temperature. Class discussion was insufficient. We added simulations that allowed students directly to investigate naturally occurring problems. After experimenting, students could generalize to related problems. Eventually we extended class discussion to more complex and ambiguous problems such as designing a plan to survive in the wilderness.

Students who gained an integrated understanding of the heat and temperature laboratory problems encountered difficulties in extending these ideas to more complicated, naturally occurring problems. On complex and ambiguous problems, students could not manage the complexity. For example, they had difficulty recognizing which parts of a problem had to do with heat and temperature. If they decided that wilderness survival concerned finding food rather than keeping warm, they often suggested superficial solutions. We saw a similar pattern when Robin, the scientist, relied on parental practices rather than insulation principles in responding to a complex everyday problem.

Naturally occurring problems also pushed the boundaries of student understanding. Some students had difficulty applying heat and temperature results because they did not understand some of the factors in the naturally occurring situation. For example, they might comprehend that objects would come to thermal equilibrium, but not understand what would happen to objects that are heat sources. Moreover, they might understand that heat flows more slowly through insulators than conductors, but not know which materials were insulators and which were conductors.

We also saw this pattern when asking experts to apply their knowledge to complex, everyday problems. Engineers who specialize in designing heat flow systems could make these connections, but chemists or physicists often were less successful.

Could we build a curriculum that would help students develop an integrated understanding of science inquiry? Would this help students understand how to apply their ideas? We tried implementing the process that succeeded for heat and temperature. We designed pragmatic scientific principles and personally relevant problems about inquiry.

Derrick Newell, an undergraduate who joined the project initially as an interviewer and interpreter of student responses, and whose undergraduate degree was in cognitive and computer sciences, was particularly interested in the nature of inquiry. He helped us design pragmatic scientific principles and interesting problems about science inquiry. He also designed additional items for the pretest and posttest and scored all of the data.

We identified pragmatic scientific principles about the nature of inquiry to unify student understanding. We added the black box activity to the CLP curriculum as an introduction to scientific models. These black boxes are illustrated in Fig. 2.21. In this unit, students tried to imagine a model of the inside of the black box (Fig. 2.22). The black boxes were constructed with shallow boxes, pick-up sticks, and washers. The box then was covered with another piece of cardboard.

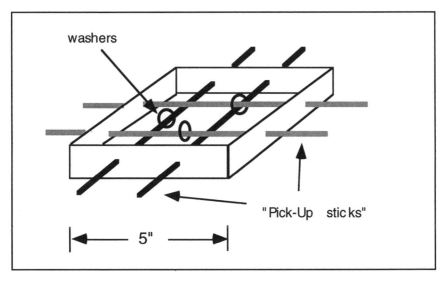

FIG. 2.21.   Black box activity with the lid open. In this reasoning activity, students tried to figure out the placement of the washers with the box lid closed.

Students could rotate the box and listen to the feedback from the washers to develop a model of the arrangement of washers and sticks inside the black box. One tantalizing aspect of the lesson involved never opening the black boxes. Students enjoyed this activity and often remembered it many years later. We found that students could understand the sticks and washers in this situation. They could recognize and visualize which washers were free to move. They were able to make sense of the feedback from the sound of the washers sliding or caught at the intersection of sticks, and they could draw representations of what they thought the inside of the box was like. Would gaining an integrated understanding of this task help students solve any other tasks?

Another source of general inquiry problems are puzzles or mysteries. Martin Covington, at the University of California at Berkeley pioneered the Productive Thinking Program, in which students solve a whole set of interesting mysteries (Fig. 2.23). This program engages students in conjecturing, modeling, and reasoning. We used similar puzzles for the CLP scientific inquiry unit.

To help students understand scientific argumentation and dispute resolution, we designed the dinosaur debate. This was the only part of the inquiry unit that engaged students in connecting personal experience to science inquiry. The debate engaged students in constructing arguments and supporting assertions with evidence. The debate was designed to help students deal with evidence such as that presented in Fig. 2.24.

The principles and activities for the nature of science curriculum are listed in Fig. 2.25. The materials were pilot tested and implemented in all the classes at the middle school during one semester. All students then studied heat and temperature and extended heat and temperature reasoning to solving naturally occurring problems. We tested students' understanding of heat and temperature as well as their understanding of science inquiry both before and after instruction.

Name:_____ Period:_____

The Black Box

Definitions

Observation: An observation is anything you can see, hear, smell, taste, or feel.

Inference: Any guess about **HOW** or **WHY** an event happened. For this activity, your inferences should be based on your observations.

Principle: General statement that summarizes how scientists investigate natural phenomena.

Prototype: An everyday example that illustrates a principle.

Evidence: Any information that either supports or contradicts an explanation. For example, an observation is a form of evidence.

Principles

Principle I: Scientists separate observations from inferences.

Principle II: Scientists use evidence to construct explanations for natural phenomenon.

1. Draw what you think the inside of the black box looked like.	2. Draw another model of the contents of the black box that was presented in class?

FIG. 2.22.   The Black Box Activity *(continued on next page)*

3.What evidence only supported your model?	4. What evidence supported both models?

Principle III: Evidence _____ *support more than one*
model.   *must/can/can not*

6. If you could you look inside the black box could you tell which model was correct?

(Circle one)   Yes   No

7 a. Can scientists always find out which model or explanation is correct?

(Circle one)   Yes   No

b. Give an example which helps explain your answer:

FIG. 2.22.   The Black Box Activity.

During subsequent semesters, we compared students who studied the inquiry curriculum with a group that had studied light and the rest of the CLP curriculum but not inquiry. Assessment items included new puzzles and mysteries, new debates, and heat and temperature questions.

Newell analyzed the scientific inquiry results and concluded that both groups of students gained in their understanding of scientific inquiry from the pretest to the posttest, but that the group with the additional scientific reasoning instruction made no special progress beyond that achieved by the students who studied light and heat. Newell was disappointed and left for the Peace Corps.

Many research groups report similar disappointing results from instruction in scientific inquiry. Students can apply their understanding to the topics they studied (e.g., black boxes, dinosaur extinction) but not to new topics (e.g., health decision making, new puzzles). Students' ideas about inquiry were not sufficient to solve these new prob-

A detective was hired to find the absentminded King's crown. The detective observed that the crown was not in the safe. The King told the detective that the last time he remembered having his crown was when he went to his study to read. He had just finished having lunch with the Queen and the Queen remembered the King wearing his crown at lunch. The king told the detective that he went to the bathroom and then went straight to his study to read. The detective concluded that the crown must be somewhere in the study.

a. What evidence did the detective use to infer that the crown was in the study?

b. Where else might the detective look for the crown?

FIG. 2.23   Mystery problems. Puzzles and mysteries that illustrate some aspects of scientific inquiry.

lems, just as our scientists' ideas about inquiry were not always sufficient to interpret everyday heat and temperature questions.

As we discuss in the next chapters, students' intuitions about scientific disputes differ substantially from the normative view. As we learned, students often believe that scientists assert their ideas without warrants. Perhaps students gain these intuitions from newspaper or television accounts of science disputes. Perhaps they generalize their own argument resolution procedures to scientists. Whatever the reason, students primarily view scientists as asserting a point of view and paying little attention to the experimental results or views of others.

Making inquiry a lifelong habit requires more than principles and isolated experimental examples. We also need to help students understand how scientists independently resolve disputes and to support students in using these same dispute resolution procedures in their own inquiry. In later chapters, we discuss debates, critiques, and projects that address these issues.

In summary, to make science ideas about inquiry accessible, we can scaffold students as they conduct valid inquiry, but we need better ways of helping students connect one inquiry to another. We need to build on students' ideas about how scientists conduct inquiry. We need ways to connect students' and scientists' inquiry. Furthermore, we need to engage students in connecting their ideas about inquiry into a coherent perspective on scientific experimentation.

REFLECTIONS

This chapter describes how our CLP partnership made scientific ideas accessible to students. The partnership's commitment to coherent sci-

A. In Alaska fossils of plants that grow in colder places were discovered with fossils of dinosaurs. Estimates are that the average temperature was 2° – 4 °C (37°F) in the coldest month and 10° –12°C (52°F) in the warmest month.

B. Mammals and birds are better able to maintain their body temperature because of their fur and feathers. They can withstand greater changes in temperature. Reptiles have more difficulty maintaining body temperature.

C. Recent studies show that the size of giant turtles helps them maintain body temperature. Some scientists think that the large dinosaurs were able to keep warm because of their size.

D. During the time before the dinosaur extinction, small, furry, insect eating and plant eating mammals greatly increased in number and variety.

E. Some dinosaurs lived in much cooler and drier climates than the swamps we usually think of as the habitat for dinosaurs. Dinosaur bones have been found in northern Alaska, where there is night for up to three months. Dinosaur bones have also been discovered in the far southern latitudes of Argentina, Australia, and Antarctica. Although the climate was not as cold there as it is now, scientists estimate that temperatures dropped below freezing. Temperatures may have been as low as -11°C (12°F).

F. Did a comet or meteorite strike the blow that wiped out dinosaurs?
Did the clouds from such an impact block out sunlight and cool off the globe? Berkeley paleontologist William A. Clemens and his colleagues think that dinosaurs could have survived such an event. Fossil evidence shows that several species of dinosaurs were probably adapted to living through winters near the poles. In the April 1991 *Scientific American* studies of bones and footprints indicate that the 6-ton to 9-ton triceratops could gallop as fast as a rhinoceros. The huge 34-ton Apatosaurus probably moved much the same way as a modern elephant. If these calculations are correct, dinosaurs were capable of traveling long distances.

G. Any theory regarding dinosaur extinction must explain why dinosaurs in Alaska, Australia, and Antarctica that were able to survive in 3–5 months of cold would have died. A prolonged period of darkness alone could have brought about the extinction only if it was longer than 5 months.. At least small, large-eyed, large-brained dinosaurs would have survived this long.

H. The types of plants changed from tall evergreen trees to low flowering seasonal plants before the dinosaur extinction.

FIG. 2.24 Students used text evidence (subset shown)
to formulate arguments to support a theory about dinosaur extinction in
preparation for a class debate.

entific understanding necessitated some substantial modifications from the original textbook version of the thermodynamics course. The most substantial change concerned adopting a heat flow model rather than a molecular kinetic theory approach to principles for heat and

Activities	Principles
Bernoulli's tube	Science is the effort to make sense of natural phenomena.
	Scientists seek to make accurate observations.
The black box	Scientists use established ideas to make sense of new phenomena.
Dinosaur extinction	Scientists' views affect their observations.
The exploding can	Scientists use observation and description to describe what they see.
PolyLine	Scientists devise hypotheses to explain what they observe.
Mysteries	Scientists devise experiments to test their hypotheses.
	Scientists have different explanations for events because they have different evidence about those events.

FIG. 2.25   Activities and principles used to teach science inquiry.

temperature. The partnership design studies demonstrated unequivocally that heat flow was both more accessible and more powerful as a model for middle school students' understanding.

At the same time, even with this more accessible and powerful model for students, the partnership demonstrated that extending understanding to naturally occurring problems and personally relevant contexts presents substantial, considerable, almost overwhelming challenges for science education. Students whose understanding of principles in the classroom seems comprehensive have great difficulty extending their ideas to naturally occurring problems. Indeed, students seem to isolate classroom and everyday complex problems. As a result, students bring to bear observed practices in homes and restaurants such as wrapping potatoes or drinks in aluminum foil rather than analyze the science principles associated with these practices. To build on these ideas, we redesigned our science activities, incorporating more complex problems. We developed new activities to help students make broader connections and sustain knowledge integration longer.

We also want students to use the methods of science inquiry more broadly and to understand their role in the work of scientists. We found that students rarely connect their personal scientific activities to those of scientists. Instead, they isolate scientists' activities from their own. We return to this dilemma in future chapters.

How does making the curriculum accessible help Lee, Sasha, Pat, and Chris to learn science? As observed in chapter 1, Lee followed the consumer pattern of associating science experiences and personal experience, but did not seek cohesive, linked understanding. Introducing personally relevant problems gave Lee a chance to make more connections than would be possible with only typical science problems.

Sasha, following the strategizer pattern, preferred memorizing to understanding and typically linked examples to new problems. The CLP approach supports this process of locating similar examples and making analogies. It broadens the scope of knowledge integration in contrast to typical courses for students like Sasha.

Pat, following the experimenter pattern, looked for wide connections, used all the features of CLP, and kept many options open. Pat made analogies, deductions, and assertions, but resisted cohesive understanding. In chapter 6 we find out how this broad set of ideas evolves in Pat's thinking.

Chris, following the conceptualizer pattern, relied primarily on pragmatic scientific principles, using a process of deduction to connect situations to principles.

Using CLP makes science accessible for all four patterns of knowledge integration identified in chapter 1. The students in the case studies need more than accessible ideas to learn science, and we address other ways that CLP promotes knowledge integration in subsequent chapters.

ASK MR. K

How did you get involved with using computers?

I have been teaching for 35 years. A little more than half my career was without computers. In 1983, I began using Apple II computers. Before that, the technology involved would have been found primarily in laboratory equipment such as thermometers or burners, and machines such as movie projectors and tape recorders.

Can you describe some of the partnerships and key people who influenced your teaching?

When I first started to teach with computers, I met Dick Merrill of Northern California Committee on Problem Solving in Science (NCCOPSIS). Dick was the science coordinator for the Contra Costa Country District. He was very enthusiastic and kept me informed of things going on in California. For example, Pacific Gas & Electric, the local utility company, used to do teacher professional development workshops on energy. We called these "environmental camps" and met on weekends over the winter. It was really neat! We had the chance to work with other teachers and rethink the kinds of lessons and activities we designed. This group ended up meeting every so often as a teacher support group. Once every month, we would take turns presenting a lesson, then have other teachers critique our teaching. We were the best colleagues. This lasted for a couple years.

How did the CLP partnership contribute to your teaching?

In the second year of CLP, John Layman was here as a visiting scholar. I also was concerned, initially, that kids were doing all this real-time data collection. I had always taught them how to graph, and here I was not teaching them how to graph anymore. But with the computer, students could set up the axes once the graph was completed and then manipulate the axes and change the graph around.

Basically it was all dumb work. I said to John, "You know, it's great that we have computers, and kids are doing that. But what's going to happen when they get to high school and they don't know how to read a data table or graph anything?" And he said, "Well, let's check and see what happens."

We set up this little experiment. We collected data and tested student ideas with an experiment about light-over-distance. We used a candle and a light probe, and we gave them a data table rather than a graph, asking them to graph the points. The graphs came out better than anything I had ever experienced when I was teaching, I think because they had learned how to manipulate the axes and resize a graph on the computer. They really understood what was going on and were able to make their own graphs. They did a great job working with the graphing, so it just took that worry away from me.

It therefore is working with people like John and Bob Tinker on the computers. I think working with the graduate students also has been one of the things that really has kept me going and excited about what I am doing because it is a continual challenge.

As a group, the CLP partnership always felt free to say, "Hey, wait! This isn't working. What's going on? Have you thought about this?" I think the challenge of being involved with a group of people really looking at how we can change to make this better and willing to change has been exciting. From my point of view, Marcia Linn has done a great job of allowing me to feel free to do things a different way.

You look at our program. I have journals from the past 15 years on my shelf. I was going through one the other day trying to find out when I had become involved with an organization. It was about the first year we were involved with the program. Every year we are seeing kids coming to better understanding.

Why is building on student ideas rather than ignoring them a good idea?

You can tell students the "right answer," but they go back to what they were thinking the minute they go out the door. Eileen Lewis and Nancy Songer both saw that in their research. Students see the classroom and the outside world as two completely different things. Kids might be convinced here in this class, but then go back to believing what they thought before.

How do I sway them? The first way is by listening to what they are saying. Then I ask kids to explain why they believe what they say. I use questions to get students to compare two situations, in a way similar to the note writing they do when using classroom software. I ask them to do predictions, explain their graphs, describe heat flow in their experiments, and talk about their conclusions. I also give students an everyday example and ask them how that relates to the principles they have written or their experiments.

Why did you select heat flow to build on student ideas?

I used the heat flow model instead of the molecular kinetic model or measurement with calories and thermometers because students found it more relevant. We used to teach heat in terms of calories. Students would learn the definition of a calorie, and we would do some hands-on experiments. For example, students would burn Cheetos or peanuts under a can filled with water, observing how much the water changed in temperature. Kids typically would have trouble with understanding ratios and calculating the energy per unit mass. They also had trouble setting up the apparatus and carrying out the laboratory activity well enough to get good results. They always had fun burning things, but after the laboratory experiments, students still had trouble connecting their experiments to their lives.

How did you use the Electronic Laboratory Notebook?

The nice thing about the Electronic Laboratory Notebook was that it was flexible enough for me to use as an interface to add principles and prototypes while students provided their own everyday examples or "prototypes" as they learned throughout the semester. It was also useful for keeping track of student ideas so I could see their thinking during an activity.

POINTS TO PONDER

- Give examples of how you make science accessible to students.
- Critique CLP measures of knowledge integration. What questions would you ask?
- Analyze the short-answer and multiple-choice questions you use and say whether they measure knowledge integration.
- How can you scaffold students to conduct inquiry?
- Describe a teaching partnership you have joined.
- Describe how technology constrains the curriculum in a discipline you teach.
- Describe a pragmatic scientific principle for a topic you teach.
- Describe several personally relevant problems for a topic you teach.
- Review the layouts of the CLP classroom. How has the design of your classroom contributed to classroom activity.
- Watch the section of the CLP film called, Can we make science accessible. Compare the CLP activities to those in another curriculum.

RELATED READINGS

Clement, J. (1990). Genius is not immune to persistent misconceptions: Conceptual difficulties impeding Isaac Newton and contemporary students. *International Journal of Science Education, 12*(3), 265–273.

Eylon, B. S., & Linn, M. C. (1988). Learning and instruction: An examination of four research perspectives in science education. *Review of Educational Research, 58*(3), 251–301.

Lewis, E. L., & Linn, M. C. (1994). Heat energy and temperature concepts of adolescents, adults, and experts: Implications for curricular improvements. *Journal of Research in Science Teaching, 31*(6), 657–677.

Linn, M. C., & Songer, N. B. (1991). Teaching thermodynamics to middle school students: What are appropriate cognitive demands? *Journal of Research in Science Teaching, 28*(10), 885–918.

The Cognition and Technology Group at Vanderbilt (CTGV). (1997). *The Jasper project: Lessons in curriculum, instruction, assessment, and professional development.* Mahwah, NJ: Lawrence Erlbaum Associates.

Vygotsky, L. S. (1962). *Thought and language.* Cambridge, MA: MIT Press.

3

Making Thinking Visible

Aluminum foil would kind of pull the cold out of the soda into the air.

Styrofoam has holes to trap air.

Temperature is how hot or cold something is.

Insulation just keeps the temperature in.

Metal spoons would attract heat when you are stirring noodles.

The difference between heat and temperature is like a baby's bottle is hot with heat and when a baby is sick he has a temperature.

Temperature will eventually get the same because the heat or the cold goes out into the air.

These examples show students in the CLP curriculum making their thinking visible. Students reveal many relevant, incomplete, and disconnected ideas, especially about their personal experiences. They hold multiple views of the same phenomenon.

In this chapter we discuss how making thinking visible can help students sort out ideas, entertain new ideas, and form more cohesive, sophisticated views. We describe how teachers model the process of connecting ideas and detecting mistakes to make the thinking of science visible. We discuss ways the curriculum can guide students in making their own thinking visible. Furthermore, we describe how technological supports make scientific ideas visible.

Why do we care about the ideas students already have? As discussed in chapter 1, students keep ideas such as "Wool heats stuff up" in their repertoire even when they add clarifying new ideas such as "Wool is an insulator" and "Wool slows heat flow." We learned that curricular features can motivate students to connect ideas such as "Wool has holes in it" and "Heat flows through 'holes' such as doors or windows."

In science, students regularly articulate a confusing set of ideas. They also spontaneously seek connections among their ideas. Effective instruction builds on the ideas students already have and promotes knowledge integration. We can carefully craft experiences so students productively build on their views.

Why not just "tell" students the right answer? As chapter 1 shows, Lee, Chris, Pat, and Sasha did add new information, but they also sometimes isolated it as relevant only in school. Moreover, not all the information was fruitfully connected. Students need to connect and reorganize all their relevant ideas. Otherwise, their everyday ideas may remain unchanged, and they may use the new ideas only on science tests if they use them at all. Students who isolate ideas rather than integrate them are at risk of concluding that science is confusing and disconnected. We need to do more than tell students new information. The thinking necessary for knowledge integration must be made visible and accessible for students.

Why does making thinking visible promote knowledge integration? The process of knowledge integration includes eliciting ideas, introducing new ideas, and encouraging new connections. When students make their thinking visible, they can identify the many ideas they have about a scientific topic. Eliciting all these ideas while adding new ideas to the mix encourages students to connect rather than isolate new information.

Instructors also can make new ideas visible to students. The example in Fig. 3.1 makes the process of heat flow visible and also elicits heat flow ideas from the reader by posing a compelling problem: Will a metal or wooden spoon feel hotter when both are left in boiling water? The animation in Fig. 3.2 illustrates the process of heat flow using a computer program called HeatBars.

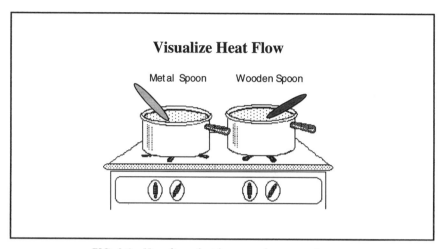

FIG. 3.1 Visualize what happens for a metal spoon
and for a wooden spoon in pots of boiling water. Describe your visualization.

Instructors can also encourage new connections by revealing authentic thinking. This can empower learners to sort out their ideas by following the model. When we first started working with Michael Clancy, a faculty member in computer science at the University of California at Berkeley, to study computer science instruction, we found that some students expected to compose computer programs from start to finish without error because lecturers in computer science described solutions without illustrating the wrong paths, alternative ideas, or errors they encountered. This also happens in mathematics classes, with many students believing that proofs progress from first to last step, yet experts generally work forward and backward. In science, students may conclude that scientists always know what experiment to do next, instead of understanding the challenge of designing novel investigations. To dispel these myths, we advocate that instructors highlight authentic examples of reasoning about difficult problems and phenomena.

Designing ways to make thinking visible requires that instructors thoughtfully analyze the mix of ideas students bring to science class. Instructors get more adept at making thinking visible the more times they teach a topic and the more opportunities they have to interact with individual learners.

The process of making thinking visible begins with eliciting student ideas, but requires careful analyzing to promote reorganization of ideas. Most ideas held by students resonate with ideas held by teachers.

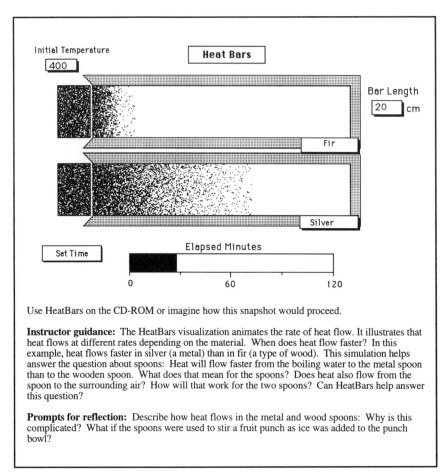

Use HeatBars on the CD-ROM or imagine how this snapshot would proceed.

Instructor guidance: The HeatBars visualization animates the rate of heat flow. It illustrates that heat flows at different rates depending on the material. When does heat flow faster? In this example, heat flows faster in silver (a metal) than in fir (a type of wood). This simulation helps answer the question about spoons: Heat will flow faster from the boiling water to the metal spoon than to the wooden spoon. What does that mean for the spoons? Does heat also flow from the spoon to the surrounding air? How will that work for the two spoons? Can HeatBars help answer this question?

Prompts for reflection: Describe how heat flows in the metal and wood spoons: Why is this complicated? What if the spoons were used to stir a fruit punch as ice was added to the punch bowl?

FIG. 3.2   HeatBars visualization: Software to encourage visualization.

Teachers have the challenge of connecting student ideas to their more sophisticated views and designing instruction that promotes reorganization of ideas. For example, both students and teachers agree that a metal desk in the classroom feels colder than a wooden table. Whereas students often connect the cold feeling with the idea that metals can impart cold, instructors instead can describe how they connect the way metal feels at room temperature with the way metal feels in an oven or hot car, noting that metals feel cold at room temperature but hot relative to, say, wood, in a sauna or other hot environment. Also, instructors might connect how metal feels in a classroom with the rate of heat flow from their finger to the wood as illustrated with HeatBars.

After eliciting student ideas, instructors can analyze the connections students have made and identify pivotal cases that might motivate students to reorganize their ideas. For example, instructors might ask students who report that metals have the capacity to impart cold to consider how metals feel in a hot and cold car. They could ask, "How do metals feel in a hot car? Why don't they feel cold? How do the metals know which way to feel? What's going on?" These questions can motivate students to reorganize their ideas about insulation, conduction, and the properties of metals. Pivotal cases such as these help students because they are natural experiments. These cases compare situations in which just one variable changes.

Instructors also might illustrate possible connections by making their own thinking visible saying, "so I know my own temperature; it's 98.6°F, but metals change temperature. Why is that?" Furthermore, instructors might describe their experiences: "For a children's picnic, I wanted to keep the ice cream bars cold. I had extra blankets. I hesitated to cover the ice cream. I thought about how I feel when I crawl under a blanket on a cold night. I wondered if a blanket would keep the ice cream cold. I tried the blanket and it worked."

Instructors might elaborate: "I have to remind myself of the principle that heat flows from warm to cold objects. In the case of the ice cream bars, the blanket slows the transfer of the heat in the air to the cold ice cream. On a cold night, the blanket slows the transfer of my body heat to the cold room." In these examples instructors encourage new, pivotal connections based on analysis of student ideas. Instructors add connections to student ideas, make their own confusions visible, and help students recognize inconsistencies.

Many student ideas are based on valid observations: Metals do feel cold at room temperature. These observations stand in the way of knowledge integration when interpreted to mean that metals can cool objects. Pivotal cases, when introduced, help to make thinking visible and encourage students to reflect, reorganize, and reconnect their ideas. Eliciting ideas, modeling the process of connecting ideas, introducing pivotal ideas, and encouraging students to rethink their own connections jointly enable knowledge integration.

These approaches motivate students to figure out how their observations connect. The following quotes from a student in the CLP program demonstrate the connections students might make:

Interviewer: *"What happens to hot and cold objects over time?"*
Student: "Well, eventually after 8 hours, a Coke would heat up and the hot chocolate will cool down. So, just it would all...."

	Most of those things unless they were heated or cooled be-fore, will already be at room temperature."
Interviewer:	*"What does it mean to be a good conductor or insulator?"*
Student:	"For the conductor … we experimented and there was like the heat source, and they put the heat source on the material, and if it warmed up real fast it was a good conductor, and if it warmed up slow it was a poor conductor."
Interviewer:	*"How?"*
Student:	"The heat energy flowed through the material, so like copper was the best because heat energy went through it really fast, … And like Styrofoam didn't. It went really slow…. "

We hope that students who connect ideas in science class will begin to believe they can make sense of science instead of joining those who remark, "Don't ask me about science, I have forgotten everything."

Three pragmatic principles synthesize our ideas about making thinking visible. The first principle states: *Model the scientific process of considering alternative explanations and diagnosing mistakes.* Instructors can help students integrate ideas by making their own thinking visible, as shown with the pivotal cases earlier. The second principle states: *Scaffold students to explain their ideas.* Curriculum materials can be designed that encourage students to explain their ideas, reducing the emphasis on mundane tasks such as copying down procedures. This frees students to think and teachers to help individuals integrate their ideas. The third principle asserts: *Provide multiple, visual representations from varied media.* Technologies that provide animations, modeling environments, and multimedia depictions of phenomena all play a role here along with drawings, print materials, and hands-on materials. To offer learning partners to diverse students, we need varied visualizations.

PRAGMATIC PEDAGOGICAL PRINCIPLES

Model the process of considering alternatives

When do explanations work for students? How can we design instruction that explains processes and demonstrates mistakes? When we started teaching about heat and temperature, we relied on the explanations in the eighth grade textbook. Textbooks typically presented a molecular kinetic model of heat and described heat as measured in calories. Students made almost no progress in knowledge integration after this instruction. They continued to express intuitive ideas such as "Heat is the higher degrees on the thermometer." If students added ideas, they learned that "calories measure heat" and "degrees measure temperature." They did not link their ideas about heat being the higher degrees and heat being calories. We sought by using heat flow to make the connections among ideas more visible.

As discussed in the preceding chapter, we also turned to the heat flow model because it made more sense to students. The heat flow model affords many more connections for students. Nevertheless, students find making these connections, or thinking, difficult. We sought ways to encourage these connections, provide models of the process, and stimulate students to restructure their ideas.

In the CLP research we developed specific methods for encouraging knowledge integration. We elicited students' links and connections in knowledge integration assessments so students got rewarded for thinking and instructors know which ideas to build on. We helped instructors provide personal accounts of the process of linking ideas and making mistakes in classroom discussion. In addition, we developed instructional materials, such as case studies, that illustrated the steps and mistakes in knowledge integration.

With the CLP approach, the teacher's assessments elicit links and connections to measure the degree of knowledge integration students achieve. These assessments serve two purposes. First, knowledge integration assessments help teachers document student progress and understand student ideas. All the student comments in this book come from class assessments or interviews. We administered a pretest before instruction began and a posttest at the end of the semester. The pretest helped us to understand the ideas students already had. The posttest served as a final exam. Although we used the same questions on both tests, the students generally thought the questions had changed. Why? Students' ideas had changed, so the questions elicited a very different set of connections after the course was over.

Second, knowledge integration assessments communicate the demands of the course to students. Many of our students were surprised to find short-answer and short-essay questions in science (Fig. 2.1). We let them know, with these questions, that we expected them to link and connect ideas and think about what they were learning.

With the CLP approach, these assessments document improvements in instruction and in learning. Changes in the curriculum from one semester to the next can be evaluated by looking for specific improvements in learning outcomes. As discussed in chapter 2, such assessments reveal steady gains in knowledge integration. The assessments allow instructors to diagnose student confusions and redesign the course to make knowledge integration more feasible in areas of confusion. Some examples of knowledge integration assessments that reveal confusions about everyday examples are provided in Fig. 3.3.

To create effective assessments, we recommend designing them in tandem with the instruction. In engineering, this is called *concurrent design* of materials and assessments. Assessment items should reinforce the visualization process, help students test their visualizations, set course expectations, and reveal student thinking to the instructor. Assessment design requires the same creative process needed in instructional design. In the CLP project we incorporated prototypes and principles in assessment to parallel their usage in the software we were using (see Fig. 3.3). For example, we asked students to connect an example to the principle: Heat energy flows faster when the temperature difference between an object and its environment is greater.

We designed assessments that tapped understanding in diverse ways to connect to the range of student abilities. For example, we asked students to draw heat flow diagrams using arrows and other representations to depict the direction and rate of heat flow (Fig. 3.4). Ideally, students also could represent their ideas using electronic, dynamic tools, not just paper and pencil. Such assessments remain to be implemented in our work.

When instructors elicit student accounts of their own thinking, they encourage the knowledge integration process for students. As Mr. K describes (see Ask Mr. K), learning to make thinking visible for students involves developing good, short questions that help students sustain reasoning and consider new connections among their ideas. For example, some students believe that heat is absorbed like water in sponges and become confused when heat flows through an object. Other students view insulators as barriers, assuming that no heat passes through them. These students have difficulty understanding the continuum between insulation and conduction.

To address these kinds of student ideas, Mr. K introduced pivotal cases around the topic of thermal equilibrium. In one pivotal case, he asked students to compare the temperature of a metal table leg and the plastic seat by just touching them, then built on their experiences. Students were at first puzzled and surprised to find that objects that feel hotter or colder than each other have the same temperature. These activities and assessments reveal the many views students hold about heat and temperature.

Instructors can draw on assessments, class discussions, individual interviews, and one-on-one tutoring to identify student ideas about heat and temperature, not just to assign grades. Mr. K uses this infor-

> **Thermal Equilibrium Principle:** Eventually all objects in the same surround become the same temperature unless an object produces its own heat energy.

It is a hot summer day and Mac has invited some friends over. Mac takes two identical pitchers of lemonade out of the refrigerator and puts one on the counter in the 20°C air-conditioned kitchen and one on the picnic table outside on the covered porch where the temperature is 40°C.

 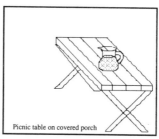

Air-conditioned kitchen   Picnic table on covered porch

a. Which lemonade will **warm at a faster rate**? (check one)

_____The lemonade on the kitchen counter

_____The lemonade on the picnic table

_____Both lemonades will warm at the same rate

What is the reason for your answer?

b. Fill in the blank to make a principle that applies to these pitchers:

Heat energy flows _____**when the temperature**

faster / slower / at the same rate

difference between an object and its environment is greater.

A wooden chair and a metal chair have been in Mr. K's class for 12 hours. The metal chair **feels colder** when you sit on it than the wooden chair, but when you measure the temperature of the chairs you find that they are both are 23° C.

a. Do you think that your temperature probe is working properly?

(circle one)   Yes   No

What is the **main reason** the objects _feel different_?

FIG. 3.3   Knowledge integration assessments.

You are shoveling snow without wearing gloves.

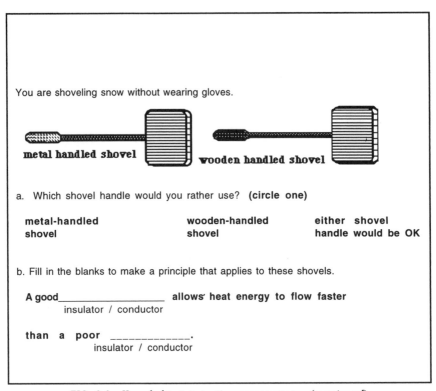

metal handled shovel   **wooden handled shovel**

a. Which shovel handle would you rather use? **(circle one)**

| **metal-handled shovel** | **wooden-handled shovel** | **either shovel handle would be OK** |

b. Fill in the blanks to make a principle that applies to these shovels.

A good_____ allows' heat energy to flow faster
        insulator / conductor

than a poor _____.
          insulator / conductor

FIG. 3.3   Knowledge integration assessments. (*continued*)

Heat energy flows only from objects at higher temperature to objects at lower temperature

In his pottery class, Rex makes a ceramic bowl and bakes it in the kiln for several hours. When he removes the hot bowl from the kiln, which direction does the heat energy flow—from the hot bowl to the cooler air or from the cooler air to the hot bowl?

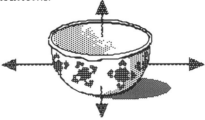

The heat energy flows from the hot bowl to the cooler air.

FIG. 3.4   A prototype in which arrows indicate direction
of heat flow.

mation to become more and more effective at interacting with students to encourage knowledge integration. To understand this process, Judy Stern, our software designer, "wired" Mr. K for sound, hooking up a tape recorder and collecting examples of his interactions with students. For example, this segment shows Mr. K using prompts to help a student understand the relationship between surface area and cooling, then design an experiment to test these variables:

Mr. K:	"What would be your guess at this point, for example, that you're going to do with surface area?"
Tyne:	"Wait! What are we supposed to be doing?"
Mr. K:	"OK, think about the lab. Which variable is it you're looking at? (pause) What is the thing you're trying to find out?"
Tyne:	"If it'll cool if it's on the flat plate or the large one ... "
Marti:	"Big surface area or small ... "
Tyne:	"Big or small ... "
Mr. K:	"OK, big or small. So, the variable you're going to change is what?"
Tyne:	"Small, wait ... "
Mr. K:	"Which variable do you want to be different on those two things?"
Marti:	"Small, here. Large, here."
Mr. K:	"Sounds good. OK?"

Mr. K often asks just the right question at the right time. He also elicits explanations to illustrate the course expectations. By the later versions of the CLP curriculum, Mr. K regularly elicited diverse student ideas and spent more time talking out loud about his own understanding of science phenomena. As shown in chapter 2, this modification to the curriculum significantly improved student performance.

Why does it help to describe wrong paths and illustrate pivotal cases? It takes considerable courage to describe mistakes and errors in reasoning, but this is a central aspect of scientific thinking. Some instructors invite students to ask them complex problems in class. These instructors then spontaneously describe their solution, often confirming that they, too, can flounder and try wrong paths. By describing mistakes and the process of recovering from a mistake, instructors provide an authentic model of scientific thinking that may surprise students.

Students need models of "science in the making" to add to their views. Many students believe that scientists are always right or that everything in the science text will always be true. More than 25% of CLP students assert that everything in the science text is true. When asked what is untrue, some say, "Last year we had a couple of wrong principles in our textbooks." Why? "Probably the people that typed it up." Others assert that the text is true, with the possible exception of some true or false questions.

Students often believe scientists disagree on details but not fundamentals. One student explained: "Two scientists may see something another one didn't." Others find that scientists like to argue saying, "Scientists never agree since they each have their own opinions."

Illustrating wrong paths can help students learn about science in the making. Wrong paths can show that scientific thinking involves a continuous process of rethinking and reorganizing ideas and developing more integrated perspectives. Every day we read articles in newspapers and magazines and encounter personal decisions that require us to think about potential contradictions and resolve ambiguities among our scientific ideas. Lifelong science learning, our ultimate goal, means that we need to prepare students to use this process regularly. Ideally, students should understand the way science progresses. Some students bring useful ideas to the discussion:

> Scientists might come to a conclusions about something such as evolution only to have it corrected by future findings.

> Scientists may discover something else to prove a theory wrong.

> Not everything in a science book is true because we don't know everything there is to know in this world yet, and some of the things in a science book are just sometimes observations.

> The science books made in the early 1900s said that going to the moon was virtually impossible. The books in the early 1400s said that the world was flat. Much of science is based on theory.

> Yes, they can find something in the experiment, and a week later they can find something else.

> Yes, sometimes scientists compare their results. Sometimes they figure it out by themselves by using 'guess and check,' but only if they can.

To engage students in the process of making thinking visible, we sought ways to make the tutoring Mr. K does more accessible to students. With Mr. K's assistance, we built prompts phrased as sentence starters into the software. These included "We predict ... " and "A prin-ciple ... " or more elaborate prompts such as "From our experiment, we found that ... " and "Something we've seen or done that gives evidence for these predictions is ... " and "It supports our predictions because ... ". For example, in response, students wrote as follows:

> A principle that helps explain something that you observed in this experiment is if the material is a good conductor it will let energy flow through freely, but if it is a good insulator it will keep heat in.

> A principle that helps explain what I saw in this experiment is that to keep an object cold you need a good insulator.

> A principle that applies to this experiment is that a good conduc-tor is a bad insulator, while a bad conductor is a good insulator. The better the insulator, the more the heat or cold will be con-tained.

Prompts help students with knowledge integration, but are less effec-tive than a human tutor for promoting knowledge integration. Prompts and reflection are discussed in chapter 5. Students can also make their knowledge integration visible when they discuss their decisions with their peers. This approach is considered in chapter 4.

Curriculum materials themselves also can explain a process and demonstrate mistakes. For example, case studies often illustrate steps and mistakes in problem solutions. Our work to design better com-puter science instruction in the CLP project was benefited by our col-laboration with Michael Clancy. Clancy and Linn developed case studies of solutions to complicated programming problems and tested them in research investigations. Case studies alerted students to the errors that program designers make, improved understanding of com-puter science, and increased the amount of material students learned in the first course. Clancy and Linn published two books of case studies that implement these ideas.

In the CLP project, we did not create written case studies, but in-stead asked students to critique reports of problem solutions authored by their peers. This approach is discussed as part of promoting student autonomy in chapter 5.

In summary, rather than telling students the "right" answer, in-structors who elicit student ideas and model scientific thinking en-courage students actively to connect their ideas and sort out their links. Studies of programming and studies of science instruction show that students learn more sophisticated ideas from instruction that emphasizes making thinking visible. Instructors can explain the process of integrating ideas and enact scenarios involving common dead ends and wrong paths that problem solvers take. Print, online, and peer-to-peer interactions can involve students in considering pivotal cases to improve their understanding.

Scaffold students to explain their thinking

How can we design classroom experiences to make thinking more visible? We can structure science so that students devote most of their reasoning power to connecting, linking, and reorganizing their ideas. We can guide the process of connecting, linking, and reorganizing so that students keep thinking about their experiences in productive ways. If students have to spend too much time thinking about or keeping track of mundane classroom details, they may not have energy to think about scientific ideas. Even when doing hands-on experiments, students may lose track of the outcome because they are busy adjusting the apparatus or cleaning up spills.

The CLP curriculum encourages students to make their ideas visible with the CLP checklist to keep track of progress in an activity: in the CLP predictions and outcomes where students reconcile their ideas; the CLP notes that elicit student ideas; the CLP principle construction process in which students abstract their ideas; and the CLP prototype examples wherein students connect ideas across examples.

The CLP checklist takes care of details so students can spend time on knowledge integration (Fig. 3.5). Judy Stern used the tapes of Mr. K talking to students while they conducted experiments and designed online tools that left more time for tutoring. Stern designed the CLP checklist to make visible the steps needed to complete any activity. Rather than ask, "What should I do next?" and "How do I do that?" students can use the checklist. Before the checklist was used, far too many questions that Mr. K answered had to do with what the next activity was. In addition, students who knew what to do next were often unsure about how to do it. The checklist provided answers to these questions, reduced the frequency of logistic questions, and enabled Mr. K to spend more time in one-on-one or small-group discussions of science.

Mr. K elaborates: "I think previously I spent an awful lot of time answering questions such as: "What do I do next? How do I do that? What's next? I've done this. Now do I get a test tube and go and do this? Well what do I do now? Mr. K, what do I do now?" Stern came up with the checklist. It provided me a lot more time to talk to kids about the science of what's going on. Technology's left me with more time to work

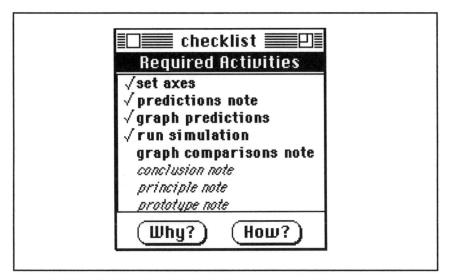

FIG. 3.5 The activity checklist frees the teacher from answering
What next? Why? and How? questions. The next activity is in bold. Gray
activities have prerequisites. Checked activities have been completed.

with kids on the side, and basically to talk and probe the kinds of things
I find valuable."

The CLP predictions and outcomes make the process of explaining
and interpreting results more visible. Students make predictions
about experimental outcomes right on the graph. Then they compare
their predictions to the results as shown in Fig. 3.6. By structuring predictions, we emphasize an essential aspect of scientific thinking. We
also encourage autonomy, as discussed in chapter 5, and improve the
impact of real-time data collection.

To structure the process of taking notes on a scientific experiment
as mentioned in chapter 2, Stern created electronic post-it notes for
students to use (Fig. 3.7, see Fig. 2.15). Students explain their predictions, describe their findings, and reconcile their predictions with
their findings. For example, here are some student notes from the
Cokes and Potatoes experiment, in which students experiment with
various materials to find a good wrap for keeping a Coke cold and a potato warm:

What we saw in this experiment is that Styrofoam is a very good insulator. Heat energy flows better through a good conductor, like
aluminum foil, and doesn't flow as well through a bad conductor
like Styrofoam.

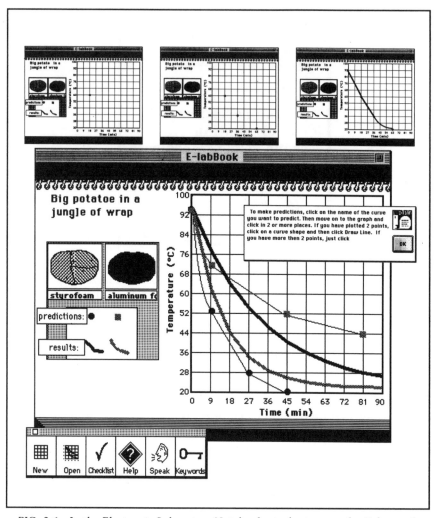

FIG. 3.6   In the Electronic Laboratory Notebook, students open the Cokes and Potatoes experiment. Students place dots on graphs to make predictions, then check their predictions against actual results (thicker curves) simulated by the computer.

Good conductors allow heat to flow easily into an object while good insulators don't allow any heat or cold energy to flow into an object.

An object in a good insulator slows down the flow of heat energy escaping.

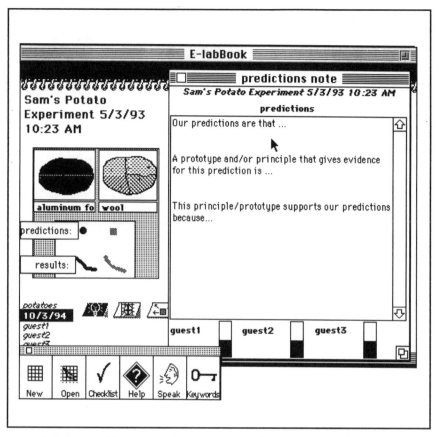

FIG. 3.7   This Electronic Laboratory Notebook notes window that prompts students to make predictions, provide a prototypical example, and write a principle.

Materials that are higher scattering like aluminum and don't absorb heat are better insulators than objects that do absorb and don't reflect. [sic]

Heat travels from hot to cold. In this experience the heat from the room traveled to the soda.

Wrapping an object in a good insulator makes the heat energy flow more slowly.

To help students synthesize their ideas in CLP, we designed opportunities for them to construct principles. For describing scientific phenomena, students need a precise vocabulary. Yet heat and temperature have many imprecise, colloquial uses. To support knowledge integration, we wanted to scaffold the processes scientists use to talk about complex, precise problems and to show the benefits of abstractions. We asked students to write pragmatic scientific principles to synthesize their experimental findings.

As a first step, as described in chapter 2, our research group tried to develop a set of pragmatic scientific principles to describe the aspects of heat and temperature that CLP students investigate (Table 3.1). Negotiating principles raised tempers and lengthened group meetings. The early version of the Mass and Rate Principle was worded as follows: "If the same amount of heat energy is added to different masses of the same material, the temperature of the larger mass will change less." Over time, it became this statement, "When only mass differs, the temperature of the larger mass will change more slowly." Later, we clarified the initial condition, adding this modification: "Initially, heat energy will flow at the same rate from both objects to a cooler surround." We sought principles with precision and power to explain personally relevant problems.

To scaffold thinking we asked students to write their own principles. Students found writing principles nearly impossible. Why were we surprised? Our research group failed the same assignment. To scaffold students in principle construction, we asked them to construct single principles after each experiment. We tried to make the thinking of constructing principles visible and provided examples of principles. Still, difficulties were the rule. Examples of principles drawn from students' work include these:

In 2 hours, the coke reaches its freezing point.

Temperature can be either hot or cold, but heat energy is the amount of heat in an object.

Two things may be the same temperature, but the larger one has more heat energy.

We tried using sentence starters such as "A principle for this experiment ... " or, "My experiments show that heat flows faster ... " or "Our principle is ... " The sentence starters elicited somewhat better answers:

A principle for this experiment is if an object is a good conductor, like the foil then it will be a bad insulator.

Our principle is the warmer the material, the warmer that material makes the object it is wrapped around.

TABLE 3.1

Pragmatic Scientific Principles: These CLP Principles Revised Over the Years, Reflect Ideas About How to Express Thermal Concepts

FLOW PRINCIPLES

- Direct flow principle: Heat energy flows only when there is a temperature difference.
- Direction of heat flow principle: Heat energy flows only from objects at higher temperature to objects at lower temperature

RATE PRINCIPLES

- Surface area principle: When only surface area differs, heat energy will flow faster through the larger surface area.
- Mass and rate principle: When only mass differs, the temperature of the larger mass will change more slowly. Initially, hat energy will flow at the same rate from both objects to a cooler surround.
- Material and rate principle: When only material differs, the temperatures of the two objects will change at different rates. Initially, heat energy will flow at the same rate from both objects to a cooler surround.
- Temperature difference principle: The greater the temperature difference between objects and their surround, the faster heat energy flows.
- Conductivity principle: A good conductor allows heat energy to flow faster than a poor conductor.

TOTAL HEAT FLOW PRINCIPLES

- Thermal equilibrium principle: Eventually, all objects in the same surround become the same temperature unless an object produces its own heat energy.
- Mass and total heat flow principle: When only mass differs, more heat energy flows from the larger mass to a cooler surround.
- Material and total heat flow principle: When only material differs, more heat energy flows from one material than the other to a cooler surround.

INTEGRATION PRINCIPLE:

- Heat energy and temperature principle: When each part of an object has the same temperature, more heat energy will flow to a cooler surround from the whole than from each part.

To scaffold the process more, there was one Macintosh utility that allowed students to construct principles using pull-down menus (Fig. 3.8). Students could select words to fill in principle statements. More students could construct principles using this approach. Furthermore, the computer could evaluate the choices students made and provide feedback. Principles of varying sophistication (Fig. 3.9) could be constructed by students and evaluated.

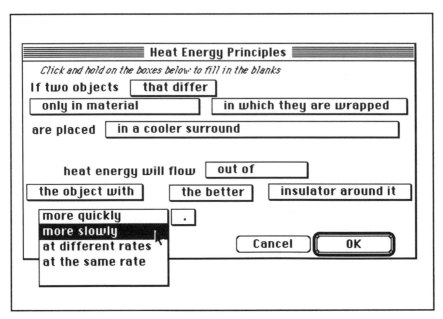

FIG. 3.8   Students build principles by selecting words
or phrases from pull-down menus.

"If two objects that differ only in size in which they are wrapped are placed
in a cooler surround heat energy will flow out of the object with the better
conductor around it   more quickly."

"If two objects that differ only in material in which they are wrapped are
placed in a warmer surround heat energy will flow out of the object with
the better insulator around it more slowly."

"If two objects that differ only in mass in which they are wrapped are placed
in the same surround, heat energy will flow out of the object with the
better conductor around it at different rates."

"If two objects that differ only in size in which they are wrapped are placed
in a warmer surround heat energy will flow into the object with the better
conductor around at the same rate."

FIG. 3.9   Sample principles that students construct using Electronic
Laboratory Notebook pull-down menus.

Some student groups became frustrated with the pull-down menus because they could not construct a principle. Others used trial and error. Because a typical principle had 5 to 10 blanks and at least four choices for each blank, few students had the patience to try the thousands of possibilities.

Stern redesigned the software so that after three failures in constructing a principle, students were encouraged to consult the teacher for needed tutoring. In the first version, students could not continue until Mr. K typed in a password. This approach reduced the trial and error method of principle construction but created other problems. If every group called Mr. K at the same time, large numbers of students were left with nothing to do until Mr. K could get to their screen. We modified this procedure to permit more tries and to encourage peer collaboration.

The group soon located better software to support principle construction. In the next version, students selected among terms and phrases to construct a principle (Fig. 3.10). This software also could identify accurate and inaccurate principles. Choice of terms and phrases could simplify or complicate the task. Offering only the words students needed for constructing a principle made the task easier than offering unnecessary and extraneous words. In addition, capitalization and punctuation could provide clues.

This new software worked best when groups of students first wrote a principle in their own words, then constructed a principle, and finally received feedback on their principle (Fig. 3.11). Constructing these pragmatic scientific principles allowed students to make their abstract ideas visible.

To encourage visible, productive links to everyday experience, we identified prototypes, personally relevant situations in which students can make good predictions about the outcome of an experiment but cannot necessarily provide an explanation. For example, students had good ideas about what a thermos will do but were less able to explain why (Fig. 3.12).

Students linked the prototype to their experiment before constructing a principle. They understood both the prototype and the experiment, so linking these two examples was easier than constructing a principle. For some students, abstracting a statement about their experiment and the prototype still proved difficult. Students explained, "Heat energy flows out of the smaller one"; "Everything will reach room temperature"; and "In 2 hours, a coke reaches its freezing point."

Does the creation of principles and connections between examples make thinking visible? These opportunities for knowledge integration make visible the process of linking and connecting ideas by scaffolding it in a step-by-step manner. Students who might not spontaneously

The first principle construction interface

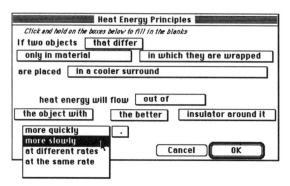

Heat Energy Principles

Click and hold on the boxes below to fill in the blanks

If two objects | that differ |
| only in material | | in which they are wrapped |
are placed | in a cooler surround |

heat energy will flow | out of |
| the object with | | the better | | insulator around it |
| more quickly |
| **more slowly** |
| at different rates |
| at the same rate | | . |

Cancel | OK

Intermediate principle construction interface

principle

| Conductivity | Hot Potatoes |
| A good conductor allows heat energy to flow faster than a poor conductor | A good conductor / a poor conductor / allows / heat energy / to flow as fast as / to flow as slow as / to flow faster than |

Late principle construction interface

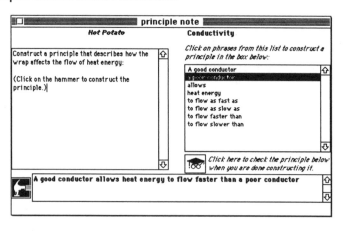

principle note

Hot Potato

Construct a principle that describes how the wrap affects the flow of heat energy:

(Click on the hammer to construct the principle.)

Conductivity

Click on phrases from this list to construct a principle in the box below:

A good conductor
a poor conductor
allows
heat energy
to flow as fast as
to flow as slow as
to flow faster than
to flow slower than

Click here to check the principle below when you are done constructing it.

A good conductor allows heat energy to flow faster than a poor conductor

FIG. 3.10 Electronic Laboratory Notebook supports student construction of principles. An iterative redesign of the principle construction feature made a complicated activity of selecting phrases simpler.

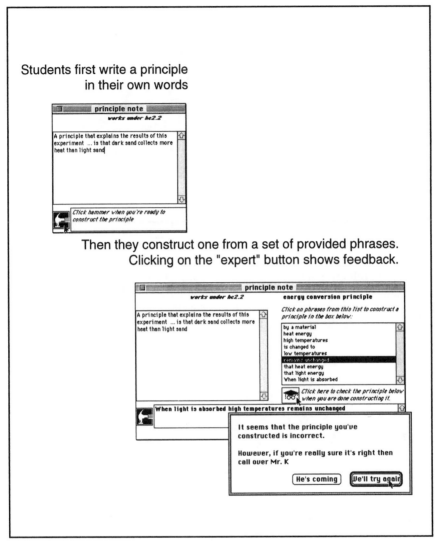

FIG. 3.11   Final version of principle construction software: Students write
a principle, get feedback, and keep working.

make connections, and who certainly could not write principles for
their experiments on their own have the opportunity, nevertheless, to
engage in some aspects of this inquiry process with these supports and
scaffolds.

We found that when we provided guidance and structure to encourage students to make their thinking visible, students learned more. For

Sam uses a thermos to keep her chicken soup warm and her Slurpee cold. How is this possible?

Since a thermos is a good insulator, it keeps heat energy from flowing as quickly so whatever is inside it tends to stay near the same temperature.

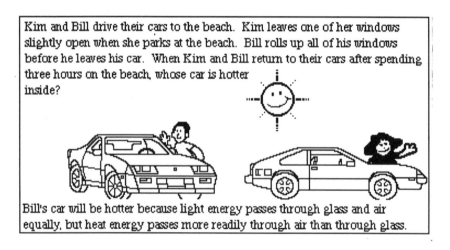

Kim and Bill drive their cars to the beach. Kim leaves one of her windows slightly open when she parks at the beach. Bill rolls up all of his windows before he leaves his car. When Kim and Bill return to their cars after spending three hours on the beach, whose car is hotter inside?

Bill's car will be hotter because light energy passes through glass and air equally, but heat energy passes more readily through air than through glass.

FIG. 3.12   An example of two prototypes used to provide everyday examples of heat and temperature.

example, students doing a CLP experiment spent more time thinking and writing than is common in middle school hands-on laboratories. Some students complained that they wanted to do experiments, not think about them. We counted this as an indicator of success.

In summary, to help students use their reasoning power for knowledge integration, we iterated to find a balance between "hands-on" science and "minds-on" science. We kept adjusting the number of required notes (initially, we had far too many). In addition we kept adding choices for students. For example, we encouraged students to choose which materials to investigate, what volumes of liquids to compare, how long to observe changes, and what starting temperature to use. All such decisions potentially can lead to an experiment that is confounded or yields ambiguous findings. As a result, students had a chance to make and correct mistakes with support from peers, software, and their teachers. To help students do independent experiments we added CLP projects as described in chapter 5.

Use multiple visual representations from varied media

Our third pragmatic pedagogical principle encourages instructors to use a broad range of media to make thinking visible. Individual students find learning partners in some visualizations but not others.

We found during the CLP project that even very short visualization experiences can have a dramatic impact. As visual thinking becomes more commonplace, students may develop the ability to generate their own visualizations. Some students need only a prompt to consider a visualization. Others need some visual alternatives. We need to encourage students to seek animated depictions for their ideas right along with verbal and symbolic representations.

The science curriculum takes surprisingly little advantage of animations and visualizations, yet these skills are crucial for success in understanding building construction, molecule interactions, and more. We can prepare students by providing visual experiences and encouraging them to think visually.

The CLP approach features many diverse visualization tools. Paper and pencil tools are used, along with tools that take full advantage of multimedia. These multimedia tools include HeatBars to animate the process of heat flow, the Continuum Line to help students represented relative rates of heat flow spatially, graphs of real-time data collections to animate trends in experiments, the Thermal Model Kit to animate the implications of design decisions, and multimedia debate evidence to illustrate connections. Offering a mix of visualization tools means that most students will find a depiction they can add to their repertoire of ideas.

Because relative rates of heat flow confused many students, the CLP project sought a good representation of heat transfer rate. Natural scientists often argue that molecular kinetic theory with its elegant mathematical representation makes thinking visible while it prepares students for future science courses. Middle school students, however, cannot visualize the process behind the mathematics required for molecular kinetic theory. They need a more accessible representation.

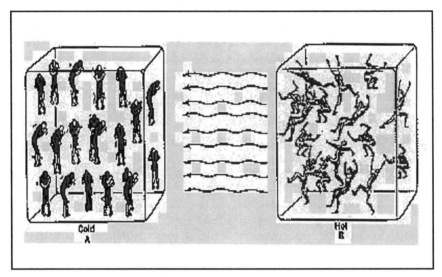

FIG. 3.13 Dancing men: Illustration adapted from a textbook representation of heat energy.

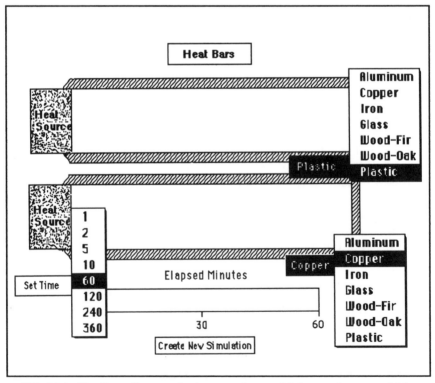

FIG. 3.14 HeatBars allows students to conduct multiple experiments quickly.

Textbooks that rely on molecular kinetic theory feature visualizations such as the one in Fig. 3.13. In this visualization, the speed of molecules is represented by the movements of individual male images. For a cold object, the people are shivering. For a hot object, they are dancing. These figures suggest that molecules in warmer objects move more rapidly. When asked, students have difficulty interpreting this image and wonder exactly what each man represents. Some assume that the men represent heat, concluding that when heat gets warmer, it jumps around more. Others liked the idea that heat might have intelligence and would know when it needed to change. Some attempted to impose a heat flow model on the dancing men, saying that the men moved from the cold to the hot, between the two sides of the representation. Students' responses to the dancing men confirmed our conjecture that molecular kinetic theory defies easy visualization for eighth-grade students.

To help students visualize heat flow, we created HeatBars and the Continuum Line. We also incorporated real-time data collection, the Thermal Model Kit, and multimedia evidence.

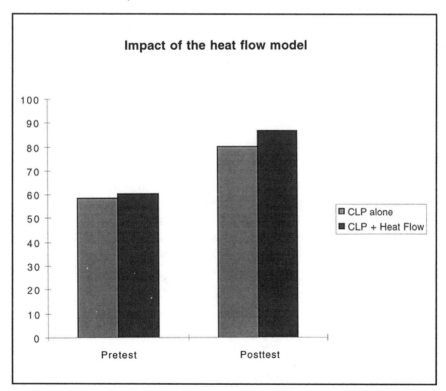

FIG. 3.15 Adding the heat flow model improves student understanding of thermal concepts.

HeatBars. Eileen Lewis and Brian Foley created HeatBars (Fig. 3.14) to simulate the rate of heat flow through an object placed on a heat source. HeatBars animates the invisible process of heat flow in a simplified, interactive visualization. This model for heat flow is similar to the historic caloric model, but stresses that heat lacks mass.

The HeatBars software program allows learners to simulate heat transfer in two bars made from different materials. Learners can select the starting temperature of the room, heat source, duration of the experiment, and bar materials. When the simulation is started, heat sources are brought in contact with the ends of the bars. A random distribution of dots in a given area represents the amount of heat energy flowing into and through the area.

Many eighth-grade students report the benefits of HeatBars. One student remarked: "The heat energy flowed through the material, so like copper was the best because heat energy went through it really fast, ... and like Styrofoam didn't. It went really slow." Another student said that "[HeatBars] showed you how different things worked. There was an experiment about how time affects the rate of giving off energy of something ... seeing how fast it did it."

Compared with molecular kinetic theory, HeatBars connects to more student ideas and experiences. One student explained: "You can use your hands and go to work instead of just trying to visualize it in your head or something. And sometimes it helps if it doesn't work in your head or something 'cause you can see it."

By animating the process of heat flow, HeatBars allows learners visually to compare the relative rates at which heat energy flows from a constant temperature heat source into the equally sized bars of various materials.

HeatBars has a remarkable impact on understanding of elementary thermodynamics. Lewis found that students in the CLP classroom who used this heat flow model for 1 hour performed significantly better than those who did not. Scores improved especially on distinguishing between heat and temperature. Posttest scores of students who used the model were significantly higher, as shown in Fig. 3.15. These results suggest benefits from animating invisible relationships to make a process more visible to students.

The HeatBars visualization directly encourages a heat flow representation. Many students map HeatBars onto their own views of how heat flows. Visual representations, such as HeatBars can add new views of scientific phenomena to the mix held by students. They might even connect to nonverbalizable ideas. Students, who cannot express themselves in words, may still report that they "see" how heat flow works. Students who characterize themselves as "visual" learners resonate

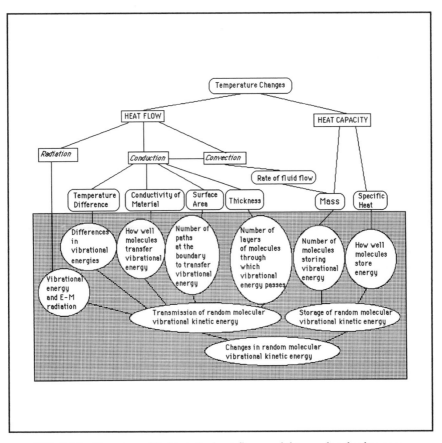

FIG. 3.16   One view of linking the heat flow model to molecular kinetics.

with such things as HeatBars. One student reported, "You don't think about having good conductors and stuff unless you actually see it and you feel it and you know. It's not real unless you do it."

Discussing a visualization such as HeatBars with peers and teachers can provide a vocabulary for students. One student used HeatBars to explain conduction to a teacher: "For the conductor ... we experimented and there was like the heat source, and they put the heat source on the material and if it warmed up real fast it was a good conductor, and if it warmed up slow it was a poor conductor."

Do students who study HeatBars learn a molecular kinetic view more easily? Lawrence Muilenberg, a former education graduate student at University of California at Berkeley trained in physics, illustrated how

Make a prediction about insulators and conductors

Where would you place the following materials on the Continuum lLne? Do the same problem again, but assume that the ends of the continuum line are labeled "conductor" and "insulator." What visualizations helped you solve this problem? Did this exercise contribute to knowledge integration?

Write the names of each of the following materials on the line where you think they belong as an insulator. Assume all the materials have the same thickness.

Materials: metal   roam   rubber   plastic
             ceramic   wool   wood   glass

|———————|————————|———————|———————|———————|———————|———————|———————|
very poor insulator   very good insulator

FIG. 3.17   Make a prediction using this Continuum Line activity. An activity to help students organize their knowledge of insulators and conductors.

students might start with heat flow and make subsequent connections to molecular kinetic theory (Fig. 3.16).

Some students make connections between the two perspectives by the end of high school. For example, one high school students remarked: "The heat from my hand is going into the can and it's like heating up the molecules in the can. That's what I'm thinking anyway because I guess it is going to an area where there's less energy because it's colder." Another student said: "Something that's hot has more energy. Like when you boil water, it has more energy, and all of these molecules, when it starts to evaporate, all of these little molecules are jumping off the surface, and because they have a lot of energy. And when you freeze it, it slows the molecules down and it has less energy and it's cold." A third student remarked: "Atoms that lack heat energy would want to take heat energy away from warmer objects."

Some students in the CLP project saw HeatBars as reinforcing a "heat as substance" model, interpreting the "dots" as "pieces" of heat. Pat was able to distinguish this view from the normative view in high school as discussed in chapter 7.

Continuum Line.   The Continuum Line representation was designed to augment HeatBars because some students in the CLP project believed that insulators all behave similarly and essentially put up a "barrier" so heat cannot flow. To help students sort out the behavior of materials, Nancy Songer designed the Continuum Line exercise shown in Fig. 3.17. Songer thought that asking students to arrange materials along a continuum line might help them visualize how insulators vary in their effectiveness. To complete the Continuum Line activity, students performed experiments and compared the insulating properties of different materials. Classroom assignments involved testing insulating properties and constructing continuum lines. Research groups in the classroom studied different materials and combined results.

For many CLP students, placing materials on the Continuum Line contributed to knowledge integration. In Songer's dissertation work with continuum lines, students successfully placed different materials and objects according to their relative rates of heat flow. Students also applied this idea to water tower designs, placing them along a continuum according to how well they would insulate the water.

Students were able to connect HeatBars results to the Continuum Line representation. They could use HeatBars results to place points on the line. These two representations both reinforced heat flow and helped students build a coherent personal visualization about the rate of heat flow and its effects on insulation, conduction, and other aspects of heat and temperature.

Students could modify the Continuum Line task to make visible barrier models and other views of insulators and conductors. For example, some students placed each item twice on the Continuum Line, once for heating and once for cooling. Others relabeled the Continuum Line to more closely reflect their views, adding a section for materials that can both insulate and conduct. Continuum Line responses revealed student confusions (Fig. 3.18). Evan and Angel labeled the end points in terms of "time" rather than "insulation," perhaps because things change temperature more slowly with insulation. Sean and Tu focused on evaporation rather than insulation. Sam and Jean predicted that wood cools faster than aluminum.

The Continuum Line helped some students think about insulation and conduction, and also assisted instructors in understanding the range of student ideas. Thus, students who believed that insulators and conductors work better for hot than for cold items had the opportunity to communicate their visualization of the role of insulators and conductors to others. Peer discussions often centered on alternative ways to design the Continuum Line. Whether students incorporate this feedback or not, the opportunity to discuss these ideas had the potential of helping students restructure their ideas and added the normative view to their mix of ideas. (See chapter 4 for further discussion of how students learn from each other.)

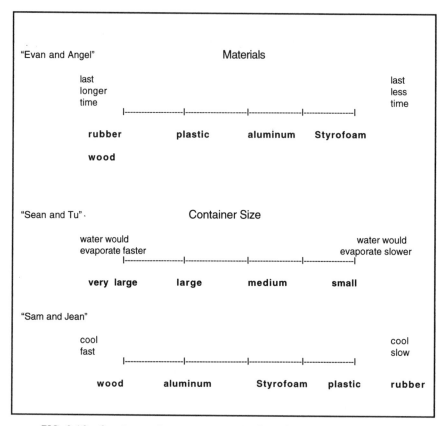

FIG. 3.18   Continuum Line responses: Analyze these student responses. Evaluate the labels for the endpoints as well as the placement of materials.

The success of the paper and pencil Continuum Line motivated Judy Stern to design an online version for the electronic notebook. Students using this feature of the electronic notebook were able to compare results of many different experiments simultaneously. The electronic Continuum Line was easier for students to access and update throughout the semester than the paper-and-pencil version. Stern also created a mechanism for students electronically to share the results of their experiments shown in Fig. 3.19. Logistic problems with sending and receiving data in the classroom made this less successful than simply posting information on the blackboard and having students incorporate it into their own worksheets.

How do students use this Continuum Line? Do they directly translate this representation into a mental image that they can inspect visually? Do they use the Continuum Line as a clever mnemonic for keeping

Exchanging Research Worksheet

KH
AH
KIRKPATRICK

1. Enter the wraps you used in your experiment.

First wrap	Aluminum Foil
Second wrap	Styrofoam

2. Use the text tool (it's the letter **A** in the tools palette) to place your two wraps on the conductivity continuum line below. "Air" is done for you as an example.

3. Use the **Network Request** option in the **Windows** menu to find a group that used **one** of the wraps you used, but **did not** use both of the wraps that you used. For example, if you used aluminum and styrofoam, you could share data with a group that used aluminum and saranwrap.

To find a group, send a request to a group asking for a **Graph.** In the space where you can describe your request say something like "Send me your potatoes graph, if your group used aluminum, but NOT styrofoam, please." (They should send you back a response of "Sorry, can't help", if their experiment does not meet your needs). If the first group you ask can't help, ask another, and so on. If a group can help, they will check **Send Graph** and then click **OK** in the window where your request showed up. Their graph should show up in a window on your computer.

When you Enter the wrap they used that is **different** from your two.

Third Wrap	Wool

4. Use the data from the graph they send to place the new wrap on your continuum line in step 2, above. Some questions that might help placing the new wrap are:

Is the new wrap a better conductor than **both** of my wraps?   **NO**
Is the new wrap a worse conductor than **both** of my wraps?   **NO**
Is the new wrap a better conductor than **one** of my wraps but not the other? **YES**

You might need to find a third group's data in order to answer the last question!!!

FIG. 3.19   (*continued on next page*)

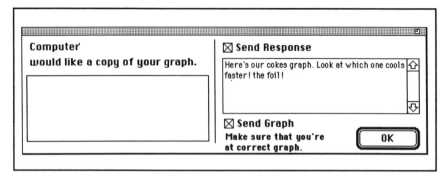

FIG. 3.19   This example is drawn from the Cokes
and Potatoes experiment. Students can share graphs, notes, and other
documents during experiments.

track of alternative materials, or does the Continuum Line become an
abstraction that individual students visualize differently? Listening to
students talk about the continuum line, illustrated alternative uses.
Pat used it to organize information saying, "Metal would probably be
first. Then wood and Styrofoam are probably about the same. And then
glass, saran wrap." Another student responded to the Continuum Line
by revealing gaps in knowledge. "Yeah. I keep going back and forth with
it. I was just going to say I would put it somewhere in the middle because I really don't know."

Real-time data collection.   Real-time data collection is an important
example of the varied representations found in CLP. As discussed in
chapter 2, Bob Tinker created real-time data collection tools for students to use in animating graphic relationships. Tinker wanted to
make visible the process underlying graphing. The real-time
data-collection tools represent the dynamic changes over time when
objects heat and cool. Bob Tinker, working with Ron Thornton, demonstrated that dynamic, real-time data collection graphs helped students
to understand complex phenomena. College students gain better understanding of mechanics as well as heat and temperature from using
real-time data collection.

In 1985, when real-time data was introduced into CLP curricula,
eighth graders immediately embraced it. Students described their
findings using dynamic language. They noticed more rapid cooling at
the beginning of an experiment when there was a big temperature difference than at the end when there was a small temperature difference.
Students describing their results meant hands flying through the air
imitating graphic changes.

Clearly, the graphs orchestrated a physical response in students, who experienced the changes they saw on the screen as dynamic relationships rather than static drawings. Our classroom research showed, as discussed in chapter 2, that students using real-time data collection integrated their understanding of heating and cooling change over time, and of graphing better than students who used paper and pencil to graph their findings.

How do students interpret graphs? We looked for ways to make students' ideas about graphs visible. Many students view static graphs as pictures of mountains, or roofs, or valleys. Bob Tinker invented a wonderful device to illustrate student ideas about static graphs: the Back to the Future Graph (Fig. 3.20). Tinker asked students whether a graph that turned back on itself was an adequate representation of cooling or heating over time. Many students accepted this graph, not realizing that time ran along the bottom axis of the graph, and therefore that the line represented going backward in time.

These examples illustrate how students interpret graphs as pictures. In contrast, dynamic, real-time data collection graphs connect the process of, say, cooling to the graphical representation. Students can "see" the relationship. They enact these relationships with their hands. They use dynamic language like faster and slower to describe changes rather than talking about static representations such as valleys and mountains.

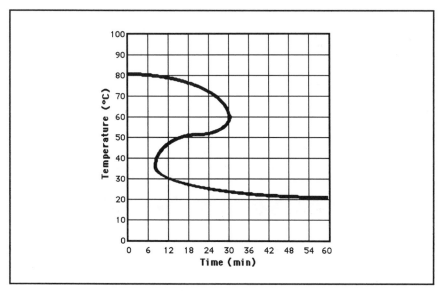

FIG. 3.20   Back to the Future: What is wrong with this representation
of temperature versus time?

Once students recognize that graphs represent dynamic relationships, how do they sort out the patterns in these graphs? The CLP partnership wanted to help students encode the shapes of graphs as relationships and to reinforce the notion that heating and cooling curves have characteristic shapes. Stern designed two choices for graph predictions. In one choice, students put a few points on the graph, and the computer program creates a continuous curve using a "spline" drawing program to create a smooth curve (Fig. 3.6).

To reinforce patterns, Stern also added a facility in which students could select among various curve shapes, put in a few points, and fit them with the shape (Fig. 3.21). The software fills in the curve the student selects. When students select shapes, they concentrate on the pattern for heating or cooling rather than on individual points. This approach reinforces the idea that the graph represents a reproducible,

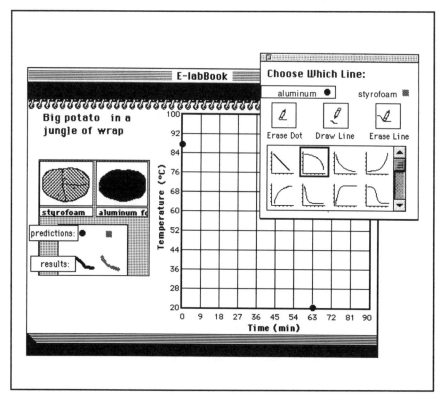

FIG. 3.21   Students can make graph predictions by drawing the start and end
temperatures with a line-drawing tool, then selecting the shape of the curve.
Electronic Laboratory Notebook draws the spline curve between the two points
on the basis of the student's selection.

continuous, physical process. We found that some groups of students preferred using shapes for their graph predictions, whereas others liked using points. This is another way to support diverse students with visual representations.

The CLP team wondered whether middle school students could be engaged to create and test models of heat flow. A modeling tool might help students distinguish thermal equilibrium and rate of heat flow by illustrating that objects reach thermal equilibrium at different times. The tool needed to represent the rate that heat flows into or out of objects when they are all in the same environment.

Thermal Model Kit. Mark Thomas joined the CLP group after completing an undergraduate degree in physics. Thomas had extensive experience writing computer programs at the Lawrence Berkeley Laboratory. He spent time in the classroom identifying students' understanding and intuitions about models. To support students' conjectures about this process, Thomas designed the Thermal Model Kit, a visualization and modeling program for middle school students, as part of his Master's thesis in the combined teacher credential and Master of Arts program (Fig. 3.22). Designing the Thermal Model Kit required representing three-dimensional objects in two dimensions. Unlike HeatBars, which compared objects with similar characteristics, students use the Thermal Model Kit to create everyday objects such as pizza boxes or insulated coolers and explore their properties. Representing the thickness of an object and its contents raised difficult questions.

As the design of the Thermal Model Kit progressed, Thomas became more and more interested in communicating complex physics issues to students. He wanted students to explain multiple interacting variables. One assessment shown in Fig. 3.23 asks students to combine mass, surface area, relative rate of heat flow, and change over time. Some students were thrilled, whereas others were confused. To help those who were confused, Mr. K built several simulations using the Thermal Model Kit so all students could explore the same issues.

The designing and implementing of the Thermal Model Kit in the classroom illustrates how the CLP partnership worked to negotiate effective instruction and shows how technology can support diverse learners. Thomas wanted to communicate complex ideas that a few students understood, and created a tool that those students found fascinating. Mr. K found a way to introduce the Thermal Model Kit by creating objects students could modify. The Thermal Model Kit enabled students to use simulations designed by Mr. K. Some students designed their own excellent projects to explore more complex questions.

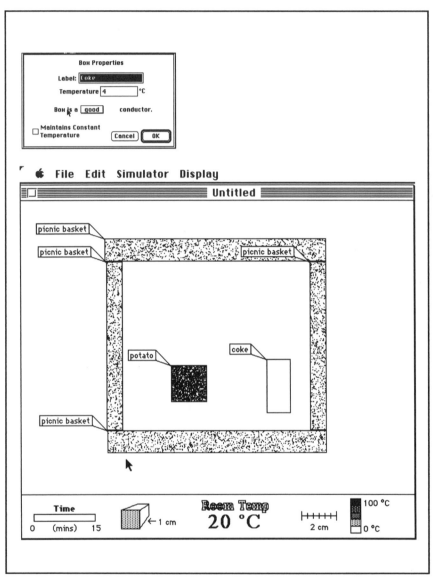

FIG. 3.22 Students construct a visual representation of an object like a picnic basket and conduct experiments using the Thermal Model Kit.

Multimedia evidence. As our technological tools in CLP became more powerful, we began to wonder about the advantages that multimedia resources might offer for knowledge integration. Claims for the benefits of multimedia permeate educational writing. Certainly, if movies taught algebra, our life would be simpler.

We had an opportunity to test the role of multimedia evidence when we redesigned our debate activities. Building on the success of the dinosaur debate mentioned in chapter 2, graduate student Rich Weinland created the How Far Does Light Go? debate using evidence in text format. Philip Bell, a graduate student, worked with CLP to compare how students interpret multimedia and text evidence in the How Far Does Light Go? debate. Bell created multimedia versions of each

One stack of 6 pancakes at 60°C is set on an aluminum cutting board at 20°C. Another stack of 3 pancakes at 60°C is set on a wood cutting board at 20°C. Room temperature is 20°C.

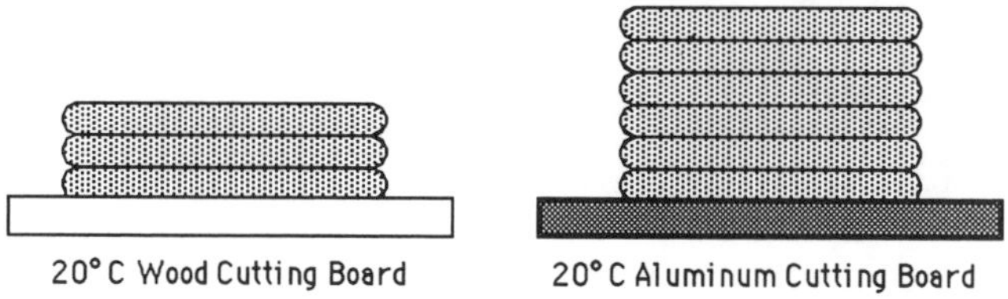

20° C Wood Cutting Board   20° C Aluminum Cutting Board

a. Which stack of pancakes will reach room temperature first?   **(circle one)**

6 pancakes on aluminum   3 pancakes on wood   they would reach room
                                                        temperature at same time

b. Explain why (or why not) one stack of pancakes would reach room temperature first. Clearly list each factor or variable that influences the outcome and explain what effect each has.

c. Draw arrows on the picture above to show how heat or cold flowed at the moment the pancakes were put on the cutting boards.

Use fat arrows to show more heat or cold flowing and thin arrows to show less. Also, use only one arrow between each pair of objects. (Don't show lot's of heat or cold flowing by using many arrows.)

FIG. 3.23   Complex assessment questions designed to measure impact of the Thermal Model Kit.

piece of evidence. To compare the impact of each evidence format, Bell created two versions of the debate. In each version, one half of the evidence was text and the other half was multimedia. Each student saw each piece of evidence in either text or multimedia. Bell found that students frequently classified multimedia versions differently from text versions. For example, the evidence in Fig. 3.24 was linked differently

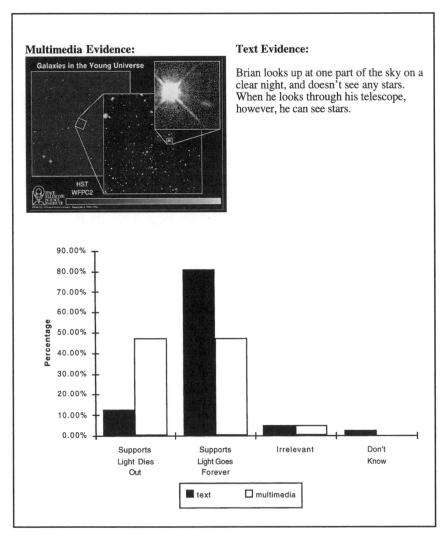

FIG. 3.24   Students view multimedia and text evidence
for the How Far Does Light Go? project differently.

depending on whether it was text or multimedia. What accounts for this changed linkage?

As we expected, students made more connections to multimedia than to text evidence in their notes on the evidence. Multimedia evidence elicited more alternative ideas than text evidence in most situations. Therefore, when many alternatives are desired, multimedia evidence can help. When a particular interpretation is desired, careful design of multimedia evidence is necessary to ensure its impact.

Designing instruction to support knowledge integration with multimedia requires serious attention to the links and connections that students might make because multimedia can motivate students to make many complex connections. Generating creative alternative ideas is part of knowledge integration, but this can become unmanageable. Designing multimedia instruction to elicit manageable levels of complexity requires iterative refinement. Over time Bell created a manageable, rich set of evidence for the debate. We discuss the design of the debate in chapters 4 and 8.

In summary, multiple diverse representations, animations, and other visualization tools can help students "see" how complex scientific phenomena work. They introduce new views of a scientific phenomena. These media offer students another way to test ideas and make connections and teachers help in diagnosing student confusions. Furthermore, they can free teachers to help students make new connections and develop more integrated perspectives on scientific events. However, not all visualizations are created equal, and some work only for certain students.

For most students, the Continuum Line, real-time data collection, and HeatBars promoted knowledge integration. Individual students found ways to represent nonnormative ideas, such as distinguishing heating from cooling using these representations. The Thermal Model Kit and the multimedia evidence succeeded only after a careful design process involving numerous iterations. Some representations, such as the dancing men in the textbook, primarily confuse students.

REFLECTIONS

All students find learning partners among the various CLP efforts to make thinking visible. Encouraging students to visualize can add a neglected dimension to science courses. Even students who rarely animate their ideas and prefer to use verbal representations for science report that online visualizations help. These approaches also get students in touch with tools they will need in future courses. HeatBars and the visible nature of heat flow serves as a turning point for many students in their understanding of heat and temperature.

Chris made this especially clear when explaining the value of HeatBars: [HeatBars] helped me understand it more. It showed pictures so you can get it. It makes you understand it more real easily.... It just like draws a picture in your mind instead of having all those words and then so you can see it."

For some students, animations such as HeatBars and real-time graphs add models to the repertoire. For example, many students add heat flow to their repertoire of ideas about heat after using HeatBars. In addition, students often view a graph as a representation of a process after using real-time graphing.

Visualizations also can promote restructuring of ideas. For example, HeatBars can demote barrier and absorption models while promoting heat flow. Mr. K can encourage restructuring when he makes his thinking about heat and temperature more visible and prompts students to think about their own ideas.

Making thinking visible can help students by simplifying the process of connecting ideas. When students have fewer ideas to keep in mind, it is easier to connect the main ideas and not get distracted. Students agree that this is the case, especially for principles. For example, one student remarked, "Scientific principles don't cover just one thing. They can also cover two or more things."

Connecting students' ideas to abstractions such as heat flow or the shape of a cooling curve increases the possibility that they may use this information in a new setting. Redesigning instruction to increase knowledge integration frequently means highlighting the connections students can use. In complex situations we all miss "obvious" connections. Helping students to "see" connections improves science learning.

Offering a rich mix of visualizations means that most students will use visualizations as learning partners. Visualizing scientific thinking can become a habit, whether students use primarily verbal modes or primarily dynamic representations for visualizing their ideas. Each of our patterns of knowledge integration can involve visualization as a learning partner. Thus, students following the *conceptualizer* pattern like Chris tend to abstract their ideas in verbal principles and prefer abstractly dynamic visual representations. Ultimately, these students articulately and consistently use verbal forms for expressing their thoughts. These students typically report that principles help them verbalize whereas visualization tools help them animate scientific processes in their minds.

Students following the *experimenter* pattern eclectically consider all the tools for visualization introduced in the curriculum. Often experimenters hold multiple views comfortably because some views make sense in the verbal mode and others in dynamic images. As Pat illustrated in chapter 1, these students can frustrate teachers when they entertain seemingly incommensurate views as they learn.

Students following the *strategizer* pattern wait for visualizations they understand and remain satisfied with descriptive accounts of phenomena long after students following the conceptualizer pattern have identified causal mechanisms. Strategizers like Sasha often defend their descriptive accounts, neglecting or ignoring the visualizations available. Of the various visualization tools in the CLP curriculum, strategizers prefer those that illuminate examples: HeatBars, prototypes, and sometimes principles appeal to strategizers. Strategizers may prefer to know results rather than use principles to generate predictions.

Students following the *consumer* pattern prefer passively to watch visualizations rather than actively integrate these ideas. Ensuring that students like Lee interact with visualizations, doing HeatBars experiments, for example, will make instruction more successful for them.

What criteria should guide the design of visualizations? Examination of visualizations and their effectiveness in the curriculum suggests several criteria for successful visualizations. The simple representations generally make the most sense to students. HeatBars implements an extremely simple and straightforward view of heat flow. The Continuum Line has a similar simplicity.

In addition, visualizations must connect to ideas students have. The Continuum Line illustrates how this works. Even students who distinguish heating and cooling could communicate their ideas and get useful feedback from peers and instructors by creating two continuum lines, one for heating and the other for cooling.

The CLP partnership found that designing effective visualizations often requires many revisions. In making the Thermal Model Kit successful, the classroom teacher and the CLP partnership both contributed. The teacher created simulated examples that students could modify. Many students used the simulated examples to test their predictions. A few students designed models to test personal theories. Thus, CLP found ways to make this tool accessible to a broader range of students.

The CLP research group considered many representations for heat flow. For example, the group discussed arrows as representations of direction and rate of heat flow. We considered fat arrows and colored arrows and various other ways to have an arrow represent both direction and rate of heat flow. None of these representations worked for very many students. For a few students whose interests extended to more complex questions, these arrows were helpful. The Thermal Model Kit implemented arrows judiciously, allowing students to test arrow placement and get feedback on their predictions.

In conclusion, CLP designed many opportunities for students to engage in visual thinking. The repertoire of visual thinking tools contributed to improved understanding of heat and temperature. The design process also revealed the difficulties inherent in creating animations, multimedia, and scaffolds that support and encourage knowledge integration.

ASK MR. K

How does technology make you an effective teacher?

Technology can be used to keep track of more mundane things such as "What should I do next" in the experiment so I can concentrate on science. I like to work with students by walking around the classroom, talking to them, listening to their ideas, and seeing the kinds of things they have created in their experiments. Technology lets me ask questions. It tends to hold students on task and keeps them thinking.

Another way is to make students aware of their partner and how their partner can help motivate the student on task.

What is your role when kids work with computers?

I'm kind of a catalyst. I try to not take part in the interaction between the kids but to throw in some ideas that will stimulate their group discussion or introduce pivotal cases. I probe kids to think. Then, I let them take it from there. Sometimes it's called coaching. I'm not real fond of that term because it tends to be one of those educational jargon words, and I think it's misunderstood. Some teachers think it means being similar to a football coach who really tells kids what they have to do to win. I'd like to think, instead, of a coach as person who stimulates discussion, somebody who asks a question or two to probe and then backs away, coming in later on as a facilitator.

Before CLP, how did you use visualization in your teaching?

Before CLP, one of the things I did a lot was to have the kids enact science. I used to space out kids to represent the distances between planets or have them pretend to be molecules and jump around. It helped kids to visualize, particularly in middle school. Of course, visual images such as films, film strips in the old days, illustrations in books and those types of things were helpful. I also did demonstrations. For example, if we were talking about densities of gases, I might have used balloons with different kinds of gases to show the problems with those different gases. Kids sometimes tested out ideas, such as inflating balloons, filling one with carbon dioxide and another with air. Before CLP, visualization was pretty much limited to kids doing things, films, and demonstrations.

How do you use visualization with CLP?

I think with technology we now see new visualizations and simulations. But it wasn't really possible in the early days to have students do experiments and observe the results. With HeatBars for example, technology allows the kids to look at the representation of heat flow in a conductor, change the conductor, change the temperature, and look at the rate again. Students also can run these simulations with different materials. Another example involves the reflection of light. Students can more or less visualize what's going on with light, also doing a simulation, building a house, making predictions, and collecting data.

How do you encourage visual thinking without computers?

Well I think if you get kids working with each other, doing labs together, this encourages kids to visualize. With chemicals, for example, they see a color change, precipitate or something. That's a visualization. But unless they can relate it back to something that has meaning outside the classroom environment, I'm not sure that much visualization takes place. I think the test is how kids are relating principles to their lives, visualizing what's going on.

What do you do when students cannot "see" connections?

I think what you do is provide some alternative activity and an alternative way to see it. Kids learn in different ways. Some things are going to reach kids. This is an advantage of technology: You can program and incorporate all those different visualizations and other things. In a CLP laboratory, you have a visualization of the graph in real time. At the same time you have such things as constructing principles, like reflecting. Therefore, I think one of the real strengths of what's going on in CLP is that it does provide a variety of ways to get kids to think.

POINTS TO PONDER

- Analyze a visualization that helped you learn a science topic.
- Select a technological visualization for a science topic. Analyze how it helps students learn.
- Interview a student using a visualization. Describe how the visualization helps the student to learn.
- Select a complex personally relevant science problem. Describe how you approached this problem by making the wrong paths as well as the solution visible.
- Analyze the assessments you use. Describe the student ideas they make visible.
- Describe the visualizations students encounter in a course you have taught. Explain how the visualizations help students to learn.
- Select one pragmatic pedagogical principle from the chapter. Describe how this principle applies to your practice.
- Watch the section of the CLP film called, Can we make thinking visible? Compare Mr. K's approach to your own.

RELATED READINGS

Collins, A., Brown, J. S., & Holum, A. (1991). Cognitive apprenticeship: Making thinking visible. *American Educator, 15*(3), 6–11, 38–39.

Gardner, M., Greeno, J. G., Reif, F., Schoenfeld, A. H., diSessa, A., & Stage, E. (Ed.). (1990). *Toward a scientific practice of science education*. Hillsdale, NJ: Lawrence Erlbaum Associates.

Gordin, D. N., Polman, J. L., & Pea, R. D. (1994). The Climate Visualizer: Sense-making through scientific visualization. *Journal of Science Education and Technology, 3*(4), 203–226.

Laws, P. W. (1977). *Workshop physics activity guide*. New York: Wiley.

Linn, M. C., & Clancy, M. J. (1992). The case for case studies of programming problems. *Communications of the ACM, 35*(3), 121–132.

Linn, M. C., Layman, J., & Nachmias, R. (1987). The cognitive consequences of microcomputer-based laboratories: Graphing skills development. *Journal of Contemporary Educational Psychology,12*(3), 244–253.

Tinker, R. F. (Ed.), (1997) *Microcomputer based labs: Educational Research and standards* (Vol. 156). Berlin: Springer-Verlag.

White, B. Y. (1993). ThinkerTools: Causal models, conceptual change, and science education. *Cognition and Instruction, 10*(1), 1–100.

4

Helping Students Learn From Each Other

I learn more from other students because I listen to other students more than the teacher.

I can know better by what the students are saying and it makes more sense.

Sometimes they can explain things better than a computer can.

Other students can help you understand what stuff means and what it can do.

Talking with classmates would be sort of like debating with other scientists to come to a conclusion over different pieces of evidence.

Orchestrating social interactions in the science classroom can speed up knowledge integration and increase the effectiveness of science instruction. We learn a great deal from each other. Most children learn how to speak by interacting with their families and friends. As adults, we consult others on every imaginable topic including interpersonal dilemmas and housing repairs. Our colleagues provide role models, guidance, reassurance, and advice. They also can confuse and mislead.

Both unintended and unanticipated consequences arise when students learn from each other. Peers can reinforce stereotypes. Young women may learn that science and mathematics are male domains. Young men may learn to take action rather than to reflect. Students may learn that only the elite can participate in scientific reasoning. Peers also can reinforce intuitions that scientists would dispute. What happens when individuals assert that the earth is round like a pancake, that scientists uncover facts, or that light dies out when no longer visible?

How can we orchestrate classroom science learning to take advantage of social interactions, promote social roles, prepare students to learn from peers in the future, and ensure that students help each other learn science? How can class interactions promote knowledge integration?

Nick Burbules, a philosopher of education, joined the Computer as Learning Partner (CLP) group as a postdoctoral scholar and encouraged CLP to contrast philosophers' accounts of the social interactions among scientists with empirical observations of students' interactions in science classes. Philosophers have long sought to distinguish colloquial "talk" from scientific communication. The rules and rubrics governing scientific communications, especially academic research reports, can obscure the actual reasoning that leads to scientific advance.

Scientific research groups typically include a status hierarchy based loosely on expertise. Investigators have authority and decision-making responsibility. Students aspire to the role of investigators and participate as "apprentices" learning the methods of research, whereas technicians carry out responsibilities defined by the leaders. In classrooms, students' status patterns may not depend on expertise in science.

Over the years, we have revisited these issues, often returning to two questions: First, how do social roles and expectations about these roles influence scientific discussions? For example, people develop personal expectations concerning which authorities to believe. Some adults respect scientists, whereas others trust the conclusions of astrologers over astronomers. Second, what shared methods and criteria govern social interactions among scientists, students, and citizens? Scientific communities develop criteria and methods for interacting in professional meetings, reviewing manuscripts from other laboratories, critiquing contributions of their peers, and communicating findings. These shared criteria of scientists may not work for students who often seek a satisfactory rather than an optimal solution to a problem such as "Which picnic cooler should I buy?"

Our CLP research offers some guidance in the form of four pragmatic pedagogical principles for designing classroom social activities to promote science understanding. Why should students listen and learn from each other? We find that classroom discussions can augment the teacher's efforts to make thinking visible as discussed in the last chapter. Furthermore, ideas expressed in the vocabulary and style of peers often communicate more effectively to students who find textbooks, hands-on experiments, or lectures confusing. Thus our first pragmatic principle asserts: *Encourage students to listen and learn from each other.*

How can we ensure respectful and productive interactions in science classes? In particular, how can students learn to work collaboratively? How can science instruction encourage healthy skepticism about social roles from the past? Most practicing scientists were White males in the 1950s. How do we design social situations so students engage in respectful discussions? Can we guide current students to develop balanced expectations so they listen to all scientists, not primarily those who fit some stereotype? Our second pragmatic principle asserts: *Design social activities to promote productive and respectful interactions.*

How can we encourage groups to base decisions on valid criteria? To help students listen and learn from each other, science classes need to develop shared criteria for scientific explanations and shared methods for exploring new ideas. When students explore new ideas using shared scientific criteria, they have standards they can apply to predictions, observations, experimental results, practical ideas, incomplete views, and persuasive messages. When criteria are explicit, students evaluate the criteria themselves as they apply them to their own work and to the results of others. They can revisit and revise their class criteria and even critique the criteria of others. They are prepared to work out criteria for future science decisions. Therefore, our third pragmatic principle states: *Scaffold groups to design shared criteria and standards.*

Which social interactions make sense for some students? Should students work in small cooperative groups, engage in debates, participate in large class discussions, critique the work of others, or jointly design problem solutions ? How can we use technology to support group activity structures? We have examined a wide range of classroom activities. Our findings show that students differ in their responses to opportunities for social interactions. Some like to have a large audience as found in class discussion. Others prefer discussing their ideas with a friend or one other student. Still others prefer to respond by writing comments on the opinions of others, by reviewing student work, or by contributing to an electronic bulletin board. On the basis of CLP experience, our fourth pragmatic principle asserts: *Employ multiple social activity structures*. These pragmatic pedagogical principles are discussed in the next sections.

PRAGMATIC PEDAGOGICAL PRINCIPLES

Encourage students to listen and learn from each other

Our first pragmatic principle emphasizes the advantages of learning from peers. We also point out drawbacks to collaborative learning that make it important to design peer interactions artfully. We often learn new scientific ideas from our friends and colleagues. Several research groups report that students understand new scientific perspectives better when they hear them in the words of their peers than when they hear them from scientists or read them in textbooks. Peers may connect an idea to a personal problem, present the idea using more familiar vocabulary, or motivate students to make new connections.

Parents have complained that their children speak a different language for years. For example, adolescents typically use the phrase "I'm all" to mean "I said": "I'm all I hate him and she's all, I do too." Teenagers also adopt phrases from rap songs such as "I'm cold chillin' with my homies at my crib" to mean "my friends and I are relaxing at my house."

Students may express scientific observations in ways that their peers understand and can later dispute. In the science classroom, peers may suggest models for scientific phenomena that contradict ideas held by experts. Students often endorse intuitive ideas that scientists would discredit. For example, students assert that sweaters give off heat, that all engineers are men, or that objects in motion come to rest. Students may believe that heat flow changes directions depending on the material, or hold a barrier or absorption model of heat transfer. For example, students, called Harry and Pam, during an interview to uncover views on heat transfer, were asked to compare equally sized blocks of aluminum, wood, and iron placed on a hot plate. Harry insisted that heat is better absorbed by some materials such as wood, but stays on the surface of iron. Pam understood and elaborated.

Teacher: "Which block will heat up faster? Why?"
Harry: "Well, if aluminum and wood, they're probably softer than iron is and so I think that they would absorb the heat like to the inside, and like if you would cut it in half it would be hot on the inside, but iron, like if you did that I don't think it would be that hot on the inside, just all the heat would stay on the outside."

Teacher:	"Which one would feel hotter?"
Harry:	"The iron."
Teacher:	"The iron would because all the heat's on the outside of it? And what about the wood and aluminum. You said they're soft. What do you mean?"
Harry:	"Well, they're not as dense, so heat could travel through it easier than it could the iron."
Pam:	"[the iron block] It's probably like hot on the bottom and then it like goes out to the sides to the top and they can't like absorb it."

The experiences and observations of scientific phenomena described by Harry and Pam would be inaccurate by scientific standards. When these ideas enter the discourse in science class, they can get scrutinized by other students, compared to alternatives, and sorted out or clarified. If they go unanswered and unchallenged, they can persist along with normative views.

Students may "borrow" an idea from someone else, but elaborate or reformulate it to explain their own position. Scientists do the same, building on the ideas of colleagues, collaborators, and historical figures. Physics, for example, is rife with examples that borrow from fundamental principles of Archimedes, Bernoulli, Kepler, Maxwell, or Heisenberg. Individuals come up with novel explanations by combining their own and other's ideas. Some of these novel ideas may prove to be scientific advances, whereas others may require substantial refinement, reformulation, or reconsideration.

In many cases, novel explanations offered by students help other students determine whether a borrowed idea improves their own account of a phenomena and whether it makes the explanations of the group more predictive. For example, these students engaged in an asynchronous online scientific discussion (see Multimedia Forum Kiosk) on the topic of whether an object at room temperature contains any heat energy.

Teacher:	"Do objects at room temperature have any heat energy?"
Hadley:	"Yes something at room temperature (it) does have energy. In this case the cooler and soda are at room temperature, but I think they will get cooler when the blue ice is added to the cooler's environment."
Angelo:	"I also agree that the ice will let off energy because when you take a piece of ice and put it in a room temperature place, the ice will melt. Therefore, it has let off the energy."

Lauren: "And now the soda will be able to give off its heat energy
              that the ice will absorb, so the soda will become cooler."

Students use peer comments to reinforce ideas such as "ice lets off cold
energy" that scientists would dispute. These disputed ideas, however,
also can spur peers to express more normative ideas such as "The soda
will be able to give off its heat energy." Getting ideas out so they help
other students reflect is a first step. To make progress in connecting
and sorting out ideas, students also need ways to decide which ideas to
promote. They need criteria to select among ideas.

Besides adding models to the repertoire, peer interactions can help
students distinguish and restructure their ideas. For example, peers
can serve as role models by talking out loud about a problem and making their steps in knowledge integration explicit. In this sense, peers
extend the role of the teacher, who in the CLP classroom talks out loud
about his process of knowledge integration. For example, students participating in class discussions expressed their preference for explanations provided by peers by saying, "Sometimes I miss what the teacher
said and I ask my classmates about things that I didn't understand" or
"I understand them more and they can tell me their opinions."

Overall, peer interactions can help support the process of knowledge integration if properly orchestrated. Peers can provide ideas for
each other. They can illustrate ways to integrate ideas such as identifying pivotal cases. They can dispel stereotypes by taking diverse roles
and can establish methods to help all students evaluate scientific ideas.

In the CLP project we designed activities so students could get new
ideas from each other. The CLP Electronic Laboratory Notebook
grounds discussion by focusing participants on concrete, testable, alternative perspectives. Students working on experiments consider alternative designs for their investigations. For example, when
conducting a cooling experiment to determine whether soup cools
faster in a large bowl than a small bowl, the group decides the initial
temperature for the hot soup at the time they begin data collection,
the duration of the experiment, and the difference between room temperature and soup temperature. If the group selects a soup temperature only a few degrees above room temperature and runs the
experiment for 2 minutes, they cannot reach valid conclusions. The
Electronic Laboratory Notebook scaffolds students to discuss conse-
quential decisions. They get feedback from the computer interface and
from each other as suggestions to control variables or vary starting
conditions (Fig. 4.1).

As discussed, students bring a repertoire of ideas to science class.
Peers can build on these ideas to enhance learning. Several Electronic

Laboratory Notebook features enable students respectfully to consider alternative ideas from peers.

When students do experiments, make predictions, or share their results, they encounter conundrums they need to discuss. For example, if one group concludes that brownies take less time to bake in a glass pan

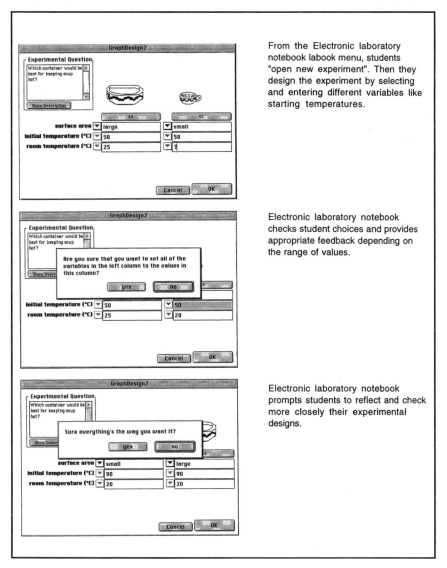

FIG. 4.1   Students design experiments and the Electronic Laboratory Notebook provides guidance and feedback.

(a better insulator) than in an aluminum plan (a better conductor), and another group comes to the opposite conclusion, the groups have the opportunity to compare their findings and sort out the differences. They might discover that one group put less brownie mix in the glass pan than in the aluminum pan. Group discussion might identify other differences between the two experiments: Were the pans the same size and thickness? How long were they each in the oven? What was the oven temperature? How did the brownies taste? The discussion could introduce the idea of a "fair" experiment in words that students understand and help students establish criteria for evaluating experiments.

The Electronic Laboratory Notebook uses Agreement Bars to encourage students to recognize that peers hold alternative ideas. Agreement bars, as shown in Fig. 4.2, help students focus on their reasons and defend their ideas. For example, Tom, Bob, Jill, and Sally used agreement bars to extend discussion. Initially the group asserted that "the small bowl will cool faster than the medium bowl. The reason we predict this is because the small bowl has less surface area." Using agreement bars, Tom and Bob agreed completely; Jill disagreed; and Sally indicated partial agreement: They discussed their predictions:

Sally: "Some of us don't agree that the small bowl will cool faster than the larger bowl. Instead, we think that the medium bowl will cool faster. We believe this from past experience and intuition."

Jill: "Why do you think that? You have to have a reason? Do you think the medium bowl will cool faster?"

Tom: "No, I don't think so."

Jill: "She might be right. Why do you believe it?"

Sally: "I don't know. I'm out of it. Just put any reason. No, if it is smaller and deeper, wouldn't it stay warmer."

After running the experiment, Tom told Sally, "You're on the money!" Sally made an accurate prediction and also, reluctantly, gave a good reason.

Agreement bars can help groups such as Carla, Toni, Alicia, and Joel identify dissenters. Here Joel disagreed yet wrote down what the other group members believed:

Carla: "You mean you think even though they're different in shape, they'll cool the same with the same amount of water? So even though the surface areas differ, you think it'll be the same?"

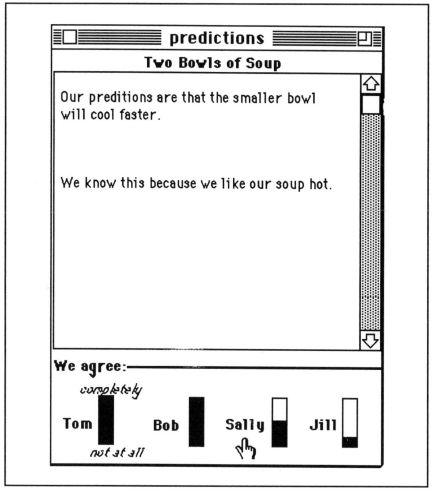

FIG. 4.2 Students can indicate their degree of agreement
with the group response.

Joel:	"Yeah."
Toni:	"What do you think?"
Carla:	"I don't know?"
Alicia:	"I'm still thinking. The big bowl has more surface area. Aren't the bowls the same size. Well, wait a second. Which one are we going to agree on."
Joel:	"I think they'll be the same. The bowls are just the same except for this like that and this one is that."

Carla: "So the one with the bigger surface area will cool faster."

Alicia: "So which one has the bigger surface area?"

Toni: "This one because it's wider than this one down there. Because this one has 200, right, and it's like this you have it all down there. Then this one is like and oval and it has it all spread out across. Well, let him write his and we'll see."

Joel: "I'll write that, and I'll just say that I kept my prediction."

Toni: "Then it's our prediction you're writing down?"

Joel: "Yeah, because most people agree with that one."

Toni: "Okay, then go."

Carla: "Do you all agree?"

Toni: "He doesn't (as seen from agreement bars)."

Carla (to Joel):"Don't you agree even a little bit?" (reference to Joel showing no agreement on the agreement bar)

Class observations reveal that, at times, self-selected group leaders can encourage a student to "agree" with the leader's view instead of discussing why the student disagrees. Here Joe, Josh, and Jim do not consider Maria's view:

Maria: "You guys aren't even asking for my opinion, but then who cares."

Joe: (Irritated tone) "Okay, fine. What do you think? She says up a little: All three, three against one." (Maria has the lowest agreement.)

Maria: "Just leave it, just leave it where it was." (bar says she does not agree.)

Joe and Jim: "Right here, right?"

Josh: "No, down a little."

Joe: "She said yes, what do you say?"

Maria: "I don't care."

Joe: "I said right there. There it is three to one, decide."

Maria: (In a disgusted tone). "No, never mind."

In addition, group members can ignore students who disagree as an interview with Billie shows. Billie decided to sit in the back away from the computer, explaining: "No, I mean, I felt okay and everything. It's just that I don't know; I don't like sitting up there; I feel better in the back." Billie preferred, "just to be able to put up a little opinion wherever it's needed." Billie was reluctant to volunteer a view saying, "Well, if they ask for my opinion, I'll give it, or if it's like they're stuck in doing something, I'll tell them we should do this, this, and that. Otherwise, I don't say anything." Billie indicated lack of argument using the agreement bars and explained, "Well, I'm not going to change my opinion just to make them happy. I'd just rather keep my opinion and find out whether I'm right or wrong." When asked why, Billie said, "I don't think that I should say I'm right, I'm right, I'm right."

These examples illustrate the diverse roles students assume in group discussions and show how students respond to the Electronic Laboratory Notebook. Agreement bars enable students to identify dissenters. Even with these supports, however, groups sometimes agree to disagree or to ignore some students.

The CLP Electronic Laboratory Notebook provides many opportunities for students to listen and learn from each other. Often students take advantage of these opportunities, but sometimes they do not.

The CLP emphasis on personally relevant problems also helps students learn from each other, although the complexity of these problems can lead to difficulties. For example, students gave thoughtful answers when the following problem was proposed to them:

> Derek is having 20 guests over for dinner. He is going to make spaghetti. He got stuck in traffic on the way home from school, and now he has only 20 minutes to cook the noodles. He has one big pan and three smaller pans. He can either cook all the noodles in the one big pan or in the three small pans. His stove has two large burners and two small burners. What can Derek do with these pans and this stove to cook the noodles in the shortest amount of time? What is the main reason for your answer? What principles from this class helped you to make your decision?

Students give diverse predictions in response:

Joe:	"The pot with 1 liter of water will heat faster is because there is less water to heat." (smaller pot is better)
Ricki:	"The smaller amount, the quicker heat energy either flows into and out of."
Rudy:	"The bigger pot will have more heat energy because it has more mass." (bigger pot is better)
Jamie:	"The pot with 1 liter will have a higher temperature Because it has less mass, so it will take less time to heat up." (smaller pot is better)
Nick:	"The molecules in the 1 liter of water could spread out more easily."

The CLP approach encourages students to recognize alternatives by asking groups to critique the work of each other. Students seem content to accept conflicting alternative accounts of scientific events. For example, two students critiquing each other's work on the Derek noodles problem reached contradictory conclusions. One student said mass is the most important variable, preferring three small pots. Another focused on the surface area in contact with the burner, opting for one large pot. To reconcile their differences, the students concluded, "We're both right."

Another pair of students, faced with the dilemma of predicting whether a small coke in the freezer would cool faster than a large Coke in the refrigerator, reached contradictory conclusions (Fig. 4.3). Instead of accepting both answers, this pair conducted the experiment, using empirical evidence to resolve the contradictory predictions.

In summary, students can be encouraged to listen and learn from each other. The CLP Electronic Laboratory Notebook provides opportunities for discussion when students make predictions, design experiments, and interpret results. For more complex personally relevant problems, students need more than opportunities for discussions. Our second and third pragmatic pedagogical principles provide additional guidance.

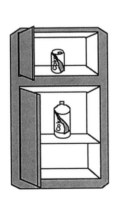

Two Cokes Problem:

Jean puts a can of Coke in the freezer and a bottle of Coke in the refrigerator. Two hours later, Jean takes them out for a drink.

a. Which do you predict will be coldest after 2 hours?

b. Which coke will be the coldest after 24 hours?

c. What is the main reason for your answer?

d. What principles from this class helped you to make your decision?

e. What evidence do you have to support your decision?

FIG. 4.3   This CLP complex everyday problem helps students integrate instruction and personal experience.

Design social interactions to promote productive and respectful discussion

Designing effective peer interactions requires that teachers find ways to address social role expectations and discourage stereotyping. The CLP team tried to increase the repertoire of social roles students encounter and also studied the design of group interactions.

Role Models.   Social roles for science and technology often are reinforced in the media. Television shows regularly ridicule women who attempt to perform technical tasks or use computers effectively. The media often portray scientists with glasses and white laboratory coats. As more and more role models of technically competent women become available, we hope for change. Middle school students are especially vulnerable to stereotype. The quest for identity and personal understanding predominates in the lives of many middle school students.

To address stereotypes in the CLP classroom, we offered students a broad range of science role models, following our theory about expanding the repertoire of models. How did we introduce role models in the classroom? First we named each computer after famous female and male scientists including Sally Ride, Jane Goodall, Isaac Newton, and Albert Einstein. In one CLP activity, students researched the scientist after which their computer was named, made an oral presentation, and posted their report on the classroom bulletin. Recently, we connected to the Internet and students now use the World Wide Web to research and report on their scientists. We post the reports on the class home page.

Inevitably some students confound the information they read from various sources on the Internet. In one amusing example students reporting on Jane Goodall gathered information from sites reporting information about research on primates. They attributed to Jane Goodall work done by other female primatologists including Diane Fosse.

A few years later, our project received a letter from the lawyers representing Jane Goodall informing us that errors had been found at our computer site. With further investigation, we discovered that the lawyers had read a student-written report with an error in attribution. We wrote back to the lawyers explaining that they had reviewed a student report and requesting their guidance concerning how best to resolve the problem. The lawyers have not yet responded.

In addition, to providing effective role models, we invited diverse scientists, including our graduate students, to visit the classroom and participate in online class discussions with students. The eighth graders often remarked that these students inspired them to study science more seriously.

The range of social roles in the classroom was not sufficient to completely discourage stereotyping by students. We sought to design group interactions so that opportunities to stereotype student contributions or to marginalize students would be minimized. We saw in the agreement bars examples that both Maria and Billie felt discouraged from participation.

Cooperative Groups.   Our design studies to promote respectful discussion were very much technology driven. The number of classroom computers dictated group size. We experimented with group size to promote respectful discussion.

Our research demonstrated that students' roles changed depending on the size of their work group. Our first grant of 16 Apple II computers established groups of two students each for carrying out experiments. Mr. K had used small groups in science for many years before the introduction of computers. Designing effective ways for groups of two to use Apple II computers presented a few difficulties (see Ask Mr. K). Mr. K asked students to switch keyboarding roles halfway through the class period, and most groups complied. Occasionally, students demanded their turn on the keyboard or preferred not to work at the computer, but Mr. K enforced this classroom equity policy. Mr. K established classroom-wide standards of respect that helped students learn from each other.

Students found effective ways to work in groups of two at the keyboard. Often one student would type and the other would monitor spelling, grammar, and content. Students discussed interpretations and next steps. Most disputes were minor. The Apple II software introduced complex problems such as how to determine which line on the graph connected to each experiential condition. Ideally, students would divide responsibility, each monitoring one line on the graph. When one student did all the work and the other student paid vague attention, project success suffered. In two-person groups this was rare, and Mr. K usually was aware the situation.

Our first grant of eight Macintosh computers (to replace the Apple IIs) necessitated that students work in groups of four around the eight available computers. Immediately, the classroom character changed. Groups of four had difficulty jointly seeing the small Macintosh screen. Individuals pushed each other aside to observe experimental results. Two students often took the front seats while the other two socialized in the back seats. Contributions to group work became more difficult. No easy arrangement of four middle school students around this Macintosh screen was possible.

Jacquie Madhok, a former biology and mathematics teacher who worked with both at risk and gifted students, joined the project as a graduate student and began observing group interactions in the classroom. Madhok noticed right away that groups with three boys and one girl or three girls and one boy were less successful than groups with two boys and two girls.

To understand the situation better, Madhok tape-recorded group interactions and studied the comments made among participants in two-person, three-person, and four-person groups. Madhok found that as group size increased, so did "put downs" and criticism of others. Students often criticized clothing or social practices of others. In the following example, two boys and a girl are trying to describe the experiment they have just conducted on insulation and conduction using different wraps such as aluminum foil and Saran wrap:

Gina: "What do we do now?"

William: "Your armpits smell bad."

Aaron: "What about the wrap?"

Gina: "We didn't wrap the pole. [correcting typing] We wrapped the potatoes."

In addition, students sometimes used social roles and school social status to criticize scientific ideas, such as mentioning a peer's ability in sports or brand of shoes. Girls encountered more criticism based on social roles than did boys.

Madhok's systematic analysis revealed that groups of two collaborated better than groups of three or four. In addition, groups with disparate gender distributions had more put downs and boys were more likely to put down girls than the reverse. Thus four-person groups with more boys than girls were most likely to put down the girl, and two-person groups composed of one boy and one girl rarely engaged in put-downs.

To improve the interactions among four person groups, we tried assigning roles to students similar to those found in research settings: investigator, result expert, equipment monitor, technology specialist, and the like. We failed. The assigned roles frequently conflicted with established social hierarchies, creating friction. We tried to define the roles more carefully, creating color-coded name tags to indicate role assignment, and arranging regular role shifts. Students rebelled by switching name tags, avoiding role assignments, or criticizing others.

The grading of jointly produced reports and products also challenged Mr. K as group size increased. Mr. K could monitor two-person groups, but three- and four-person groups were more difficult. Mr. K asked students to grade each other using class-established criteria. These grades helped Mr. K determine final grades. Developing shared criteria for grading group products also alerted students to appropriate behavior and expectations as discussed in the next pragmatic pedagogical principle.

We ultimately concluded that the small computer screen intensified impediments to group interaction. Mr. K's extensive experience in orchestrating group work was insufficient to overcome the small screens. We scrounged, begged, and borrowed more computers until we had students working in groups of two again.

Four-person groups might succeed with larger computer screens that allow all students to interact. However, school-wide expectations concerning gender roles and leadership make it difficult to design four-person groups that promote new social roles. One unanticipated consequence of introducing computers into the classroom was that social stereotypes were intensified.

Group Discussion The CLP partnership also designed class discussion to promote productive and respectful discussion. We experimented with various forms of technology-rich, online discussion.

Most science classes make use of class discussion. However, class discussion frequently reinforces social roles instead of contributing to knowledge integration. Numerous research studies have documented that boys participate more than girls in class discussion. Boys also shout out answers, whereas girls usually raise their hands, contributing to the imbalance.

In our CLP classroom, we monitored the students who participated. We observed that the classroom teacher called almost equally on boys and girls and discouraged the shouting out of answers. However, boys still dominated the discussion, making about 50% more contributions than girls (Fig. 4.4).

More importantly, only 15% to 20% of the students participated in face-to-face class discussion. More than half of the students continuously remained silent. If only a few students participated, we could not be sure of eliciting the full range of student ideas. In addition, class discussions rewarded rapid response, not reflection. Students spent little time connecting ideas or warranting assertions. Furthermore, class discussions when male voices dominate reinforce the view that men do science.

Sherry Hsi, as a graduate student on the CLP project, designed an online discussion tool to increase equitable and reflective class discussion. Hsi hoped to take advantage of the best aspects of classroom interaction. Working initially with Christopher Hoadley, another

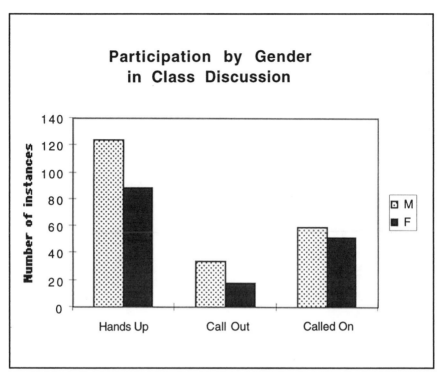

FIG. 4.4 In science class, boys contribute more because they call out more
answers and raise their hands more frequently.

graduate student, Hsi designed the Multimedia Forum Kiosk illustrated in Fig. 4.5. The Multimedia Forum Kiosk environment allows
learners to engage in scientific discussions with peers and permits the
teacher to audit student ideas more carefully.

A stand-alone, asynchronous electronic discussion tool, the Multimedia Forum Kiosk uses two representations of discourse to support discussion of science topics: opinions and arguments. Multimedia discussion
starters in the form of digital videos anchor student comments. Eighth
grade students are asked such questions as "Which kind of pan should I
use to bake brownies: aluminum or ceramic?" Each student then enters
his or her own interpretation as a text comment, reads the comments of
other students, and adds to an ongoing discussion. Student comments
are represented visually as face icons and the structure of discussion is
recorded graphically in the form of argument trees.

The Multimedia Forum Kiosk allows groups of students to discuss
science topics presented with multimedia evidence such as this ques-

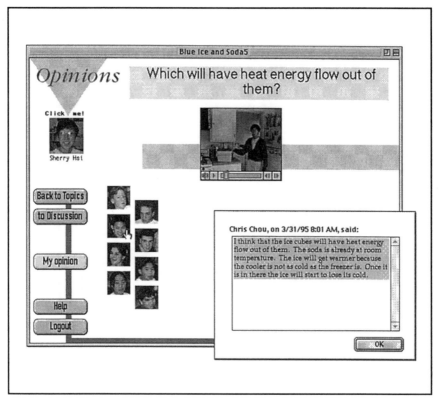

FIG. 4.5 The Opinion Area of the Multimedia Forum Kiosk allows students to see multimedia evidence illustrating a science question, enter their opinions, and read the opinions of their classmates.

tion: What happens to a plastic cooler containing a soda at room temperature and blue ice? Students contribute their opinions and participate in a group discussion (Fig. 4.6).

In the Discussion Area, students either create a new topic or respond to a comment (Fig. 4.7). The electronic format makes the discussion visually explicit. Students indicate the relation between their contribution and the ideas already presented. Thus, students indicate the links among ideas. Students reading the discussion can easily identify areas of controversy. Furthermore, students can "see" how others respond to their comments.

Hsi investigated ways to design a productive discussion. She compared groups of 8, 15, and 30 students, drawing students from the same class and from different science classes. She permitted students

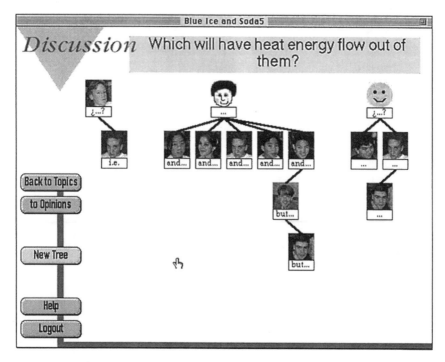

FIG. 4.6 The Discussion Area of the Multimedia Forum Kiosk allows students
to discuss their ideas about a science question.

to participate anonymously or required that comments be attributed
to a name and a face. In the anonymous condition, students were assigned a unique cartoon face and their names were hidden from peers,
but known to the teacher (Fig. 4.8).

Students preferred to participate in discussions with peers from different classes. Groups of approximately 15 had the best discussions.
Groups of 8 students did not disagree enough. Groups of 30 were confusing to participants, rather like class discussions with 32 students.

Students participated equally in anonymous and attributed conditions. When given a choice, girls preferred anonymous contributions
more often than boys. Girls reported expressing their ideas more freely
in the anonymous condition. Sometimes, girls converted their anonymous contributions to attributed contributions if responses of peers
were favorable.

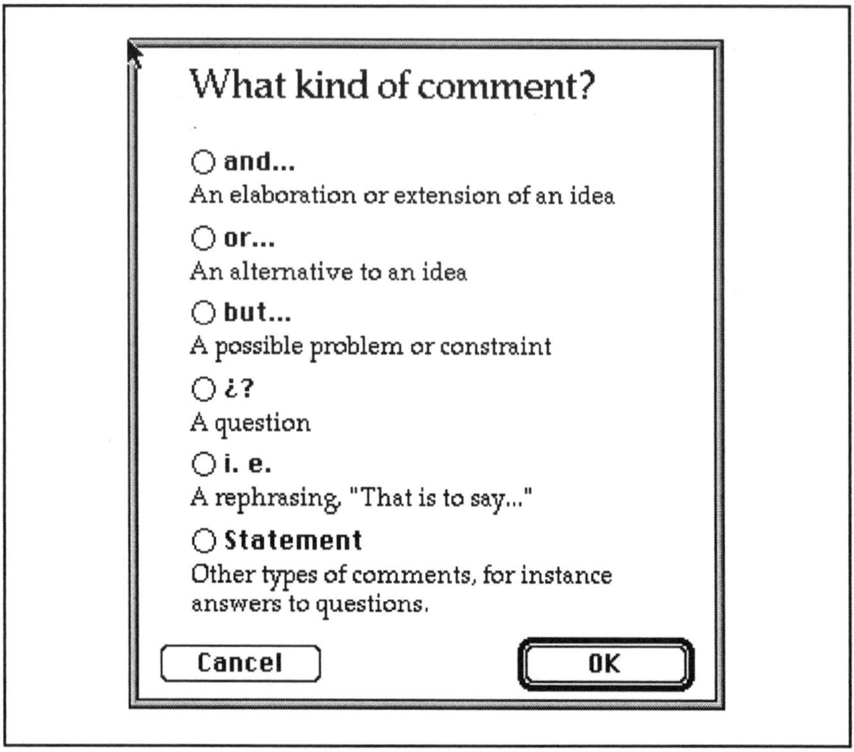

FIG. 4.7   To make a comment in the Discussion Area of the Multimedia Forum Kiosk, students select a category to label their comments.

Hsi found that electronic discussion permitted more students to participate in science discussions than a class format (Fig. 4.9). Nearly 90% participated electronically compared with 15% in class. Moreover, students who used the Multimedia Forum Kiosk were not necessarily those students who traditionally do well in science.

Hsi also found that Multimedia Forum Kiosk discussions were more gender equitable than classroom discussions. Boys who typically shouted out answers, raised their hands more quickly, or were called on by the teacher in face-to-face classroom discussion were less prominent in online discussion (Fig. 4.10). Girls participated equally with boys in the electronic discussion and contributed high-quality explanations. Girls expressed less apprehension about participating in electronic discussion, finding it less embarrassing and confrontational. Moreover, school reputation and status did not get in the way of discussion. Ideas could always be contributed anonymously if students feared reprisals.

In addition, the Multimedia Forum Kiosk encouraged knowledge integration in ways that classroom discussion did not. The electronic discussion motivated students to defend their ideas and judge contributions based on their defense. Overall, 42% of the comments had multiple backings or explanations. Almost 80% of the comments had at least one backing. For example, the following students backed their explanations of heat transfer between a plastic cooler, ice, and a warm soda:

Gail: "I feel the blue ice will give off cool energy keeping the soda cold. When you take something out of the freezer, you can see the cold. If you take something out that is room temperature, you can't see the heat come off."

Val: "I think that you are correct on your statement. The heat energy will flow out of the ice pack, and some of the coldness will be absorbed by the warm coke. I wonder, though, how is it that you can see cold air?"

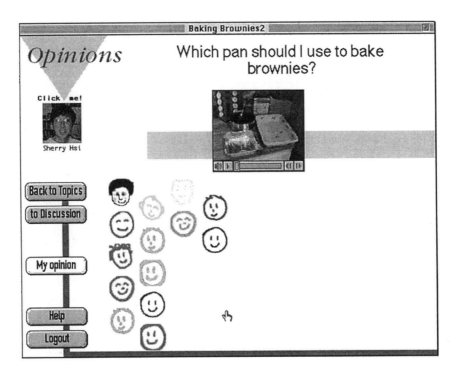

FIG. 4.8   To participate in an anonymous discussion, students are assigned unique cartoon faces.

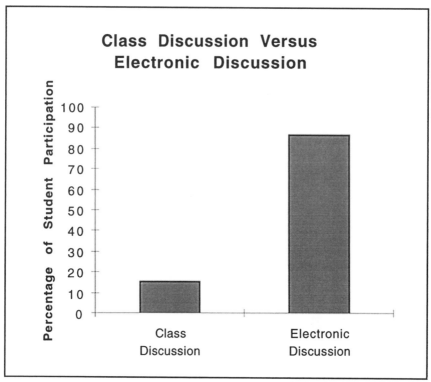

FIG. 4.9   Compared with class discussion, electronic discussion provides more opportunities for students to participate.

Jules: "I agree that the coke would become cooler after the ice was placed in the cooler. However the coke can would have heat energy flowing out of it and it would go throughout the cooler, making the ice get warmer or start to melt."

Angel: "I think that none of the objects will have heat energy flow out of them, because the ice will just change the surrounding temperature [sic] to the temperature [sic] of the ice. So, basically the temperature [sic] will just change."

Ari: "I think that the ice will have heat energy flow out of it because it is going to make the soda colder. I don't think that the soda will have heat energy go out because the ice is the one that is getting warmer."

Asynchronous discussion offers a useful alternative to class discussion. It allows greater participation, extends the time that the teacher can spend with students, and enables access before and after school, as well as during recess and lunch breaks. Students can participate anonymously; teachers can require participation; and groups for discussion can come from several different classes, schools, or geographic areas.

A benefit of peer discussion is that students provide scientific explanations in words that their peers can understand. Student arguments, their lines of reasoning, various interpretations, and explanations can be seen in argument maps. Teachers can use these same maps to monitor class views and guide further understanding. Students learn that students do not all agree. One student remarked with wonder that peers disagreed about the interpretation of science problems.

Class discussion limits the number of students that can participate at one time. Electronic discussion that is asynchronous can provide

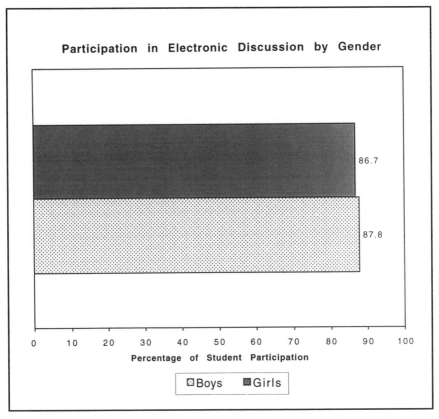

FIG. 4.10 In electronic discussion, compared with class discussion, boys and girls participated more equally.

and encourage self-paced reflection and opportunities to participate in science discussions. The Multimedia Forum Kiosk was designed to promote more scientific discussion among students and help support knowledge integration in science, helping students consider more ideas, elaborate their ideas, and motivate knowledge revision.

Who participates the most in electronic discussion? In the CLP project, all students reported interest, but in some cases small groups of boys formed Kiosk Clubs, spending their lunch hours and after school time in Mr. K's classroom. These students dominated the machines, so CLP redesigned access to the machines to promote equity. We used a signup sheet and limited access to 10 minutes at a time.

To understand classroom discussions better, we asked students to compare class and electronic discussion. Boys reported that a benefit of electronic discussion was its asynchronous format, which allowed them more flexibility in their schedule to participate in discussions. Girls compared with boys reported more instances of fear, ridicule, and possible embarrassment in class discussion. For example, one girl reported: "I dislike participating because I'm afraid of asking a stupid question. Sometimes when you say something, the class might start laughing at you, and I don't like to participate in class discussions unless I know the answer, and I speak softly so no one can hear me." The online discussion with an anonymous option permitted all students to contribute and get feedback.

In summary, we designed effective small-group and class discussion by incorporating and reacting to technology. When technology dictated group size, we tried many designs but were limited by small computer screens. We found asynchronous electronic discussions far more productive and respectful than whole-class discussions. For both small-group and class discussion, effective design included selecting group size carefully. Small groups of 2 and class discussion groups of 15 proved optimal.

Class discussions and small-group discussions were most successful when the topic was controversial and clearly defined. Thus, class discussions about designing an experiment were most successful. Similarly, small-group discussions about predictions for experiments were better than open-ended discussions.

Designing effective small-group interactions for science learning involves an iterative and incremental process of design and redesign, as used in all of our CLP work. We found that small groups of two generally worked best. With significant attention to social roles and accessible computer screens, larger groups might also succeed. When teachers must use larger groups, we believe students benefit from experiencing a mix of same-sex and half-male, half-female groups. Class discussion about social roles and expectations also contributes to the success of group interactions in science classes.

Scaffold groups to design shared criteria and standards

Why do groups need shared methods and criteria? To reach consensus, groups need to agree on which ideas are important and deserve promotion. Parents and their children illustrate the dilemma when selecting a good movie. Children may prefer movies with animals or animations, whereas, parents may select movies with prosocial messages or well-known directors.

Students come to science class with varied criteria for scientific validity. They may equate opinions with research findings and view hearsay as fact. For example, when middle school students judge the validity of two assertions in Fig. 4.11, they have varied responses. Some assert that both are correct, whereas others ask for more information before making a decision. Sometimes they support their beliefs by citing advertisements (e.g., "Choosy mothers choose [this brand of peanut butter]").

Students need to develop criteria for interpreting opinions and statements from authorities. As observed in chapter 3, some students believe that every statement in the science textbook is true, with the possible exception of the true-false questions. The reader will remember the student who believed the textbook might be wrong be-

---

An East Coast research group found: Peanut butter is good for you because it is high in protein. A West Coast research group found: Peanut butter is bad for you because it is high in fat.

    a. Why do the scientists reach different conclusions? **(check one)**

_____Both groups are right because scientists have different opinions.

_____Both groups are right, but the groups need more information.

_____Both groups are wrong, so the groups should resolve disputes.

_____One group is wrong because one group made a mistake.

    b. Explain your answer.

    c. What research is needed to help people decide whether to eat peanut butter?

FIG. 4.11   An assessment in which students are asked to judge the validity of scientific claims and evidence used to support the claims.

cause, "probably the people that typed it up" had made errors. Students can benefit from classroom activities that analyze scientific criteria.

How can student groups establish shared methods and criteria? Students, as compared with scientists, start with a much smaller set of shared criteria, and classes often neglect this topic or assume students have established criteria. Students can develop shared criteria when they jointly critique experiments.

The CLP partnership designed a class critique activity for Electronic Laboratory Notebook reports. We created a report that included many typical examples of incomplete or unwarranted reasoning. Using small-group and whole-class discussion, students critiqued this report and created a set of class criteria. The criteria were posted so students could use them to assess their own reports. Figure 4.12 illustrates ideas from a typical class.

In the CLP curricula students get to experience setting criteria for critiquing personally relevant projects as well as Electronic Laboratory Notebook projects. One example asks students to critique a study com-

---

Use proper grammar and punctuation. Proofread all your work.

Use bold, clear titles to show different parts of your report.

Include graphs, diagrams, and illustrations to clarify report.

Be precise and concise. Don't use pronouns like "it" or "this."

Make sure that what you write makes sense, and stick to the topic.

Answer all the questions thoroughly and clearly.

Principles should be clear, make sense. .

Don't contradict yourself in one note.

Compare the data you collected with what you thought would happen – your predictions.

Make sure your everyday life examples match your principle.

FIG. 4.12   Criteria that students created for judging reports
on laboratory experiments.

paring rock music and classical music fans (Fig. 4.13). Students initially select a wide range of criteria. Some point out confounding variables or errors in methods. Some conclude that rock music fans like loud sounds, so rock music should be played loudly. Others complain that classical music fans are "old" and probably suffer hearing losses. Still others advocate measuring the hearing ability of the listeners first. Some students have no criticism, and others have trouble de-

A scientist (audiologist) predicted that people who listen to heavy-metal music will damage their hearing. To test this prediction, the following experiment was conducted.

The scientist gave a hearing test to:

      200 people who listed to classical music and
      200 people who listen to heavy-metal music.

The results of the hearing test showed that the people in the classical group had better hearing.

The scientist said, "This proves that heavy-metal music damages people's hearing."

The fan group Heavy Metal Forever said, "No way, the experiment was not done right and proves nothing."

a. Do you agree with the scientist or the fan group?

      _____fan group (rock music)
      _____scientist

      Give the main reason for your choice

b. If you were going to do this experiment, what might you do differently?

FIG. 4.13   Huh? activity asking students to critique an experiment

termining which confounds are important. For example, do sound experiments yield different results on Tuesdays than on Thursdays? Does it matter whether the listeners are fans of Beethoven or the Beatles? Scientists find these potential confounds somewhat amusing. Students often find them worthy of experimentation.

Students revise their criteria as they critique more experiments. For example, Mr. K encourages students to critique their peers' nonnormative ideas. The CLP portfolio activities that engage students in critique are discussed in chapter 5.

Citizens may require methods and criteria for complex, personally relevant problems that differ in emphasis from criteria used in scientific practice. For example, citizens typically want a good answer, not necessarily the most rigorous answer. Consumers might want to find one product that meets their criteria rather than the whole list of products. *Consumer Reports* illustrates how difficult it is to establish shared criteria for complex personal decisions. Reading *Consumer Reports,* citizens might disagree with the standards used for comparing products differ. Not everyone values quick operation over ease of repair or vice versa.

Activities in the CLP classroom engage students in discussing criteria for personally relevant problems with their peers. All the problems students will face cannot possibly be addressed in a classroom. However, students can learn to consult peers jointly and identify sensible methods and reasonable criteria for a range of personally relevant problems.

Perhaps these activities will prepare students to critique spontaneously the criteria used by advertisers and practice this skill. Advertisers frequently promote specific methods or criteria for product decisions that showcase their brand but may not convince consumers. Toothpaste companies may claim that their brand is preferred by "leading" dentists. Shampoo companies may claim that their brand is used by famous salons or that it "makes your hair smell like peaches!" Helping students critique advertisements to recognize whether the claims are relevant to their own concerns offers a valuable opportunity.

In summary, we all need to reason about the scientific problems we face in our lives. Often we learn by listening to the ideas of others and by asking others to critique our ideas. Establishing an environment in which students discuss each other's ideas and try to reach consensus prepares students for future science-related decisions.

To prepare students to be lifelong science learners, we need to design instruction that alerts citizens to the process of selecting methods and criteria. Furthermore, we need instruction that empowers citizens while providing a firm foundation for students who ultimately choose careers in science.

Use multiple social activity structures

The fourth pragmatic principle, *using multiple methods to orchestrate peer interactions in science classrooms*, recommends offering a mix of social experiences so students can find ways to learn from peers. These activities include class discussions, small-group work, class debates, peer critiques, and online electronic discussions.

Multiple social activity structures allow students to take on a series of social roles and to learn new roles. When students take a stand in a class, they learn to create coherent arguments and respond to criticism. Critiques allow students to offer conflicting explanations and evaluate peer responses. Online anonymous discussion permits students to try out new social roles. In projects, students can specialize just as scientists specialize in an aspect of their field.

For example, one CLP approach encourages students to specialize in a science project. As specialists, students have the opportunity to gain understanding of how to become an authority and to learn the power an authority has on group decision making. Students might become more skeptical of authorities after taking the role of authorities. They also might learn more about the specialized topics they choose to study by teaching others the information they have learned. Students benefit from teaching others because their classmates scrutinize the advice they give. When teaching, students might encounter questions that require increased research and lead to improved knowledge integration.

One successful approach is a CLP portfolio activity, in which students draw on class laboratories to explain an everyday problem to a younger sibling. (Fig. 4.14). The younger sibling may be skeptical or very accepting of everything said by the student. The student learns by teaching the sibling and responding to the questions asked by the sibling.

Taking on the role of an expert or specialist also helps students understand the nature of expertise. In many cases, students will need skill in selecting an expert or in knowing when an expert is needed.

Classroom debates offer another promising way to orchestrate peer interactions. Over the past 15 years, the CLP project has experimented with several formats for classroom debates. Initially, classroom debates were designed to help students understand scientific inquiry as mentioned in chapter 2. The dinosaur extinction, earthquake, and How Far Does Light Go? debates used paper and pencil materials. (Fig. 4.15). Students worked on their debates while others used the computers. The debate format helped to illustrate scientific reasoning and solved a logistic problem, reducing group size at the computer.

All CLP debates ask students to review a set of evidence. Students analyze each piece of evidence and consider how it supports or refutes

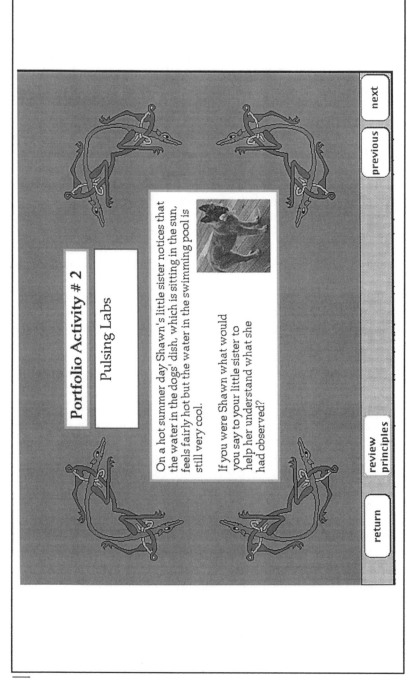

Portfolio Activity # 2

Pulsing Labs

On a hot summer day Shawn's little sister notices that the water in the dogs' dish, which is sitting in the sun, feels fairly hot but the water in the swimming pool is still very cool.

If you were Shawn what would you say to your little sister to help her understand what she had observed?

return | review principles | previous | next

FIG. 4.14   A CLP portfolio activity in which students take the role of specialist.

Group: _____ Date: _____ Period: _____
Members: _____

Dinosaur Extinction: Who Knows Why?

Several theories have been proposed to explain why dinosaurs became extinct. Your group
has been assigned a theory and given evidence and information about some of the dinosaur
extinction theories. Organize your evidence and information into the three categories below.
Write the letter that is on each piece of evidence and information under the category in
which you place it.

Supports your theory	Irrelevant to your theory	Contradicts your theory

Within each category, organize the information in ways that will help you in the panel
discussion.

1. What did you decide were useful ways to organize the evidence and information within
   the categories?

2 a. Do you think scientists know why dinosaurs became extinct?

   yes_____   no_____

   b.   What are your main reasons for your answer?

3. Summarize the evidence for your theory.

4. What are the weaknesses in your theory?

FIG. 4.15   Students select a dinosaur theory, make predictions, and
plan a class debate.

the debate questions. In all the debates, students in small groups construct one or several arguments in preparation for the class debate. The class debate follows several formats. Sometimes students debate the view they support. At other times students debate an assigned view. During debate, one student presents the argument of the group, and other students ask questions. These debate activity structures engage students as collaborators and critics. They allow students to play roles common in scientific research.

Individuals participating in debates advocate a particular point of view. They examine evidence from the standpoint of their advocacy role and develop an argument based on that evidence. This opportunity to play the role of advocate allows students to gain insight into the process of science.

Running a classroom debate efficiently demands some careful planning. To engage students, all groups are asked to come prepared to debate. Groups are called on randomly to present arguments on each side of the debate. New groups present rebuttals, and students who are not selected to debate or rebut are called on to ask specific questions.

Debates can equitably involve all class members while illustrating how peers form a coherent argument. For example, in the debate on dinosaur extinction, students support one of these theories: the meteorite theory, the earthquake theory, or the disease theory. Students generate additional theories as shown in Fig. 4.16. When students formulate an argument for a debate, they have the opportunity to express coherent scientific ideas and support assertions to convince others. In preparation, a small group assembles evidence and formulates an argument. They also discuss possible weaknesses that supporters of other theories might raise.

For the dinosaur debate in the CLP project, we supplied text evidence relevant to the various theories (see chap. 2, Fig. 2.24). Each group of five students organized their evidence and crafted an argument. To help students plan for the debate, we asked them questions such as "What evidence would be useful in designing this theory?" They were asked to do this assignment: "Write two questions you think a good theory of dinosaur extinction should answer." These activities took several class periods.

During the debate, the classroom teacher modeled good questioning practice by asking additional follow-up questions to encourage comparisons among theories. Each student participated in the debate, taking one role or another, and the teacher graded the contribution of each student. After the panel discussion, students filled out a questionnaire and voted on their preferred theory. (Fig. 4.17).

Whatever Became of the Dinosaurs? A List of Theories

Did they fail to adapt to a changing environment? (global cooling theory)

Were they victims of a huge meteorite hitting the earth?(extraterrestrial impact theory)

Did an enormous volcano make the earth unlivable for dinosaurs? (volcanic eruption theory)

Did earthquakes knock over the ungainly beasts? ("I've fallen and I can't get up" theory)

Did widespread smoking lead to lung cancer and fires in bed? (Gary Larson theory)

Was it due to an unfounded rumor that "Tar pits are fun to swim in"? (Mark's tar pit theory)

Did cosmic radiation mutate them all into salamanders? (De-evolution theory)

Did they scratch themselves to death after being bitten by thousands of primitive mosquitoes? (Marcia's "5000 bites will kill you" theory)

Did aliens kidnap them in order to keep Elvis company?(weekly world news Theory)

Was this a plot by school teachers to find something for kids to work on? (science murders theory)

Or are they all still waiting in line at the Department of Motor Vehicles? (bureaucratic evolution theory)

FIG. 4.16 Some fanciful and realistic theories students suggested for dinosaur extinction.

The debate structure ensures that each student contributes to class discussion. It also encourages thoughtful and well-prepared contributions. Students find the debate compelling and often spend time outside of class preparing and discussing the issues in dinosaur extinction.

When the CLP classroom connected to the Internet, we formed a new partnership called the Knowledge Integration Environment. Philip Bell converted the How Far Does Light Go? debate from paper and pencil to an online activity using the Knowledge Integration Environment software. He tried several formats, settling eventually on a format in which students reviewed evidence on the Internet instead of text evidence and used this evidence to construct an argument and carry out the debate. In the course of designing the evidence for this debate, Bell compared multimedia and text evidence as described in chapter 3. Bell

Group: _____ Date: _____ Period _____
Members: _____
Name of Group's Theory: _____

Day Two: All Class Panel Discussion

Today you will be part of an all-class panel discussion. During this discussion, it is your job to find out as much information as you can on OTHER theories of dinosaur extinction and the evidence for those theories so that you can determine which theory is the most convincing.

Choosing Jobs

PRESENTER: Choose <u>one group member</u> who will give a 2 – 5 minute description of your theory.

MODERATOR: Choose <u>one group member</u> who will help run the panel discussion. These people will time presentations, make sure each group asks questions and gets some answers.

PANELISTS: Choose <u>one or two group members</u> who will ask 2 good questions (the best ones from your group) to other groups AND answer the questions directed towards your group.

The Panel Discussion

Begin the panel discussion with each group's presentation by the PRESENTERS. Next, let each MODERATOR take a turn in letting PANELISTS speak one at a time. MODERATORS need to be sure that the QUESTION/ANSWER portion of the panel discussion runs no more than 15 minutes.

After the panel discussion:

1. Do you accept your group's theory as a good one for explaining dinosaur extinction?

    Yes _____   No _____   I am still not sure _____

2. Which ONE theory (from all the presentations) do you find most convincing?

3. What is your main reason for why that theory is most convincing?

4a. Is there one theory that you would eliminate?

   b. Why or why not?

5. Why do scientists disagree about the best theory?

FIG. 4.17 Worksheet used to guide activities during and after the class debate on dinosaur extinction

also designed SenseMaker to help students organize evidence into theories and integrate their ideas. Using SenseMaker, students wrote notes to explain how evidence connected to their theory (Fig. 4.18).

Students discussed how they might connect evidence to their personal experiences as shown in the following classroom excerpt:

Pat: "You said you could see headlights far away (referring to a particular piece of evidence). What if they were farther away—I mean a lot farther away. Would you still be able to see them?"

Sandy: "Like a mile away?"

Dale: "A mile away."

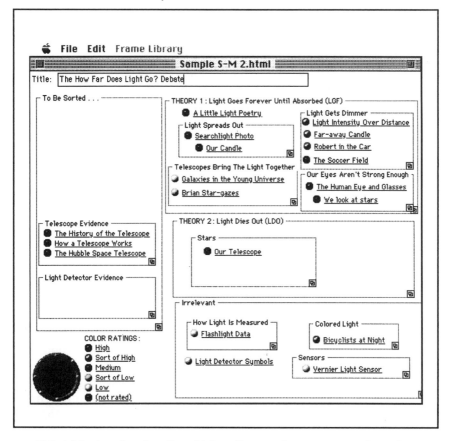

FIG. 4.18 A tool such as SenseMaker allows students to prepare for a class debate. Students organize pieces of evidence into different frames that can support two competing theories on "How Far Does Light Go?" or into a frame of irrelevant evidence.

Pat: "Like say 3 miles away? Three hundred miles?"

Dale: "Other evidence is like when you are up in an airplane, when you're real high and you look down and you can still see the city lights."

Pat: "Yeah, that's true."

Terry: "If the clouds are in the way, it just gets absorbed."

Dale: "... and it's a clear night—there's nothing in the way—and you can see the city lights."

In another example students discussed their views of telescopes and stars. Note that these students discuss the role of visual activity in determining how far light goes:

Jean: "Okay, well, you said that you can see the stars, but a star gives off so much light in the beginning. It could be getting dimmer all the way along, so if you were further away from it, you wouldn't be able to see it. So, how can you ...? Because in another one of those theories it said that you can't see some of the stars. You need a telescope to see it, proving that light is getting dimmer all along."

Tien: "Stars are there all the time. Just because you can't see them doesn't mean they're not there. There can be clouds blocking them."

Jean: "No! But it's saying light doesn't get to us, and if we can't see the light ... "

Tien: "Just because we can't see the light doesn't mean the light isn't there."

The SenseMaker software encourages students to prepare for the debate by distinguishing ideas and refining connections. In the How Far Does Light Go? debate, visual acuity determines many initial predictions. Students assume that if they cannot see light, then it is not there. In recent versions of the debate, students also search for evidence on the Internet. They find evidence that convinces them and share it with others.

For example, in one debate students located a night goggles advertisement that became a pivotal case in the debate. The advertisement included a movie showing what can be seen with and without goggles. Whereas many students found the telescope evidence confusing, most endorsed the night goggles as illustrating the limits of visual acuity.

When students are required to vote on alternative accounts of scientific phenomena in a debate, they commit themselves to a particular perspective and explain why they prefer that approach. For example, when students vote on what caused dinosaur extinction, they defend their viewpoint and support their assertions with evidence. This form of classroom interaction requires students to articulate their criteria. The class debate engages students in considering these individual criteria and developing class criteria.

Effective classroom discussion also occurs when groups debate evidence and discuss criteria. Groups can compare their SenseMaker arguments and discuss how they organized the evidence (Fig. 4.19). Discussing group products such as SenseMaker arguments overcomes some of the drawbacks of typical class discussion because no one student is individually responsible.

In summary, science classes can help students learn to rely on peers and experts to solve personally relevant problems they regularly encounter as they become competent citizens. A wealth of activity structures best serves this goal. All these activity structures implement mechanisms for supporting knowledge integration with peer interactions. In all cases, students add new ideas, explain ideas to their peers,

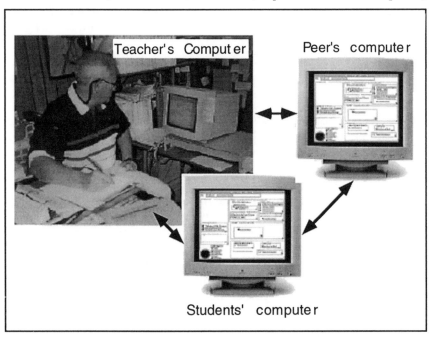

FIG. 4.19   During classroom presentations, Web-casting facilitates comparison of groups arguments by making their thinking publicly visible. SenseMaker arguments of the group who is presenting are displayed throughout the classroom.

borrow ideas from each other, observe the process of knowledge integration, debug each other's knowledge integration approaches, and develop critiquing, investigating, and reformulating skills.

Class discussion can succeed when efforts are made to include all the voices in the classroom and when knowledge integration goals predominate. However, the limited time available for class discussion can silence some students and reward superficial comments. Much evidence and observation of classrooms suggest that even the best class discussion engages only a proportion of the students.

Reflecting on differences between the methods and criteria used by students and those used by scientists can help us design these varied activities for lifelong science learning. Students need to select methods and criteria that make sense in their lives. The methods and criteria used by scientists often need to distinguish valid from invalid claims. Contrasting methods and criteria will help students understand why scientists speak with more authority than citizens. Citizens also will gain respect by distinguishing the methods of scientists from those of citizens. Exploring contrasting methods and criteria ultimately can improve students' understanding of the nature of science. Debates, critiques, discussions and role reversals all will contribute to this goal, and each activity will benefit some students so the mix succeeds.

REFLECTIONS

Better designs for small group work, project critiques, group discussion, and class debates mean that more students listen to the ideas of other students, get feedback on their own ideas, and engage in the process of knowledge integration. To improve face-to-face discussion opportunities, several avenues seem promising. Orchestrating debates, encouraging small group discussions, and setting up turn taking mechanisms all will help. Overall, we found that increasing the repertoire and effectiveness of social activity structures in the CLP classroom provided more social supports for learning.

Instruction that uses multiple activity structures provides opportunities to meet the needs of each individual learner. For example, in online discussions, anonymous and attributed roles give students more choices. Anonymous discussion allows students to take risks and voice an opinion in science or put forth an alternate explanation for scientific phenomena. On the other hand, attributed discussion permits readers to judge the validity of a comment on the basis of its source and author. The asynchronous format also means that students cannot interrupt each other. More students voice opinions when using an electronic forum than when participating in large class discussions.

Small-group face-to-face discussions (with three or four students) can silence some students by appealing to the brand of shoes they wear or their success in sports. Software support tools such as Agreement Bars, however, can balance social roles in small groups. Teachers, alert to status issues, also can monitor student group activity and help orchestrate productive interactions.

Designing activity structures and being sensitive to social roles can help promote respectful discussion, a useful skill in lifelong learning. When a classroom community develops shared standards and criteria, they are better able to engage in serious discussion of scientific ideas, explore scientific controversies, and allow students to take ownership of ideas.

Providing roles and encouraging students to specialize in a preferred domain can help the group appreciate different social roles. As Mr. K describes, students naturally assume certain roles in the classroom. Some students spontaneously specialize in troubleshooting various technological tools such as HeatBars, SenseMaker, or the Thermal Model Kit. Others take the role of critic. Still others become expert in one aspect of the science topic such as insulation materials. Having students exchange roles provides opportunities for understanding different viewpoints.

Our case study students preferred different social activity structures, but all found ways to include peers as learning partners. Sasha preferred a social context for science learning and recounted views of Mr. K in giving answers to questions. Sasha took advantage of the social context of the interview, encouraging the interviewers to elaborate and give feedback. Pat recounted views of peers in answering questions. Pat seemed content to hold multiple views of science topics, in part because some other students agreed with each of the views. Chris liked classroom debates, enjoying the opportunity to connect experiments and principles. Lee pointed out the advantages of peers as learning partners. Lee gave credit to students who helped with class assignments and explained the advantages of having a good partner when doing a project.

We refined social activity structures in designing the CLP curriculum. Through trial and refinement, we identified those that work best in CLP with these students. Students in other contexts might succeed with a different repertoire of activity structures.

Despite caveats about group learning, students can learn from each other if activities are well orchestrated. Middle school students might find knowledge integration and reasoning about science more understandable when students rather than teachers describe the process. Depending on the topic, students may trust their peers more than they trust adults. Certainly, students have more opportunities to consult peers than they do to consult adults or experts, so they benefit from developing skill in learning from peers. For lifelong learning, peers become more and more crucial as learning partners.

ASK MR. K

When did you start organizing kids into groups?

As far back as I can remember, I usually organized kids into pairs or larger groups for projects. It partly grew out of a necessity based on the amount of equipment and laboratory materials available. Also, in the beginning of CLP we looked at the literature, which helped me see the value of group work as an exchange of ideas between kids.

Did you adapt your teaching style to include group work?

I think group work was compatible with my style. Outside of those first 3 or 4 years when I was still very new to the game, I tried to get away from any kind of a lecture format and instead tried to talk to the kids during their activities. When I started teaching, I was introduced that very first year to a book of activities that a high school teacher in Southern California had put together. It was an old book with many activities that used very simple materials. I started using this approach to a large degree, which helped to get me away from any kind of lecture and textbook reading format. I encouraged getting kids to do work on projects instead.

What are some strategies to help get students to work together better?

When we had groups of four, we tried assigning roles to students and role-playing, but it didn't work too well. Kids didn't always take the roles they were assigned. Some students, for example, didn't see themselves as team leaders or data recorders. In fact, we often had kids that just assumed the role they wanted or felt most comfortable filling. Some kids really wanted to manipulate the equipment. They got frustrated if somebody else wasn't doing it fast enough, or right, and take over. We tried role-playing for a year, but it became superficial.

When we had more computers, students worked in pairs. They would switch roles (such as between working the computer and handling the measurement probes) during the activity. Also, to avoid bad mixes, I made sure students didn't have the same partner in every laboratory activity. Sometimes I had to assign students to a particular group.

Do you remember some tough cases of kids who resisted working together?

I remember groups of three that just could not work together, usually as a result of some conflict outside the classroom. In those cases, I worked especially hard to listen to students and point out good ideas each person contributed. Of course, I asked questions. For more troubled pairs, I put a timer on the table and told kids to switch roles every 10 minutes, for example, change who was operating the mouse or keyboard. They always begged me not to start the timer because they did't want to look funny in front of their classmates. In my 25 years of teaching, I've only had to do that a couple of times. I think the best way is to model for them really how groups need to work together. I ask each student to report their contributions to the group.

How do you engage a large group of students in a discussion?

One way to organize a discussion is to present what I call a "complex problem," such as how does a radiometer work? Or, why does one balloon end up on the ceiling while another remains on the floor. I choose problems that lack easy explanation. Often, I use groups to discuss laboratory activities. The reason I don't use large class discussion so much is that a relatively small percentage of the students get involved. I think students don't want to look dumb in front of their peers.

How do you encourage both boys and girls to contribute to discussion?

We noticed that many boys raise their hands right away and then say nothing when you call on them. Girls often take a little longer to raise their hands, but use the time to think out good ideas about things. Therefore, we had the idea of waiting, counting to 10, giving everyone a chance to think and raise their hands before calling on anyone. There are other techniques, but this seems to work.

What activities help students work together?

Probably one of the kids' favorite activities is the How Far Does Light Go? debate. I was taken by surprise the first time the kids got so enthusiastic about it! Even though they don't support a view they are assigned, they really identify with it and debate it well. Kids say things like "I don't believe this because … ." It's interesting how strong a position kids can take even when initially they didn't buy into the point of view they are defending. I think it really helps kids if they must sit there and ask questions about what people are debating and presenting to the class. They learn how to form questions in a way that will put the presenters on the spot but get them to think about how the evidence supports their point of view. They have to deal with evidence that doesn't support their point of view.

How did electronic discussion fit into your teaching?

Number one, electronic discussion extends the discussion. It has helped to extend learning beyond the classroom. Every year more kids access the discussion at home or in the library. More than half of the kids now have access.

I think electronic discussion is a very valuable tool because it allows kids to reflect, consider, and try to solve some complex problems. For example, I love the problem of explaining walking on the grass compared with walking on the sand and discussing why sand feels different, not an easy explanation. You see kids start to talk about what's happening.

Does electronic discussion take time away from class?

Electronic discussion actually extends class discussion. You know the classroom is overflowing before school, after school, and at lunch, and students are entering comments in the discussion. Last year we really emphasized the need to read other people's ideas and support what they are saying as evidence. I saw a lot more of the kids using evidence to support their points of view. I think as we learn to use the tool, it has become a very valuable tool, and of course it gets everybody involved. In a normal class discussion you may have 15% of your kids taking part, but with electronic discussion we're talking about probably 90% of those kids taking part, almost 100% this last semester. They have that choice of getting involved as anonymous, so they don't feel like anybody's going to be criticizing them specifically. I think that is helpful.

Does electronic discussion change class conversations?

I don't have hard data, but from a teacher gut-level feeling, I would say yes. I think my feeling is partly because I see kids in classroom discussion giving their ideas and saying what supports their idea. Furthermore, I think its in electronic discussion where we really stress the need for students to support their thoughts and ideas, and I think that's rubbing off. I see it happening in the CLP laboratory notes that the students are writing. They're putting in more evidence now.

POINTS TO PONDER

- How do you use social supports in your teaching?
- What shared methods and criteria do you use to select group activities?
- Watch yourself or a colleague run a class discussion. What do you observe?
- Do you engage students in social roles?
- Who is more vocal? Who participates? Boys or girls?
- What caveats have you found in group learning?
- How to do see the potential benefits of group learning? Can it improve learning?
- Describe specialists or roles that your students play in your instruction.
- Think about the kinds of group activities in your teaching. Can technology be used to support these?
- Think about some changes in your classroom that necessitated changes to group arrangements. Compare these with a colleague.
- Watch the section of the CLP film called, Can students learn from each other? Compare the debate activity to activities in classrooms where you teach or observe.

RELATED READINGS

Brown, A. L., & Campione, J. C. (1994). Guided discovery in a community of learners. In K. McGilly (Ed.), *Classroom lessons: Integrating cognitive theory and classroom practice* (pp. 229–270). Cambridge, MA: MIT Press/Bradford Books.

Keller, E. F. (1983). *A feeling for the organism: The life and work of Barbara McClintock*. San Francisco, CA: W.H. Freeman.

Linn, M. C., & Burbules, N. C. (1993). Construction of knowledge and group learning. In K. Tobin (Ed.), *The practice of constructivism in science education* (pp. 91–119). Washington, DC: American Association for the Advancement of Science (AAAS).

Pea, R., & Gomez, L. (1992). Distributed multimedia learning environments: Why and how? *Interactive Learning Environments, 2*, 73–109.

Sadker, M., & Sadker, D. (1994). *Failing at fairness: How America's schools cheat girls*. New York: Maxwell Macmillan International.

Wellesley College Center for Research on Women. (1992). *How schools shortchange girls*. Washington, DC: American Association of University Women Educational Foundation.

5

Promoting Autonomy
for Lifelong Science Learning

Don't ask me about science. I can't understand it.

I don't remember a thing from my science classes—except how obscure it was.

Your field is science? Excuse me, I just remembered a phone call I need to make.

Far too many people report forgetting everything they ever learned about science. Far too few seem interested in remedying this situation. For many, almost any activity is more appealing than learning about science.

Worse, people tend to dismiss science entirely rather than seek a domain or discipline of science in which they have expertise. In music, for example, individuals are likely to prefer classical, country, rock, or jazz, and perhaps dismiss the others, but they are unlikely to dismiss all at once—at least until the science of sound enters the discussion. Similarly, individuals might reject modern art but embrace impressionism, or reject classical art but embrace folk art—at least until the discussion turns to the science of light and color.

How can we encourage students to revisit and build on the science they learn in school? Can we prepare students eager to add to their scientific knowledge?

In the Computer as Learning Partner (CLP) curriculum we sought to promote *autonomous learning*. Autonomous learners are disposed to update their knowledge to solve personal problems or to improve their employment prospects. They spontaneously use the knowledge integration process to make sense of novel science information and attempt to integrate new information. For example, an autonomous learner might connect advances in laser technology for cataract surgery to ideas about light. Autonomous learners might connect heat and temperature to advertising for wilderness clothing that features new materials such as Gortex™, Thinsulate™, or microfibers. Homeowners might use insulation ideas to interpret R values and understand the mechanism that makes double-paned windows effective. We hope to prepare students who will conduct scientific inquiry regularly. This means students should find science personally relevant.

We described the CLP use of personally relevant science in chapter 2. Some learners find most of science personally relevant, whereas others dismiss science entirely, as the following conversation among eighth graders illustrates:

Sol: "You use science to help you out every day. For example, if you got sick, you could use science to get a medicine to cure you. Science is everywhere."

Jay: "But what about when we learned about the brain. Who is going to care how that works. Why would we need to know why the brain works if we aren't going to be doctors."

In the CLP projects, we successfully communicated the relevance of science. Most of the students started CLP believing that none of their science courses had been relevant to their lives. By the end of eighth grade, over 75% reported that science was relevant. When interviewed in high school, even more students reported connections between the CLP class and their lives.

The CLP approach succeeds by narrowing the gap between school and everyday science and engaging students in investigating personally relevant questions. However, CLP did not succeed at promoting autonomy with personally relevant problems alone. Experimentation, gathering information, and reaching conclusions also was not sufficient. How did we motivate students to critique results, reflect, and spontaneously engage in knowledge integration?

Autonomous learners see science as personally relevant and spontaneously integrate ideas. They connect science ideas and experiments, critique science articles and assertions, and carry out sustained investigations of scientific issues that interest them. Autonomous learners recognize when science topics have an impact on their lives, seek accessible science information, and make sense of the information they encounter. We synthesize CLP's pedagogical approach to promoting autonomous lifelong learners in four pragmatic pedagogical principles.

Our first pragmatic pedagogical principle, emphasizes making connections between science instruction and personally relevant problems and recognizing the benefits of these efforts. It states: *Engage students in reflecting on their own scientific ideas and on their own progress in understanding science*. When students reflect on their own science ideas and seek more sophisticated understanding of a personal problem, they make the connections necessary for lifelong learning. If students also reflect on their own progress in learning science, they begin to establish a habit of lifelong learning.

Many students "give up" on science because they cannot make sense of scientific claims, news articles, advertisements, product labels, Internet sites, self-help publications, and other sources. Science courses often ignore this serious problem. In the CLP project, we designed activities that enabled students to experience the benefits of knowledge integration.

Examining a label from a jacket designed for wilderness survival illustrates the challenges of connecting science ideas to everyday problems. (Fig. 5.1). The label in the figure shows the layers in the jacket and describes the reasons the fibers impede the flow of heat. Students with a barrier model may wonder why one fiber is better than another because relative rates of heat flow are suppressed in a barrier model. Students who studied molecular kinetic theory will not easily connect their knowledge to this diagram because it relies on heat flow, not a molecular model. A heat flow model helps to interpret this label, although to validate the claims, students need information about the relative rates of heat flow through the various materials mentioned. Without this information, and information about fibers that might have been used instead, readers can accept the claims, research the claims, or dismiss them as hype.

Knowing what information to gather, gathering additional information, and making sense of the information are important activities that science classes typically address with "hands-on science." As discussed

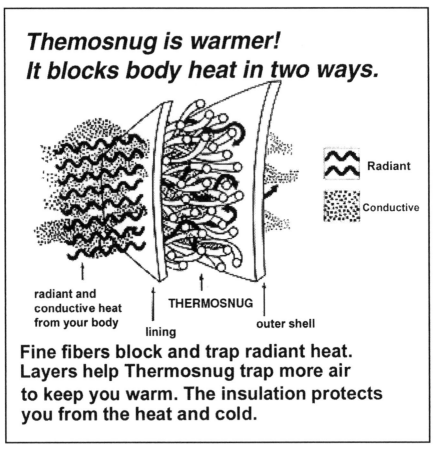

Themosnug is warmer!
It blocks body heat in two ways.

Radiant

Conductive

radiant and
conductive heat   THERMOSNUG
from your body   outer shell
                              lining

**Fine fibers block and trap radiant heat.
Layers help Thermosnug trap more air
to keep you warm. The insulation protects
you from the heat and cold.**

FIG. 5.1   Students use this fabric label from a Gortex jacket to critique
different models of heat flow.

in chapter 2, this process must be carefully crafted to achieve knowledge integration rather than isolated knowledge or frustration. To interpret the label in Fig. 5.1, citizens need skill in critiquing its claims
and skill in locating relevant information. To prepare lifelong learners,
CLP designed activities to help students connect experiences such as
interpreting this label to their other science knowledge.

In designing the CLP curriculum, we researched many ways to help
students reflect and make connections among ideas. We created a repertoire of strategies for encouraging students to reflect. We also designed personally relevant problems that promote lifelong learning
because students revisit them after they complete science class.

Our second pragmatic pedagogical principle, emphasizing the stance toward science knowledge necessary for lifelong learning, states: *Engage students as critics of diverse scientific information.* To become effective critics students need practice using their analytic approaches and criteria to assess science information they encounter such as news articles, Internet sites, advertisements, product labels, and more. They need to distinguish promising, persuasive, and bogus claims. They need strategies for resolving conflicting claims. They need to decide when to seek new information, and they need to determine when they have sufficient information to make a decision. These are dilemmas faced by both sophisticated science researchers and citizens. Citizens commonly encounter claims from news accounts, advertisements, product labels, and the like that require some critical evaluation. As the jacket label in Fig. 5.1 illustrates, this critical evaluation typically requires specific knowledge of scientific domains such as microfibers, as well as a set of shared criteria for evaluating scientific claims.

To help students become effective critics of personally relevant topics, we need to support the typical activities of citizens: making sense of articles, labels, advertisements, Internet material, or news accounts of scientific phenomena. Indeed, the barrage of scientific claims that citizens face about many personally relevant problems such as healthy eating habits, weight management, product selection, or exercise discourages many from attempting to make sense of science. Fear of radiation, pollution, or natural forces such as earthquakes makes understanding of difficult concepts like relative risk seem even more complicated. When facing debilitating disease, individuals may abandon the usual safeguards and accept any possible remedy. Moreover, with new technologies, including computers, lasers, or cloning, come very challenging ethical and scientific dilemmas.

Furthermore, students need to distinguish their goals from those of others, especially those of natural scientists. Citizens typically seek less precise solutions than research scientists. Citizens want jackets that keep them warm in the wilderness. Few need the protection necessary for an ascent on Everest. As demonstrated in chapter 2, pragmatic models often help more than abstract models of scientific phenomena in critiquing claims about everyday problems. Just as the heat flow model makes sense in evaluating claims about jackets, the source-detection model of light will work for critiquing claims about sunglasses, windshield glass, or study lamps.

Can we make critiquing tasks manageable for students and citizens? In the CLP project we struggled with this challenge. As described in chapter 2, science learners often have a disposition to "cognitive economy": Many avoid questioning conflicting results. In this chapter, we describe some promising ways to prepare students as critics. We have created critiquing activities and devised effective ways to use the debate context in science to engage students in critiquing each other.

To prepare students to conduct personal projects autonomously, our third pragmatic principle states: *Engage students in varied, sustained science projects to illustrate the broad range of science activities and meet the needs of diverse learners*. Students need to deal with a range of projects learn and how to gauge their progress.

What counts as sustained work depends on the experience of the learner. Projects that overwhelm some learners are too easy for others. Projects should involve some choices in scope, criteria, emphasis, methods, and desired outcome. Students who develop skill in choosing, refining, evaluating, seeking help, and completing projects while still in science class, will be set on a path toward selecting and completing projects in the future.

We define projects as complex, multistep activities in which individuals or groups choose alternatives, incorporate scientific information, reconsider their ideas, and advance their understanding. Projects involve reflecting and making connections, our first principle of autonomous learning. They also involve critiquing and weighing ideas, our second principle of autonomous learning. We distinguish projects from other activities by their sustained, iterative nature and their culmination in a solution or decision.

Successful project work involves determining when to stop working. Premature solutions may end up being superficial or wrong. Furthermore, at some point further effort on a project may add little benefit. Therefore, projects involve a multitude of choices, and students typically need to seek guidance and gain experience to make these choices well.

How do projects connect to scientific inquiry as practiced by natural scientists? Scientists rely on established methods, but also devise new methods to match novel questions. Citizens also need an established inquiry process to become successful lifelong science learners.

Our fourth pragmatic principle, capturing this process, states: *Establish a generalizable inquiry process useful for diverse science projects*. This process of abstracting and refining an inquiry process is the central goal of instruction for lifelong learning. It builds on a principle from chapter 2 that states: Scaffold science activities so students understand the inquiry process.

Many science courses reduce scientific inquiry to the mindless application of a formulaic process for conducting science experiments called the "steps of science reasoning" or the "scientific method."

Such formulas rarely apply to life outside class and contribute to the frustration with science that citizens often report. Instead, students need a robust process that supports the many paths to knowledge integration illustrated in the case studies presented in chapter 1. Students should know when and how to define problems, predict outcomes, design investigations, set goals, seek expert advice, interpret results, make decisions, critique evidence, and repeat these activities until the solution satisfies their personal goals.

Students also need good models of the inquiry process practiced by scientists to apply scientific ideas judiciously and to select reasonable criticisms of ideas put forth by scientists. For example, students often complain that scientists disagree rather than acknowledge healthy debate of science topics. Students also need a sense of their own process of knowledge integration to guide their learning as they conduct scientific inquiries. Knowing one's own biases, be they for information presented in "scientific" looking tables, for testimonials from public figures, or for ideas presented with sophisticated vocabulary, is essential for successful lifelong learning as discussed in chapter 6.

Taken together, the pragmatic pedagogical principles in this chapter challenge the designers of science instruction to communicate a rich, balanced view of the inquiry process and prepare students to use inquiry throughout their lives. In the CLP curriculum, we investigated ways to communicate this process so it becomes robust and useful. Our findings, linked to the principles, are detailed below.

PRAGMATIC PEDAGOGICAL PRINCIPLES

Engage students in reflecting on progress and ideas

Our first principle is a call to encourage reflection to promote autonomy. When asked, students often link ideas they had not linked before or identify gaps in their reasoning that need to be filled. We already have described a variety of CLP activities that prompt students to record their predictions before conducting experiments using the Electronic Laboratory Notebook. After collecting their results, students can compare their findings with their original predictions. We prompted students to reflect on the gaps and connections between predictions and results. The students often noticed links or gaps, saying for example, "Foil is no better than not wrapping the drink at all."

Designing experiments to encourage reflection took several iterations. Initially we used worksheets to sequence student activities and to pose questions that encouraged students to integrate their ideas (Fig. 5.2). We replaced questions with "sentence starters" such as "The

Names: _____ Period: _____

Heat Bars

In this activity, you will be using a program called HeatBars to study how heat flows through different materials. The program calculates how long it takes for different parts of a bar to heat up when a source is touching one end. After examining the different materials, you will put all the materials into a continuum line for best to worst conductor.

Use the HeatBars program to test different materials against each other.

Experiment	Materials	Observations	Conclusions (which is a better conductor)
1			
2			
3			
4			
5			
6			
7			
8			
9			
10			

FIG. 5.2 Worksheets used in CLP to help structure activities and encourage reflection before the Electronic Laboratory Notebook was developed.

Names: _____Period:_____

Sound Sources

Sounds are all around us. We hear sounds almost all the time. In this lab, we will look at where sounds start. The first task is to find 7 things that make different sounds. For each of your sources of sound, fill in a column on the table below (an example has been done for you.)

Describe the sound source	Example: Violin	1	2	3
How does the source produce sounds?	When you pluck the strings, they make sound.			
Describe the typical sound that this source makes.	The sound is a clear tone.			
Describe how the sound changes over time.	The sound slowly fades away.			
What variation on the typical sound can you make?				

FIG. 5.2 *(continued)*

reason we think this ... " and elicited more reflection. We added prediction and observation activities, as described in chapter 2, to focus attention on the experimental results. As discussed in chapter 3, the Electronic Laboratory Notebook permitted us to deliver prompts and feedback online, allowed students to draw predictions, and provided online feedback on principles. These activities all promoted knowledge integration.

Our initial prompts in the Electronic Laboratory Notebook directed students to reflect on a specific connection. We also added more general prompts that asked students to complete sentences such as "The problem with this experiment is ... " or "This helps explain our personal experience ... " Students complained that we asked too many questions. Classroom observation showed us that students were unable to distinguish prompts we thought asked for different types of reflection. Nevertheless, students wrote long explanations in response to the prompts.

In the next version of the Electronic Laboratory Notebook, we reduced the number of prompts and created general prompts. We also changed the prompting software to allow students to request more specific prompts. These modifications increased student satisfaction, did not change the number of words students wrote in response to prompts, and helped more students to reflect.

In class, Mr. K often asked reflection questions instead of giving students specific answers, saying for example, "Before I answer the question, what do you think?" "What is confusing to you so far?" or "What do you need to know to answer your question?" These questions led some students to clarify their ideas.

Evidence showing the benefits of reflection questions comes from Eileen Lewis' dissertation interviews. Lewis interviewed randomly selected groups of students studying CLP. During the interviews, she asked students "Why?" "What makes you think that?" "Why do you think it happened that way?" "What's another explanation for this?" and related questions to clarify ideas about science. Students who were interviewed learned more than students who were not selected for interviews. The interviewed students had the opportunity to practice autonomous reasoning and benefited from this reflection practice.

To promote autonomy we also need to help students learn when to ask their own questions. We must enable students to identify gaps in their own reasoning. We need to prepare students to "find" science problems in their lives and resolve them.

Activity design involves a trade-off between supporting students as they conduct a project, experiment, or inquiry and encouraging them to design their own inquiry. Students who spontaneously generate connections among ideas, identify gaps in their reasoning, or provide explanations can lull instructors into complacency. Teachers might assume that all the students are doing this. How can we enable more students to look for gaps in their reasoning and become autonomous?

Betsy Davis studied the impact of what she called "generic" prompts and "directed" prompts in her dissertation using the Knowledge Integration Environment Software (see chap. 8 for more details). Generic prompts ask students to complete sentences such as "We are wondering about ... ," whereas directed prompts start with phrases such as "We think this experiment supports the argument because ... ." Surprisingly, she found that generic prompts helped students locate gaps in their reasoning more than directed prompts.

Looking more closely at the results, Davis found that students who described themselves as autonomous responded to generic and directed prompts equally well. Generic prompts as compared with directed prompts helped students who were less inclined to be autonomous. For these students, directed prompts could often be answered without knowledge integration, but generic prompts required some reflection and connection of ideas. Our case study student Sasha illustrated the benefits of generic prompts. Sasha gave good student answers to direct questions but tended to make new connections when asked to give reasons for answers.

Davis's results made clear that all prompts are not alike. Designing prompts to help students become autonomous means carefully studying how prompts work in practice. Teachers often seek to match specific, directed, or generic prompts to students. Our results suggest the advantages of offering students a mix of prompts. Both teachers and students will benefit by experimenting with a variety of prompts. Students may begin spontaneously to ask themselves reflection questions. Teachers will gain insights into how students reason about science.

Engage students as critics

Successful lifelong learners evaluate the science information they encounter instead of accepting it uncritically. Our second pragmatic pedagogical principle to promote autonomy states: *Engage students as critics of diverse scientific information.*

Science courses often neglect opportunities for students to serve as critics. Yet critiquing prepares students for complex independent projects. Any complex project that builds on other work requires students to analyze and critique sources.

Critiquing scientific claims can overwhelm students because they have no idea where to begin. Students need a set of criteria to help them select the most personally relevant scientific claims for further scrutiny.

Students encounter many claims in advertisements and news articles. In many cases the authority of the sources or their relevance of the claims are sufficient reasons to dismiss the claims. Testimonials from rock stars about wilderness attire might be dismissed on the basis of source authority. Claims that clothes will appeal to friends may be irrelevant.

Critiquing activities are surprisingly rare in the science curriculum. When students do critique, they may use only criteria such as neatness and grammar or base their critiques on personal likes or dislikes. They need opportunities to develop and apply scientific criteria to a broad range of claims, including those made by their peers and those in popular publications.

Critiquing activities may be neglected because they take instructional time and often appear superficially unproductive. Students may seem to "go in circles" if they lack compelling alternatives to the claims. For example, in our programming work we observed students trying the same program again only to have it fail once more because they could not figure out an alternative.

We already have described some ways to make critiquing activities accessible. In chapter 2, we described how pivotal cases help students generate alternatives. In chapter 3 we showed ways to make the process of considering alternatives more visible to students. Students may benefit when teachers describe their own floundering. In chapter 4 we discussed how peers can serve as lifelong partners to help others generate alternatives. A typical online Multimedia Forum Kiosk discussion included several plausible alternatives for most problems (Figs. 4.5 and 4.6). In this chapter, we discuss manageable critiquing activities and show how instructors can support students as they take on larger and larger projects.

What does it mean to critique an experiment, advertisement, or science article? Often students critique science generally, dismissing things they do not agree with or understand. To promote knowledge integration, critiquing activities require analysis of both obvious links among ideas and more subtle connections. Thus, to critique an advertisement claiming that a new picnic cooler is "safe," students need to understand what the authors mean by "safe," as well as what readers of the advertisement might infer. Will the cooler keep food safe from spoiling? Is the cooler unlikely to injure the user? Moreover, how does this claim connect to the users' desire for a cooler that will not tip over in the car trunk?

To critique successfully, students need to apply appropriate standards or criteria. General statements such as "It doesn't make sense" or "It is not relevant" need backings to qualify as critiques. As we discussed in chapter 4, students benefit from negotiating effective criteria to evaluate claims successfully. Often, such criteria can be designed best with peers as learning partners. After students complete science classes, they often will need to critique science advertisements, political messages, and policies. Peers generally will serve as their learning partners in these situations. Ideal student critiquing activities directly connect to personally relevant projects and to relevant science ideas.

The Internet offers a wonderful opportunity to critique science communications. Traditionally, students in science classes view texts and teachers as authorities, often accepting these communications uncritically, believing that everything in the science textbook is true. With the availability of Internet information, interpreting statements from a broad range of individuals becomes crucial to effective science education. Students need to evaluate the authority of sources as part of science learning. In our new partnerships, described in chapter 8, we create critique activities using Internet evidence.

In our Internet activities, we ask students to interpret labels for wilderness gear, coolers, antiheat ice cloth shirts, solar energy, gadgets, and thermal windows (Fig. 5.3). We expect students to use the heat flow model taught in science class, skills in critiquing claims, and criteria they developed in collaboration with classmates.

In summary, critiquing activities implement a process well known in science. Scientists regularly critique the work of peers using established criteria. Peer review often determines promotion, publication, and grant approval. This process is much less coherent for students or citizens. Students learn to critique by observing mentors, participating in group discussions of research results, and responding to review of their own work.

Engage students in varied science projects

Our third pragmatic pedagogical principle to prepare autonomous, lifelong learners states: *Engage students in varied project experiences.* Projects permit students to use reflection and critiquing spontaneously.

Citizens, scientists, and students all endorse hands-on experimentation as a motivating component of science instruction. Yet projects are rare. Why? Teachers often complain that students lack motivation for the projects that science classes can support. In the early versions of the CLP, students were only mildly interested in comparing the cooling curves for large and small volumes.

Designing an interesting, feasible project requires considerable skill. Many students lack ideas for projects, and some select unrealistic goals such as building a solar car, creating a video game, or finding a

Keeping Your Cool in the Summertime
by Rocky Reporter and Jana Journalist

Summer is a time for fun and sun, but when it gets too hot, watch out! We've figured out how to beat the heat this summer. To keep your house cool this summer, do your cooking outside. Outdoor cooking attracts heat away from the house and keeps everyone cool. The new solar ovens are the best, using up lots of heat that otherwise would heat houses.

Claim 1: Energy conversion principles indicate that black attracts heat

When made correctly, solar ovens use energy conversion principles to put heat to good uses. Solar ovens often have black lids to make them heat up faster. We asked local residents why the black lids worked. One woman interviewed reports: "I've seen it happen myself. When my friend Bill and I went to the beach, Bill stayed cool longer in his white T-shirt than I did in my black dress." Obviously, black items attract the heat better than white items.

Claim 2: Heat sources cause the temperature to go up

Why move the ovens outside? Everyone knows that anything that gives off heat will heat up the space it's in. So because ovens heat up kitchens, moving them outside will cool the house down. This works best in houses with small kitchens because studies show that heat sources heat up small rooms faster than large rooms.

Claim 3: Ovens and other objects use up sunlight, thereby lowering temperatures.

The third point, then, is that having a solar oven outside would keep your house cool by using up some of the sunlight that otherwise would have entered your house and made it hot. Students performing an experiment on the greenhouse effect determined that the heat can be trapped in containers where light can get in easily but heat can't get out. This is similar to what happens in a greenhouse for plants. We've experienced the same phenomenon when we left our cars in the sun with the windows shut; the heat built up quickly. If possible, leave the windows open and keep the shades drawn so less sunlight comes in. The solar oven uses up heat in a way similar to how the new a shirt does. The shirt reportedly keeps you cool because it is dipped in a special chemical. The manufacturers say that this chemical can keep you cool even in the hottest weather.
You can see, then, that the answer to the question "How can I stay cool in the summertime?" is clear. Just cook with a solar oven and use other items to use up the sunlight, and you'll stay nice and cool while everyone else is sweating.

FIG. 5.3   Students are asked to critique an article from a newspaper that makes claims about heat and temperature.

new organism when asked to come up with a project. Scientists also find designing their next experiment challenging.

Even with realistic, accessible projects, students often lack ideas about how to proceed. For example, students designing an energy-efficient house may need help to identify which variables or questions are important.

Finally, science projects take instructional time. Sometimes, as students flounder or convert a science project into an art project, teachers conclude that projects are not worth the days devoted to them.

These issues concerned us as we created projects for CLP students. We introduced student projects with "aliens on tour" designed by Nancy Songer. Students were asked to design clothing and dwellings for aliens coming to the United States (Fig. 5.4). Working in groups of two, the students jointly designed dwellings and clothing for one type of alien: Kulebeings, Sizzlepersons, or Equilibs.

The students were eager to design clothing and dwellings for aliens. However, they had considerable difficulty connecting their project work with their classroom laboratory experimentation. A number of students approached their project more as an art activity than as a heat and temperature activity. One group designed their oral report as a news account of the landing of aliens and their subsequent housing and

---

Project "Aliens on Tour"

It is the year 2062 and you currently are living on the planet Zumtar. On the basis of your reputation as an expert in heat energy and temperature, you have been given the following assignment: Three tour buses of important aliens from different origins have just arrived on the planet Zumtar. Your assignment is to use the evidence below to design various products for the aliens to make their visit on Zumtar as enjoyable and comfortable as possible.

The Equilibs

Equilibs are known for rapid adaptation to new environments. Initially, when they move into either very cold conditions or very hot conditions, Equilibs appear sluggish and lazy. Their body temperature adjusts to the outside environment as quickly as possible, and once it does, they function very well. Equilibs are cold-blooded, and their ideal body temperature is identical to the environment in which they are located at the time.

The Kulebeings

Commonly referred to as "the cool ones," the Kulebeings need to be kept cold in order to function well. Kulebeings also are cold-blooded, and their ideal body temperature is 0.0 degrees Celsius.

The Sizzlepersons

The Sizzlepersons are commonly referred to as "the hot aliens." They need to be kept warm to survive. These aliens are cold-blooded, and their ideal body temperature is 40.2 degrees Celsius.

FIG. 5.4 Aliens: A sample student project.

clothing problems. Many project reports neglected connections to the heat and temperature activities from class or failed because students really did not understand what it meant for an alien to be cold-blooded.

For her dissertation, Helen Clark sought projects that connected to science class. She created small, medium, and large projects. Students could select from among groups of projects. They then were required to perform two small projects, one medium project, and one large project throughout the semester.

Project examples appear in Fig. 5.5. Students selected the project they wanted to perform, the methods for carrying out the project, the evidence they needed to reach conclusions, and whether they wished coaching help.

Clark found that students selected projects for superficial reasons. They preferred projects that looked easy and connected to what they knew. Often they made poor decisions. For example, the Derek and his noodles question sounded easy to the students but was difficult because the variables compensate for each other. Figure 5.6 shows students comparing answers about Derek and his noodles, but failing to resolve the differences among their views.

Student projects varied in the degree of creative thinking, use of evidence from classroom experimentation, and consideration of alternatives. To create class criteria, students reviewed each other's projects. Efforts to develop shared criteria led to interesting class discussions and improved project outcomes as shown in Fig. 5.7.

How do we assess projects? Clark devised several measures of knowledge integration to use in assessing projects. She developed the holistic criteria given in Fig. 5.8. In addition she graded projects by combining the separate warrants used to justify conclusions, giving credit for class experiments, personal observations, and use of science principles.

Many projects rated poorly on these measures. Consistent with our goal of encouraging spontaneous knowledge integration, Clark designed coaching opportunities for students. When students asked for coaching, they received feedback on their reasoning, and were reminded of class criteria. Clark experimented with two different coaching approaches. First, she motivated a large number of reluctant graduate students to serve as personal coaches for 180 eighth graders as they completed projects. Each eighth grader was assigned to a coach. Students sent their first drafts to their coach by e-mail. The coach reviewed the draft, made comments, and returned it to the student for further action. This dialogue could have several iterations (Fig. 5.9). Graduate student coaches initially gave both helpful and unhelpful comments. Clark analyzed successful comments and devised a

Small Project:

Movie theaters or playhouses both use "special" lighting. After visiting either one, draw a picture explaining how the theater was lit. Explain what you think are the reasons why the lights may have been placed or angled the way they were. What was the effect on you as you tried to "see" different things in the theater? (for example, the aisles versus the screen)

Medium Project:

Jennifer has a 2-liter bottle of coke. Ted and Lisa each have one 12-ounce can of Coke. They all left their Cokes out on the kitchen counter overnight. Jennifer put her Coke in the freezer. Ted put his in the refrigerator. Lisa wrapped her coke in Styrofoam and then put it in the freezer.

      a. Which Coke will be the coldest after 1 hour?

      b. Which Coke will be the coldest after 24 hours?

      c. What is the main reason for your answer?

      d. What principles from this class helped you to make your decision?

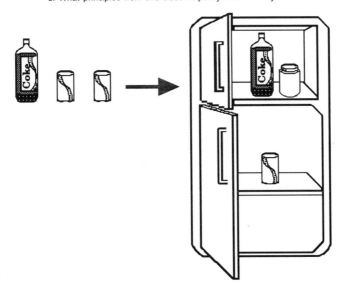

Large Project:

Tape-record or videotape yourself teaching a younger child about any of the principles studied in class. Be sure to find ways to communicate these ideas so that they can be understood by the child. Choose words and images that make sense to the child's age group. Ask the child to explain and give examples. Be sure to ask questions to see if the child understands. Plan an entire lesson. Submit lesson plan, and tape, and provide reflections.

FIG. 5.5 Small, medium, and large portfolio projects.

Dr. Conduction critiques Dr. Insulation's solution:

Dr. Insulation also has her own conception on how to solve Derek's problem. He finally decides he would cook all the noodles in one large pot. He feels that it is the fastest way because it is only one pot and heat energy flows faster through a larger surface area. Her ideas for cooking the spaghetti are very realistic and the way she presented his sob story was very creative. Dr. Insulation seems to understand the principles of heat energy as well as the principles involving equilibrium. Besides giving the answer that she felt was right, she took the time to explain why she thought it would be fast. She also provided a backup plan in which she suggested making a Greek salad.

Dr. Insulation and I came up with different answers, and I obviously thought that mine was right, but now I'm not so sure. I suggested using three small pans, one small burner, and two larger burners. Dr. Insulation preferred using one large pan, although she never stated which burner type to use. Her answer, in my opinion, is either right or we are both right. All the principles that I used to emphasize my solution worked for hers as well. We even used the same reasoning. We both felt that our answer would enable the water and spaghetti to heat up the fastest. Dr. Insulation's answer probably would have been right if she had said to use the large burner as well as the large pan. Overall, I felt that her solution as well as the way she presented it, were creative, well thought out, and very realistic.

FIG. 5.6   Students' compare their recommendations to Derek,
who is preparing noodles for dinner.

coach instruction program. Coaches succeeded in motivating knowledge integration when they related evidence from personal experiences that contradicted the conclusions in projects and asked students to consider specific revisions. For example, comments such as the following were helpful: "On the next revision I want you to explain how the heat gets into the water," and "Look over your report from the pulsing lab and see if you can connect the principles in that lab to your explanation." Less helpful comments included these: "What other factors might be influencing how warm the water gets?" and "What activities have you done in class that are similar to this question?"

Helen found that students benefited from being coached (Fig. 5.10). For example, in the small project, (Fig. 4.14), coaches were found to

Linda describes the problem:

In the morning, Jennifer put her Coke in the freezer. Ted put his Coke in the refrigerator. And Lisa wrapped her Coke in Styrofoam and then put it in the freezer. We had to figure out, we had to predict what the temperature would be after 1 hour and after 24 hours.

Nomi critiques Linda's report:

I critiqued Linda's report. I was very impressed after reading her paper. The only minor detail I think should be changed would be to simplify her report. Some sentences were awkward and hard to understand. Besides that, her predictions seemed to make sense and were very realistic. However, our predictions differ. I predicted that both Jennifer and Lisa's Cokes would be coldest after one hour and Linda predicted that Lisa's Coke would be the coldest. After 24 hours, I thought that Jennifer's Coke would be the coldest and she predicted that all Coke will have reached equilibrium with their surroundings.

Linda critiques Nomi's report:

I critiqued Nomi's report. After reading the paper, I felt that it answered the main problem well. The reasoning behind the prediction was a little vague. The paper is different than mine because I went into more detail about how and why the heat energy was flowing a certain way. The materials that the containers were made out of was not taken into consideration. No evidence or references to the previous lab was given. This essay is organized and easy to understand logical order. The format is neat and clear. Correct grammar and spelling use. The sentences are complete, and it's obvious the paper has been carefully proofread for errors.

Nomi describes the next steps:

After writing our reports, we were curious to what the results would actually be, so we did the experiment and got these results.

Linda describes the results after 1 hour:

Okay, after 1 hour, Ted's Coke was the warmest at 13° C. Lisa's was second warmest at 10° C and Jennifer's at 5°C. Now, Nomi had predicted that Lisa's and Jennifer's Coke would be about the same temperature or equally the coldest and I had predicted that Jennifer's Coke—no Lisa's Coke would be the coldest, so we were both wrong.

Nomi describes the results after 24 hours:

Okay after 24 hours, Ted's Coke was still warmest at 2°C and Lisa's and Jennifer's Coke were the same at -10°C. I predicted that Jennifer's Coke would be coldest and I was obviously wrong. And Linda predicted that all the Cokes would have reached equilibrium with their surroundings, and she was right.

Linda and Nomi analyze their experiment:

Okay when doing the experiment according to the description given on the medium lab, we found out that it wasn't very realistic and we had some problems. Uhm, after 1 hour, we had opened the Cokes to measure the temperature, and so we had to put them back in the fridge and the freezer open, so that may have changed the temperature slightly. And after 24 hours, Lisa's Coke, because it was open, expanded and spilled all over the fridge, our freezer, and when we opened Jennifer's Coke, it like erupted like a volcano for about 30 minutes. And my mom drank Ted's Coke the night before so we had – we used a different soda that had been in the fridge for about 2 days.

FIG. 5.7 Students critiquing each other' project on the "Two Cokes" question.

1 point – No science principle mentioned, descriptive only (bowl is smaller)

2 points – Mentions principle, but is inaccurate or incomplete (small things get hotter)

3 points – Accurately restates principle without elaboration or connections (if same heat is added than smaller object reaches higher temperature)

4 points – Clear and accurate understanding of single principle and adds elaboration and or context. (e.g., If same heat is added to two objects, then the smaller object has less space, so heat is more dense like in the lab where we heated the small and large beaker, so it reaches a higher temperature)

5 points – Clear and accurate understanding of principle and also ties in one or more additional principles from the same or related topic area (e.g., The light from the sun hits the water and changes to heat energy which warms both the bowl and the pool, but since the pool has more water and surface area it doesn't reach as warm a temperature)

FIG. 5.8   Holistic grading: These categories were used to rate the quality of small projects.

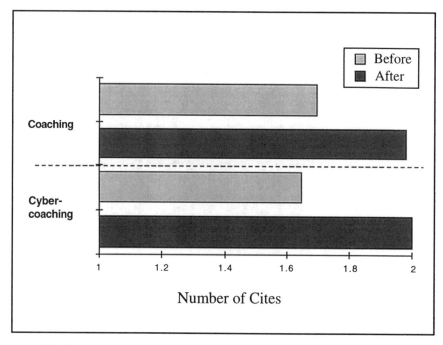

FIG. 5.9   Students benefit from coaching both from a human coach and a cybercoach.

elicit good explanations and revisions (Fig. 5.11). The student quoted in the following excerpt filled in gaps in reasoning after being coached. Before coaching:

> If my little sister [Jaime] asked, 'On a hot day why is the dog dish usually hotter than the pool?' I would say to her, "Well Jaime, the dog dish holds *less* water than the pool, so it *can adjust* to the *temperature* of the air *quicker* than the pool."

After coaching:

> If my little sister [Jaime] asked, 'On a hot day why is the dog dish usually hotter than the pool?' I would say to her, 'Well Jaime, the dog dish holds *less water than the pool, so it can adjust to the temperature of the air quicker* than the pool. Tell you what, let's *make lemonade'*. I would show her that in a big glass of lemonade you need *to add more sugar to make it as sweet* as the small glass.

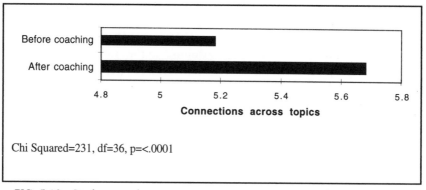

Chi Squared=231, df=36, p=<.0001

FIG. 5.10   Students made more connections to topics across the curriculum as well as links to everyday life examples after coaching.

Helpful: On the next revision I want you to explain how the heat gets into the water.

Less helpful : What other factors might be influencing how warm the water gets?

Helpful: Look over your report from the pulsing lab and see if you can connect the principles in that lab to your explanation.

Less helpful: What activities have you done in class that are similar to this question?

FIG. 5.11   An example of coach prompts that elicited both less and more helpful revisions on projects.

Then I would explain to her that it's the *same thing with heat. You need more of it in a big* pool to make it as warm as the small dog dish.

Clark also observed that coaches made many similar comments on the projects used in the CLP classroom. To make coaching more efficient, Clark designed the CyberCoach, which allowed coaches to select from a list of coaching comments that had been used previously for the project they were coaching. A form letter was created incorporating the selected comments. The coach then added a personal note and sent the coaching comment to the student.

How did this work? To our surprise, students liked the CyberCoach comments. Although some students recognized that the letters were electronically generated, they treated the comments seriously. The personal remarks were sufficient to convince students that an individual had designed the coaching comments they received.

Coaches liked the solution as well. Nearly 90% of the form letters were able to use some coaching comments from the database. Coaches required only 10% of the time to generate a unique coaching comment (Fig. 5.12). Of course, this comment then could be added to the database. Students coached by use of the CyberCoaching system were as likely to improve their projects as students who were coached personally.

Clearly, students reflect on their ideas and benefit from coaching when they seek to be coached. Coaches can efficiently provide comments when the project has been coached previously. We can imagine expanding this facility to include coaching on a broader range of projects. Use of the CyberCoach means that coaches need less training than would be the case if they individually developed their coaching

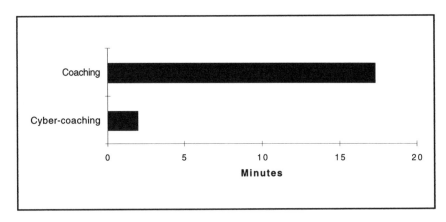

FIG. 5.12 Human coaching takes more time than cyber coaching.

styles. The CyberCoach helps new coaches by modeling how to design appropriate comments for eighth graders.

When students reflect on their science experiments, critique experiments, and conduct projects, they also improve their knowledge integration for the science topics they study. All three of the pragmatic pedagogical principles described so far work by getting students to identify gaps in reasoning, generate links among ideas, critique alternatives, and reach coherent conclusions.

Establish an inquiry process

Our fourth pragmatic pedagogical principle, seeking to generalize the process of knowledge integration, states: *Establish a generalizable inquiry process suitable for diverse projects.* What conditions enable students to generalize the reasoning they learn in science and spontaneously engage in knowledge integration? College faculty often complain that entering students cannot "think." Students often retort that faculty members do not understand how they think.

Do students think differently from scientists? Most parents of teenage students would agree. If we look closely at how students think about science, we see that students do link and connect ideas. However, they often make connections that scientists would criticize and they frequently miss connections that seem straightforward to scientists. In the case studies in chapter 1, we see many examples of this.

Scientists integrate their ideas productively because they select the "right" information and draw on a great deal of related knowledge they can use to interpret questions. Students appear to lack this skill when they focus on superficial information. With CLP, we tried several approaches to teaching a generalizable inquiry process. Derek Newell, as described in chapter 2, designed a scientific reasoning unit to teach principles such as how to control variables, how to design comparisons, how to critique results, and how to evaluate evidence. In this scientific reasoning unit, students solved mysteries, critiqued medical decisions, evaluated news articles, and engaged in the dinosaur extinction debate.

We compared students who studied scientific reasoning with those who did not. We found no impact of this scientific reasoning unit on posttest performance or other indicators of autonomy and knowledge integration. Students could describe the abstract principles but did not use them to critique their heat and temperature experiments. In subsequent versions of CLP we tried to make inquiry more accessible to students.

Several aspects of this reasoning unit seemed promising. The debate project discussed in chapter 4 helped students learn to use evidence to support their arguments about dinosaur extinction and develop shared criteria for evaluating claims.

We also found that we could engage students in inquiry by scaffolding them as they performed multiple laboratory experiments using the Electronic Laboratory Notebook. We could motivate students to identify gaps in their reasoning by using prompts, and we could engage students in critiquing many personally relevant experiments. These activities prepared students to carry out more complex projects and take advantage of coaching. This series of activities led to more and more independent, sustained inquiry by students.

Students benefit from accessible science projects that regularly engage them in the process of selecting and applying criteria. These experiences enable students to reason like scientists in a discipline they understand. Making connections to inquiry processes, ensuring that students encounter these opportunities in every science class, and helping students learn to locate necessary information for normal problems all offer promise for lifelong learning.

Even so, we cannot promise that CLP students will always reason scientifically. Indeed even scientists complain that they cannot make sense of some complex problems. Students need sensible criteria for the topic they are studying. They must have a healthy skepticism about criteria proposed in advertisements, by authority figures, or by others. They also need to select projects matched to their knowledge. Developing criteria with peers as learning partners can help students form robust standards.

Our results suggest that CLP helps students become autonomous. To assess autonomous lifelong learning, the CLP team studied how students critique solutions, solve novel problems, carry out projects, and perform in high school. We concurrently designed assessments to match instruction. Students were asked to apply classroom learning to novel problems. For example, in labs, students investigated different materials. They made predictions about which wrap will work best, recorded starting and ending temperatures of the soda, and synthesized their work in a principle. For assessment, students explained an everyday example using the experimental findings and critiqued conclusions of others. Later, on the final examination, students solved a new problem using the same principle.

When students apply a principle to a new problem, or conduct a project using the principle, educators sometimes call this "transfer" of understanding from one context to another. Students might explain how the insulation and conduction principle would work to keep a pizza hot rather than keep a drink cold. This can be difficult. Readers may recall that our case study student Lee concluded that materials work differently depending on whether they insulate hot or cold objects. After studying early versions of CLP, students could answer the Continuum Line question (see Fig. 3.16) better than the Water Tower questions (Fig. 5.13). Few students could apply the results of their experiments to new, complex problems. By the eighth version of CLP, as interviews with Lee, Sasha, Chris, and Pat illustrate (chapter 1) students were better at solving personally relevant problems. This ability flourished in high school as discussed in chapter 7.

Overall, CLP helps students apply science knowledge to more and more complex problems, use science information in personally relevant problems, and critique projects conducted by others. In summary, many try to teach "the scientific method" like we did in the scientific reasoning unit described in chapter 2. This approach is far too abstract for most students. Students might agree that experiments need to be fair, methods should be respectable, and arguments require supporting evidence. However, in their own experiments they lack criteria to determine what constitutes a fair experiment, relying on methods others would dispute and supporting their ideas with questionable evi-

---

A company called West Coast Water decided to build a series from water towers of different materials for storing large amounts of rain water. As part of their selection process, they needed to determine which material and design choice would be best for longterm outdoor storage. Using the following materials and design choices provided, what choices would you recommend?

MATERIALS

Stryofoam   rubber   wood   plastic   aluminum

DESIGN CHOICES:

1 very large tower   3 large towers   5 medium towers   10 small towers

Which material would be the worst?_____

Give examples that help explain your answers:

List here any class experiments that you were reminded of or were helpful in solving this problem.

FIG. 5.13   Students apply results from their insulation and conduction experiments to water tower design.

dence. Should they use an advertisement as evidence? Is a case study convincing to the audience? Should they control for the time of day, the source of water, the phase of the moon, or the latitude of their classroom when experimenting with heat and temperature? When they disregard these variables, might they also dismiss altitude, a factor that influences many aspects of heat and temperature.

Abstract general principles make sense only when buttressed by intensive, detailed knowledge of the problem context. Criteria must be developed locally and tailored to each experiment. When science classes help students understand the complexities of inquiry, students will develop an integrated understanding of the more abstract principles scientists recognize as part of the scientific method.

TECHNOLOGY AND INQUIRY

Designing activities to promote autonomous, lifelong science inquiry remains complex. In the CLP curriculum, technology contributed to the promotion of autonomy and offers promise for other designers.

First, we found ways of using technology to sustain reasoning. "I'm done" and "What's next?" are frequent comments of students doing projects. With the Electronic Laboratory Notebook, students needed to complete all the steps of an inquiry on the checklist before concluding that they were finished with it. Furthermore, the checklist and help screens guided students to seek online answers to questions, an autonomous learning skill. This technology sustains reasoning and provides a model of the inquiry process.

Second, technology in the CLP project supported autonomy by providing sentence starters or prompts for reflection. Student worksheets initially served this purpose with sentence starts such as: "The reason I believe this is … " or "The main reason for my answer is … ". Delivered electronically, these sentence starters encouraged students to connect their ideas, reflect on their own intellectual work and identify gaps in their reasoning. As noted, this reflection process succeeded more often when students had useful criteria to guide the process. In the first version of CLP, in which students used a molecular kinetic model, their reflections often lacked scientific grounding because they could not connect the theory being taught to their experimental observations. The heat flow model improved students' reflections, giving them criteria to use for explaining their observations. Many students, however, used absorption or barrier models despite their introduction to heat flow.

Third, computer diagnosis of faulty methodologies spurred revision of ideas. As discussed in chapter 3, for example, if students designed an experiment to compare two wraps for a potato to keep it warm and actually selected the same wrap in both conditions, the computer would ask them whether they wanted to vary that condition to gain more understanding from their experiment. In this case, the technology augmented class critiquing opportunities and prompted students to recall class ideas. Most students responded to prompts by modifying their experiments, but they may have concluded that "the computer told me to do it" instead of reflecting on why.

Fourth, the Internet supports the process of establishing criteria in electronic discussion. For example, individuals suffering from rare diseases identify each other on the Internet and form discussion groups that can negotiate shared criteria for symptoms, treatment, and personal expectations. Physicians report that patients engaged in these support groups often become more articulate in describing their own problems and better at distinguishing one symptom from another. In addition, such support groups can help patients set realistic goals, identify treatments that might not be available in their local area, and debunk quick fixes. Using online discussion to help students develop shared criteria, recognize alternative viewpoints, and engage in sustained reasoning has great potential for lifelong learning and is part of our Knowledge Integration Environment (KIE) partnership.

Fifth, the Internet permits students to search electronically for relevant information, an aspect of autonomous learning. We found in the CLP classroom that even a search of the local database for experiments similar to one's own could confuse some students. Often students were more successful with a peer as a learning partner. Effective science instruction could start earlier to help students develop criteria for searching. These skills ultimately will help students become lifelong learners and use electronic databases in their own lives.

Sixth, technology can help with the search for information, as well as with evaluation of the materials located. An effective curriculum can combine technological opportunities for search and experimentation with class and group opportunities for knowledge integration for the purpose of selecting valid evidence. Technological tools such as SenseMaker (see chapter 3) can prompt students to employ criteria discussed in class settings or in electronic discussion forums.

Finally, coaching and CyberCoaching also stimulates students' autonomous efforts to explain observations. Our research suggests that students who respond to coaching make substantial improvements in knowledge integration. Sometimes students ignore this feedback. and at other times they never seek it in the first place. Students poised for autonomous reasoning already recognize the value of getting feedback on their work. Teachers can offer unsolicited feedback to help students recognize the benefits.

Technology helps promote productive inquiry but is not sufficient. Some students seem eager to finish science work before they really have begun to think scientifically. Technology is effective in sustaining reasoning, a necessary but not sufficient condition for autonomous learning. In addition, technology in conjunction with teacher-led classroom activities can help students develop shared criteria, not only for scientific conclusions, but also for the methods, evidence, and comprehensiveness of their projects. Technological environments can prompt students to use the criteria they develop as a class. These tools, however, may break down when students carry out more independent projects.

REFLECTIONS

Why do students see science as personally relevant only rarely, whereas they often build on their understanding from other disciplines? Is the gap between activities performed in science and the science used by citizens larger than similar gaps in mathematics, literature, and government? Do students view school science primarily as relevant to careers in science?

The CLP project found many ways to help students become autonomous learners. For example, students need criteria for valid criticism of their own or others work. In CLP activities, students establish criteria for each step. For students conducting more independent projects, finding valid criteria distinguishes success from failure. Students with well-integrated ideas will have more connections to potential criteria. Yet students frequently neglect knowledge integration, fail to seek specific criteria, and apply superficial criteria such as neatness.

Students differ regarding their willingness to undertake projects that require autonomy. Their project selections strongly align with their self-assessments of project difficulty. Students, such as Lee, who fit the consumer pattern, often fail to undertake a project at all. Students such as Chris, who fit the conceptualizer pattern, prefer theory comparison projects in which they can analyze the strengths and limitations of various accounts of scientific phenomena. Students who fit the strategizer pattern, such as Sasha, choose projects that require a critique of their own and someone else's experiment. These students want to solve problems in collaboration with others and believe that the least amount of intellectual effort is required for a critique. These students often settle for superficial critiques, so their projects often turn out to be quite easy. Students who select projects in which they have the opportunity to design such things as picnic hampers tend to fit the experimenter category. Experimenters such as Pat draw on many examples. Design projects help these students develop criteria for selecting among alternatives.

Students vary with regard to soliciting coaching on their projects. Some students seek critical comments whereas others conclude that they have the right answer. Our research suggests that autonomous learners monitor their own performance, recognize the need for coaching, benefit from coaching, and perform more successfully. We need to design instruction that motivates a broader range of students to identify when they need coaching.

In the CLP project, we started with the view that students needed reasoning principles, prompting, and support to become autonomous. We added personally relevant problems and required reflection and critiquing to enhance knowledge integration in class. We could sustain reasoning experiments in class, but did not improve spontaneous scientific reasoning, so we added projects of various sorts. We found that students who conduct projects, discuss their ideas, and seek coaching become better in carrying out projects on a broader range of topics.

Our experiences demonstrate that reflection, critiquing, and criteria development go hand in hand. The CLP approach engages students in critiquing class projects, asks students to critique the work of others, and encourages students to engage in sufficient self-criticism to warrant a request for coaching. As a result, many students become more effective investigators.

ASK MR. K

How do you help students become autonomous science learners?

I don't always provide the answers right away! Sometimes kids get mad at me when I answer their question with another question. How else do you get them to reflect?

Do you need to know lots of science to do science projects?

Teachers ought to be modeling the way to learn new things in the classroom. No one is expected to know all the answers, but anyone can stay interested and excited about finding out about the question. I like to think of teachers as doing co-investigations with students and asking good questions. If teachers explore together with students, and get excited, they can illustrate ways of thinking about a topic. I think we do kids a disservice when we hold the same naive views and approaches to learning that they have. Neither teachers nor kids have all the answers.

With reform efforts such as "integrated science," teachers are asked to teach things that are unfamiliar. For example, I could teach biology, but I just wouldn't do as good a job as my fellow teacher who knows what student ideas to build on. I could provide connections to biology examples from the CLP curriculum. Over time I would begin to learn how to teach biology concepts better.

Lifelong learning is important to teachers as well as students. When I get to explore with students, I learn something too.

What are the main advantages of group science projects?

First, the key thing is that it allows the kids to build on each other's ideas and understandings. Therefore, you have that exchange of ideas. Second, group learning really models the way scientists work. It's important to show kids the process of knowledge integration too. Group learning also teaches kids to value other people's opinions, to accept or critique them, and to use evidence to support their point of view. One not so obvious benefit is that students who have special needs become a part of the discussion. Student partners can help each other.

What are the challenges or disadvantages to group projects?

One disadvantage is that it's hard for some kids to be receptive to working with a partner, particularly if they are paired with a kid who has a learning difficulty. The student often will just do all the work for the other student. That's something technology can't monitor, but the teacher can try to get students to collaborate, share their work with each other, and respect each other. Assessment also is hard. For example, in pairs, one individual can do a lot more work than another. How do you evaluate that? If the person who doesn't put in the effort still gets the same grade, it gives kids the wrong message sometimes. It is very difficult to monitor this continually when you have 30 to 32 kids.

How do you deal with students who can't work with others?

Sometimes, when a student has outside problems at home and I think it's unfair for them to take from their partner, I ask that student to sit out. Usually, that's over in 2 days and the student wants to take part in what the other kids are doing because it's more fun. One of the difficult things is to deal with those kids who just aren't doing anything. Hopefully, we can provide enough activities and things to keep their interest in some way.

Do some kids benefit from working together?

Yes, I found that when I put kids who are trouble makers together, they realize that they can't rely on the other person to do the work. Somehow, they end up pulling it together and getting the project finished. Actually, it surprised me because I didn't think that was going to happen. I thought they would sit there and do nothing. When these students are with more motivated partners, they can learn to rely on somebody else rather than do the work themselves.

How do you develop shared criteria?

You need to do some kind of investigation, some experiments, and develop criteria. Here's an example. Say you tell the kids a vacuum cleaner doesn't work. How do you know what's going on? We write guesses on the board and discuss how you test the validity of these things. Students also learn what makes a good question. One criteria students discover is that a good question is testable. It's trying to get kids to think through, from a simple example, the kinds of questions you ask to solve the problem.

POINTS TO PONDER

- Describe how you can tell when students learn autonomously in a course you teach. Create an autonomy checklist to keep track of progress for each student.
- Describe the projects or independent activities students undertake in a course you teach. Describe the guidance or scaffolding provided for students doing projects.
- Analyze the guidance provided by technology in a course you teach. Describe how technology could be used to encourage more autonomy.
- Interview a student who is doing a project. Provide coaching and analyze the response of the student.
- Interview students about their views of scientific inquiry and analyze how these align with the views of inquiry they encounter in science courses.

- Analyze the scaffolding for the inquiry process available to students in a course you have taught and describe improvements.
- Select one pragmatic pedagogical principle from the chapter. Describe how this principle applies to your practice.
- Watch the section of the CLP film called, Can students become lifelong learners? Compare the CLP approach to your own experience as a lifelong science learner.

RELATED READINGS

Dewey, J. (1938). *Experience and education*. New York: Collier Books/Macmillan.

Hutchins, E. (1996). *Cognition in the wild*. Cambridge, MA: MIT Press.

Kafai, Y. B. (1995). *Computer-based learning environments and problem solving*. Hillsdale, NJ: Lawrence Erlbaum Associates.

Papert, S. (1968). *Mindstorms*. New York: Basic Books.

Scardamalia, M., & Bereiter, C. (1992). A knowledge building architecture for computer supported learning. In E. De Corte, M. C. Linn, H. Mandl, & L. Verschaffel (Ed.), *Computer-based learning environments and problem solving*. Berlin: Springer-Verlag.

Student Learning Partners
Revisited

When we left Lee, Pat, Sasha, and Chris in chapter 1, we wondered about their learning trajectories and how the Computer as Learning Partner (CLP) instruction would contribute. In this section we revisit these students in high school and discuss the implications of CLP for lifelong learning.

We examine several aspects of lifelong learning. In chapter 6, Learning Partners and Science Inquiry in High School, we ask students to describe the learning partners they used in eighth grade and those they used in high school. In addition, we characterize students' ideas about science inquiry and the nature of scientific research.

In chapter 7, Building on Middle School Science in High School, we ask students to revisit heat and temperature concepts they studied in eighth grade and assess their learning trajectories. We also examine how these students respond to a short activity about the science of light and assess their learning trajectory between tenth and twelfth grades for this topic.

We look for changes in patterns of knowledge integration, wondering whether the consumer and strategizer patterns persist and whether more students use the experimenter or conceptualizer patterns.

We report that the rich set of learning partners CLP designed met the needs of the diverse students we studied. In general, students had more sophisticated ideas in high school than in middle school. We conclude that CLP set students on a path towards lifelong science learning.

6

Science Learning Partners and Science Inquiry in High School

Do students build on the learning partners we designed for the Computer as Learning Partner (CLP) curriculum to become more autonomous learners in high school? Does CLP also help students understand the nature of science inquiry?

To see how students exploit the rich set of learning partners in the CLP curriculum, we revisited Pat, Lee, Sasha, and Chris in high school. We asked them which learning partners in CLP they found useful, then contrasted this with the learning partners they used to solve problems in interviews and on assessments.

To understand how students' ideas about science inquiry had changed since middle school we posed several sorts of questions. We asked students about the way science progresses and how scientists resolve disputes. We also asked students to critique specific science experiments to see if their general inquiry skills had developed. Because CLP did not teach directly about the progress of science or science dispute resolution we anticipated that students might add ideas to their repertoire, but did not expect that they had sorted out their ideas. For critiquing experiments, we expected that both CLP and subsequent science courses could provide specific science disciplinary knowledge that would enable more effective critiques.

We looked at the responses of Lee, Chris, Pat, and Sasha. We also looked generally at CLP students who followed the consumer, strategizer, experimenter, and conceptualizer patterns, distinguishing views of science learning from views of science inquiry because students also distinguish these topics.

When students reflected on science learning, they all told us what they liked and disliked. Students vary considerably in their ability to tell us how they learn. Generally, they liked the CLP curriculum better than prior science courses for its many distinct features: the computers, the labs, the teacher, the visualizations, the everyday problems, and the limited number of homework assignments. Students complained about the topic: heat and temperature or physical science in general. Most middle school students preferred biology, perhaps because of its relevance to their lives. We respond to this preference in our new partnerships, described in chapter 8, by emphasizing connections between biological and physical sciences.

Students' insights into their own learning varied widely. Some students described themselves as autonomous learners. Others could not give an answer. Some predicted their scores on tests and grades in courses accurately, whereas others were constantly surprised. We assessed students' *self-monitoring*: their ability to describe their own learning (Fig. 6.1). Chris, for example, said, "I'm here to learn, so while I am learning I want to understand." Others described themselves as "cognitive economists" doing the minimal amount of work to get a grade. Sasha, as mentioned earlier, asserted, "I don't need to know why," and buttressed this assertion with the report of earning and A in the course.

"Because . . . just because the teacher explains it right doesn't mean that I can understand it correctly. When I know . . . when I do a problem right, then I know definitely I have it right."

"You just wouldn't know the right answer, and if somebody tells you what the right answer is, it's better to know."

"Memorizing facts is always an easy way to understand more. If one was made to memorize facts, he would easily understand a new concept based on those facts."

"I would like to memorize facts better than trying to understand complicated material because it is easier for me to do."

FIG. 6.1   Students hold different views about their own science learning.

Students who followed the consumer and strategizer pattern compared with those who followed the experimenter and conceptualizer patterns, had less insight into their own science learning. Students who followed the experimenter and conceptualizer patterns frequently expressed insights into their own science learning partners and reported learning autonomously. Lee and Sasha, compared with Pat and Chris, illustrated these distinctions in our case studies.

SCIENCE INQUIRY

Our case studies revealed only a few connections between the students' views of their own learning and their views of science inquiry. Furthermore, the students' views of science inquiry lacked coherence. They held diverse views of science and scientists (Fig. 6.2). Those following the conceptualizer pattern, more than other students, expected scientists to establish and use scientific principles (Fig. 6.3). But most of the students held many, varied disconnected views of scientists and of science. Their views of scientific disputes and criteria for critiquing experiments were similarly disjointed.

Strikingly, Lee, Pat, Chris, and Sasha learned about science inquiry much as they learned about heat and temperature. They started with diverse, incompatible ideas, but they linked their ideas and reflected on their views when prompted. Because these topics rarely occurred in the curriculum, the students learned haphazardly and developed idiosyncratic views.

For example, when asked whether everything in the textbook will always be true, Pat said, "No, there may be older textbooks that aren't up to date." Pat elaborated, pointing to textbooks that neglect space exploration. Pat mentioned that some aspects of science are difficult to investigate, such as extinct animals. Pat primarily focused on ways that

---

"From what I've seen, atoms and molecules are studied in science. Both 'scientists' studied and used atoms in experiments are famous for those studies. So, they are scientists."

"Science is always growing. New science "breakthroughs" or just new ideas happen constantly, expanding current ideas."

"Scientists may have different ideas based on what they found. They add their own experiences and ideas (interpretations too) to reach their own conclusions."

FIG. 6.2   Students hold diverse views of science and scientists.

"I think that the ideas we learned in class do connect with one big idea. For example, when we learned about light, we learned about how it changes into different energies, how it is reflected, how it is absorbed, how far it travels, what the intensities are, etc. I don't expect all of the things we learn to be connected, but I think that in all of my classes the little things we learn help us understand the main idea the teacher wants us to learn."

"Textbooks from a while back probably had principles that have today been proven wrong, so I believe maybe in the future ideas that we have today [in textbooks] will be studied further and more will be added to the principles or they'll be changed."

"A lot of the principles in textbooks are just theory while some may be true. Like if you said hydroden was a gas, that would be true, but if you said that the Big Bang formed the universe that would be just theory."

FIG. 6.3   Conceptualizers expect science to connect to principles
or big ideas.

scientists accumulate knowledge, not on dispute resolution. This view of scientists accumulating knowledge was consistent with Pat's propensity to add new ideas to the mix when learning science.

Lee emphasized disputes rather than accumulation of knowledge, viewing scientists as extremely independent and experiments as potentially wrong. Lee said, "Scientists, they'll all get different answers," then elaborated, "They can all be different experiments and come out with different answers and some of them are wrong." Lee thought scientists disagree because "they all have different ideas and they all do different experiments and come up with their answers." Lee expressed the belief that, "they agree on just like little things like the colors of something." Lee viewed scientists as doing experiments, coming up with different results, and disagreeing. This view of scientists paralleled Lee's personal reluctance to resolve discrepancies.

Consistent with Sasha's minimalist stance toward science knowledge integration, Sasha had many views of scientists and science inquiry, reporting that scientists have different opinions, different theories, and get different results. Sasha saw science inquiry as disjointed saying that scientists might, "start with the same data, but everyone goes in different directions with that data so they come out with different results." Sasha went on to explain that scientists would "agree on facts but they disagree on opinions." Like most students, Sasha had difficulty distinguishing facts and opinions and had not connected views of science inquiry.

Chris believed that new principles or findings can change the "facts" of older science textbooks and asserted, "The scientists could agree on one idea about something ancient. A few years later they might think of a new experiment to add on, constantly improving or replacing their old idea." Chris also asserted in response to a news article, "It means that different scientists have different opinions about things based on what experiments she or he has done." When asked to explain, Chris said that people disagree because they might have different evidence, and when scientists are more in agreement, "there's more evidence for it or something."

Here, Chris viewed scientists as a community responding to similar information. Chris expressed contradictory ideas, sometimes asserting that scientists connect, reorganize, and even integrate ideas, but also expecting disagreements that do not get resolved.

Most students enter eighth grade with a mix of ideas about how science progresses and about how scientists interact. We examined the development of these ideas in the case studies.

To understand how students interpret science inquiry, we asked students to critique specific results and arguments from scientific experiments in diverse fields including human development, disease, and nutrition. We looked to see how the students analyzed experimental designs and reported findings. We analyzed how the students used knowledge of the science topic and their ability to reason scientifically to critique these problems. We examined how the students distinguished experiments conducted by scientists from experiments conducted by students.

We asked students to critique news accounts of science findings and experiments reported by students. We probed students about their analyses of these situations, especially asking whether they needed more information to evaluate the claims, whether the methods used by the researchers are valid, whether new research might change the conclusions, and whether they questioned the logic in the assertions. Students varied along all of these dimensions.

Science courses often aspire to teach science as a way of thinking especially about arguments such as those in Figs. 6.4 and 6.5. In listening to students responding to these questions, we realized that often such reasoning requires information that students simply do not have. Students may not know whether studies using rats have implications for humans. Students also may not realize their need for information to help them evaluate the questions. Because the CLP curriculum provided information relevant to the rods problem in Fig. 6.5, we contrasted student critiques of this problem with critiques of other problems.

A university researcher believed that interesting, educational experiences in early life lead to larger brains. She took one litter of rats and placed each rat in its own, empty cage at birth. She took another litter of rats and placed all of them in a single large cage filled with toys, mazes and exercise wheels.

When all the rats were adults, she measured the brain size of each rat. The rats raised alone in the empty cages had smaller brains than the rats raised together in the interesting environment.

Based on this experiment, she concluded that children who have interesting, educational experiences in preschools will grow up to be more intelligent adults than children who do not attend preschool.

a. Do you think the conclusions will be accepted by other scientists?   (circle one)

      yes   no   cannot predict

b. Why or why not?

A preschool teacher disagreed with the researcher. She said that the rat experiment could not be used to explain the advantages of preschool.

c. How could the researcher convince the teacher that she was right?

d. How could the teacher convince the researcher that she was right?

FIG. 6.4   Rats: An item used for science inquiry tests after the CLP curriculum.

LEE: A CONSUMER

We earlier described Lee's pattern of reasoning in eighth grade as that of consuming science ideas. Lee had followed the consumer pattern of isolating ideas, rarely giving explanations in discussing science learn-

Erin, a scientist, compared three rods: one made of plastic, one made of diamond, and the other made of copper. All of the rods were the same length and thickness. Erin placed the end of each rod into a beaker of boiling water (100°C).

After 10 minutes, she measured the temperature at the other end of each rod. The diamond rod was the hottest, the copper rod was second, and the plastic rod was the coolest. Erin concluded that diamond was the best conductor of heat and that copper is a better conductor than plastic.

a. Do you think the conclusions will be accepted by other scientists? (circle one)

     yes   no   cannot predict

b. Why or why not?

Max, another scientist, disagreed because he knew that copper is an excellent conductor of electricity and he said no one uses diamonds in their electrical equipment.

c. How could Max convince Erin that he was right? (circle one)

   1. Tell her the right answer.

   2. Describe an experience to support his conclusion.

   3. Design an experiment to show that his answer was correct.

   4. Other _____

d. What is the **main reason** for your choice?

e. How could Erin convince Max that she was right? (circle one)

   1. Tell him the right answer.

   2. Describe an experience to support her conclusion.

   3. Design an experiment to show that her answer was correct.

   4. Other _____

f. What is the **main reason** for your choice?

FIG. 6.5   Rods: An item used for science inquiry tests and interviews.

ing or science inquiry. When faced with a contradiction, Lee tended to distinguish situations and avoid making connections.

Learning Science

Lee expected to "consume" science knowledge in science class instead of actively making sense of science. Lee explained learning in the CLP classroom: "Well I like it. It's easier to learn without the book because you're like explaining it. But I don't know." Lee clarified, "when Mr. K is explaining something and he demonstrates it with different things that helps me...." "Like when we touched the mouse pad and then we touched the leg to the desk, the mouse pad seemed warmer but they were both the same temperature." When asked if the explanation improved learning, Lee said, "Yeah, but I don't really understand it." Lee had low expectations for personal science learning and did not seek to resolve uncertainties such as this one.

Consistent with this view, Lee preferred the parts of CLP that do not require a response from the students. Thus, in doing CLP experiments that included design, prediction, explanation, graphs, principles, and prototypes, Lee preferred watching the graph because "the graph is easier to understand." Lee had a general perspective on the experiments, saying, "most of them were good." In class, Lee preferred explanations and demonstrations by the teacher.

Lee had minimalist intellectual goals in eighth grade, saying "I'd rather memorize things than understand them. If it gets complicated I don't enjoy it, and then if it gets boring then I daydream. Complicated material. I never understood it. I would take tests and it was mostly memorizing words and facts." Lee looked to the teacher and the graphs for material to memorize and gave up when the situation required mental effort.

In high school Lee recalled computers and experiments from eighth grade, reporting that in CLP we did "a lot of stuff on computers and I was usually always last, and I was really confused with stuff." Lee explained that it was difficult to carry out the experiments, fill in notes, and write principles saying, "It was just the work, and I was really stuck.... I would try hard as I could, and I just couldn't ... sit around most of the time.... I just didn't want to do the schoolwork." Looking back at eighth grade Lee reported being completely unmotivated to understand in all classes, not just science.

Lee's views of science learning coincided with performance on assessments and in interviews. Lee was comfortable coming to interviews and answering "I don't know" to question after question. If really pushed by the interviewer, Lee cited the teacher as an authority with comments such as "Mr. K said it would happen," or cited an observation such as "people wear wool" or "I saw it." Lee gave similar responses on assessments, making some progress by reporting results and teacher comments.

Lee behaved consistently and had excellent knowledge of personal learning practices in eighth grade. Lee accurately described the eighth-grade science experience, asserting, "We did some experiments" in CLP, but "I didn't understand them." Lee described a lack of motivation, attention to superficial information, and avoidance of work. For Lee, making connections among ideas constituted work. In contrast to this minimalist approach to school, Lee reported spending considerable out-of-school time training animals. We wondered whether Lee eventually would connect this interest in animals with school science courses.

Lee, in twelfth grade reported not using ideas from CLP in other classes. Lee said, "I think I understand it about the same." Lee's views of science learning, however, had changed in high school. Lee explained, "Well, whatever ... all the stuff I've ever had to memorize I've just forgotten, so I don't know if memorizing works, I mean, I'm sure it would work on a test or something, but in the long term it doesn't do any good.... I know I understand it really when I go over it, or like tell someone, explain it to someone. If ... if I know enough to explain it to someone else, then I understand." We see here that Lee's accurate self-monitoring had paid off. In high school Lee realized eighth-grade patterns of observing and memorizing were not sufficient for lifelong learning. In addition, Lee's motivation to learn had improved.

Lee's increased interest in learning science connected school and career goals. In eighth grade Lee had asserted that "anyone can learn science if they try" but did not try. Lee also had seen limits on personal science learning in eighth grade saying, "I don't know. Like I don't think that some person can just come and invent something because you need to like know all the little wires and stuff. I couldn't do it." In high school, Lee had changed to a new school and developed a much more interactive relationship with science. Lee reported that this new teacher "would explain every vocabulary word and make sure you understood every step." This personal attention provided reassurance about science learning that Lee seemed to need. Lee also reported a connection between learning biology and a career.

Science Inquiry

Lee responded to questions about science inquiry with minimalist answers, making little progress on this topic.

Lee saw scientists as disagreeing with each other and reaching different conclusions from the same scientific results. Lee described scientists by saying, "They all have different ideas." Lee in eighth grade had not looked for coherence in learning science. Similarly, Lee had not expected scientists as a group to offer a coherent account of science. Lee had not even expected scientists to check their answers. Lee said, ' scientists figure new things out all the time because they could have written the wrong thing and then found out it was wrong."

Lee was reluctant to critique experiments of others or news accounts of scientists' experiments. Lee generally said, "I don't know" or asserted that scientists "all have different ideas." The rats question was an exception. In eighth grade Lee had said, "Maybe if you took the mice from the same litter, then divided them up we could see what happens," critiquing the use of two different litters for the comparison. This answer seemed motivated by Lee's experience training animals. When asked this question again in twelfth grade, Lee raised other concerns as well saying, "She should do an experiment on actual children, watch the ones who did attend preschool, and then watch the one's who didn't." This question elicited more detail than other critiquing questions, perhaps because Lee could connect it to knowledge about animals gained from out-of-school experience.

Trajectory

Lee had made little progress in science learning and possessed a good understanding of personal learning practices. This self-monitoring ability enabled Lee to adopt a new disposition toward understanding science in twelfth grade.

This change came along with a coupling of school and career interests. By twelfth grade, Lee had aspired to some position in a hospital and recognized the importance of learning science. Lee's interest in hospital work stemmed more from experience training animals than from school experience. In chapter 7 we see whether this new view of science learning leads to a better understanding of science concepts.

Lee's understanding of science inquiry changed little during middle school and high school. This makes sense because courses neglect these topics, and Lee does not autonomously make connections.

Lee entered eighth grade with a passive, reception model of learning. Lee believed science was memorizing words and facts "because that's all school is." Lee found learning partners in animated graphs of experiments and teacher explanations.

In high school Lee started to adopt a pattern reminiscent of some experimenters, connecting science learning to out-of-school experience in training animals.

Maturity, and eventually interest in a science-related career enabled Lee to take a new stance toward science learning. We hope that other students who initially follow the consumer pattern eventually also become motivated to make more connections among scientific ideas. We wonder how science courses could help students such as Lee start on the path to knowledge integration earlier. In eighth grade, Lee had believed that memorization was the best way to learn science. Perhaps an emphasis on knowledge integration earlier in school would establish a better balance between memorization and understanding.

SASHA: A STRATEGIZER

We described Sasha as following the strategizer pattern in the eighth grade. In describing science learning and characterizing the nature of science, Sasha had followed the strategizer pattern of satisfying class expectations while resisting autonomous reasoning. Sasha wanted the teacher, the interviewer, and the curriculum to provide concrete explanations that could be memorized. Sasha had come to science class with a long history of success with this pattern. The reader may recall that Sasha cited ideas memorized in fourth and fifth grade when asked questions in eighth grade.

Science Learning

Sasha had articulated the strategizer approach to science in eighth grade. Sasha combined a professed reliance on memorizing with pride in course success. Sasha accurately described learning facts but not explanations. The reader may recall Sasha's assertion: "I don't need to know why." Sasha elaborated: "For me, memorizing the facts is easier, understanding them, I don't always understand, and teachers kind of move on and I am a little slower than some people, but in science I am not that good at it, but memorizing facts is easier for me because I can refer back to it in my mind." Nevertheless, when asked if science is too complicated to understand, Sasha said "That's false. I am understanding most of this stuff. I am getting an A in this class, and science is definitely not my best subject."

For Sasha, memorizing was easy. Sasha recalled detailed results from elementary school. Sasha memorized class experiences but did not seek to understand explanations. At every opportunity Sasha complained that CLP labs required explanations. For example, looking back from twelfth grade Sasha said, "I didn't really like the labs because they were so long and just like.... It's kind of like these, similar to these interviews, where he'll ask you a question and then he'll say, 'Explain your answer' and ask you a question, 'Explain your answer!' You know what I mean? I don't know. It wasn't that much of a hands-on experience kind of thing. I don't know."

Sasha viewed science learning as doing experiments to build up a set of examples rather than to abstract principles by reflecting on the results. Sasha wanted to keep doing new experiments instead of explaining what the experiment's results meant, connecting one experiment to another, and creating principles. This meant that Sasha found CLP experiments frustrating. However, to succeed in CLP, Sasha found a way to memorize CLP findings and apply them in classroom tests.

These contradictory ideas about science learning contributed to the strategizer approach. Sasha translated this frustration with giving explanations into a dislike for CLP topics. Early in the eighth grade Sasha had said, "Science is total confusion and it's just hard, especially when we're dealing with topics such as heat that I don't enjoy, that don't really seem fun. Dissecting is more fun, I guess, even though I won't use that either. But, it's still more fun." Nevertheless, Sasha had seen some connection of CLP science to life outside of school, saying, "Well, some of it does, I guess. I agree partially, because like with the Cokes and stuff, wrapping them in aluminum foil … that has to do with what's outside of school. And learning about plants and stuff. I have learned about that in science, and that has to do with stuff outside of school." And Sasha had liked Mr. K, the teacher.

Sasha resolved this ambivalence about school success, the relevance of science learning, and understanding science by finding ways to satisfy course requirements while avoiding opportunities to elaborate on science ideas or make new connections among science topics. The CLP curriculum met Sasha's learning needs. Sasha found CLP examples, details, animated graphs, and teacher explanations consistent with memorizing class experiences, satisfying course expectations, having fun, and spending a minimal amount of time on science.

From the experiments, Sasha preferred examples and even details to principles, but offered some surprising insights as well. Sasha said, "The examples are better because you can see something. Those are more real than a 'good conductor allows heat energy to flow faster than a poor conductor.' You can memorize facts with that stuff. You don't actually learn something until you can apply it, I think, and things like this–it's better." In spite of preferring examples, we noted that Sasha accurately described a science principle. We wondered what Sasha meant by this statement about learning by applying ideas. We will return to it when Sasha describes chemistry class.

When asked to distinguish details from examples Sasha said, "I think that the examples are better…. The details are good, but the order would probably be these [examples] and then the details, and then these are like way back there, principles. When you're saying examples and stuff, you can talk about the principles a little bit, but use it in the examples and you don't just give just the principles."

For Sasha, examples and details were easier than principles to memorize and use in science classes. Sasha could apply examples by analogy and found this satisfying. Principles did require more mental effort because they are abstract. Principles must be instantiated whereas examples only require making an accurate analogy. Both of these skills are part of scientific reasoning, but Sasha preferred making analogies.

Sasha emphasized this focus on examples when evaluating the features of CLP experiments. Sasha preferred the animated graph because the graphs captured the results and require less student effort than hand-drawn graphs. Sasha remarked, "The way the graphs turned out was good," and "We did temperature probes, and those were better than graphing by hand." Sasha also liked the experiments because they seemed "real" and connected to everyday problems. Sasha liked the real-time data collection experiments better than the simulations because hands-on experiments were more fun and more "real." For Sasha, "Its not real unless you do it yourself".

Sasha's reluctance to figure out how principles apply to new situations was consistent with views of teachers and peers. Sasha preferred that teachers make science thinking visible and disliked having to figure out which ideas satisfied class expectations. Sasha extended this preference to the interviews, encouraging the interviewers to explain rather than answering the explanation questions asked by the interviewers. Sasha also monitored the social context, knew how peers approached science, and tried to do as well or better than others.

In the CLP curriculum Sasha found many useful learning partners including examples, details, and teacher explanations. Sasha recalled this information and accurately applied it, usually by analogy, in interviews and on assessments. Sasha also memorized principles, but accurately reported that these were less helpful. Principles failed to help Sasha because they were too abstract to apply directly or by analogy. Sasha did not seek the understanding necessary to instantiate a principle in a new situation, preferring instead to map a new situation onto a class example. For Sasha, CLP examples were especially compelling because they applied to everyday situations.

The CLP examples presented Sasha with a conundrum. Sasha on the basis of past courses had rejected physical science as too abstract and embraced mathematics because examples could be applied to new problems. The CLP approach disrupted this view by offering personally relevant problems in physical science. We wondered how this would contribute to Sasha's interpretation of future science and mathematics courses.

Reflecting in twelfth grade, Sasha reiterated impressions of CLP. Sasha said, "I liked Mr. K, but I don't really care about how heat energy works and all that stuff. All I remember was the long labs, and that I didn't like them very much. But it didn't seem like science to me. It wasn't very interesting to me." Sasha liked CLP better than most high school courses until chemistry. Sasha reported that chemistry "changed my view."

Sasha said about chemistry, "I learned a lot in that class. That was my favorite class, chemistry. I don't really like life sciences all that much. I didn't really like sciences all that much until I got to that chemistry class. I'm more of a mathematical kind of, I mean, I think more about that kind of thing. It was easier. There were, because, more word problems and when I understand how to do something I can figure it out and do it."

Sasha began to clarify this preference for making analogies rather than applying principles. Sasha connected memorizing and applying formulas, saying, "In chemistry there was a lot of memorization." Sasha commented about formulas: "Yeah, that's a lot of chemistry that I like is where it ties in with math stuff. So, yeah, I like that." For Sasha, applying formulas in chemistry drew on mathematics and fit into the category of memorizing. Sasha clearly liked chemistry because solving problems involved making connections to mathematics. Furthermore, Sasha was able to use the process of applying examples to make sense of chemistry. This helped explain Sasha's earlier comment about applying ideas so you understand. Sasha saw memorizing examples as a form of applying knowledge to new problems.

Sasha had a number of perspectives on chemistry in twelfth grade. Sasha described chemistry as "real" because it was fun and interesting to see the teacher "blowing stuff up and stuff like that rather than laying it out on the computer." Sasha reflected on what makes an experience interesting and said that even chemistry labs "weren't that interesting." And Sasha praised the efforts of the chemistry teacher to make thinking about chemistry visible. Sasha contrasted the text and the teacher's explanation saying, "When I read it in a textbook, most of the time it doesn't make sense no matter how many times I read it." But teachers "can explain things. If you don't get it one way [they will] explain it some other way, make it so you understand it. I don't really like reading out of the textbook because more often than not, like out of the textbook, it's memorizing facts."

Sasha clarified how teachers help explain ways to apply examples, saying, "Even with chemistry, doing word problems, I would go back to the textbook. I would see how they did it. I would figure, that must be the little step, you just do this. But I don't understand why I'm doing that. When it's explained you can understand the reasoning behind something." Finally, Sasha linked "doing it yourself" to a "really good feeling when I finally understood." This comment helped us understand how Sasha used examples to make sense of chemistry.

Sasha went on to distinguish the process of explaining and being told, saying "Explaining is the important thing. Explaining is better than being told." Sasha discussed making autonomous connections saying, "Sometimes it's better to go and relate little things to what you know already before you get into the whole new concept. Sometimes it's better to figure out the new material before, and then look back and see how it relates, and it's better to do that." Sasha maintained a preference for examples, first saying, "If you see the example first and then you can use the principles to help you understand what you're looking at. I think the example should be introduced first before the principle." Here Sasha builds on the preference for memorizing examples to incorporate explanations.

A combination of interest in mathematics, teacher explanations to connect examples, and links between chemistry and mathematics, enabled Sasha to begin the process of what we called autonomous learning in chapter 5. Sasha found this experience satisfying. In chemistry, Sasha identified a form of explanation that made sense.

Sasha illustrated the potential for students who initially follow the strategizer pattern to become more like conceptualizers. For Sasha, the reasoning valued in chemistry enabled autonomous reasoning. In chapter 7 we analyze the implications of this reasoning pattern for high school science performance.

Science Inquiry

Sasha's views of science inquiry in high school reflected the disinterest in explanations articulated during CLP. Sasha expected scientists to view the same experiment and reach different conclusions. For the rats experiment and the rods experiment, Sasha said that "some scientists will [agree] and some won't." Sasha identified superficial factors that might cause scientists to reach different conclusions. For rats, Sasha conjectures, "If they didn't have the same mother, attention at home. All sorts of reasons." For rods, Sasha says, "Diamonds would be way too expensive." Sasha also recognized the value of replication, saying "You can't come to this conclusion with just one test." These answers seemed to reflect Sasha's analogical approach to science that neglected the big picture.

In twelfth grade, Sasha's answers were more coherent. Sasha made more connections, sounding like an autonomous learner when critiquing experiments. For rats, Sasha said that the results would not always be true, that "she needs to try different things such as mixing the litters (maybe one family is different)," that "brain size does not always mean more or less intelligence also," and that "the brains of rats are different than the brains of children. Even if you did set up the large cage similar to preschool, the way they would react is different. It depends on the child and other childhood experiences, not just preschool." Sasha, instead of rejecting explanations, warranted criticisms with evidence and connected one critique to another. For a peanut butter nutrition question, Sasha advocated knowledge integration instead of rejecting it: "They are looking at different aspects of the peanut butter. They both need to look at the whole picture. They need to ... see if the good things outweigh the bad."

Between middle school and high school, Sasha connected some disparate ideas to build a more coherent picture of scientists and scientific research. Sasha relied on this more comprehensive view of scientists in high school critiques.

Trajectory

Sasha in eighth grade followed the strategizer pattern of satisfying class requirements rather than seeking coherent understanding. Several CLP features, including principle notes, visual models, and teachers who make thinking visible, pushed Sasha to make connections. Sasha complained about constant requests for explanations. Often, Sasha convinced teachers and interviewers to provide the explanations. Sasha succeeded by memorizing the explanations.

In eighth grade, Sasha relied on external indicators such as class grades instead of monitoring personal understanding. Sasha denied interest in science, saying, "It's not an interesting subject to me. I don't understand it well enough anyway. I have bigger and better things to do in my life." In chemistry, for the first time Sasha experienced the satisfaction of making connections and understanding relationships. This satisfaction translated into an interest in chemistry and a new view of science learning. In twelfth grade Sasha said, "I like to figure things out and many times it feels like a puzzle when I'm doing labs."

In high school Sasha's awareness of science extended to some insight into the social context of science learning. Sasha believed that boys and girls had similar plans to follow science careers but complained that "there's this big flap about girls not getting enough attention in science." Sasha believed the situation was complicated because some teachers "flirt" with the girls. Sasha reported, "I think that the science teachers that I've had don't think about it that way. They probably don't even consciously know that they're doing that and like favoring girls a little bit. I think it's just like their individual personalities."

Sasha's career goals changed with more science course experience. In eighth grade Sasha looked for a career that involved mathematics. In tenth grade Sasha seemed to dismiss engineering, saying, "I was thinking about going into engineering, but then I don't think I'm going to be doing that." In twelfth grade, Sasha said, "I don't want a career specifically in science but something that would tie the two together, like engineering, we use science and math."

Engineering appealed to Sasha for the same reasons that chemistry was satisfying. Sasha said, "I'm thinking about being some kind of an engineer, but I really don't know what kind of engineer. I like it when it's kind of a puzzle. You've got to figure it out. And when you finally get it, it feels good. So, that's what I like is stuff that can be figured out. That's probably why I don't like physics very much."

Sasha's view of science understanding shifted between eighth and twelfth grades. In eighth grade Sasha had advocated memorizing and could recall both experimental results and teacher explanations. In twelfth grade Sasha memorized formulas to succeed in chemistry and found connecting mathematical formulas to chemistry satisfying. Sasha avoided explanations, preferring applications of examples. In CLP, while complaining about studying heat, Sasha applauded the connections to practical problems. In twelfth grade, Sasha's career interests involved solving puzzles. Perhaps CLP had helped to set this process in motion by offering a wide range of learning partners. Perhaps Sasha's views will change again.

Could the CLP curriculum have provided the satisfaction that Sasha first experienced in chemistry, or did that satisfaction require more experience and maturity? How can we serve students like Sasha better? Will courses in integrated science enable students such as Sasha to experience more personal satisfaction? We return to this question in chapter 8.

PAT: AN EXPERIMENTER

Pat followed the experimenter pattern in eighth grade and high school. In describing science learning and science inquiry, Pat generated many ideas, looked for new views, and resisted straightforward conclusions.

Science Learning

Pat had responded enthusiastically to all the learning partners CLP had offered including graphs, teacher explanations, personal experiences, experiments, and principles. During eighth grade, Pat had rejected only the CLP prototypes, describing them as "picture-ones" and reporting that they did not help with learning science. Pat recalled dislik-ing the computers saying, "The computers and I didn't work well together." Pat had embraced most CLP features, gaining a diverse set of ideas from them. Pat said, "I'd rather do an experiment" and "doing the graph, actually like graphing it" helps. Pat also said "Writing the principle" helps "maybe" because "its all the information" and "you can understand it."

In responding to all these opportunities Pat accurately asserted, "I keep switching." Pat postponed connecting ideas, preferring to keep trying out new ones. To keep all these ideas in mind, Pat recognized the value of memorizing, saying about math facts: "I'm glad I memorized it." Pat also believed that in science, understanding helps "if you had to explain it on a test or something." Pat connected these views at the end eighth grade, saying, "I can memorize easier" and "memorize if you un-derstand."

In CLP, Pat had memorized new information from labs, experiences, experiments, and discussions, and then experimented with diverse ways to connect these ideas. Even pragmatic science principles gained and lost status as Pat made sense of problems, although Pat acknowl-edged that principles are "like the rules."

In twelfth grade, looking back on CLP, Pat described the process of considering all information and experimenting with various connec-tions. Pat said about principles and prototypes, "I think they help. Sometimes they make me more confused because they give you an idea … because you need to know more than what they tell you." Here Pat ar-ticulated the difficulty Sasha reported when using principles. Pat re-ported that details "are useful to me. I like to know everything about the experiment, even if it is not relevant to the experiment, and then figure out by myself what is relevant and what isn't." Pat had excellent insight into personal science learning practices.

What happened when Pat could not figure something out? Pat said, "If I still didn't understand it, I'd probably go look it up in the textbook, then, uhm, take some notes down from the textbook and find, pinpoint what I don't understand specifically, and then I'd probably ask friends or if my teacher was a good teacher, I would ask before class or some-thing."

Pat reported drawing on a wealth of information including facts, ex-periments, personal ideas, and social interactions, continually seeking new connections, and autonomously carrying out a process of knowl-edge integration. The CLP learning partners all supported Pat's ap-proach to science learning. But, then, Pat made this quite easy, remarking in twelfth grade, "I mean, there is no way I don't like to learn except when they say, 'Here is a book, read it, and learn it.'"

In high school Pat became even more adept at explaining this process of knowledge integration. Pat said, "I like to see it, I like to do labs, and I don't like rote memorization. But I think memorizing helps because you need to have the facts ready and clear, not to memorize but just so you know. I like to have things told to me and then sort of memorize them and make the connections myself. I don't really like to jump into something and have to find it out.... I like to prove rather than find." Pat explained, "Like we did this lab with indicators in physiology. You had all these solutions and indicators, and you are supposed to drop it and see what happens but you could do it by research first. So, I'd have much rather researched it first and figured it out and then tried it and it turned out as I'd predicted. You know, find the facts and then prove it for myself.... Rather than just doing it , ... I want to know what I am looking for." Pat looked for experience in planning and conducting experiments, not mindless investigation.

Pat's reaction to science classes rested on this opportunity to put ideas together autonomously and reach conclusions. The CLP curriculum introduced this idea. Pat praised labs "that are kind of open-ended but guided and you have to figure things out." Pat distinguished the CLP class from other science classes, saying, "It was a different way to learn science. I mean he [Mr. K] didn't have much of lectures. It was more of an individual 'go at it' kind of thing."

Although Pat liked CLP, Pat preferred life science in high school because life science courses permit more autonomous reasoning. Pat said, "I liked my life science classes better than chemistry, a lot better than I liked chemistry. I always have an easier time because it seems more real and chemistry just seems too abstract; I don't like physical science. I like the lung does this and the heart does this, but not these little atoms come together because of electronegativity.... It's just really not my thing."

Pat criticized chemistry labs for being too dangerous. Pat described the "diffusion" labs: "They said show this somehow, but they should have given us a little more guidance. I mean, I'm kind of cautious and I don't want to just start mixing chemicals, but we had a couple in chemistry where it was like okay, just do the lab and I didn't want to do it, I didn't want to make an explosion. But I like trying to figure it out for myself. I don't want to just read about it." Pat had a strong desire to figure out science ideas autonomously as long as the inquiry process was grounded in understanding of the topic.

Between eighth grade and high school Pat had gained more and more insight into personal learning practices. Pat's account of the role of memorizing in knowledge integration showed remarkable sophistication. The CLP curriculum easily had met Pat's needs, and Pat confirmed the importance of many CLP efforts to make science accessible to autonomous, responsible knowledge integration. In CLP, Pat could use knowledge integration practices with confidence.

Science Inquiry

Pat answered questions about science inquiry and critiqued scientific findings by generating more and more ideas. Pat retained these ideas instead of reconciling them, following the pattern observed in the eighth grade study of heat and temperature.

Pat viewed scientists as discovering whole new disciplines such as "space" or "computers." Pat reported that scientists disagree because they hold different opinions, saying, "One scientist may believe something can hurt you and another believed that it can't." Pat also believed that scientists disagree because they have incomplete information, saying about an endangered species that some scientists "thought they were all extinct and then they found some." Pat also said scientists make assertions that "people believe" and then later research proves them wrong.

On the eighth-grade posttest, Pat had offered some more insights. Pat described scientists as "discovering something else to prove a theory wrong." Pat said that scientists both "discover things" and "change them."

In high school, Pat described situations in which scientists might consider only some of the data and be criticized by other scientists who do their experiments on "different people." For example, Pat said that scientists would criticize the assertion that "milk makes you healthy" because some people are allergic, so "it's not proven." Pat entertained more and more sophisticated ideas while remaining open to new views.

Pat experimented with the terms "theory" and "principle." Pat initially said principles are like facts that say "when two things go together." Later, Pat reported that the prism and the soap bubbles (Fig. 6.6) can be explained because "it has the same theory." Pat explained, "The light bends in the prism and the soap bubbles, so I guess it's a principle." When directly asked what a principle is, Pat cited a class principle saying, "Heat energy flows from a hotter thing to a colder thing." Pat held several ideas about theories and principles and did not reliably distinguish between these terms.

In critiquing scientific experiments Pat often looked for alternative ideas or explanations. For example, Pat requested more evidence for both the rats and rods experiments on the eighth-grade pretest. When asked to analyze the rats experiment (see Fig. 6.4). Pat questioned the generalization saying, "They'd have to do it with humans." Similarly,

In science class Jennifer observes sunlight go through a prism and sees a rainbow on the wall. The teacher explains that sunlight has light of all colors combined in it. Jennifer sees that when the different colors go through a prism, they bend at different angles. This causes the colors to separate.

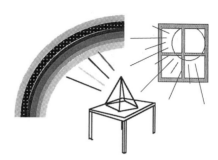

That weekend, while Jennifer is washing the dog, she sees rainbows of colors in the soap bubbles.

Do you think what Jennifer learned in her science class could explain what is happening in the soap bubbles? **(circle one)**

    yes   no   cannot predict

What is the **main reason** for your answer?

FIG. 6.6   An item used during student interviews to probe their views on the nature of science.

Pat critiqued the rods experiment saying that to compare glass and diamond as conductors you would need to do the experiment "a lot of times with different pieces of glass."

At the end of eighth grade, Pat had a more sophisticated distinction between the rats experiment and the rods experiment saying, "Well, okay this one [rods], I think she was using the same ... material or subject, you know? And uhm, she proved it. But with the rat one, she wasn't. She thought she got an answer for a different question." Pat accurately reported that the conclusions from the rods experiment could be generalized to the materials already studied, whereas the conclusions from rats go beyond what was studied. The CLP curriculum had encouraged Pat to reason autonomously, perhaps spurring these new insights.

Pat maintains a skeptical stance toward science experiments, which is consistent with a disposition to reason autonomously. Pat raised competing hypotheses for a question about causes of colds (Fig. 6.7). Pat said the researcher "did not factor in things like temperature, bacteria, family history." In addition, Pat questioned the basic science saying, "Each cold is a different virus. She may conclude that the kids are more susceptible to being sick." Furthermore, Pat asserted that new results can modify conclusions from prior research, saying, "Scientists might come to a conclusion about something like evolution, only to have it corrected by future findings."

Pat attributed to scientists a reasoning process fraught with uncertainty, and readily changed, but also distinguished, valid and speculative conjectures. This parallels Pat's own approach to science learning.

Trajectory

Pat followed the experimenter pattern of knowledge integration in making sense of science concepts such as heat and temperature, science learning, and science inquiry. Pat generated many ideas and kept considering all of them. Pat enjoyed considering new connections and could pursue this process because memorizing was easy. Pat made reasonable connections when necessary for assessments, but kept options open. In chapter 7 we see how Pat connected heat and temperature in high school.

Pat made progress while maintaining many ideas and adding more because of excellent self-monitoring. Pat recognized the need for knowledge integration and accurately described why it was going slowly. Pat seemed aware that understanding science means being prepared to incorporate new research results. Pat seemed to resist coher-

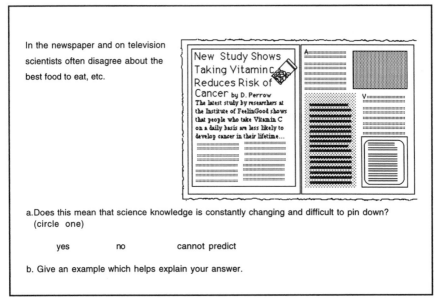

FIG. 6.7   Students explain their views about science inquiry in response to this question.

ence at the level of individual science topics while developing a robust understanding of the complex pace of scientific advance.

Pat's propensity to make connections rather than reach conclusions is reflected in excellent ability to critique scientific assertions. Pat used rich connections among ideas to identify potential threats to the validity of scientists' claims, to suggest a competing hypothesis, to question the scientific basis for claims, and to point out ambiguities.

Pat liked science and saw science learning opportunities as equitable. Pat believed men and women have equal opportunities and noted that now "it's more allowed by society." Pat pointed out that "most of my science teachers are male."

Pat's career plans reflected this same willingness to keep options open within the biological sciences field. In eighth grade, Pat had said, I plan on being "a biologist or doctor" and by twelfth grade Pat said, "an MD of some kind" and "maybe a surgeon." Pat elaborated, "I want to major in biology ... medical school, probably. I didn't want to go pre-med because I want to have the option if I wanted to become a botanist or something else along the way, I could have a choice."

CHRIS: A CONCEPTUALIZER

We earlier described Chris as a conceptualizer. In depicting science learning and in characterizing the nature of science Chris followed the conceptualizer pattern of seeking coherence and understanding at an abstract level. Unlike Pat, the experimenter, Chris focused on a few ideas and ignored pesky details to maintain a coherent view.

Science Learning

Chris had found principles and visualizations the most useful CLP learning partners. Chris preferred "visual learning," and CLP had offered animated graphs, the HeatBars visualization, and other resources that Chris readily used. Principles enabled Chris to combine experiments coherently and explain new situations. Personally relevant problems convinced Chris that some details are useful. Chris reported, "I learned about the rate of cooling of things."

Chris came to eighth grade believing that science was mainly important for people who want to become scientists or science teachers. At the end of eighth grade, Chris explained why science can help everyone saying, "Now I know what to do to keep things hot or cold," and "Life Science can help a lot." Chris distinguished between courses such as CLP that help all students and courses relevant primarily to a career in science.

Chris had excellent insight into personal learning practices. Chris had started eighth grade with the view that understanding science, not memorizing, is the best way to learn. Chris could distinguish understanding how something works from recalling an answer. Chris said, "Just memorizing doesn't answer why it happened nor how it happened." In eighth grade, Chris reported using principles, prototypes, visualizations, discussions with peers, and interactions with the teacher to learn science, and concluded, "I understand what is being taught." Chris reported seeking to distinguish valid evidence from observation and opinion. Moreover, Chris reported that in CLP "the things I learned are things I didn't know or didn't understand before." Therefore, Chris saw the work of science as understanding and used CLP learning partners to achieve this goal. Chris looked for coherent accounts of science and preferred to reach conclusions rather than hold options open.

Looking back from high school, Chris recalled that eighth-grade science was "pretty easy" because "all our questions were answered either in lab or by the teacher." Chris said, "Most of the time I understood it." Chris complained that some science classes never provide the answers that were available in CLP saying, "I like experiments if we are told the right answer afterward ... and if we have questions along the way they are answered and not just told to figure it out and we'll go over it later." Chris looked for coherent explanations and appreciated that CLP offered principles, the HeatBars model, and teacher explanations to help interpret experiments. Chris said of CLP experiments, "I use it to understand something else or have a new experiment." Chris criticized classes in which labs do not connect to principles or subsequent activities.

Chris displayed unusual insight into the advantages of visual learning opportunities, which is compatible with the conceptualizer pattern of seeking coherence among ideas. Chris often remarked, "I am a visual learner," and went on to monitor personal practices accurately.

Chris explained the importance of visual learning in CLP saying, "I mean for me to learn, I need, just reading it out of the textbook is hard. I need someone to draw a picture for me. Maybe not a physical picture but like, how do you think of it. Or uhm, do a demonstration. Just something where I know what's happening ... also, if I can do it myself or recreate the process." Chris explained how the online real-time graphs made science visible in eighth grade saying, "It was just because you could see it. I mean with the graph things you could see or track things as they were happening. You can see obviously doing more than the other one is. I see it and I understand it."

To explain the value of HeatBars, Chris described how HeatBars work, saying, "For the conductor ... we experimented and there was the heat source and they put the heat source on the material, and if it warmed up real fast it was a good conductor, and if it warmed up slowly it was a poor conductor." This helped Chris to understand. Chris recalled, "The heat energy flowed through the material, so copper was the best because heat energy went through it really fast, really quickly. And Styrofoam didn't. It went really slow and took a long time." To explain the value of HeatBars, Chris said HeatBars "helped me understand it more. It showed pictures so you can get it. It makes you understand it more real easily.... It just draws a picture in your mind instead of having all those words so you can see it."

Chris, contrasting CLP and chemistry, said, "Right now I don't like physical science.... I don't like things that I can't grasp. You know like in chemistry. I don't like things that I can't see what I'm doing, or there's no chance that I can see what I am doing. Or I just have to believe that it's true 'cause that's what I've been told, and that's what's been proven."

How does this approach work for learning chemistry? In chemistry, as in the CLP curriculum, Chris looked for useful learning partners instead of remaining frustrated. Chris missed the explanations and principles from CLP, but found a way to learn. First, Chris took advantage of lecture notes provided on the blackboard by the teacher saying, "Like this year, we had the notes on the board. We'd copy them.... Just the note taking was boring, but like if I have to be taking notes, I'd rather have it be organized. I don't like it when the teacher lectures while we are taking notes on our own because it's like what should we take?" These notes organized chemistry ideas, making thinking visible to Chris.

Chris also built on a view of memorizing articulated in eighth grade: "I think uhm, memorizing is only good for a test that's about to happen. I mean I usually go for it, just for understanding it, and then memorizing will come with that. I think that understanding is real important." To implement this goal for chemistry, Chris described a knowledge integration process using the class notes as an organizer, "Well, for my chemistry class, I never study until the night before. I was clueless for the whole chapter, and then I start studying and everything would come together, and I would just try to memorize it as fast as I could. Uhm, that was my plan and it worked. I could never like put it together until all of my notes were in front of me and I looked through it and finally I could put it together. I would remember [the lecture], and that would be helpful.... I just couldn't get it together until the last night. I tried but it didn't work."

Chris explained how this process resulted in understanding, not memorizing: "Oh it was understanding. I, uhm, unless the test was straight like, states and capitals or something like that I don't try to memorize.... If I put a picture in my head then I can understand a lot more and I memorize it a lot more because I can always refer to the picture." Chris created a picture from the class notes and other materials. It should be noted that Chris called this both memorizing and understanding, whereas for Sasha, chemistry learning seemed like memorizing. Comparing chemistry learning with CLP learning, Chris described combining principles and prototypes in a similar way saying, "I would have a whole bunch of those [prototypes]." For both classes, Chris explained, "It wasn't like the idea was flat out there. I somehow had to fit it in."

In eighth grade Chris had tended to wait for a principle instead of attempting to fit examples around a principle. Between middle school and high school, Chris reported attempting to connect more experiences to the material learned in eighth grade while forgetting some of the details from eighth grade. Thus Chris said that in eighth grade, "I would have had more background information.... I don't have all the ideas I had then." Chris described a process of connecting CLP to subsequent experiences. Chris said of CLP ideas, "I don't really think about, I just say, I should have wrapped that Coke, or I should have used a wooden spoon. I'm more aware of what effects using certain items will have. But I don't really think about heat and temperature and what's actually happening." We wondered how Chris's self-descriptions of fitting information around principles and gathering new insights would play out in the high school heat and temperature interviews.

The CLP curriculum had provided a firm foundation by offering the abstract principles and rich explanations that Chris prefers. The CLP approach also may have pushed Chris to think more about links between these principles and personal experiences. We predicted that Chris would apply principles more broadly in the high school interviews. See chapter 7 to find out how this worked.

Science Inquiry

Chris followed the conceptualizer pattern in sorting out ideas about science inquiry. Chris had started eighth grade with several useful ideas. Chris believed that "If you know the scientific way, then you can change somebody else's mind." Chris asserted that scientists primarily disagree because they have different evidence saying, "Some people can really believe one principle, and there are some people that can totally disagree and have something that ... contradicts. They have different evidence. Well maybe ... there is more evidence for it or something."

Chris distinguished fact and opinion and attributed visual thinking to scientists. Chris explained that scientists believe the earth revolves around the sun "because they know it is a fact. We've seen it." Chris's belief in visual learning is reflected in this assertion. Chris said that scientists accept results when "they can see it," assuming that by watching the earth and sun scientists can see which one goes around the other.

In contrast, Chris said scientists would disagree about whether animals can predict earthquakes. To explain, Chris offered a counterexample saying, "Since we can't tell ... if we knew when earthquakes are going to happen, I mean we could test the dog to see if he could predict it." By the end of eighth grade, Chris had additional distinctions between fact and opinion saying, "A fact is something that is true and ... it's just ... there, and an opinion can change." In high school Chris continued to autonomously expand these views of scientific thinking.

Chris uncritically accepted experimental results in eighth grade but questioned them later. Chris accepted experimental assertions, endorsing the results of the rats experiment (Fig. 6.4) saying, "Yeah pretty much. I mean, they, 'cause they, get to experience more and their knowledge keeps growing," and the rods experiment (Fig. 6.5) saying, "It's an okay experiment." At the same time, Chris distinguished between the rats experiment and the rods experiment saying, "Rats are different. Than ... metal rods. I mean, you can use the same metal rod different times or use the same metal or anything, but you can't use the same rat more than once."

In high school Chris was more cautious about experimental findings from rats saying, "Other scientists may have done a similar experiment and they got different results," and concluding that this result could not be tested on children because it would not be "good for the kids who are going to be alone."

In contrast, Chris believed that disciplinary knowledge about insulation and conduction conferred respect for the rods experiment saying, "The experiments prove it," and "a conductor of heat and a conductor of electricity are different things. The diamond might be a better conductor of heat and the copper for electricity."

After learning more about insulation and conduction, Chris analyzed both rats and rods more carefully. The CLP curriculum not only permitted Chris to develop a more sophisticated critique of these experiments, but also motivated Chris to connect science principles to everyday problems.

Trajectory

We saw in chapter 1 that Chris waited for principles instead of trying to deal with the messy connections in complex examples. We see here that

Chris has begun to anticipate connections between messy examples and principles.

Between the eighth grade and high school, Chris autonomously and systematically had constructed understanding of personal learning practices and science inquiry. The CLP principles and visualizations had made sense in eighth grade. Looking back at eighth grade Chris described revisiting CLP principles and building on them. We see how this view of science learning is reflected in the heat and temperature interviews in chapter 7.

Chris took a straightforward stance toward equity and careers. Chris expected that boys and girls would have equal opportunities in science, but noted that all but one of the science teachers in middle school and high school had been men. Chris believed that if anything, there were more girls in the 4-year science program. Chris believed that "guys are the science teachers and guys have the top grades in science." This was actually inaccurate because girls earn higher science grades. Chris may have based this conclusion on the propensity of boys to contribute more to class discussion.

The rich set of images of science employed between eighth and twelfth grades coincided with Chris's career goals. In eighth grade Chris had said, "Some things in science are really interesting and sometimes I want to know more about them, but I don't want to make a career of it." In twelfth grade Chris was planning to pursue a career in medicine, saying "I had life science since seventh grade. I didn't really seriously think about it until I shadowed an emergency room doctor. But that made me really want to do it. I'd been like medically inclined for a while."

REFLECTIONS

The CLP curriculum offers learning partners for the diverse students described here and for nearly all the eighth graders we have studied. Each student resonated with some of the course features. Pat, following the experimenter pattern, incorporated almost everything, remarking, "There is no way I don't like to learn." In contrast, Sasha, following the strategizer pattern, wanted results and explanations to memorize. Lee, following the consumer pattern, liked watching the graphs and letting other students do the work. Chris, following the conceptualizer pattern, preferred principles and visual, animated models such as HeatBars.

The students varied in their insights into their own learning practices. Students with good insight into knowledge integration became autonomous learners, whereas students who saw themselves as passive or memorizers, ended up settling for less knowledge integration. Pat and Chris both learned autonomously, monitored their own progress, and revisited class ideas. Sasha held many diverse views of personal learning practices that only started to converge in twelfth grade. Lee displayed a glimmer of insight into knowledge integration in twelfth grade.

These students built understanding of science inquiry between middle and high school, but their learning was rather idiosyncratic because little of their formal instruction had addressed these issues. Autonomous learners made more progress than students who were less autonomous.

Students' progress in critiquing science connected to their knowledge of the science topic. In the beginning of eighth grade, Chris, the conceptualizer was the least critical, seeming to rely on the view that experiments prove things. Lee, Pat, and Sasha each made connections to personal experiences to analyze the experiments they were asked to critique. Lee drew on a relevant out-of-school activity to offer a sophisticated critique of the rats experiment. The other students gave more superficial answers. For the rods experiment, Pat raised questions about replications of the findings, Sasha disputed the results based on the cost of diamonds. Lee was skeptical, and Chris was convinced.

By twelfth grade, Chris and Pat had developed some rich images of science experiments and use these to offer sophisticated and targeted criticism of all the experiments. Chris connected valid evidence and often asked for disciplinary knowledge. Pat made creative links to possible confounds. Greater willingness to think about the problems also enabled Sasha and Lee to offer more cogent reactions. The least valid criticisms came from a view of scientists as perverse rather than systematic. Knowledge of the science topic helped Pat and Chris to offer more sophisticated criticisms.

These results suggest that science classes such as CLP contribute to understanding scientific inquiry by allowing students to practice critiquing in disciplines they understand. The CLP emphasis on jointly establishing criteria and applying them consistently also helps students offer sensible evaluations of scientific claims. Nevertheless, CLP students, like scientists, are limited by their knowledge of the relevant discipline.

ASK MR. K

What do students think it means to learn science?

If you ask kids what learning science means, they will say it's dissecting frogs, learning the vocabulary or definitions in textbooks, or memorizing what scientists have already done. They sometimes say things such as science is doing the same experiment that a scientist did long ago rather than designing their own experiments. They don't see science as being inventive or creative.

When did you discover how students view science and science inquiry?

I didn't really think about students' views of science until I started working with people from Berkeley such as Eileen Lewis, Marcia Linn, and Batsheva Eylon. I then started asking kids about their ideas and listening. Kids said some really strange things when they didn't believe what they saw. Students differed in how they viewed science. Some said science was changing. Others said it was a static field with no new discoveries.

How do you contribute to student beliefs about science?

As a teacher, I try to get kids to realize that science is available to them and that they can be scientists too. For example, they can do this by just being curious, making their own observations, and trying to apply the resulting principles we ask them to make in class to every day experiences.

Another thing I try to do, as a teacher, is to get students to gain confidence in themselves and be more autonomous rather than just let their partner do everything. Part of this is having kids see themselves as important in the learning process. I accept the questions and answers that kids provide. Even if a kid provides a less acceptable answer, I try to expand on this idea, play this out in discussion, and see where it goes. This helps bring kids into the discussion and gets them to participate in science class.

Does CLP help students learn how to learn science?

I, for one, have seen kids who take biology in the ninth grade after CLP and say it was a really different science experience for them.

Although they had to memorize biology terms, they could also make use of ways they learned in CLP. Students knew what learning approach to take depending on the teacher and the curriculum. We just provided another way to learn about science. Even though the teacher and teaching style might have been different in their later science classes, they had learned the CLP way and could use this later if they needed to.

In another case, I was talking to a girl who was here last year and not really focused in science. She was very social and more interested in her social life. She told me she had realized that this was because the kids she hung around with at school weren't interested in learning. Being with partners who believed learning was important changed her beliefs. She still struggles in school, but seems more conscious of how she learns.

POINTS TO PONDER

- Describe your personal views of the nature of science. Explain how science advances, how scientists resolve disputes, and how "facts" get established.
- Interview some students about the nature of science. Analyze the repertoire of models of the nature of science students might bring to science class.
- Interview a science researcher about the nature of science. Compare the views of this expert to the views of students.
- Select a course you have taken using technology. Compare the learning partners students use in CLP to the learning partners you encountered in this course.
- Analyze the comments made by students in this chapter about opportunities for boys and girls in science courses.
- In Appendix A, analyze the interview of Lee and identify a student you have taught who resembles Lee.
- Watch a classroom section of the CLP film and look for the science learning partners that each student uses.

RELATED READINGS

Ames, C. (1992). Classrooms: Goals, structures, and student motivation. *Journal of Educational Psychology, 84*(3), 261–271.

Covington, M. V. (1998). *The will to learn: A guide for motivating young people.* Cambridge, UK: Cambridge University.

Linn, M. C., & Songer, N. B. (1993). How do students make sense of science? *Merrill-Palmer Quarterly, 39*(1), 47–73.

Schoenfeld, A. H. (1989). Explorations of students' mathematical beliefs and behavior. *Journal for Research in Mathematics Education, 20*(4), 338–355.

7

Building on Middle School Science in High School

How did Pat, Sasha, Lee, and Chris employ CLP ideas and assess CLP experiences as they continued in high school? When we left these students in eighth grade we had several questions.

For Pat, we wondered whether science ideas would converge. Pat added ideas but neglected contradictions.

For Lee, we worried that CLP had not provided a firm foundation. Lee gained some new ideas in CLP but infrequently connected these to other ideas. Lee had a tendency to isolate cases rather than make connections. Would Lee eventually connect diverse ideas?

For Sasha, we wondered how future interactions with science and science teachers would go. Sasha sought right answers but rejected thinking about the problems. Instead, Sasha often convinced the interviewer to provide hints or even answers. Sasha disliked physical science. How would Sasha respond to life science?

For Chris, we expected continued success but wondered how novel materials, situations, and problems would be handled. Chris looked for abstractions but tended to ignore specific and potentially confusing situations. Would Chris be able to use CLP ideas for novel problems?

PAT IN HIGH SCHOOL

Pat displayed invention and creativity in eighth grade. Pat expected to give explanations and sought connections among observations, class ideas, and comments by teachers or peers. Pat made many unique connections. For example, Pat struggled to sort out the role of holes in insulation. Obstacles and observations motivated Pat to add new ideas to the mix. Pat seemed comfortable with the idea that several explanations could apply to a problem. Did Pat seek coherence or continue to generate new possibilities?

After Biology: Tenth Grade

At the tenth grade interview, Pat recalled the CLP class as "fun." Pat liked "working on computers." Pat said it "really taught us this stuff." Pat preferred life science but reported that the CLP class made physical science "more interesting than I thought it was going to be."

Pat responded to insulation questions first by trying to recall class ideas. When asked about the best wrap for keeping something cold Pat said "we found out" in CLP that "it's not aluminum." Pat explained that "metal is a conductor and that's what most people use." Pat recalled, "Plastic wrap or bubble wrap I think was the best." Pat had trouble recalling why bubble wrap worked, saying, "Because uhm, I forgot what he [Mr. K] called it. I'm trying to remember.... There were little heat currents or something that would. They were called. Oh, I'm confusing myself."

When asked to describe what happens, Pat offered a mix of ideas, following the pattern found in eighth-grade responses. Pat said, "Foil would kind of pull the cold out of the soda into the air," and elaborated, "The cold moved right out onto the metal because metal is a conductor and then it would be released into the air," but then contradicted, "I forget if it happened that way or if the heat in the air, like the metal pulled the heat in from the air into the soda." To summarize, Pat said, "I forget if the cold left or the heat came in, but it's probably both," following the eighth-grade pattern of holding several alternative ideas.

Pat recalled many ideas from eighth grade and willingly tried various connections among them. As in eighth grade, Pat concentrated on generating ideas and explanations more than on achieving coherence.

Next, the interviewer encouraged coherence by asking if there could be both heat and cold. Pat said "It could also be just me," and explained "I really never kind of understood whether there was both or not." When the interviewer asked if "there is such a thing as heat energy and cold energy," this triggered Pat to recall more information. Pat said,

"That's what it's called, heat energy.... I'm not sure if there's cold energy or not. I guess there could be, but I think it was maybe just heat energy.... The more I think about it I think there was only heat energy, but I'm not sure."

Pat now used the recollections spurred by the term "heat energy" as a starting point to explain how insulators and conductors contribute to the warming of a soda. First, Pat posited an active role for metal saying that metals "attract heat." Pat said, "Then the metal, like the foil, or I guess on the can maybe I'm not sure.... So whatever is in the little metal particles attract heat and so they would, the heat energy would kind of be sucked on to the can and would go into the soda and warm it." Second, Pat recalled "something with how the air is an insulator" and connects to the "air pockets" in Styrofoam wrap saying, "The Styrofoam wrap, that's really porous. So then the air kind of holds in the little holes and then it insulates against heat energy coming in." Pat used terms such as "porous" and "insulates" rather loosely.

When asked to explain "insulates," Pat offered "opposite of conducting." To elaborate, Pat gave a range of possibilities: "I know what it is, but I can't describe it. Conducting is like, uhm, it attracts the heat and holds the heat right there and let's it go. Like a metal wall I guess if this makes sense, hot on this side and cold on this side. Then the metal wall would pull all the heat energy into it and it would like leave and go into the cold."

Pat gave a similar range of explanations for an insulator: "Well, I know that air is an insulator. Let's see, I'm trying to describe it. I guess if you had the same situation, but the wall was Styrofoam sheeting or something like that, the air would kind of get stuck in the pockets and that doesn't let the heat enter ... or doesn't. The air is not metal, so it doesn't pull the heat as fast, but eventually the little heat particles would diffuse through the wall, but it doesn't have the initial pull on all of it."

Pat expected metals actively to "attract," "pull," or, "suck up" heat, displaying an intuitive sense of potential energy. Pat followed the pattern from eighth grade of giving many responses, some supported by scientific evidence and some not, in response to probes from the interviewer. When the interviewer asked for clarification, Pat often gave scientifically accepted responses. For example the interviewer asked, "Is heat matter? You said 'heat particles'?" and Pat responded, "No ... I guess heat energy." When asked what would happen with the "Styrofoam wall," Pat said, "Neither Styrofoam nor metal would keep it cold forever, but Styrofoam is better." In these answers, Pat incorporated a remarkable set of ideas from eighth grade and made new connections among ideas while sorting out the alternatives and including normative ideas in the mix.

In responding to questions and problems about insulation, Pat went through the process of recalling ideas from eighth grade, adding new ideas, generating conflicting alternatives, and sorting things out. It should be noted that Pat wanted to explain insulation and conduction but initially was thwarted by incomplete recall of the heat flow process. A small hint, hidden in a question intended to clarify Pat's thinking, spurred Pat to give a rich, connected set of ideas. This shows how Pat's mind worked, not just connecting class ideas or observations, but also incorporating incompletely understood concepts such as "porous" from biology.

This example illustrates the difficulties in designing assessments. If we had used only the responses before the "heat energy" hint, Pat would have earned a low score. On a multiple-choice question that had offered "heat energy" and "cold energy" as alternatives, Pat probably would have selected the scientifically normative idea. Furthermore, if the multiple-choice item had offered "heat energy," "heat and cold energy," or "cold energy" Pat might have selected the longer answer. It's hard to predict.

Pat's performance in the whole interview revealed a process of making multiple connections and then seeking coherence. Coherence seemed less important to Pat than making rich connections. Pat anticipated that future courses and experience would provide additional perspectives and remained ready to consider new ideas.

Pat pulled all these ideas together toward the end of the interview when describing how it would feel to hold a metal nail on an ice cube. Pat first recognized a conundrum saying, "Like the heat energy would go from my hand to the nail, but it would also get like cold." Then Pat clarified the situation saying, "What's it like? Is it hotter outside or am I in a freezer?" Moreover, Pat attempted to use heat flow to pull everything together saying, "Then if my hand is hotter than the nail, it [the nail] should warm up too. So, ... the heat would go from my hand to the nail? ... I guess it would go up to the ice, ... but I'm not sure." Pat not only eventually recalled CLP class ideas, but also connected them to novel ideas and could explain complex situations.

Pat followed this same pattern when discussing the distinction between heat energy and temperature, starting with the first idea generated in eighth grade, saying heat and temperature are the same. Then Pat stated a CLP class idea saying, "Everything has some, has some amount of heat energy," and agreeing that when a freezer is turned down a small ice cube compared with a large ice cube "would cool down faster because it has less heat energy in it." This motivated Pat to connect the ice cubes situation to an earlier question and pose a principle: "More matter would have more heat energy."

Pat then wondered, "Heat energy and temperature, that's the same thing, right?" The interviewer asked Pat if heat energy and temperature are the same. Pat responded, "They could have the same temperature but not the same amount of heat energy. I wasn't sure." After considering a question about heating water Pat concluded "I think there'd be more heat energy where there's more matter." Pat kept adding class ideas and sorting out the meanings of terms in the context of specific examples.

For Pat, thermal ideas were firmly connected to problems rather than abstracted in principles. Pat recalled CLP principles and CLP class ideas in the context of problems. In tenth grade, Pat not only recalled this information but used it as a basis for sorting out new, complex ideas and situations. The CLP curriculum had provided Pat with specific examples, principles, and a disposition to combine this information. Between eighth and tenth grade, Pat's conclusions had increased in coherence.

Pat recalled class thermal equilibrium ideas more rapidly. For objects in both a hot trunk and a cold ski cabin (Figs. 7.1 and 7.2), Pat clarified the situation to be sure thermal equilibrium applied. For the cabin, Pat asked about possible breezes. For the trunk Pat asked if the sun shone directly on the objects. To explain how wood and metal feel at thermal equilibrium, Pat first recalled a class experiment and gave a vague explanation: "I just remember like when we had to touch the table, it felt cold and the wood parts don't. I think it's because your hand is warmer and so it feels colder on the metal." Then Pat clarified this connection by verifying the relative temperature of the hand and the objects saying, "If the degree measure is colder than your hand, then it would feel cold." For the hot trunk, Pat said the metal would feel hotter "because it's a conductor." For wood, Pat tried to recall a group of ideas about air. For the cold cabin, Pat said wood doesn't feel cold. It has to do with the air that's inside of it.... Inside the wood ... because, well, it's porous." For the hot trunk, Pat said, "They wouldn't feel as hot.... Little air pockets? It has something to do with little air pockets. Why can't I remember?... Because the air insulates it." It should be noted that Pat set high standards for explanations and recognized when they had not been met.

In summary, at tenth grade Pat struggled to recall CLP ideas and principles, added ideas from biology, and organized ideas primarily around examples. In discussing insulation, besides reexamining the range of eighth-grade answers, Pat added new vocabulary from biology. Therefore, Pat said heat would eventually "diffuse" through the Styrofoam "because everything's moving and stuff."

Later Pat used the term "isotonic" to explain thermal equilibrium saying, "If heat energy had a brain, it would want to make everything

You and a friend are buying materials for a project and have purchased several long strips of aluminum and several long strips of wood at a hardware store. You place the strips in the trunk of the car. It is a hot day and you and the friend stop at another friend's house on the way home. You leave the strips of metal and wood sitting in the trunk of the car. When you return several hours later, you and your friend have different predictions about the temperature of the strips of metal and wood in the trunk. Your friend thinks the wooden strips would be hotter than the metal strips. You say the metal strips would be hotter than the wooden strips. Who is right? Why? (Probe students' understanding of and conditions for thermal equilibrium.) What would happen if you touched the metal strips? What would happen if you touched the wooden strips? Why?

FIG. 7.1   Car trunk: An item used to interview students in high school.

You arrive at a ski cabin in the winter and no heat was left on. The room thermometer reads 5˚C. What can you predict about the temperature of the objects in the cabin? Why? Did you always think about the objects in a room this way? What happens when you touch some of these objects in the room (e.g., cast iron stove, small pile of wood, a plate, a chair, a fork)?

FIG. 7.2   Ski cabin: An item used to interview students in the 8th, 10th, and 12th grades.

isotonic. I think that's right. Well, equal. And with the environments and what's in it that's why like a soda would heat up on the outside so that everything's the same."

Pat pounced on hints such as heat energy when the interviewer mentioned them. Pat looked for coherence, promoting compelling recollections such as the idea that only heat flows, the distinction between heat and temperature, and the nature of heat energy. Pat built on CLP ideas, connecting them to ideas from biology such as isotonic, porous, and diffusion. Just as in the CLP curriculum, Pat made connections through examples rather than more abstract ideas such as equilibrium. For Pat, the rich, complex, personally relevant CLP examples enabled connections to new ideas. Pat had a more robust understanding of thermal events in tenth grade than in eighth grade.

In tenth grade Pat drew more on principles than in eighth grade. In addition, Pat recalled details of class experiments about insulation, mass, and thermal equilibrium and applied them to novel problems. How would this process look in twelfth grade?

After Physiology and Chemistry: Twelfth Grade

Between tenth and twelfth grades, Pat studied physiology and chemistry. Pat, like most CLP students, reported little or no subsequent instruction on thermal topics and expected some diminished understanding in twelfth grade. Pat said that CLP topics did not come up in biology or physiology, but did in chemistry. Following past practice, Pat made connections around examples, saying that these ideas came up "in chemistry when we talked about metal substances, and ionic substances and bonds, and that some are conductors and that kind of thing." Although Pat had connected biology ideas in the tenth grade interview, Pat asserted, "I took biology and physiology and we didn't talk about it."

Pat reported understanding CLP ideas "about the same" in twelfth grade but explained "it was fresher in my mind then [eighth grade]." Pat said CLP ideas played a role in day-to-day thinking, explaining "I don't sit down and say, 'Oh, I have these two cakes. Which one has more heat energy?' Not in those terms exactly, but I am sure it's in my subconscious."

On the basis of eighth and tenth grade performance, what prediction can be made about Pat's twelfth grade responses: Will Pat, as in tenth grade, express uncertainty and need time to recall and connect ideas? Will Pat rely on non-normative ideas such as porous materials, cold energy, or metal actively sucking up heat? What will Pat say about "holes" in materials? How will Pat support conclusions? Will Pat's responses reflect progress since tenth grade or some regression?

When asked about insulating a cold drink in twelfth grade Pat sounded confident, considered new issues such as practicality, and recalled class findings: "I think the best thing was wool, I know it wasn't aluminum. We talked about air being a cushion and metal being a conductor so even air is better than aluminum.... Practically, I wouldn't choose wool. I would choose saran wrap™ ... because wrapping it in a sweater would be a little awkward." When asked to explain why, Pat rejected a tautology: "You can't say a conductor conducts." Pat settled on a CLP view of heat transfer: "It takes the heat energy from the air, the surroundings, and transfers it into the can, into the soda?" In elaborating, Pat interjected the notion of metals "attracting" heat or "pulling it into the can." In responding to a later question, Pat connected to porosity, air, and practical examples to explain insulation: "I would put Styrofoam as an insulator because it has a lot of air. Anything porous is a good insulator, ... because it has a lot of air and insulates well.... That's why you put that pink stuff in houses 'cause it is cushiony ... and it holds the air in the walls."

Pat in twelfth grade, has both a more coherent and a more confident view of insulation phenomena than in eighth or tenth grade. Pat sustained the approach of connecting new ideas like porosity and retaining them if they prove useful. In twelfth grade Pat still struggled to distinguish between heat energy and temperature, but could give coherent examples.

Pat compared a small and large ice cube heating from - 40° to 0°, clarifying that it is important to measure at the center of the ice cube (Fig. 7.3): "If you were measuring from the center, ... it would take the heat energy longer to reach the center of the larger one 'cause it has to pass through all that extra ice than if it went straight to the center of the smaller one." Pat said "Temperature is the measure of how much heat energy there is," but remained uneasy. Pat then offered another distinction by referring to the ice example: "The big block of ice had to gain more heat energy to get up to 0° because there is more mass." Here Pat distinguished heat energy from temperature using the normative scientific view.

For thermal equilibrium questions in twelfth grade Pat started with the class result: "They are all the same temperature but they feel differently." Pat also asserted that even well-insulated objects will reach equilibrium with their surroundings saying, "Eventually the heat energy from the air would flow into the can and warm the soda until it's room temperature." To explain why, Pat said, "It was one of those equilibrium things," and to distinguish how things feel, Pat relied on rate of heat flow "because the heat energy flows from the metal to my hand better than it does from the wood," and ... "because metal is a conductor, it's more noticeable."

Pat could coherently explain new situations and distinguish objects on the basis of rate of heat flow. Pat said, comparing objects and a child in a room, "They [the objects] should all be at room temperature. But they're not going to feel like it.... A child ... if you stuck it [a thermometer] in a child, it would be 98°, hopefully. No matter how long you leave a child at room temperature, it's not going to be 60° or whatever because a child has its own source of heat energy. Its skin might be 60° or maybe if you touched his clothes, they would feel at room temperature. A metal plate would probably feel colder because if the heat you bring with you in your hand there is a big difference because of the conducting. The hot chocolate ... the liquid would be at room temperature and the cup too, but it wouldn't necessarily feel that way depending on whether it was metal or something else. The table would be at room temperature. Styrofoam would be at room temperature. I think the cold Coke would be at room temperature, but if you touched the can, it would feel colder because of the conductivity."

You have stored a big block of ice in your freezer. You want to compare the temperature of the big block of ice to a small ice cube that also was in the freezer. How do they compare? Are the blocks of ice the same temperature? Why? Probe students' understanding of thermal equilibrium. What could you say about the heat energy of the large block of ice compared with the heat energy of the small block of ice? Do cold things have heat energy? (Ask students to give examples of things that have different amounts of heat energy.)

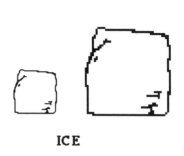

ICE

a. What would you have to do to cool these two blocks of ice from 0°C to –40°C?

b. What would you have to do to warm these two blocks of ice up from –40°C to –20°C?

c. [Ask if students are confused] Suppose you wanted to melt the blocks of ice. What would be different for the big and small blocks?

FIG. 7.3   A heat and temperature question asked during the high school interview.

Pat offered similar coherent answers when relating heat conductivity to thermal equilibrium, drawing on class experience as well as personal examples. For example, Pat predicted that a metal platter will cool faster than a ceramic tile platter taken out of the oven, saying, "Terra-cotta, I think ... because the metal will release the heat energy into the air. Do you want to know why? Do you want to hear my thought process?... These terra-cotta plates and you put them in the bottom of your bread basket to keep the rolls warm.... It holds the heat in, and the heat rises through the buns.... I've seen them. I think those are pottery and not metal because I think once you take the metal out, the heat will just go. If you have a cookie sheet when you are baking cookies, you can touch the cookie sheet in, like, a minute and you can use it again in a couple of minutes. But I don't think you can with the terra-cotta thing. It wouldn't feel as hot as the metal, but it would hold the heat longer. It wouldn't dissipate as fast."

Similarly, Pat relied on a sound view of heat flow as well as personal experience to discuss shoveling snow with a metal shovel and no gloves (Fig. 7.4). Pat said, "The heat energy from your hands is flowing into that part of the metal, and then you have an equilibrium.... But there's not enough heat in just your hands to heat up the whole shovel. So when your hands aren't, the heat energy's leaving from the shovel into the air, and if you touch it again, there's a big difference between the heat energy in your hand and the amount of heat energy in that part of the shovel." Pat said gloves would reduce the personal impact of the cold shovel "unless you were wearing really cheap gloves."

Pat connected to chemistry ideas when asked how metals attract heat. First Pat said, "It just happens." Then, to explain, Pat used phrases from chemistry saying, "Oh, there's excess" and "It lacks equilibrium." Pat imported many new examples but also relied on the CLP class ideas as a foundation. Pat referred to metals "attracting" heat but primarily talked about heat flowing, leaving, going, and dissipating.

When Pat attempted to connect concepts of equilibrium from CLP and chemistry, the examples created obstacles. Pat said, "Like these are atoms and these are like heat waves transferring, and so even so, you want an equilibrium and energy, but it's different from saying you want your carbon atoms to be balanced.... I think so," but then went on to consider similarities saying, "I mean, I guess you could say the metal table atoms are lacking in heat energy and therefore it would want to take the heat energy away from the platters, so I guess they are the same: they just seem different.... They're consistent." Here, as in eighth and tenth grades, when prompted Pat looked for coherent connections.

In twelfth grade, Pat remained poised to add new ideas, following the autonomous reasoning pattern CLP encouraged. Pat relied on CLP ex-

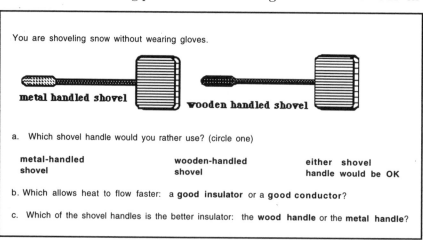

FIG. 7.4 Shoveling snow: An example of items used on the pretest and posttest assessments to measure changes in students' understanding of insulation and conduction.

amples, some CLP principles, and, importantly, on the CLP process of knowledge integration. In twelfth grade Pat relied less on authorities like Mr. K, and more on experiments, reproducible examples, and useful abstractions. Pat preferred examples to principles.

Extending CLP Reasoning to a New Topic: Light

How did Pat reason about a new topic? To find out we asked questions about light in tenth grade (Fig. 7.5). Then we provided a very short (1 hour) activity following the CLP model of predicting, experimenting, and forming principles. In twelfth grade, we asked related questions about light.

In the tenth grade, Pat displayed the process of making and analyzing connections and of using promising connections to reach more

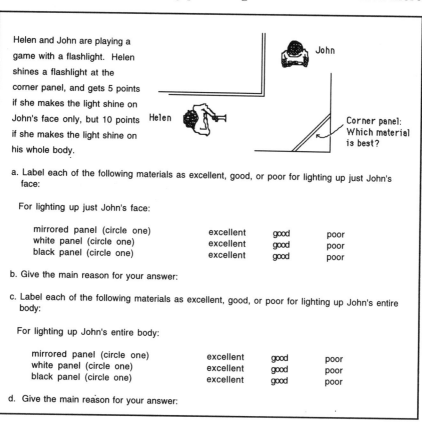

FIG. 7.5   An item used on the pretest and posttest as well as during the interviews to probe students' understanding of light, light propagation, and reflection.

valid conclusions in responding to questions on light, a new topic. Pat had a good understanding of reflection and absorption, but at first did not connect light to vision. When asked about seeing a book by shining a flashlight on the ceiling, Pat demonstrated this process of making and analyzing connections. Pat considered variables such as the color of the ceiling, the strength of the flashlight, and even the angle of the flashlight: "Let's see, the light would go up and hit the ceiling. This is in a house right?... It would, uhm, hit the ceiling. I'm assuming the ceiling would be white because most are. It would reflect down. I mean if you had a black ceiling, it would probably be absorbed.... I think would depend on the flashlight, how big the flashlight was.... If the beam was big enough, then the light would go up and kind of break and come down in an arc, and I'm not sure with this flashlight if she could see 'cause the light would kind of be like that. Do you know what I mean? But if it was a big enough flashlight and the arc went like that, then she would see."

To describe the role of light in vision Pat had several ideas. First, Pat said the light "might have to reflect," and that it would "reflect into the air" or "maybe on the ceiling." Later Pat connected vision to the book saying, "If the paper had eyes, it could see" because the light reaches it. Pat then considered how the light would have to reflect "to my face, to my eyes."

Pat connected these ideas and used others as well to explain coherently why it is easier to see a white shirt than a black shirt at night: "Okay, you could see the white T-shirt better than the black ... because light reflects off of white, but it's absorbed into black. That's why you want to wear a white T-shirt on a hot day. I'm not sure where the light was coming from.... Well, if equal light was shining on them and everything like that then the light would bounce off the white T-shirt and come back to your face." Pat extended these ideas to consider why sunglasses work, again connecting to a rich set of ideas. Pat considered how the color of the sunglasses influences vision saying, "They'd look more the shade of the glasses. If you had brown lenses, they'd look brown." Pat also connected to the type of lenses saying "if you had UV protection, it would be a little altered." Pat also connected ideas about absorption saying, "I guess it absorbs the light a little.... So the light still comes through so you can see.... Kind of changes the amount of light, I think."

Later, Pat acknowledged that this process of connecting ideas about light to explain how sunglasses work was learning, saying, "I learned stuff ... 'Cause I didn't understand how like light worked, and I think it was kind of cool that I got the right answer or very close."

In twelfth grade Pat recalled material learned about light in tenth grade, remarking "It's not fair; we only did this once years ago." Parallels between Pat's response to the question about which is best for lighting up a room—black walls, white walls, or mirrors—and Pat's response to the first tenth grade questions about heat were apparent. Pat reported many ideas, but did not sort them out. Pat said, "Black panels was bad in it just absorbs. Maybe the mirrored panel diffracts, then the white panel focuses." Then Pat said, "I might have those backward." Clearly, Pat would have liked a hint to sort these ideas out.

On subsequent questions, Pat relied on observations. To explain sunglasses Pat said, "Light is sort of absorbed. The rest goes into your eye. You need light to see clearly and to see bright colors." To explain how far light goes, Pat emphasized visual activity saying, "To see it the light has to reach you," and "if you can see it pretty clearly, it will probably go past you." When asked to explain how far light would go outside, Pat expressed uncertainty saying, "If it was outside and it wasn't bouncing off of anything, it would just go on. It's hard to say how far it would go."

The interviewer seemed rushed, and Pat clearly wanted some hints to stimulate recall. Pat left this topic open for further input instead of reaching hasty conclusions. In addition, Pat distinguished observations based on visual activity from the question about light propagation.

These responses reinforced our insights into Pat's mode of thinking and illustrated gains in sophistication. Pat, for both heat and light, resisted superficial connections.

LEE IN HIGH SCHOOL

Had Lee continued along the path of isolating situations to avoid making connections? In eighth grade, when confronted with contradictions, Lee had asserted, for example, that what worked for hot objects did not work for cold objects. In high school, did Lee seek more connections across situations?

After Biology: Tenth Grade

In tenth grade Lee had trouble remembering eighth grade, saying "I don't know" frequently. As in eighth grade, Lee seemed either disinterested or lacking in confidence in science.

Responding to tenth-grade insulation and heat energy questions, Lee offered a range of ideas. To explain how to keep a drink cold, Lee said, "I don't know.... Usually people wrap it in tin foil, but we learned that it doesn't work, and I don't remember what did work. I think it was paper or something like that…. That's what Mr. K told us." Lee offered several disconnected ideas about temperature, air, and amount of liquid to explain how a small and large milk shake would change after they were poured. First, Lee said the small one would "be colder," but when probed Lee said, "Oh, I meant it'd probably be warmer because it has less liquid, so it loses temperature faster," and explained "The air…. It warms the soda." Lee concluded, "I never understood what heat energy was."

In tenth grade, Lee recalled the class idea about thermal equilibrium saying, "They'd all be the same temperature of the room." To explain, Lee overgeneralized, saying that even the child would be "the same temperature as the air." Lee could recall that wood and metal would feel different, but could not explain why. Hints and prompts were not sufficient to resolve contradictory recollections.

After Integrated Science: Twelfth Grade

In twelfth grade, Lee gave far more elaborate answers and showed a disposition to offer a wide range of ideas but not to select among them. Describing a cold Coke on a table, Lee said that over time it "will drop down to room temperature." Lee explained using air as a vehicle for transporting heat, saying, "Just 'cause the surrounding temperature, the air around it, the cold air would like go out of the soda and the room temperature air would go in." Lee said that because the can is metal it "absorbs different temperatures really easily." When asked to sort out these ideas, Lee decided that it is not the air but the "temperature," and "like, the heat" that is going into the soda.

Lee elaborated on the idea of wrapping a soda in paper to keep it cool, saying, "Paper would kind of be helping the cooler air [stay] in, and like keeping the, keeping the hot air out. Uhm, paper … uhm, paper's different from like just the can, 'cause the can absorbs the heat better than the paper." Lee posited an active role for paper, saying it is "helping the cooler air." Lee distinguished metal from paper on the basis of "absorbing" heat. Although Lee drew on non-normative ideas such as temperature absorption, barrier models, and active roles for molecules, these answers reflected more sophistication than eighth grade or tenth grade answers. Lee seemed to be starting the knowledge integration process by generating a repertoire of potential explanations.

Lee showed a similar disposition to explain when asked what will happen if a large and small ice cube are placed on the table. Lee predicted that "the smaller one would melt quicker" because "there is less ice surrounding it, keeping it cold." Lee distinguished ice on the outside of an ice cube from ice on the inside. When asked which ice cube would cool faster in a - 40° freezer, Lee said "maybe the bigger one" and explained, "just because its probably already colder." Here Lee used an idea many eighth graders initially expressed: Larger things at room temperature are hotter or colder than smaller objects. This idea probably reflects the observation that it takes longer to heat a larger mass with the same heat source. Lee also could imagine why the smaller ice cube might cool faster saying, "because there is less of it."

Considering a wood and metal spoon for stirring boiling noodles, Lee followed the same pattern of generating many ideas. Lee used absorption as the process of heat transfer, and talked about heat and temperature interchangeably. Lee said, "I don't know.... It'd be that just steel is hotter—gets hotter.... So it's ... it absorbs a bunch of heat out of the noodles.... I don't know. The heat ... it, the spoon just absorbs the heat from the water, and when you take it out it'll start to cool down, but the wood absorbs the heat too, but it just doesn't feel as hot. Uhm, they're both absorbing the temperature. Hot temperature and cold temperature." At twelfth grade for the first time Lee tried giving explanations. As a result, Lee generated contradictions and sounded rather like other students when they first made connections in eighth grade.

Lee, in twelfth grade discussing thermal equilibrium, often relied on an idea from eighth grade: Objects would all reach the same temperature although this idea was not applied to the large and small ice cube at 0°. Lee learned a normative answer for thermal equilibrium in eighth grade. Everything has the same temperature. Because Lee did not connect the answer to the explanation, this normative view could be overgeneralized when Lee asserted that a child would reach thermal equilibrium and ignored when Lee considered how fast the temperature of ice changes. Lee connected some ideas but not others in responding to questions about thermal equilibrium. For example, Lee considered the "absorption" idea when discussing why wood and metal feel differently at thermal equilibrium, saying, "I don't know if the wood absorbs more." Lee also connected the idea of conduction, saying, "Maybe the metal would be hotter because it is a good conductor of heat." When asked about a metal and pottery platter. (Fig. 7.6), Lee again looked for an explanation saying, silver probably would stay warmer when both were removed from the oven, "cause silver's kind of like a metal, so uhm, it'd probably hold a lot more heat. And uhm, the other one, the other one's heat would be ... it's hard, because once you start thinking about it, it can like reverse what you're saying. 'Cause the metal is a good conductor so it would absorb the full air, ... I think it would cool off quicker." To explain how they would feel, Lee said, "If it was in the oven, and I touched them, the metal one would be hotter, and, 'cause it absorbs more heat than the dish would." When asked to summarize Lee said, "Uhm, the metal feels hotter when you take it out, so I think that it will stay hotter longer, but then I'd also think about, uhm, metal absorbs temperature quickly, so it would absorb the coolness." Lee held several unresolved views but could elaborate and consider alternatives.

Remarkably, Lee not only elaborated but also monitored the elaboration. Lee said, "Once you start thinking about it, it can like reverse what you're saying."

In this interview, for the first time, we got some insight into Lee's thinking. Lee still responded with, "I don't know" to many questions, but rarely followed the eighth-grade pattern of resolving contradictions by isolating cases. Indeed, when Lee elaborated, we saw that some uncertainty may have stemmed from having too many unresolved ideas instead of too few ideas, as seemed likely in eighth grade. Indeed Lee recalled far more eighth grade information in twelfth grade than reported in tenth grade, or even in the last eighth grade interview.

We wondered whether reticence in eighth grade had prevented Lee from distinguishing heat, cold, temperature, air, and related concepts. Alternatively, Lee may have gained confidence and maturity between eighth and twelfth grade that made it possible for Lee to reflect on these concepts in twelfth grade.

This twelfth-grade interview allowed Lee to generate and inspect these diverse ideas but not to resolve them. The heat absorption mechanism, asserted for the first time in twelfth grade, took precedence over heat flow and interfered with knowledge integration in the twelfth-grade interview. Many students who consider absorption in eighth grade compare absorption and heat flow and eventually settle on heat flow. With more time Lee might also sort out these models.

You place a silver platter and a pottery platter in an oven at 450°F for three hours. Which will stay warm longer when removed from the oven, the silver platter or the pottery platter?

a. Explain your reasoning.

b. How do the rates of cooling compare when they are first removed from the oven? After they have been sitting out for a while?

c. What would affect cooling?

FIG. 7.6 Platters: A question presented to students during the high school interview.

Lee's answers, like Pat's, illustrated the challenges of assessment. Lee would give correct multiple choice answers for most questions about thermal equilibrium but lacked a mechanism to explain the phenomena. At the beginning of the interview, Lee and Pat gave similar answers to questions about heat flow. After reflecting, Lee would give confusing, contradictory answers involving absorption, heat flow, and temperature flow, whereas Pat would give more coherent answers. Moreover, only careful analysis of Lee's responses would reveal that Lee had begun to engage in scientific reasoning that, with nurturing, might converge on more normative and robust understanding.

Which is better for a test: Lee's tenth-grade disposition to report a valid observation and say "I don't know" instead of giving an explanation, or Lee's twelfth-grade compelling, revealing account of possible explanations for the cooling of pottery and metal platters? Many scoring rubrics would reward the tenth-grade response more than the twelfth-grade response. Yet the twelfth-grade response was the first evidence that Lee could make rich connections and reach robust conclusions.

In summary, in twelfth grade, Lee made more connections than in eighth grade. At times, Lee added ideas about absorption, distinguished heat from air, and distinguished conductors from insulators on the basis of rate of heat transfer. Lee used heat and temperature interchangeably and described both heat and cold being transferred. Compared with eighth grade, Lee pushed ideas much further. Lee used ideas from eighth grade, including thermal equilibrium, metal as a conductor, and wood or paper as insulators, to sort out new ideas. Lee could articulate a sophisticated conundrum when describing how fast a metal and pottery platter would cool. Once Lee attempted to connect ideas, the CLP experiments and observations helped, and Lee made substantial progress in twelfth grade. Lee ended up with many unresolved ideas, but Lee's newfound confidence and autonomous reasoning boded well for the future.

Light

In tenth grade, Lee mostly said "I don't know" when asked about light. Lee offered several ideas about why it is easier to see white than black at night, saying white "shows up, it's brighter, it glows," and "it's easier to see."

In twelfth grade, Lee drew on the results from the tenth-grade reflection activity. For the reflection question (Fig. 7.5), Lee said that the white "would be good for lighting up his body," that the black would not "light him up at all," and that the mirror "would light up his face more than his body."

Lee offered several ideas about how sunglasses work including the explanations that they "darken" because the "shade of the lens is darker," and that they would be "blocking" the light.

When asked how light works, Lee gave a reasonably sophisticated answer, saying light comes "like from the sun" and is "just reflecting off of objects." Lee said that objects can be seen when "light goes into your eyes."

When asked to explain how far light goes, Lee asserted in one answer that light goes as far as you can see it. In another answer, Lee distinguished detection from light propagation. These answers were not resolved.

Overall, Lee made substantial progress in generating potential explanations for light between tenth and twelfth grades. Lee, however, did not seek connections or distinguish situations.

SASHA IN HIGH SCHOOL

Sasha had resisted explanations in eighth grade. Although this pattern seemed well established, it conflicted with Sasha's desire to succeed in school, as chapter 6 clarifies.

In tenth grade, Sasha attempted to recall CLP class results and regularly reported "I don't remember." As in eighth grade, Sasha resisted giving explanations and attempted to convince the interviewer to answer the questions by constantly asking for feedback.

After Biology: Tenth Grade

In discussing heat and thermal equilibrium in tenth grade, Sasha seemed to isolate each question, instead of seeking a coherent set of explanations. Therefore, responding to questions on heat, Sasha said that heating water is "taking the cold out of it." When describing large and small milk shakes, Sasha said, "Twice as big would have more heat energy," and on the basis of experience with milk shakes, "The bigger one is going to stay cold longer, right?"

Sasha gave a set of answers that did not connect to each other, which is consistent with memorizing ideas in eighth grade. When asked to clarify the distinction between heat and temperature, Sasha combined uncertainty with incoherence and said "I don't know." When probed, Sasha distinguished between heat and cold energy. At times, Sasha described heat as actively removing cold, and asserted that a bigger object means more heat or temperature.

In these answers, Sasha posited both heat energy and cold energy, making coherence difficult. For example, when a Coke heated up, Sasha said, "The cold is leaving." In discussing what happens when someone holds a metal nail on an ice cube, Sasha described two processes, one for heat and another for cold: "The heat from your hand will go into the nail and then the nail will heat up and melt the ice. The cold is coming out of the ice. Eventually it's going to get your hand cold, so it won't work for that long. So it'll start melting the ice faster at first, and then as your hand gets colder then it will slow down. Does that make any sense?" Sasha seemed aware that these answers lacked coherence and hoped the interviewer would help.

When the interviewer probed, Sasha kept recalling snippets from prior discussions. For example, Sasha reflected on the temperature: "Why does your hand get colder? Because the cold from the ice is going out and into the air, is it going to go through the nail? A little bit, it will, yeah, because, yeah, a little bit it will but also, so the nail is going to be kind of in between temperatures."

In discussing thermal equilibrium, Sasha followed the same pattern, attempting to recall phases from class, trying out descriptive ideas, and seeking explanations from the interviewer. First, discussing metal and wood strips in a hot car trunk, Sasha said, "The metal one is going to be a lot hotter than the wooden one, because the metal conducts the heat more." Then, when probed, Sasha recalled another answer: "I think the metal, no they have to be the same temperature. It's just that you can't feel it, or something, I don't know." When asked to distinguish metal and wood, Sasha connected to conduction of electricity saying, "The metal one, uhm, this is the one that I didn't know. If you touch an electric outlet with a metal something so you're going to get shocked, and if you touch it with wood then you won't. Metal conducts a lot better than wood does."

Sasha recalled several alternative models for heat and temperature, inferred additional answers from the interviewers' comments, and focused on interacting with the interviewer rather than making sense of the answers. Sasha managed to motivate the interviewer to provide some feedback. The interviewer recounted pragmatic scientific principles from CLP and encouraged Sasha to reflect on the CLP experience. Sasha paid attention. Sasha seemed pleased to have convinced the interviewer to "bend" the rules and provide some feedback.

By tenth grade Sasha's memorization model had broken down. It never had worked very well in CLP because Sasha had memorized examples rather than explanations. As Sasha predicted, memorizing was not sufficient for responding to tenth-grade questions. However, Sasha's excellent social skills motivated the interviewer to help, and Sasha could connect diverse recollections.

At the tenth-grade interview Sasha followed the eighth-grade pattern, but also got the interviewer to recount CLP principles. In twelfth grade, Sasha made many more connections and displayed a reasoning process not apparent earlier. Sasha applied principles from CLP for the first time in twelfth grade and gave much more coherent explanations for many thermal events.

After Chemistry: Twelfth Grade

In the twelfth-grade interview, Sasha incorporated the equilibrium and system concepts from chemistry. Sasha also specifically explained that the information provided by the tenth-grade interviewer had led to reflection on CLP experiences. This is consistent with Sasha's earlier recall of information attributed to teachers in third or fifth grade when responding to eighth-grade questions. It should be recalled that during eighth grade, Sasha had looked for correct predictions, but had resisted learning explanations, even asserting that it was not necessary to learn why things happen. As a result, Sasha had not made connections among eighth-grade ideas and could not apply them in more situations in tenth grade.

In twelfth grade, discussing thermal equilibrium, Sasha recalled and applied the concept consistently. In addition, Sasha connected thermal equilibrium to the systems equilibrium concepts from chemistry. For example Sasha said that a conductor "helps to get the whole system at equilibrium."

These ideas permitted Sasha to make connections that ultimately resulted in distinguishing heat energy and temperature. Sasha displayed a new confidence and disposition to make connections in twelfth grade.

For the ice cube question, (see Fig. 7.3), Sasha explained that big and small ice cubes would melt at the same rate, but that the small one would melt first saying, "Just because it's smaller. They would probably melt at the same rate maybe, but because there's less of it, it would go first." When asked to distinguish heat energy and temperature, Sasha said cold things have heat energy: "Yeah, they do, I think the larger one would. There's one thing I'm not really sure about is heat energy. I think the larger one would probably have more heat energy. Just because it's bigger, I guess they would stay cold longer. I don't even know hardly what heat energy is. Is heat energy the same as temperature? I don't think so. I think heat energy has something to do with ... temperature is how much heat it has. I don't know!"

When asked to explain what happens for both ice cubes to get from 0° to -40°, Sasha made connections to distinguish between heat energy and temperature: "The heat that they had in them, even though they're cold they have heat in them, and the heat that's in them would have to leave and go out of them for them to get down to minus 40. So that would probably be heat energy, right? Heat energy is probably the amount of heat they still have in them, while temperature is just. Temperature and heat energy are different. I can't ... I don't know. Because there's more of it to get down to minus 40, so it has more heat energy in it probably, and so more of that has to leave, or has to get out of it for it to get down to minus 40." These chains of reasoning made Sasha's process of knowledge integration visible, and represented a substantial change in disposition toward thinking about science.

In twelfth grade, Sasha used the concepts of insulation and conduction to explain why objects at thermal equilibrium feel differently, a connection missing in tenth grade. For objects in an oven, Sasha said, "Back to the conductors, wood is not a very good conductor, and when you touch wood, the heat from it doesn't go into your skin as much as in metal which would go into your skin and burn you." For objects at room temperature, Sasha gave the same answer, not connecting to the relative difference in temperature between one's hand and the objects. Sasha said, "The wooden table and Styrofoam would probably not feel very warm. Cooler than say, the metal plate, or uhm, the liquid or whatever that is, ... Hot chocolate and Coke and the apple would probably feel warmer."

But for the question about using a snow shovel, Sasha made the connection between the flow of heat from the shovel to the air (see Fig. 7.4). Sasha said, "The heat would be going out of it in that situation but let me see.... The bottom end would get colder faster, I don't know." Sasha went on to consider the flow from one's hand to the shovel: "Oh! The heat from your body is probably going into the shovel a little. I didn't think of that. I don't think it would be enough though. I think right under your hand it would stay warm. But if you moved your hand it would ... I don't know. After a while of doing that, you know, with your hand in the same spot, it probably would not feel cold to your hand."

The interviewer asked about shoveling for an hour. Sasha said, "Probably wouldn't feel cold even then right where your hand was because the more you're shoveling, the warmer your body's going to get. Right under your hand I think it would stay, not warm, but it wouldn't get cold I guess you could say." Sasha buttressed this response with recall of a principle from the prior interview and CLP saying, "This is another thing I remember. I don't think that ... no, the cold doesn't move. It's just the movement of heat."

As in eighth grade, here Sasha preferred to report on recollections instead of making connections. At times Sasha reported conflicting ideas without seeking to resolve them. However, in several instances such as distinguishing between heat and temperature, Sasha sorted out ideas and reached new conclusions.

For example, in discussing the properties of ceramic tile, Sasha employed a knowledge integration approach saying, "It would probably be on the insulator side when you feel, when you're standing on a floor tile or whatever, it feels cold usually and so ... I think it might be similar to brick or something like that where it wouldn't let heat pass through." To elaborate, Sasha said, "I'm relating it more to bricks where it would keep the heat in or keep the cold out. In some ways it seems like it could be similar to metal where it could get really hot like that, and that's not at all like wood and Styrofoam and stuff." Later, in distinguishing a silver and pottery platter Sasha noted the need for consistency saying, "Pottery is more of an insulator. The silver's a far better conductor than the pottery, and so heat would go out of it quicker."

In all of these responses Sasha relied solely on heat energy and viewed heat as "going," "traveling," or "moving." Sasha in twelfth grade also posited differential rates of heat flow to distinguish materials. Sasha often mentioned the constraint that "only heat flows," but did not always consider which direction heat would flow. For example, when describing use of a snow shovel to shovel snow, Sasha continued to give some inconsistent responses. Sasha preferred to predict the results and either knew the reason or expressed uncertainty.

When confronted with apparent inconsistencies in twelfth grade, Sasha sometimes tried to sort out ideas, sometimes tried to motivate the interviewers to provide the answer, and sometimes said "I don't know." Compared with responses in the eighth and tenth grades, Sasha engaged in more knowledge integration.

Did CLP contribute to Sasha's success in twelfth grade? Sasha definitely used information distinguishing heat and temperature from the tenth-grade interview, in which the interviewer had "bent" the rules to provide some feedback. Sasha also reported specific results from eighth grade about which materials conduct well and about thermal equilibrium. Moreover, Sasha reinterpreted ideas about relative rates of heat flow from eighth grade, using the constraint that only heat flows, established in tenth grade.

As recounted in chapter 6, Sasha reported that high school chemistry catalyzed an interest in science. This new interest seemed to dispose Sasha toward making connections and giving explanations. During twelfth grade Sasha no longer asserted that explanations are unnecessary and even gave explanations at times. This combination of a firm foundation from CLP and a propensity to make connections from chemistry resulted in more knowledge integration. This qualitative change in behavior in twelfth grade was consistent with Sasha's reflections on science learning reported in chapter 6. Sasha not only started to make more connections, but also reported satisfaction when ideas fit together.

Light

In responding to tenth-grade questions about light, Sasha introduced the idea of "light rays bouncing off the ceiling" and "sun reflecting off sunglasses." When asked why white is easier to see than black at night, Sasha displayed the propensity to memorize and recall information, saying, "Because I don't know why it's easier: Oh, because the black doesn't; Oh, the light doesn't bounce off the black as well. Then you get hotter. I remember this from third grade. The darker colors conduct light or heat, or something more. I remember now. We said that light would bounce off of the white T-shirt, and it would make it easier to see." As in eighth grade, Sasha relied on an excellent memory to respond to these questions.

In twelfth grade, Sasha recalled results from the tenth-grade light activity and looked for connections among ideas. Sasha distinguished absorption and reflection and, when prompted, recalled experiences with walls and mirrors in response to the question asking for a comparison of a black, white, or mirrored panel (see Fig. 7.5) "It wouldn't be the black for either of them. The black absorbs light, and the white it would reflect off of the mirror.... In some ways it probably absorbs the light a little bit. For his whole body I would say the white and I'm not sure how much of a difference just his face is. What would it look like if the light came over from the flashlight to the mirror. I'm not really sure about. It would probably, like it opens up a little bit. I still think the white would probably be better for even just his face. Actually, the mirror would probably be better. The white would reflect it in all different directions, and the mirror would probably be more of a straight shot for just his face. Because.... [Can you draw it?] Well, with the mirror it would be more of a ... that kind of a thing you know ... just his face. But with the white, it would be reflecting light every which way." Sasha elaborated when prompted by the interviewer, looked for connections to experiences with mirrors, and asked for tools to draw the relationship, all signs of knowledge integration.

To explain the role of sunglasses, Sasha generated several alternatives from class and other experiences. Sasha said that they "shade" your eyes and also that "sunglasses absorb the light so it doesn't go into your eyes. Sunglasses filter out certain kinds—not certain kinds of

light, not even certain colors, but it is like different things that it ...
They filter out the harmful stuff is all I know." Sasha followed the pattern of giving several answers and hoping the interviewer would help
sort them out. When the interviewer didn't cooperate, Sasha generated
more possibilities.

Sasha followed a similar pattern to explain how far light goes. Sasha
distinguished detection of light from how far it travels saying that in
the daytime, light goes just as far. Sasha elaborated, "But you wouldn't
be able to tell that it was going that far. The light still travels the same
distance." Sasha distinguished a candle from a flashlight, asserting
that "more" light will go further. "Probably, because with a flashlight
you can ... all the light is directed towards one.... I mean it's all going in
the same direction instead of spreading out, and it would probably go
further because it's focused more on one direction."

As a stunning indication of both knowledge integration and a new
propensity toward autonomy, Sasha spontaneously returned to an earlier question in the twelfth-grade interview. At the end of the
twelfth-grade interview (that included doing an activity about How Far
Does Light Go? with a partner), Sasha spontaneously elaborated about
How Far Does Light Go? and also complained about the partner: "We
both kind of knew that, I mean, we wanted to believe that light goes on
forever, but then there were things like, how can it? If it gets down to
one proton or one atom or whatever it is, then it reached a certain point
and it can't get any smaller. Then there's the concept of even if you
can't see it like there, but we wanted to go through and see the examples. We only got through like the first three and a half or whatever."

The interviewer asked whether there was enough time. Sasha complained, "We would have, had we not been discussing every little detail." Sasha seemed excited about making the connection between the
How Far Does Light Go? question and a microscopic model of light. We
saw here for the first time the sort of reasoning that had led to the connections in chemistry described in chapter 6.

Sasha took advantage of the social context to make sense of science
in a way that many classes and most assessments fail to support. Sasha
wanted more opportunities to discuss science, looked for elaboration
and answers from the interviewer, and found working with a partner
stimulating as well as frustrating. Social interactions contributed to
Sasha's knowledge integration by supplying links and information, but
also by motivating Sasha to make autonomous connections.

Typical individual assessments would not have prompted Sasha to
make the connections displayed in twelfth grade. The CLP interview, in
contrast, clearly helped Sasha to demonstrate a disposition to learn
and to integrate ideas.

CHRIS: HIGH SCHOOL

How did CLP contribute to Chris's learning in high school? Chris asserted that CLP ideas were never revisited in later science classes, saying, "Biology doesn't deal with that whatsoever," and "In chemistry ... we didn't talk about the way it actually happened ... just how it affects systems ... like if you add heat to a system which way the reaction will go."

During these interviews, Chris struggled to connect the images of heat from CLP to later science experiences, talking about heat as "a force" and saying that objects "limit heat" or "give up heat" when placed in a cooler environment. Chris expressed the heat flow idea of CLP as "heat goes." And Chris remained cautious.

After Biology: Tenth Grade

At the beginning of the tenth grade interview Chris, discussing insulators and conductors, generated both a rate of heat flow and a barrier model. Chris said, "Heat from outside is gonna come in." [An insulator] "keeps the heat energy in" (or out depending on relative temperatures). Comparing conductors with insulators Chris said, "Heat can go faster ... more in and out ... faster." Later discussing thermal equilibrium, Chris attributed an active role to heat saying that metal at room temperature feels colder than wood because it's "taking the heat from your finger" faster than "with the wood."

As the questions continued, Chris started to autonomously connect ideas and to promote the heat flow model over both the barrier model and the active role of heat model. Chris said, for example, that Styrofoam "does keep what's in there in. But there's not much in there. It doesn't conduct anything. Well it does, but not as fast."

Chris held a robust view of thermal equilibrium and connected the normative model with insulation and conduction. Comparing the way wood and metal feel Chris said, "Probably it's not that cold. [Wood] doesn't feel cold. Cause it's not conducting the heat from your fingers. Well, it's doing it, but not doing it as fast."

These ideas form a part of Chris's science knowledge that no longer is closely tied to eighth grade. When asked where this information was learned, Chris said, "I don't remember. I think I learned it in Mr. K's class."

After Chemistry: Twelfth Grade

In the twelfth-grade interview, Chris repeated this process, generating many models, using vocabulary loosely and eventually connecting the most promising ideas. In twelfth grade Chris again considered a barrier model when talking about Styrofoam, saying that Styrofoam "insulates the temperature of the can of Coke, or it doesn't let heat go through." It should be noted that Chris also spoke of "temperature" when the normative response would be "heat." Soon, however, Chris discussed several alternatives, and at the same time sorted out these ideas, saying, "I think of wool as making something hot. But then if wool is an insulator and it really just keeps your body at the same temperature rather than heating you up, then it might just keep it cold, but that not really like.... I see it two different ways. That's what I think, you know when I think of wool ... wear it in the winter to keep yourself warm.... If I think of it another way, it's keeping you warm. It's not making you any hotter than you were. So, in that way I would think it would keep the soda the same temperature as it was."

Chris connected ideas more richly in twelfth grade compared with eighth grade. Chris made connections between heat, temperature, thermal equilibrium, surface area, direction of heat flow, rate of heat flow, and aspects of proportional reasoning when explaining what happens to a large and small ice cube placed on a counter: "Well, temperature is more like a measurement. I mean heat is a thing, like a, like a force or something, I don't know, and heat makes something the temperature that it is. The smaller one is going to melt faster, or not faster, but it would disappear first 'cause there was less to melt. The heat from outside is warming it up, the surface of it, and then eventually it melts all the way. I don't think it would just uhm, well, it might go faster just because there's less surface area for the heat to get to. The smaller one would be gone first, or be more melted, just because there's not as much to melt."

In twelfth grade Chris used CLP ideas confidently and carefully to distinguish speculation from experimental evidence. Asked to place objects on a continuum from best to worst insulator, Chris first ordered objects studied in CLP, saying choices are based on "what I remember from class," and, "what I've touched maybe, or what I've experienced." To place a new item, ceramic tile, Chris first asserted that it probably didn't conduct saying, "I think of ceramic floor tile and I don't think it conducts very much either, so I don't know where I'd put it. I mean, I'd probably put it closer to the Styrofoam."

The interviewer introduced a conundrum, pointing out that metal and ceramic tile both feel cold to the touch at room temperature: "Have you ever stepped on ceramic tile barefooted? It's usually cold. It always feels cold. It never feels warm to me." Chris used this information cautiously saying, "Based on this, I would say that it's a good conductor, but just 'cause I feel the metal is cool and because the ceramic floor tile is cool."

Later, when ceramic platters came up, Chris distinguished metal from ceramic and again asserted that more information would help: "I don't know. Ceramic tiles are a bit, you know, I don't have much experience with them besides stepping on them. I would think that the silver, I think they'd both be the same temperature, but I don't think they'd feel the same though. Because silver is a metal it would feel hotter." Chris treated the information supplied by the interviewer with respect, but, as in eighth grade, waited for more evidence before reaching a conclusion.

In discussing thermal equilibrium in twelfth grade, Chris connected the system idea from Chemistry, explaining what happens when a muffin is removed from a hot oven: "The heat was going out of the muffin into the environment, and I don't think the heat would be significant enough to change the temperature of the environment."

By the end of the twelfth-grade interview, Chris connected coherent ideas, used the term "heat" accurately, and converged on normative views. Chris discussed rate of heat flow rather than a barrier model, describing heat as "going" faster or slower instead of describing objects as "taking" heat. For example, in contrasting a metal and wood handle for a snow shovel, Chris said, "You're warmer than the handle, and so the heat from your hand would go to the shovel and you would feel how cold it was, whereas the wooden handle, that conducts less than the metal, so it wouldn't go as much. The heat is not going from your hand to the wood as much."

These excerpts show how Chris, when revisiting CLP questions in twelfth grade, generated multiple ideas for heat and temperature situations, kept considering alternatives, and looked for valid evidence to reach conclusions. Ultimately Chris autonomously reintegrated CLP ideas to weave a well-connected argument, promoting rate of heat flow notions over barrier models or absorption models and relying on known insulators and conductors to anchor interpretations of novel materials. Chris's tendency to wait for class principles in eighth grade showed up in twelfth grade as a disposition to distinguish observation from experimental results and to reflect carefully on new situations.

Light

In responding to questions about light, Chris followed the pattern of generating multiple ideas, looking for connections, and distinguishing observations from experimental results. Once more, Chris illustrated this propensity for autonomous reasoning.

The power is out in your home, and you are looking for a book to read with a flashlight.

a. What must happen for you to see the book?

b. Explain everything that happens that allows (or does not allow) you to see the book.

c. Explain what you see when you flash the light at the ceiling.

FIG. 7.7   An item used in 8th, 10th, and 12th grades to interview students about their understanding of light and the role of eyes in seeing.

In tenth grade before instruction, Chris drew on careful observation to respond to the flashlight question in Fig. 7.7. Chris reported experience with flashlights: "I don't know. I found that if you put the flashlight up, you see more in the room than if you hold it down on the ground." Chris described how light illuminates a book: "Well, it wouldn't [need to] be on the book. It would just light areas near the book, but you can just see 'cause it's, the whole thing, is lighter."

Chris reported that sunglasses work "because sunglasses are shielding you from the brightness.... It's not blocking it. It's just tinting it." Chris asserted that objects need to be in your field of vision and have light on them to be seen. For example, Chris said that you could see a car parked on a dark street "if any light reached the car." Interestingly, before instruction Chris did not distinguish light reflection from light absorption.

In twelfth grade Chris reported no memory of the light activities from tenth grade, but did distinguish absorption from reflection. When asked to consider the difference between light reflecting off a wall and off a mirror, Chris said that white reflects and black absorbs. For the mirror, Chris could not offer an explanation.

Later in the interview, Chris asked the interviewer to return to the question saying, "I thought about it." Chris now described several relevant experiences: "When I think of the bathroom and you shine a flashlight in the mirror, there's like a little pattern or something, where you shine it and it doesn't reflect much ... but then there are certain glass type ... that have that mirror, and they can blind you." Then Chris related these experiences to the question the interviewer asked earlier: "You can reflect it so that the light is on the person ... like at a concert or something, you see where the sun is hitting someone with glasses." These targeted examples clearly answered the light question and also revealed that Chris autonomously reflected on novel questions and relied on personal experience.

Between the tenth- and twelfth-grade interviews, Chris had learned some principles about reflection and absorption and used these to sort out answers to the light questions. For the light topic, Chris followed the same pattern of seeking principles, clear-cut examples, and connections to answer the questions. This approach allowed Chris to give more and more sophisticated answers both from one interview to the next and also within an interview. Chris looked for principles when connecting ideas and delayed reaching conclusions until principles became available. Chris expected science classes to provide the principles but, when pushed, would also generate principles from compelling evidence and incorporate sound examples.

The CLP curriculum had provided the principles and coherent experiments that helped Chris reach conclusions. At each interview Chris recreated valid, robust explanations, but not before also considering colloquial terms and incomplete observations.

Chris followed an established, effective reasoning process that had started in eighth grade. In eighth grade Chris had resisted speculating and waited for answers. In twelfth grade, Chris combined both principles and compelling experiences. This process worked well for the light topic.

Chris was the sort of student who will succeed on most forms of assessment. Chris liked principles that often form the basis for science tests, be they multiple choice, essay, or short answer. Chris used examples but preferred principles. When confronted with complex examples, Chris preferred to get more information. Assessments relying substantially on complex, ambiguous problems often give an advantage to students such as Pat. However, Chris will give answers that are solid and uncontroversial.

Chris followed a coherent path to knowledge integration, incorporating science content into coherent understanding, often not distinguishing specific ideas. Furthermore, Chris persisted in sorting out ideas until settling on a coherent answer. Chris often kept reasoning until all available evidence supported an answer or, as illustrated for light, returned to the topic with more ideas until a coherent response emerged. Chris focused on the main issue in a question and could neglect ideas in a question when reaching coherence.

REFLECTIONS

Lee, Pat, Sasha, and Chris completed the twelfth-grade interviews with more understanding of CLP ideas than they had at the end of eighth grade. They each drew on a different set of CLP learning partners and beliefs about learning as described in chapter 6. The CLP curriculum had served as a firm foundation for these students. The others we studied in high school had similar trajectories. (Fig. 7.8). This progress and more sophisticated under- standing in high school stands in contrast to most studies, in which students forget what they learned in earlier classes.

Pat drew extensively on the heat flow model, and also exemplified the CLP ideal of continuing to connect more ideas autonomously. Pat in

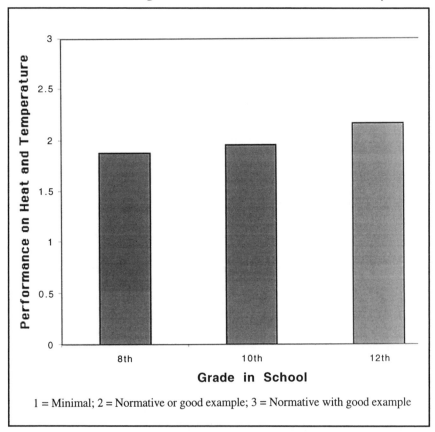

1 = Minimal; 2 = Normative or good example; 3 = Normative with good example

FIG. 7.8 Progress from middle school to high school. Students who took the Computer as Learning Partner curriculum in the eighth grade made gains in high school.

high school still tended to prefer adding new ideas rather than reaching abstract views, and this stood in the way of success in chemistry. It did fit well with Pat's interest in biology and medicine, in which analyzing new cases is central to effective practice.

Lee seemed rather lost at the tenth-grade interview, primarily repeating fragments recalled from eighth grade. In the twelfth-grade interview, Lee tried to make connections for the first time. Lee displayed a new-found confidence in reasoning when reflecting on the process of thinking about science. Lee, at the twelfth-grade interview, offered the first evidence of ability to reason autonomously. In this effort, Lee drew on some ideas such as heat absorption that interfere with reasoning, but also used some experimental evidence from eighth grade to distinguish heat and temperature.

Sasha continued to resist giving explanations in tenth grade but clearly recognized that the interviewer wanted them. As in eighth grade, Sasha tried to use the social context to convince the interviewer not only to ask, but also answer the questions. In twelfth grade the ideas provided by the tenth-grade interviewer combined with insights from chemistry allowed Sasha to craft more sophisticated answers. Sasha found chemistry easy and interesting, using successful approaches from learning mathematics to deal with many of the problems. Sasha's career plans in engineering were consistent with this success.

Chris in high school continued to seek and use principles and to apply them carefully to more problems. Chris could identify connections between CLP and chemistry at the molecular level, demonstrating that the heat flow model can connect to molecular kinetic theory. Chris's autonomous approach to learning succeeded for both CLP and chemistry. Chris planned, like Pat, to study medicine, in which this approach also had promise.

All four students engaged in knowledge integration about both heat and light, although only Chris had endorsed this approach in eighth grade. All these students balanced memorization and understanding by twelfth grade. Memorizing ability had determined quite different paths. Sasha's confidence and ability in memorizing interfered with understanding. Lee's false confidence in memorizing eventually gave way to alternative learning activities. Both Pat and Chris used a mix of memorizing and understanding. Pat's eagerness to understand each detail often obscured the big picture, Chris's reliance on the big picture sometimes suppressed useful details.

Pat, Lee, Chris, and Sasha all exclaimed, "I don't know" at times, but they meant different things. Pat said "I don't know" when unable to reconcile a set of examples including personal experiences. Lee initially said, "I don't know" when unwilling to make connections, and later to indicate confusion. Chris said, "I don't know" as a prelude to neglecting an idea that did not connect to the others. Sasha initially used "I don't know" when asked to explain, and to encourage others to explain. Later, Sasha continued to use "I don't know" to elicit feedback. The CLP approach makes students uncertain. Generally, as these interviews show, this uncertainty motivates a healthy effort at knowledge integration.

These students relied on diverse learning partners and found different cases pivotal. Lee eventually found the "feel" of metal in hot and cold surroundings pivotal for abandoning the distinction between heating and cooling. Lee began to understand the notion of temperature relative to one's body.

For Pat, the relative rate of heat flow had played a pivotal role in eighth grade. In high school, the idea that holes can trap air permitted Pat to integrate a complex set of observations.

Sasha dramatically illustrated the impact of understanding temperature relative to one's body temperature. This had occurred in eighth grade when Sasha explained objects at room temperature and in an oven, but really connected to complex situations in the twelfth-grade interview, in which Sasha suddenly generated a long set of connections to explain shoveling snow.

Chris found the first CLP activity, probing your surroundings, pivotal for understanding thermal equilibrium and regularly built on the distinctions between insulation, conduction, and thermal equilibrium. For Chris, the HeatBars visualization captured complex ideas about relative rates of heat flow that eventually supported connections to molecular kinetic theory. Chris's comment that HeatBars "draws a picture in your mind instead of having all those words" captured the value of visualizations as learning partners.

In conclusion, these high school interviews illustrated how CLP had formed a firm foundation for science learners. All the students we followed not only had improved their understanding of the scientific topics, but also persisted in their plans to study science. These students are typical of CLP students in that they both build on their ideas about science and expand their scientific interests.

ASK MR. K

What do students visiting from high school say about CLP?

Many students come back to visit while they are in high school.

They remember CLP as a fun class. They want answers to the scientific reasoning activity with the black box. I used to tell kids that I would tell them what was in the box only when they were high school seniors. They had to guess how the box was arranged, make predictions, and test them out with the box by shaking it. In fact, some students did come back and ask me. Kids stayed curious!

Kids who returned to the class remembered the "Cokes and potatoes" lab and joked about wrapping foil or wool around a soda. They really enjoyed that lab because it tied to their everyday experiences and made science more relevant to them.

I remember there were at least two of my eighth graders who became students at the University of California at Berkeley and met one of our research partners. One student said that many of the concepts he was learning in first year physics he had already learned in eighth grade! Another student remembered the computers and measuring with probes as being the most fun.

How do you deal with kids who have trouble with autonomous work?

I recognize that there will be diverse learners, failures, and difficult cases. As a teacher, I learn from those failures. Oftentimes, students have difficult home situations too that interfere with being motivated to learn or working with others. Many kids do have the ability but are stubborn. Sometimes I get surprised by pairing students together. Maybe I think they wouldn't get any work done, but they learn to not rely on each other and become more independent in carrying out a lab. As teachers, we need to keep high expectations of kids and guard against labeling them.

How can the CLP approach help design instruction for light?

With light, the models that build on student ideas are things such as the conservation of energy or a light-source transmission model. Thinking about light as spreading out until absorbed connects to personal experience. I worked with CLP to create principles for light.

POINTS TO PONDER

- Predict the patterns of knowledge integration for several students you have taught. Compare your predictions with the patterns of learning described in this chapter.
- Describe a student you know whose learning trajectory surprised you. Explain why students might use new learning patterns.
- Ask a student to describe the learning partners they find most useful. Analyze whether these learning partners contribute to knowledge integration.
- Interview a student about his or her career plans. Compare the responses with those given by students in the chapter.
- In Appendix A, add annotations to the 10th and 12th grade interviews for Pat following the patterns from interview 1-5.
- Discuss how students use learning partners. Analyze the learning partners in courses you have taught.
- Reflect on the comments of the current and returning students at the beginning and end of the CLP film. Connect these views to the progress of Pat, Sasha, Lee, and Chris.

RELATED READINGS

Bruer, J. T. (1993). *Schools for thought: A science of learning in the classroom.* Cambridge, MA: MIT Press.

Driver, R. (1983). *The pupil as scientist?* London, England: Open University Press.

Schwab, J. J. (1962). *The teaching of science. Elements in a strategy for teaching science in the elementary school.* Cambridge: Harvard University Press.

Wiser, M., & Carey, S. (1983). When heat and temperature were one. In D. Gentner & A. L. Stevens (Ed.), *Mental models* (pp. 267–298). Hillsdale, NJ: Lawrence Erlbaum Associates.

New Design Partnerships

To create a designed rather than a decreed curriculum, we need new design partnerships. These partnerships can create innovative instruction, conduct design studies, and report their findings so others benefit. In this section we synthesize the CLP experience to guide technology planning and professional development planning and describe new partnerships that readers can join.

We provide pragmatic pedagogical principles to help partnerships become learning communities. We illustrate planning for technology and for professional development, with examples from the CLP sound unit and the CLP light unit.

Chapters 8 and 9 organize our pragmatic pedagogical principles around technology planning and professional development as follows:

Chapter 8: Planning for Technology in Education

Helping individuals, schools, and policy makers can create technology plans that support innovation. This involves

- planning for fluency in information technology
- collaboratively investigating alternatives and learning from experience

- participating in a community of learners.

Chapter 9: Partnerships for Professional Development

Helping teachers, administrators, policy makers, and technology experts can create professional development programs to promote knowledge integration. This involves

- using technology as a teaching partner
- using scaffolded knowledge integration as a partner for curriculum innovation
- learning from other partnerships and from experts in related fields
- creating new professional development partners.

We describe how the CLP experience led to new partnerships that readers may want to join. The Knowledge Integration Environment (KIE) project, involving many of the same people who participated in the CLP partnership uses Internet resources to promote knowledge integration. The Web-Based Integrated Science Environment (WISE) project responds to calls for integrated science. The Science Controversies On-line: Partnerships for Education (SCOPE) project hopes to improve student understanding of the nature of scientific advance by connecting scientists researching current controversies with students in schools around the world.

We hope that our CLP experience will motivate readers to form partnerships in their local areas. We also hope that partnership activities will make sense for individual teachers, administrators, and policy makers interested in improving their practice. Individuals might want to join online partnerships with others who have similar interests. Our web site identifies current opportunities.

Planning for Technology
in Education

Can school districts, states, universities, and industry design plans for technology that support its effective use in education? How do these groups cope with the many frustrations, trade-offs, conflicting demands, sudden advances, and outrageous costs? Some advocate waiting until leaders from business, industry, government, computer science, or some other group create an ideal plan for education. We must resist these tempting invitations to give up in frustration or defer to "experts" in some other field. We all have seen well-meaning yet woefully inappropriate "solutions" for education, some even naively asserting that technology can replace teachers altogether. We need, instead, to take the planning process seriously and actively plan, analyze, and replan in partnership with leaders from relevant fields.

Does everyone need to use technology? Technology with all its frustrations plays a growing role in all our lives. Everyone complains that modern copiers shred documents; new telephones refuse customers' credit cards; computers destroy valuable files; electronic mail ruins friendships; and powerful software steals hours of time from users. Despite these and other frustrations, few would return to less technologically rich times. These same complainers can no longer imagine being productive without instant access to copy machines (remember carbon paper?), laser printers (remember teletypes?), fax machines (remember telegrams?), automated teller machines(ATMs) (remember bankers' hours?), spreadsheets (remember double-entry bookkeeping?), or even cell phones (remember being stranded on the roadside?).

We define technology planning broadly to include decisions about whether to have technology, which technology to select, how to achieve equity, and which curriculum to implement. Our CLP partnership set out to help students benefit from technology. We made curricular and logistic decisions in tandem, but often found ourselves responding to technological constraints or wondering how to deal with technological "opportunities."

PLANNING PARTNERSHIPS

Planning partnerships face a huge challenge and often get overwhelmed by economic and logistic decisions. We offer some suggestions and experiences to help partnerships create technology plans that focus on pedagogy. In the next chapter. we discuss planning for professional development.

Creating and sustaining fruitful technology planning partnerships is challenging, risky, rewarding, and frustrating, but far superior to accepting default options. On the basis of CLP experience, we recommend forming multidisciplinary planning groups representing all the major stakeholders. In schools, partnerships might include teachers, administrators, technical staff, parents, potential donors of resources, evaluators, and pedagogy researchers. We all will benefit if we motivate policymakers and the technology industry to join us in designing and regularly rethinking the roles of technology in education.

Inevitably, these groups will hold a variety of models of teaching and learning, making planning contentious and difficult. Partnership members may assert that they learned without technology, questioning the value of technology for current learners. Individuals who loved science and independently sought to learn more, may assume that all students start out as autonomous learners, like Chris, needing only access to technology to find ways to use it productively. Pedagogy researchers may emphasize idealized benefits of technology instead of considering local constraints.

In earlier chapters, we describe benefits of partnerships using our CLP project as an example. In our work, the partnership brought multiple perspectives and negotiated effective solutions as discussed in section II. For example, our technology partners advocated real-time data collection as used by experts, and the partnerships designed the Electronic Laboratory Notebook to incorporate this technology into instruction that made sense for all students. The diverse expertise in the CLP partnership also enabled us to make informed decisions about complex issues such as selecting a network provider or creating a technology budget. We kept in mind our goal of using technology to promote integrated understanding, but we also developed some more specific criteria to make decisions.

Our partnership started with a varied set of views, learned from experience, integrated new ideas, and became better at planning. Our partnership's learning followed knowledge integration processes similar to those followed by students in the CLP curriculum. In this chapter we synthesize what we learned in pragmatic pedagogical principles and provide examples to guide the learning of new design partnerships.

Individual teachers, administrators, industry representatives, parents, and others concerned about technology develop their own understanding when they participate in a planning partnership. Often individuals face obstacles to their own learning such as inadequate opportunities to learn technology, outmoded technological resources, and pressure from advocates of technology to embrace every innovation. To succeed, a planning partnership needs to help individuals learn about technology while developing a partnership perspective.

Partnerships benefit from supporting each participant as they autonomously develop their own expertise. If participants become frustrated and alienated, the whole partnership suffers. The CLP partnership nurtured new members, listened to their concerns and enabled them to become effective users of technology. Some of our best ideas came from newcomers complaining about something we thought was "straightforward."

Partnerships also, as a group, face learning challenges and need to locate and use outside experts as new technologies become available. The CLP partnership relied on a few members and several consultants to make network provider decisions. The rapidly changing costs, opportunities, and options meant we faced many frustrations and spent resources in ways that, in retrospect, were unwise. We publicized our failures in hopes of helping others.

PRAGMATIC PEDAGOGICAL PRINCIPLES FOR PLANNING

Our first pragmatic principle recommends goals for individuals and planning partnerships struggling to identify effective uses of technology, create resources for instruction with technology, and support groups designing innovative uses of technology. We recommend that groups and individuals *plan for fluency in information technology*, and offer a variety of strategies for achieving and sustaining this goal.

Our second pragmatic pedagogical principle recommends that the diverse members of a partnership *collaboratively investigate alternatives and learn from experience*. To succeed, partnerships need to listen and learn from each other, create preliminary plans, conduct design studies, and iteratively build on successes or failures.

Our third pragmatic pedagogical recommends that planning groups *become a community of learners*. We hope to engage partnerships in assessing progress, tailoring innovations to local conditions, and communicating their successes and failures to others. If we combine the insights from many classroom investigations, we can enhance understanding of technology and education and help schools make better decisions.

We hope to motivate many technology planning partnerships involving people with expertise in fields such as technology, curriculum, and computer networking. We hope this volume also will spur communities of planners that cut across district, geographical, and age lines to identify promising approaches for everyone.

Plan for fluency in information technology

We have described how CLP designed technological environments to promote lifelong science learning. We often worried that students would spend too much time learning technology or that students adept with technology would have an advantage over others. At the same time, we demonstrated that learning technology tools often amplified science learning because students could understand topics such as graphing or heat flow that traditional instruction taught less successfully. We also noted that technological enhancements offered new paths to success and enabled some previously unsuccessful science learners to learn science.

Mr. K reported that students classified as "learning disabled" achieved more in CLP than in the traditional course, in part because CLP relied less on reading and more on thinking. Learning science with technology also motivated some students to become more proficient technology users. Often these same students who were classified as having problems learning ended up being classroom technology experts.

The CLP partnership negotiated a complex role for technology in science courses. We describe this as helping students become fluent in information technology. We wanted to prepare students so they regularly could improve their understanding of technology and make the best choices for using technology in their own science learning.

Today's college graduates and tomorrow's high school graduates should be fluent in information technology. Individuals fluent in information technology can do the following:

1. ***Plan and carry out personally relevant projects using appropriate technology*** e.g., create a multimedia, interactive presentation; use real-time data collection to investigate home insulation materials; use a simulation to compare designs for a solar car.

2. ***Manage a complex task requiring trade offs and decisions about technology*** e.g. select a presentation design that works over the Web at diverse schools of business; create a personal web page to communicate a new use for real-time data collection; research best use of Internet technologies.

3. ***Cope with unintended or unanticipated consequences of using technology*** e.g. repair broken links to your personal web page; deal with questions about intellectual property; post answers to frequently asked questions; respond to inequitable access to technology.

4. ***Test technological solutions and incorporate results into the next version*** e.g., access your personal web page with a different browser and fix any problems that arise; teach a technology unit and improve software on the basis of student responses.

5. ***Debug technological problems*** e.g., fix problems with movies or animations that crash; investigate why computers fail to run or printers crash; improve response times.

6. ***Locate and use information needed to complete a technology project*** e.g., search for related uses of real-time data collection and link to your web site.

7. ***Collaborate with others to carry out a larger technology project*** e.g., help create a web page for a club or sport team; join a partnership to create a middle school curriculum using real-time data collection.

8. ***Communicate results from technology projects to diverse audiences*** e.g., create print, multimedia, and interactive reports on your project.

9. ***Plan for rapidly changing technologies*** e.g., plan to upgrade to new versions of software; research purchase decisions, deal with year 2000 problems.

10. ***Reflect on progress in learning technology and seek opportunities to keep uptodate in workplace or personal technology activities*** e.g., decide when to learn a new web design tool; assess need for a new interface for a classroom software program; evaluate strengths and opportunities.

FIG. 8.1   Ten capabilities for fluency in information technology.

Our first pragmatic pedagogical principle encourages new partnerships to negotiate a similar goal. Recently, a National Academy of Sciences committee defined fluency in information technology (FIT) as shown in Fig. 8.1. These criteria for fluency in information technology capture our goal of promoting lifelong technology learning. They align with calls to prepare middle school students who are as "comfortable with the keyboard as the chalkboard." They respond to calls for technology standards to go along with standards in mathematics, science, and history.

What does fluency mean? Just as individuals fluent in Spanish or Japanese can use the language to solve personal problems, carry out complex projects, and meet workplace requirements, so we envision that fluent users of information technology will incorporate technology into many aspects of their lives. In addition, just as fluent speakers of languages constantly add to their knowledge in areas relevant to their lives, so we envision that fluent users of information technology will continuously update the ways that they use technology to lead satisfying lives.

Fluent language users specialize. Journalists become expert in communicating to a broad audience. Biologists develop vocabulary relevant to their needs. Hobbyists from crossword puzzle enthusiasts to sports fans develop terms that others find irrelevant. Similarly, those fluent in information technology specialize in applications, tools, and skills relevant to their work, leisure, and educational needs.

Specifically, science learners fluent in information technology can use technology effectively while they carry out personal and school projects. Fluent science learners also can evaluate new technologies, select technologies that will help them succeed in science, and learn new technologies they need for their work. Ideally, science classes will introduce relevant technological resources that students can use in subsequent courses. Fluent users will be prepared to update their use of technology regularly for science activities at home, at school, and at work.

Establishing a planning process.   Partnerships of learners, administrators, parents, leaders, experts, and others can work together to ensure that technology promotes fluency in information technology. We anticipate a many-layered planning process.

To plan for a school, district, or state use of technology, partnerships need to consider the full range of courses, not just science. Ideally, a plan for technology will promote its fluent use in every course and also set students on a path toward lifelong technology use.

This goal of fluency in information technology applies to students, members of planning partnerships, all classroom teachers, and all citizens. Science students are fortunate that they start on this path early and learn gradually. Planners often need to become fluent rather quickly.

Helen Clark, a postdoctoral scholar with the CLP project, worked with a variety of school districts to establish technology plans. She started with interested teachers, helped them implement technology in their classes, then formed a school partnership to create a technology plan. Clark observed that successful educators started by learning to use technology for their own activities. In the Ask Mr. K section, Mr. K describes how he developed his own fluency with information technology by taking a programming course at the Lawrence Hall of Science when Apple II computers first appeared.

Clark worked with teachers to reflect on successes and failures and encouraged groups to identify fruitful uses of science and mathematics software. She identified four elements leading to personal fluency in information technology along with success in planning for science and mathematics instruction with technology. She called them personal, peripheral, project, and pedagogical elements of technology use.

The *personal* element of information technology use involves enhancing existing personal practices by using technology for personal activities such as designing a class newsletter. The *peripheral* element of technology use involves enhancing existing classroom practice with technology, for example, by using a web browser to get current information for a class activity such as following the progress of the Iditerod in Alaska. Peripheral use also might include participating in online discussions with other educators about using technology. The *project* element of information technology use involves designing new curriculum activities with technology and supporting students in conducting projects. Projects can involve all aspects of fluency as defined in Fig. 8.1. Students might design weather stations, model traffic flow, or create alternative goals. Teachers might design new uses for online resources such as bird migration data. Clark also identified the *pedagogical* element of technology use as efforts to incorporate technology into pedagogical philosophy and practice. Participating in a partnership such as CLP provides a community to support educators as they rethink instruction in light of technology.

Creating a successful school technology plan means negotiating among the varied views of technology held by the planners. Plans need to support development of fluency for the planners, for each course using technology, for the series of courses students might take, and for students who will need fluency in information technology in their lives. All these plans demand the same knowledge integration process we describe for learning science in previous chapters. We start by discussing how planners negotiate a view of technology in education.

Negotiating a view of fluency in information technology.

To illustrate the planning process, we discuss how partnerships can assess alternative roles for technology. We advocate using computers to promote fluency in information technology. We contrast fluency with other perspectives.

Many view computers as "productivity tools." Word processors, spreadsheets, and databases suggest the advantages of computers as tools to enhance the productivity of individuals who previously used typewriters, calculators, and double-entry bookkeeping. Some even dispute claims of productivity, pointing out that word processors help individuals generate more but not better prose, and that grammar checkers often mislead writers. From a fluency perspective, we hope students will learn to evaluate refinements of these tools and find ways to use them effectively.

Fluent users of productivity tools learn from their mistakes. For example, Linn decided to learn the "style" feature of her word processor when collaborating with Clancy. She then taught Clancy who "went wild" creating over 50 styles using computer science names such as "xq," "lp," and "xsh." Consequently, Linn had to devote more time to learning how to give styles multiple names so she would know whether "lp" referred to "left paragraph," "let's play," or "last part." Fluent users of technology make productivity decisions by analyzing both short term and long term benefits. Short-term frustrations sometimes can pay off—ultimately styles helped Linn and Clancy collaborate effectively.

Scientists often view computers as "visualization tools," which have fueled scientific advances. Supercomputers create animations, real-time displays, or simulations of phenomena such as the structure of molecules, the dynamics of severe weather, and the impact of earthquakes. These tools, like productivity tools, have advanced rapidly. Some critics argue that visualizations are no better than filmstrips. Educators often complain that expert tools primarily confuse students. Therefore, fluent users of information technology need to select tools carefully. Many prefer the weather channel to interactive computer weather visualizations. However, amateur pilots eagerly master the complexity of online weather tools.

Many view computers as "computational" devices and advocate learning computer programming. Does fluency with information technology require that all citizens learn to use the computer as a computational device? Most scientists learn a programming language (Fig. 8.2). Others argue that only certain disciplines need deal with the computational features of technology. They suggest that most citizens will remain consumers of expert computations. As shown in Fig. 8.1, boundaries between programming and writing scripts for architectural software or designing a personal home page has blurred. Fluent users will apply computational approaches to problems, but may use scripts for a spreadsheet or a web-design tool instead of a traditional programming language.

Some view computers as "electronic libraries" calling for Internet resources to replace libraries, pointing out that everything from airline schedules, sports statistics, health hints, and international maps are but a mouse-click away. Others dispute this claim, arguing that the Internet is confusing and often wrong. Fluent users of information technology need to evaluate the validity and reliability of information

---

Linn's Personal Planning

As a Stanford undergraduate I used a mainframe computer primarily for statistical analysis. I punched cards, submitted them to a Burroughs 5500 computer, and collected printouts the next day. I could not do all the analyses I wanted to conduct using existing canned programs. I already had tried other available canned programs and creative combinations of existing programs. Maybe I could learn to write my own computer programs? It might be easier than dealing with the canned programs. I already had spent hours testing and debugging the punched cards I had submitted, so writing my own programs might be just as easy.

I consulted with Dick Atkinson and Pat Suppes, faculty members who designed computer tutors. They encouraged me to learn programming, pointing out added benefits besides writing statistical programs. Deciding which computer language to learn was harder. Statisticians advocated FORTRAN, the language used to write the statistical programs I had used. Psychologists suggested that I learn LISP, a new language used in artificial intelligence. Stanford offered a new introductory programming course in ALGOL on the Burroughs 5500 machine. I sensibly selected the ALGOL course because it was available to undergraduates.

FIG. 8.2   Should I learn computer programming?

available electronically—a goal we address in the Knowledge Integration Environment (KIE) partnership.

The image of "computer as matchmaker" has charmed many writers who see computers as connecting learners to experts. Some argue that students and teachers can access scientists using electronic mail (e-mail). Others point out the advantages of chatrooms or listservs where individuals with similar hobbies share information and help each other succeed. Still others point to online tutoring for homework available from several commercial vendors.

These groups argue that social matchmaking can enhance technology use and learning. Others dispute these claims, arguing that practicing scientists simply lack the time to help every student. Even providing guidance to the 1 million teachers in the United States and more worldwide proves daunting for the university scientists or even the industry scientists.

As reported in chapter 5, having expert knowledge is only the first step. Communicating with diverse audiences is difficult. We address this challenge in our Science Controversies Online: Partnerships in Education (SCOPE) project.

The CLP project used technology as a learning partner. Many dispute this role, asserting that computers hinder instead of help learners. They point to "help" systems that offer no guidance and time wasted learning to use complicated software. Clearly, not all computer applications serve as learning partners, and not all courses help students make computers their learning partners. As we described in section II, each planning cycle required trade-offs between the time and frustration of adding a new tool and the time and frustration of dealing with outmoded technology. The challenge of designing the best uses of technology constantly faced CLP. Starting with Apple II computers, we replanned to incorporate Macintosh computers, more powerful computers, larger computer screens, more powerful software, better real-time data collection, a classroom network, color monitors, and the World Wide Web. Often we adopted technology too soon, suffering when computers crashed and students became frustrated.

The partnership often reflected on what students needed to know about technology to use computers as learning partners and to become lifelong technology users. We also worried that students would spend too much time learning "technology" and not enough time using computers as learning partners.

In the early years of the CLP project, many students came to science class with little computer experience so we sought learning partners that students could use easily. We devoted the first week of class to activities that introduced the computers. We encouraged students to teach each other and to figure out new tools themselves inasmuch as communications is an essential aspect of fluency with information technology. Today, in our partnerships, students can build on prior experience with computers in school, libraries, and homes. We spend less time introducing computers, seek to build on what students know, and pay special attention to equitable access to technology. We keep refining our technology plan to achieve fluency in information technology.

Individuals and partnerships developing fluency in information technology will explore trade-offs, get feedback from peers or local experts, and discuss options. Almost everyone has an opinion (often strongly held) about technology, and peers often have relevant experiences.

All the elements of knowledge integration discussed in section II can help planners distinguish and redesign alternatives. Planners can start with small projects and gradually scale up. Small projects may not illustrate all the features and frustrations of larger projects, but decomposing a goal into a series of steps that can be more easily accomplished is part of fluency with information technology.

Frequent reflection means less time spent going down fruitless paths. No matter how well plans are made, unanticipated benefits and consequences inevitably will arise. Nobody welcomes roadblocks and frustration, but they are realities along the path to fluency in information technology.

We found in our programming research that simply prompting students in the laboratory to explain what they were doing led many to replan and solve their problems faster. Individuals often describe themselves as "blind" to alternatives when following a plan. Partnerships benefit when they stop and review their plans. The CLP team established a regular cycle of reflecting, assessing progress, and replanning, a cycle that was repeated every semester. The schools that work us with typically establish an annual cycle.

In summary, planning for fluency in information technology requires the same knowledge integration process we described for science learning. Contrasting models such as productivity, matchmaking, or computer programming; and creating innovative solutions will substantially increase the benefits of technology for education.

Collaboratively investigate alternatives and learn from experience

Our second pragmatic principle describes collaboration of partnerships based on the CLP experience. How can policymakers, school-site administrators, informed parents, government agencies, state departments of education, textbook developers, and regulatory groups regularly collaborate? Often, policymakers hold models for fluency with information technology that differ substantially from those held by school-site educators. Diagnosing differences in models, negotiating criteria that might help distinguish among these differences, and dealing with trade-offs often can resolve policy disputes.

Technology collaborations face a vast array of value-laden decisions (Fig. 8.3). In establishing a technology plan for a school, trade-offs between costs and benefits, between reliability and leading edge applications, between open-ended and rigid uses of technology, between discovery and scaffolded investigation, between plug-and-play applications and those that require considerable user expertise, between platform-independent and specialized platform choices, between immediate costs and long-term costs, between programs focused on all students and those targeted to specific groups such as gifted, handicapped and remedial students, all play a role.

Frequently, partnerships can gather evidence instead of making premature decisions. For example, a school might reject computer maintenance contracts without consulting other school districts and later discover that repair bills combined with the costs of lost opportunities to use the computers make the contract valuable.

Partnerships may hold an array of perspectives on fluency in information technology. Individuals from business and industry may suggest a business productivity model advocating the use of business software augmented by the Internet. Teachers may dispute this model as unlikely to promote knowledge integration in science. Industry leaders may retort that workplace preparation is more valuable than understanding science. Scientists who use visualization and animation software may advocate using technology to illustrate ideas. Educators may question the cost of computer animations, arguing that filmstrips and

---

Issue: Should we place all the computers in one classroom like a computer lab, or have a single computer in each classroom?

Issue: Should we spend resources on software courses or buy software tutorials?

Issue: Should we emphasize basic technology literacy or teach computer programming, or incorporate technology in existing courses?

Issue: Should we hire one school technology coordinator or train multiple teachers to do software installations and diagnose computer malfunctions?

FIG. 8.3   Illustrative trade-offs that technology planners face when deciding where to place computers or how to spend resources.

movies are already available. Software developers may offer highly interactive science software enabled by simulated online experiments. Educators may want to assess whether software involves pressing buttons or science inquiry.

Often, partnerships can agree on a technology goal for their school, district, or class at some future date. For example, a group might agree that "all students graduating from middle school in the year 2005 will use technology for sustained complex projects in math and science." The school also might select assessments to measure goal achievement (Fig. 8.4).

Listening and learning from others.   Understanding the arguments of hostile parents, policymakers who detest technology or individuals

Computers as tools	• All students have earned a computer proficiency award for Level I Author a story with graphics using best effort keyboarding techniques • Ability to create a graphic image to communicate • Ability to organize, sort, and report data using a database software program. • All students knowledgeable of responsible uses of technology • Coordinate elementary skills with middle school and with high school expectations
Computers as resources and access to resources	• Every classroom will be equipped with at least one computer capable of acting as resource guide • Resources, and computer capable of acting as resource guide research library of more than 200 titles • All students will be able to complete a resource search using age-appropriate tools • Networked Internet access in all classrooms
Technology to support curriculum	• Support curriculum model integration of technology with instruction • All classrooms will be using such curriculum units as appropriate • There will be a mechanism for teacher exchange of ideas and materials
Computer programming and authoring	• Multiple student-authored projects using such as MSWorks and HyperStudio
Infrastructure	• Site self-sufficiency for installation, purchasing, maintenance and trouble shooting • Adequate hardware and networking.
Staff development	• All staff personally proficient in technology • All staff using technology in a curriculum where appropriate

FIG. 8.4   An example of a technology plan from middle school.

offering large technology donations will enhance the plan. Decision-making software tools and online discussion forums might be used both to consult widely and to focus discussion on planning (Fig. 8.5). Techniques such as polling and voting can ensure an open-ended, responsive planning process and foster frank, productive sharing of opinions.

It is easy to use technology to collaborate and consult others. Currently every group from genealogists to philatelists has an online community to discuss which technology tools to learn and use. The success of online health networks that often help individuals suffering from rare diseases to articulate their symptoms and evaluate alternatives attests to the value of learning from others. Science educators may benefit from comparing technology plans, critiquing each other's plans, sharing resources, or helping each other locate useful technologies. For example, we encourage individuals and groups to discuss the distinctions between "computer as productivity tool" and "computer as learning partner." Groups might report on successes with off-the-shelf software and seek help with dilemmas.

We can help each other develop criteria for planning discussions. Often, choices are obscured. For example, large numbers of individuals

Name of Approach	Description
Private opinions, summary	Ask each member to write opinions and submit them to a moderator. The moderator summarizes all the positions and presents this to the group.
Forced opinions	Each member is asked to formulate a position ahead of time before joining a discussion.
Cascading opinions	One member voices an idea. Two members are asked to build on that idea, but also suggest at least one alternative. Two more members add ideas to each individual member's ideas until a list of alternative ideas is generated.
Open forum	Each member voices opinions while being able to hear the opinions of others, adding to the discussion. A moderator encourages participation from all.
Anonymous forum	All members are anonymous and participate in an online forum moderated by a facilitator.

FIG. 8.5   Online approaches for polling group members on technology plans.

initially took programming courses that frustrated them and even turned them against technology. Currently, we encourage learners to take courses in science, art, or music and learn about relevant technology. Indeed, some experts report learning to use things such as library search tools and discovering that they wanted to learn more about technology.

Resolving complex issues.

Resolving complex issues.   Some issues continuously plague planning collaborations. For example, everyone wants equitable access to technology, but schools cannot solve this problem alone. Our computer programming research revealed the difficulties of school-based access. Frequently classrooms had eight computers for 32 students. Programming classes met 4 or 5 hours per week in 50-minute blocks, sometimes for only 8 weeks. A quick calculation revealed that individual students, even if computers were used continuously for the full class hour, would get fewer than 10 hours of access during the course. Using a home computer for a weekend would put an individual far ahead of a student using computers only in class.

Fluency in information technology requires experience interacting with the technological tools. Schools and universities have discovered that providing public access computers will never meet the demand for technology access. Rather, any effective access plan must include out-of-school access for all participants. Some students might access computers in libraries, community centers, or faith communities. Others will access them at home. Ensuring equitable access must be our highest priority. Yet, we cannot place this burden solely on schools.

Another problem that plagues planners is responding to new technologies. Although technology changes rapidly, schools may implement a computer laboratory, an Internet connection, or a software suite, and expect it to persist for many years. For example, our new KIE partnership using the Internet was invited to work in a school that wanted to study Life on Mars. Our Life on Mars unit, developed in partnership with classroom teachers and NASA scientists, was set to run for 4 to 5 school days. Then we learned that teachers could reserve the computer laboratory for only 2 days per month. We assumed that negotiation was possible. The teachers asked if they could trade 2 days in February for 2 days in March, thereby allowing 4 days in March for the Life on Mars unit. This proved impossible. The unit ran the last 2 days of February and the first 2 days of March.

Establishing goals for computer laboratories also challenges planners. Incorporating Internet resources can pit innovation against established practices. One school that joined our partnership had previously used the computer laboratory for drill typing and for computer games to "reward" students. Students and some teachers resisted adding science activities that required sustained reasoning. Major discussions centered on the role of the computer laboratory. Eventually, the group agreed to emphasize sustained reasoning and projects instead of eye–hand coordination games.

Planners also are plagued by decision timetables. Decisions about service providers, maintenance contracts, software purchases, whether to have computer labs or computers in classrooms, and whether to teach science or word processing often must be made with limited or even inadequate information. Instead of performing pilot tests and gathering information, large donations or sudden availability of funds may necessitate rapid decision making.

Donations of technology to the CLP classroom led us to experiment with group size as discussed in Chapter Four. Many schools face the difficult decision of deciding whether to accept donations of discarded equipment from industry. As the President's Committee of Advisors on Service and Technology (PCAST) concluded, these donations often "cost" more than they are worth.

Donated equipment may support only cumbersome software, require extensive maintenance, or restrict decisions about pedagogy. The same factors that motivate businesses to upgrade to more powerful computers also may determine the technology selections of schools. Donations may work for some courses yet fill the computer laboratories and preclude further innovation.

Few information technology plans anticipate the many dilemmas likely to arise. Schools wired on Netday frequently discover that the wires connect only to actual active computers 2 years later. Costs of Internet connectivity fluctuate wildly, and few find effective mechanisms for predicting future costs. Technology may not lead to the learning outcomes desired. Students may learn how to use complex technological tools but not the science, mathematics, or literature the tools were designed to teach. Furthermore, students may learn with the tools in class but fail to use them for homework.

Instead of viewing these challenges as frustrations, we encourage planners to view them as opportunities for experimentation and research. Documenting the existing and new conditions as well as their impact on all of the participants will greatly aid other groups engaged in similar planning activities.

Because technology changes rapidly, planners will face new challenges that make old mistakes obsolete. Wireless networking may replace expensive or earlier solutions. Free online resources may improve on cumbersome products, and some applications may even become easier to use. Partnerships that regularly replan to achieve the goals of fluency in information technology generally have the best plan.

Ideally, planners will design assessment methodologies that complement their plans. Given the complexity of implementing any technology plan, a variety of indicators make sense. Most schools report information about costs and benefits. Measuring the impact on the information technology fluency of teachers, administrators, and students is more challenging.

For example, most information technology plans have concrete goals of establishing equitable access to information technology. To measure the more abstract goals, such as increasing the lifelong benefits from technology, requires the design of assessments.

Assessment of fluency in information technology typically requires analyzing the projects performed by teachers, students, and others using the aspects of fluency in Fig. 8.1. As a first step, asking educators, students and even parent volunteers, initially to describe their fluency with information technology; and then chronicling change in these over time could inform the planning process. See Fig. 8.6 for ideas about measuring fluency in information technology.

In summary, technology planning brings together stakeholders with diverse needs and expectations including teachers, students, administrators, parents, librarians, industry leaders, technology experts, and business professionals. The many trade-offs in this complex situation mean that planning includes recovering from failure, dealing with unanticipated consequences, and incorporating new advances as a regular process. Educators' concerns can get lost, especially when the planners lack time and resources to investigate educational benefits. Planning that ensures the best possible outcome for students and schools typically involves researching alternatives and negotiating goals. This sort of planning requires flexibility, willingness to reconsider alternatives, skill in articulating trade-offs, and graciousness in the face of failure.

Form a community of learners

We, as a field, need ways to investigate progress and report successes and failures so others can use them. This volume is one approach. In addition, new design partnerships need ways to report their findings to others. Our third pragmatic principle says *form a community of learners* among partnerships and evaluate innovations.

Partnerships will vary in what they count as evidence demonstrating effective use of technology in educational programs. For example, some prefer standardized tests, whereas others disparage anything

School Technology Plan: Assessment	

Students are proficient in basic technology.
 	
All students by completion of grade eight can use technology as a tool to access information, analyze and solve problems, and communicate ideas.
 	
Student can create a project using at least three tools (e.g., word processing, database, spreadsheets, desktop publishing) and incorporating other technologies such as graphics and multimedia.
 	
Students can demonstrate knowledge of responsible uses of technology. Students are taught how to make appropriate, ethical uses of the technology in their daily lives.
 	
Equity is maintained. All students should have the same opportunities to succeed with these technology goals regardless of which school in the district they attend. Within schools, students should have equal access regardless of which teacher they are assigned, and wherever possible, home access should not be assumed nor required to meet these goals.
 	
Goals are accomplished within the existing curriculum activities and classroom practices.
 	
Technology is presented to children as a tool that enables them to find, access and manage information, to communicate with others and to express their creativity.
	All curriculum planning in the district considers the application of technology where appropriate to enrich students' educational experience.
	
	Some of the major areas in which technology offers promise toward better learning or higher levels of engagement include these:
	
	Simulations and visualizations
	  New software offers ways to demonstrate complex scientific phenomena that are not observable to the eye such as molecular structures or anatomy.
	
	Collaboration and networked activities
	  Students can engage as researchers and collaborators on statewide or national projects with students in other schools.
	
	Supports for project-based explorations
	  Our students frequently engage in sustained project-oriented studies. These can be published using various technology tools such as HyperStudio and the Internet, which serve as a synthesis activity for the work.
	
	Drill and practice on basic skills
	  Programs exist for both school and home use which help make repetitive drill requirements such as math facts more engaging.

FIG. 8.6 Using a variety of assessment indicators can help groups define goals and implement technology plans. For example, here are indicators drawn from a technology plan from a local K–8 school in California.

measured using a multiple-choice format. Some rely on examples of what they consider "good" or "bad." Others regard "anecdotes" as useless and distracting. To succeed, planning communities need to negotiate a shared view of assessment.

In the CLP partnership, for example, we have reflected on whether the CLP curriculum helps students on standardized tests. As discussed in conjunction with the case studies in chapter 7, multiple-choice items would not capture the ability to reason about novel problem or reconstruct understanding that Pat, Lee, and Sasha displayed in high school. These students probably would perform much like students following the traditional curriculum on multiple choice items but outperform others on items requiring knowledge integration such as short essays and larger projects.

Conducting design studies and case studies. The CLP knowledge integration perspective was established using design studies in which innovations were studied in diverse classrooms and case studies wherein trajectories of students were documented.

In the CLP curriculum we designed assessment concurrently with instruction so we could measure and evaluate our effectiveness. Our success in improving knowledge integration over eight versions of the curriculum support our approach (see chapter 2). As discussed in chapter 10, students in the traditional program made no progress on knowledge integration questions in eighth grade or high school. We found that CLP promoted knowledge integration, but multiple-choice tests cannot distinguish this form of understanding from more superficial ideas.

Many mistakes and failures in the CLP design studies had to be remedied along the way. For example, students did not engage in knowledge integration when we emphasized molecular kinetic theory. The first version of the Thermal Model Kit made sense to only a very small number of students. Our efforts to orchestrate peer interactions included many failures: The agreement bars helped some groups but hindered others. In many cases, students evaluated their own and other's work on neatness or length instead of evidence of knowledge integration. We needed more strategies to help peer groups establish helpful criteria for class work instead of discouraging students from discussing alternative interpretations of scientific observations.

The CLP studies also explain when many proposed "quick fixes" fail. Innovations always need iterative refinement in new settings to become effective for students. For example, collaborative learning requires careful design to promote knowledge integration.

Mechanisms also are needed to ensure that materials created to build on the ideas of one group of students work for others. Critics of innovation often claim that programs developed by one creative teacher or school will not work for typical teachers or schools. These critics may even point to other teachers who fail with the innovation as "evidence" for their view. Arguing instead that innovations require tailoring to local conditions to succeed, we offer methods for assessing individual innovations to help teachers and partnerships localize innovations.

Consider an analogy. A friend serves a terrific fish stew and all the guests rave. You try the same recipe, but yours tastes more ordinary. Do you assume that the recipe works only for your friend, or do you check on the source of the fish, the type of cooking pots, the cooking times, whether fresh herbs were used, or the like? Furthermore, suppose only some of your guests like the dish. Do you blame the recipe or check to see if they like any fish dishes? Tailoring a recipe to new technology and audiences has some parallels with adapting innovations to new teachers and students.

DESIGNING A LIGHT CURRICULUM

This chapter describes how teacher Rick Weinland planned an innovation following the scaffolded knowledge integration framework described in section II and shows how the CLP partnership built on Weinland's experiences and eventually created some new partnership opportunities.. Four versions of a unit on the science of light are described, highlighting the planning and iterative refinement process as well as the technology decisions and assessment.

Version 1: What should students learn about light?

Rick Weinland, a high school science teacher, joined CLP to do a Master's project. Weinland chose to use the CLP pragmatic pedagogical principles to create an innovative unit on the science of light. He immediately faced the question of what to teach. Weinland, like many teachers, had access to a new technology: probes that measure light intensity and display results on the computer screen. Moreover, Weinland had evidence from his own teaching that the typical textbook unit emphasizing geometric optics did not connect to students' ideas or interests. He listened to members of the CLP group explain why heat flow works for teaching about thermal events. Weinland sought a similarly effective model for the science of light, already knowing that it would not be based on geometric optics.

Following the CLP approach, Weinland interviewed students to identify the ideas they bring to science class and the problems that interest them. He sought problems that would make light problems personally relevant and take advantage of light probes. Weinland asked students questions such as "How do sunglasses work?" and "Why can you see white shirts better than black shirts at night?" In checking on what other researchers reported about student ideas, he found that students commonly think of objects as surrounded by a "bath" of light and do not connect the vision process with light. Weinland learned from these interviews that light probes might confuse students because, like students' eyes, they had real limitations in light detection.

Weinland concurrently designed a unit and assessment questions that encouraged students to distinguish visual acuity and light propagation. As mentioned in chapter 4, he asked students whether light goes on forever or dies out. Students might conclude that light dies out if they cannot see it, or they could base their answer on conservation of energy and argue that light goes on forever even if the eye does not detect it. Experts also find this question intriguing because it allows discussion of the wave–particle duality at its extreme. In fact, as noted in chapter 7, Sasha in our case studies connected the debate to this issue.

On the basis of interviews, results reported by other researchers, the limits of the light probes, and consultation with the CLP partnership Weinland created the first version of the light unit. This unit featured experiments about light intensity, light over distance, and reflection. Students designed the lighting plan for a house and engaged in the debate about how far light goes.

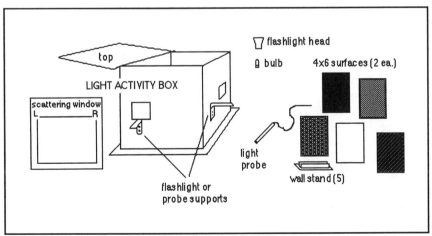

FIG. 8.7   Materials used in the activity, "Sylvanna's house" to explore the nature of light, light reflection, light scattering, and light intensity.

Mr. K found the use of light probes challenging in the classroom be-cause ambient lighting interfered with detection. Fortunately, the classroom had been used previously for teaching photography, so an-cient curtains could be closed. Students complained that the room got very hot, so fans also were added. As shown in Fig. 8.7, Weinland even-tually built "shades" so students could block classroom light in their work areas.

Weinland followed the pragmatic pedagogical principles and em-ployed many of the activity structures from CLP including experi-ments, design projects, and debates, to promote knowledge integration. He believed that helping students understand factors in-fluencing light propagation including absorption, reflection, and scat-tering would contribute to integrated understanding of light. Weinland wanted students to identify the reflection properties of mir-rors, as well as white and black surfaces. He hoped to help students dis-tinguish light propagation from visual detection, and he wanted students to understand the role of light in vision. Weinland encouraged students to connect these aspects of light problems with personally rel-evant problems such as how to light their study area and how to explain the workings of a greenhouse.

To assess progress Weinland designed knowledge integration assess-ments along with the unit. Some items and student responses appear in Fig. 8.8. On the assessment, administered before and after instruc-tion, students demonstrated substantial progress.

Weinland discussed these results with the design partnership. Ev-eryone agreed that his problems encouraged students: They wanted to know why sunglasses work and wondered whether or why light died out. Pretest results revealed students' lack of models showing the re-lationship between light and vision. Consequently, the unit added a powerful and accessible model of light as coming from a source, being detected, and continuing until absorbed (Fig. 8.9). Students liked the unit, and Weinland found it a big improvement over a geometric optics approach.

Weinland, in collaboration with CLP, however, concluded that the technological environment, which consisted of probes and worksheets, was too cumbersome and made learning inefficient. Students fre-quently lost track of their offline materials because they had become accustomed to keeping all their records in the Electronic Laboratory Notebook. Worksheets scaffolded knowledge integration for the stu-dents who used them, but students who needed the most support often were confused. Many students postponed responding to prompts they would have answered immediately in the electronic format.

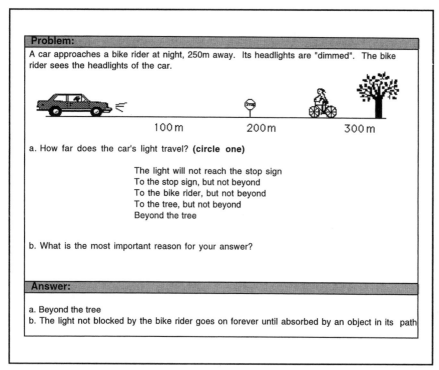

Problem:

A car approaches a bike rider at night, 250m away. Its headlights are "dimmed". The bike rider sees the headlights of the car.

100 m   200 m   300 m

a. How far does the car's light travel? **(circle one)**

The light will not reach the stop sign
To the stop sign, but not beyond
To the bike rider, but not beyond
To the tree, but not beyond
Beyond the tree

b. What is the most important reason for your answer?

Answer:

a. Beyond the tree
b. The light not blocked by the bike rider goes on forever until absorbed by an object in its path

FIG. 8.8   Problems assessing knowledge integration in the light curriculum.

Version 2: Can students learn about light with the Electronic Laboratory Notebook?

The partnership agreed to implement the light unit using the Electronic Laboratory Notebook. How would this work? Temperature-sensitive probes used graphs showing heating and cooling over time. In contrast, intensity experiments often yielded single data points that might have been displayed best in tables.

Weinland, working with Brian Foley and Judy Stern, converted some of the activities to the Electronic Laboratory Notebook format (Fig. 8.10). The house design and How Far Does Light Go debate remained worksheet based (Fig. 8.11). The Electronic Laboratory Notebook activities allowed students to gather information, make results visible, and reflect on findings more easily. Pretests and posttests suggested improved understanding of reflection and absorption. Case studies in chapter 7 showed that students using some of these light activities built on them 2 years later.

Measuring the effects of light over distance proved difficult. How could students verify that, although intensity diminished, the area illuminated increased? How could it be communicated that light does not die out, but rather spreads out?

As an answer, Weinland designed the light intensity activity, in which students estimated the diameter of the illuminated area and computed the area. To conduct this experiment, students held a light probe in the middle of cardboard-backed graph paper. While one student took an intensity reading, the other traced the circle of light made by the source on the graph paper. Intensity and area data were collected for at least 4

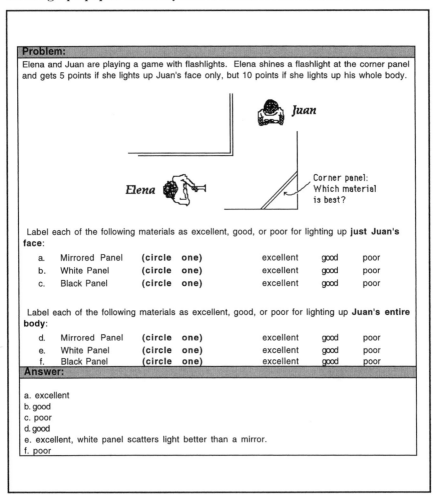

FIG. 8.8   Light assessments (*continued*).

LIGHT PRINCIPLES:

Energy conversion principle: When light is absorbed by a material, that light energy is changed to heat energy.

Reflection principle: More light bounces off a good reflector than off a good absorber.

Scattering principle: High-scattering reflectors reflect light in many directions while low-scattering reflectors reflect light mostly in one direction.

Light transmission principle: The more transparent a material appears, the more light energy is passing through the material.

Light intensity principle: The intensity of light detected by a receiver decreases as the distance from the light source increases.

Role of eyes in vision principle: To see an object, light must reflect off the object and then enter your eyes.

Light leaves source principle: Light sources convert other sources of energy into light energy.

Light source intensity principle: Different light sources can produce <the same> <different> light intensities.

FIG. 8.9   Light principles: As with the heat and temperature principles, we developed principles for understanding light.

distances. Then the students determined the area of each circle (each square of the graph paper was 1 cm^2). Bar graphs were used to chart area and intensity. As the distance increased the intensity decreased. Students were asked to reflect on what these graphs meant and come up with an explanation for what was happening to the light as distance between source and receiver increased.

Most students found the activity extremely esoteric (Fig. 8.12). No progress in understanding was found. Weinland dropped the activity, but CLP retained the assessment item, hoping that other activities would help students understand this topic.

For his Master's thesis, Weinland reported on the benefits of this new, accessible model of light. He advocated light-intensity probes for teaching about reflection, absorption, and scattering, showing how a carefully designed set of activities could help students make sense of personally relevant problems such as how sunglasses work.

The CLP experience gave Weinland a head start, but substantial planning and iterative design were needed, and many technology problems required solutions. The resulting light unit offers teachers an al-

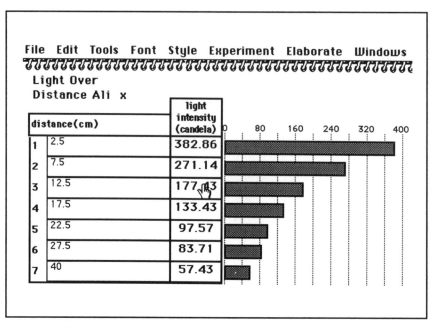

FIG. 8.10 Students work in pairs testing the light intensity over distance of various light sources like glow in the dark sticks, flashlights, and small light bulbs. Using the Electronic Laboratory Notebook, students enter the distance of a light probe from the light source as measured along a yard stick. The software generates the bars.

ternative to geometric optics that interests students and connects to relevant problems. Students studying this unit have used their ideas after they finished science class. Weinland's assessments allowed other teachers to monitor student progress, assess success, and use student answers to tailor their program.

The CLP partnership, while excited about the light unit, was concerned about student understanding of energy and, specifically, links between light and heat. To link light and heat, the partnership designed a "greenhouse" activity. Dawn Rickey, a chemistry graduate student, created an activity in which students measured the temperature of air in two liter coke bottles partially filled with water. In one bottle, Alka-Seltzer tablets created "greenhouse gases." In the other, no greenhouse gases were present. Each bottle had a temperature probe. The bottles were placed equally distant from a light bulb. The experiment "worked" but the technology was complicated. Consequently, students had trouble connecting the results to their understanding of energy (Fig. 8.13). The partnership sought other solutions. We tried to create a "light model," and a light-to-heat energy conversion activity was designed.

Version Three: Can we make thinking about light visible?

The third version of the light unit centered on using technology to make thinking visible. Can a model of light propagation enhance the light unit? Can technology enhance the *How Far Does Light Go?* debate? About this time, Philip Bell joined the CLP partnership as a PhD student with an engineering background. Previously he had designed activities using probes. As discussed in chapter 4, Bell continued to refine the *How Far Does Light Go?* debate.

To enhance the light unit, Bell first tried to create a computer-based light model that had the same impact on student understanding of heat propagation as the HeatBars software had on student understanding of heat. After trying many alternatives, Bell concluded that tech-

---

HOW FAR DOES LIGHT GO ACTIVITY:

Principle: The light rays emitted by a source get spread out over a larger and larger area as they travel farther from the source. As a result, the intensity of light detected by the eye (or any other receiver) decreases as the distance from the source increases.

Prototype: Four students are sitting around a table, taking a test. To be fair, each should have an equal amount of light. Which of the following tables would be fairest?

Investigate what happens to the light intensity detected as the detector is moved away from the source.

Light source: 200 W bulb

Distance:	25 cm	50 cm	100 cm	200 cm
Intensity:	_____	_____	_____	_____

How would you explain why this happens?

A young student looks goes outside one sunny day, and that night looks up at the stars. Because the sun light was so much more intense than the star light, does this mean the sun is a stronger light source than any of the stars?

Yes_____   No_____

What is the main reason for your answer?

FIG. 8.11. The How Far Does Light Go? activity worksheet

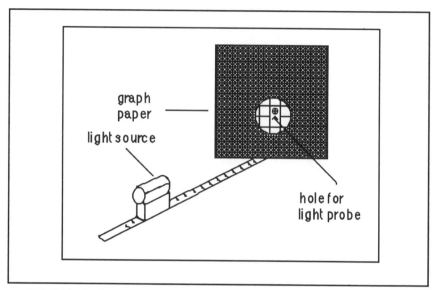

FIG. 8.12   Light intensity activity: Apparatus for light intensity experiment.

nology would not easily help. He found models that helped students understand light but ran too slowly on the classroom computers, and models that confused students. For example, students who had a "bath of light" model, and therefore believed that light fills a space, often used architectural models in which the software program renders the lighting of a particular scene to reinforce this model. Bell also found models that confused the CLP partnership. Finding a dynamic accessible model for light currently remains a challenge.

The partnership also faced several other challenges at this point. Better links among energy activities were still needed. Students wanted even more personally relevant problems. We were sure that students could gain better understanding of the nature of science, and many students wanted more connections to biology. Our work with many teachers convinced us that we needed activities readily tailored to new situations.

The CLP partnership engaged in a reflective planning process, seriously considered an exciting new technology the Internet, and wrote a new proposal defining the KIE as a new partnership. The KIE partnership built on CLP's expertise in using classroom computer networks. Many members of the CLP partnership, including Mr. K, participated.

Version Four: The Knowledge Integration Environment

The fourth version of the light unit resulted in a new partnership. The How Far Does Light Go? debate was our first KIE activity. The KIE enabled us to respond to several concerns.

First, students wanted more examples that tied science activities to their own interests. Using the Internet, students could locate personally relevant debate evidence.

Second, we wanted to improve students' ability to critique accounts of scientific phenomena. The Internet accesses a broad range of information about science that is worthy of criticism. One exciting example we found was an advertisement for an "antiheat ice-cloth shirt." Students could critique this ad easily, but still, when pushed in a debate, they used it to buttress their argument. Essentially, students "forgot" the source of the information and quoted the conclusion just as the advertisers intended. The KIE partnership enabled us to conduct design studies to improve critiquing ability.

Third, we wanted to encourage students to integrate their knowledge across more topics. Many students prefer biology to physical science, whereas some rejoice when they begin to study chemistry as the case studies in chapter 7 illustrate. We wanted to try designing activities that enabled a more integrated approach to science. Using Internet evidence allowed broader connections.

Finally, we sought an environment that enabled teachers to tailor activities easily to local conditions. Teachers could create or locate Internet resources to add to our KIE activities.

In collaboration with the partnership, Bell created the KIE software to deliver evidence to debaters using the World Wide Web (Fig. 8.14). As discussed in chapter 3, Bell contrasted multimedia and text evidence from the initial version of the debate activity in this first study. His results revealed the challenges and difficulties of using online resources for students' science explorations. No straightforward relation between multimedia and text depictions emerged. In some cases, text evidence helped students form a more cohesive argument, whereas in other cases multimedia evidence helped. Bell completed a dissertation study on the How Far Does Light Go? debate and used the results to improve the KIE software.

The four versions of the light unit illustrate the planning, localizing, and iterative refinement process that schools pioneering with new technologies might consider. This process took place in conjunction with numerous logistic decisions including when to upgrade computers, when to create new software, and how to connect to the Internet. The final version of the curriculum appears in Fig. 8.15.

Name_____Period _____

1. A diagram of your experimental setup for the Greenhouse Effect Lab is shown below. Fill in the boxes by stating what each object represents when the containers are to be used as models of the Earth.

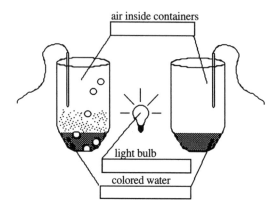

air inside containers

light bulb

colored water

2. How can the model shown above help you understand global warming?

3a. Suppose that instead of adding colored water to the containers, you add clear water. How will this effect the absorption of light? (check one)

_____Clear water absorbs much more light energy than colored water does.

_____Clear water absorbs much less light energy than colored water does.

_____Because they are both water, colored water and clear water have about the same ability to absorb light energy.

3b. How would your <u>experimental results</u> (your graphs) have been different if you had used clear water instead of colored water in this lab?

3c. Write at least one principle from a previous experiment that helps explain your answer. (See last page for a list of principles).

FIG. 8.13   The Greenhouse activity study of energy conversion.

4. Suppose that instead of adding Alka-Seltzer to one of the containers, you fasten some plastic wrap around the top of it (as shown below) and then run the experiment. You find that the effect of covering the container with plastic wrap is the same as adding Alka-Seltzer.

a. Does one of the materials you are comparing (air or plastic wrap) allow light energy to pass through it more completely? (check one)

_____Air transmits light energy much better than plastic wrap does.
_____Plastic wrap transmits light energy much better than air does.
_____Because they are both highly transparent materials, air and plastic wrap have about the same ability to transmit light energy.

b. Does one of these materials (air or plastic wrap) allow heat energy to pass through it more easily? (check one)

_____Air transmits heat energy much better than plastic wrap does.
_____Plastic wrap transmits heat energy much better than air does.
_____Because they are both highly transparent materials, air and plastic wrap have about the same ability to transmit heat energy.

c. What evidence do you have to support your answers?

d. When you turn the lightbulb on and run the experiment, will the air inside one of the two containers reach a higher temperature? (check one)

_____The container that is left open to the air will reach a higher temperature.

_____The container that is covered with plastic wrap will reach a higher temperature.
_____Both containers will reach the same temperature.

e. What is the main reason for your answer?

FIG. 8.13   The Greenhouse activity (*continued*).

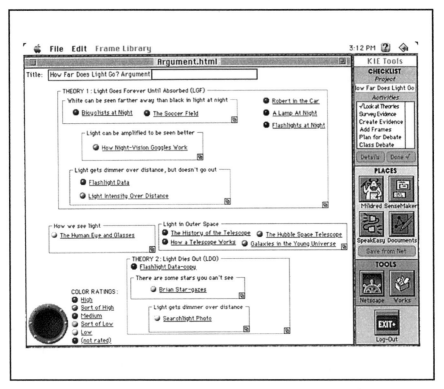

FIG. 8.14   KIE Software: This student uses SenseMaker to sort different pieces
of evidence found on the Internet to support two different theories about light.

For CLP, learning goals and technology opportunities motivated
these decisions. The primary goal was to improve science learning
while taking advantage of technology. We also sought a software environment that would permit new partnerships to tailor innovations
more easily.

All four aspects of the scaffolded knowledge integration framework
synthesized in section II contributed to the success of the light unit
and to the effectiveness of the KIE partnership.

First, following the principles in chapter 2, the group explored accessible models of the science of light. A model that emphasized a light
source and a light detector fit with student ideas and interests; geometric optics did not. This source-detector model proved effective for
understanding a vast array of light issues and a series of person-
ally-relevant problems that appeal to students. Discussions with experts in the science of light confirmed this choice. Many believed that

the How Far Does Light Go? question would provide students with a firm foundation for future science courses.

When we added Internet resources, the CLP partnership had lively debates about how to use the Internet evidence. Linn, for example, located historical references to ancient telescopes on a web site in Italy, and saw the benefits of adding student understanding of the global community to the unit. Most of the learning partnership disputed Linn's claim, citing a pragmatic pedagogical principle about making science accessible.

Week #	CLP Activity	Topic
1	Polyline	Nature of science
2	Pulsing 1 and 2	Heat and temperature
3	Light sources	Nature of light
4	Reflection, detection	Nature of light
5	Sylvana's House Reflection, scattering	Nature of light
6	What you see	Nature of light
7	Light over distance	Nature of light
8	How Far Does Light Go?	Nature of light
9	Potatoes and Cokes	Insulation, donduction
10	HeatBars	Insulation, conduction, heat, temperature
11	Hot chocolate	Insulation, conduction
12	Probing your surroundings	Thermal equilibrium
13	Thermal Model Kit	Insulation, conduction, Heat, temperature, thermal equilibrium
14	Sound activity	Nature of sound
15	Greenhouse effect	Energy conversion
16	Portfolio activity	All (except nature of science and sound)

FIG. 8.15 The CLP curriculum focused on energy including light and sound, not only heat and temperature.

Second, following the principles in chapter 3 about making thinking visible, we sought a light model that would provide a visualization of the process of light propagation. We were unsuccessful in identifying or creating such a model. Students, however, do make their thinking visible when they debate about light propagation. As discussed in chapter 2, the KIE SenseMaker tool was particularly influential, allowing students to sort out their ideas and support their assertions with well-organized evidence. In addition, light-intensity probes made important aspects of light visible in experiments about light. However, they were less central than the temperature probes were in our thermal phenomena units. Probes illustrated the reflection and scattering effects of various materials. Other questions about the nature of light, including how far light goes and the mechanisms behind sunglasses, only partially connected to light-intensity probe findings.

Third, following the principles in chapter 4, the debate helped students listen and learn from others. In addition, Sherry Hsi incorporated the Multimedia Forum Kiosk discussed in chapter 4 into the light unit. Students discussed such questions as, "Should we paint the walls of the multipurpose room white, or put in mirrors?" (Fig. 8.16). In the KIE partnership, the SpeakEasy discussion tool built on the success of the Multimedia Forum Kiosk.

Fourth, we promoted autonomy in understanding light with both prompts for reflection and science projects such as the How Far Does Light Go? debate project. Helen Clark designed additional light projects. For example, one project asked students to design an appropriate light plan for their study space at home. Another project asked students to explain why the floor lighting in a theater allowed them to find their seat without interfering with their vision of the movie.

Cybercoaching as discussed in chapter 5 helped students to perform these projects. The KIE partnership made the project easier to implement in science classrooms. Assessments demonstrated the impact of these refinements. Students studying the final versions of the light unit were far more successful than students studying the first version. In addition, on the light intensity question, experience with the How Far Does Light Go? debate improved performance. This surprising finding, even though the experiment was unsuccessful, convinced us that the unit as a whole promoted knowledge integration.

In summary, the complexity of technology planning necessitates tight cycles of trial and refinement. The design of the light unit shows how the pragmatic pedagogical principles give planning partnerships a head start on using technology effectively. Weinland used the pragmatic principles in section II to add a new topic to the CLP project. Bell, working with CLP, created new software responding to the limits

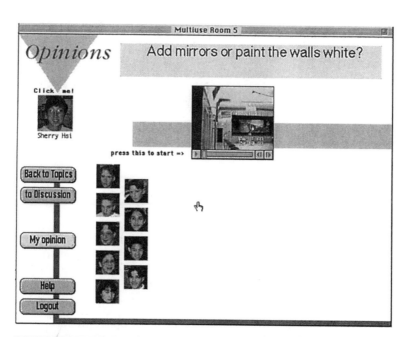

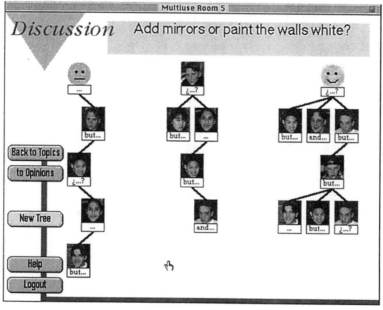

FIG. 8.16.   Paint the walls. (*continued on next page*)

Sample Comments:
I would add mirrors. Mirrors reflect light. Whenever the light reflects, then there is more of it making the room brighter. I've seen this before when you put a flash light or candle light next to a mirror.

But what if you open a window when it's really, really sunny outside? The light would just reflect itself off all the mirrors and just keep bouncing off and it wouldn't stop unless you closed the window or the light ran out of space.

I completely agree that windows would be a bad idea. If you had a window them you would blind yourself from the incoming light.

This may be true that the multipurpose room is ugly, but mirrors could also brighten up the room. I think that the white walls would be a better choice but I can't really say why. Can anyone who agrees with me that white walls is better, explain it to me?

In my experience, white barely reflects any light.

FIG. 8.16.   Paint the walls: A discussion topic on light from the Multimedia Forum Kiosk asking students to help improve the lighting conditions of the school's multiuse room.

of the Electronic Laboratory Notebook to support a debate. Many teachers all over the world have used the online version of the How Far Does Light Go? debate, often adding new Internet evidence relevant to their students.

NEW DESIGN PARTNERSHIPS

We invite individuals and groups engaged in technology planning to join our new partnerships such as the Web-Based Integrated Science Environment (WISE) and the Science Controversies Online: Partnerships for Education (SCOPE). These partnerships enable teachers and schools to use the computers as learning partners and also to tailor partnerships to local needs.

Our WISE partnership extends the KIE partnership to integrated science. Integrated science instruction enables students to explore relevant and enduring science problems such as global ecology, space exploration, or cures for disease, while connecting their learning to local issues and expertise. Many locations on the Web can support such learning activities by providing quality information from credible sources. Furthermore, teachers can make science come alive for students by incorporating local issues and examples. Thus, California schools might investigate the impact of earthquakes on land use; schools in Alaska might study glacial ice to analyze global climate change; whereas Florida students might look at mosquitoes as carriers of disease. Local scientists can provide valuable expertise to help partnerships succeed.

The WISE activities draw on the breadth and diversity of resources from the World Wide Web to meet school system needs for integrated science curricula. The technology used in WISE helps students bridge disciplines, critique biased or persuasive messages on the Internet, triangulate various sources of information, and use multimedia resources effectively. Most importantly, students who perform WISE projects are supported in knowledge integration, connecting diverse sources of evidence with their own ideas through personally relevant activities.

Integrated science instruction should prepare students so they continue to refine their ideas about central, relevant science topics such as health or global ecology, even after they have completed science class. Integrated science has the potential to teach coherent ideas that students continue to use instead of isolated ideas that students readily forget. Classroom activities can include important skills that will serve students throughout their lives such as critiquing information, supporting arguments, creating designs, or collaborating.

To prepare lifelong learners, our WISE partnership incorporates successful technology supports such as prompts for reflection that encourage students to integrate and test their ideas. These supports also amplify the effectiveness of the teacher by handling logistic aspects of the course, such as keeping track of the parts of a project that remain to be completed. As they complete WISE projects, students critique evidence from the Web, use it to inform designs and support arguments, participate in electronic discussions, perform experiments (at home and in the classroom), publish their data to be critiqued by peers, and so forth—all activities designed to foster essential lifelong learning skills.

Our SCOPE partnership builds on the KIE and the WISE partnerships and specifically addresses the nature of science. One project engages students in exploring frog deformities. Over the past few years, an apparent increase in physical deformities among frog populations has been observed. In fact, middle school students in Minnesota used the Internet 2 years ago to bring media attention to the phenomenon when they published their field observations. Currently, several competing hypotheses are being vigorously explored and debated in the scientific community.

The deformed frog controversy represents a complex, multidisciplinary problem involving environmental, genetic, and chemical arguments. A multidisciplinary partnership between integrative biologists, classroom teachers, educational researchers, and computer scientists designed the activities. This collaboration design included an urban middle school setting. Activities enabled a diverse range of students, including English language learners, to participate successfully. Because this is a current scientific controversy, students not only learn about a cutting-edge science topic, but also experience central aspects of the scientific process itself. Our design studies document shifts in students' images of science when they explore an authentic scientific controversy. Students develop a much more dynamic understanding of the process of scientific progress while developing a more integrated understanding of the science content.

REFLECTIONS

Achieving fluency in information technology requires a never-ending planning process. Many resist technology, emphasizing the frustrations users inevitably encounter. Yet technology is here to stay and we can use it to promote lifelong science learning.

Many argue that education should wait until the tools mature. We argue instead that educators must take a seat at the planning table to ensure that technology-enhanced learning environments meet educational needs and that schools participate in refining and enhancing them. Partnerships can conduct small and large-scale investigations, widely sharing the results to inform the planning process.

For example, investigations conducted by the CLP partnership yielded criteria for curriculum design that enabled more and more efficient decisions. Our pragmatic pedagogical principles capture these criteria. These principles give partnerships a head start on new designs. The KIE partnership efficiently designed software to tap the power of the Internet by building on the CLP design experience. We were able to find ways to make the Internet a learning partner for knowledge integration because we already had in place a set of agreed-on criteria and powerful examples. Our new partnerships offer opportunities for more teachers and schools to plan for lifelong learning.

ASK MR. K

How can we help teachers use technology in meaningful ways?

It's not easy to use technology. It is frustrating. Teacher's can buy software off the shelf or build some software project on their own. Either way, they will encounter frustration. The best way to get teachers involved is to find good teachers to model how technology can be used. It's all about sharing and trusting other teachers, getting into a group, sharing your ideas with other colleagues, and building on each other's ideas just as we do for the kids.

When did you decide to use technology in your teaching?

In terms of the modern technologies, I think it began when I attended a seminar at Berkeley sponsored by the Hewitt foundation and organized by Marcia Linn. I also began hearing more and more about people using computers, and I was interested in working with kids using computers. The first funded grant was from the Wheels of the Mind program at Apple Computer.

Marcia asked me, at that point, if I would be interested in getting involved. I had taken a class at the Lawrence Hall of Science beforehand which was a little bit of Basic programming. It was not anyways near the kinds of things we do today. I also started to see the potential of technology in my teaching when we started using probes connected to the computer and software such as Rocky's Boots that could get kids to think and work together. When the kids did the real-time graphing of temperature using the computer, they were more focused on the science and less on the routine collection of data points. I think this made a big difference.

Has technology changed the way you teach?

Oh, it has incredibly. A big part of my teaching used to be setting up, replacing broken parts, and taking down equipment for science experiments. The computer has given me more time to work with kids, to discuss ideas. I think the big thing for me is the fact that it's enabled the kids to get away from just thinking about carrying out procedures with equipment and data gathering and instead think about the science.

I think another really significant thing in the last 8 years or so has been getting kids to think about problems and the process of science. We were able to give them some structure along the way when the Macintosh came out, whereas the Apple IIs were used mostly to gather data. The first Macintoshes (SEs) enabled us to design the "scaffolds" and model the kinds of things and the types of thinking we wanted kids to do. Therefore, technology has changed the way I teach by letting me go into a program and design the kind of things I want to happen, while still leaving it open-ended for the kids to explore what you can do with it.

How do you help students integrate their ideas about light?

Well, consider the example of why we see something. We go through a series of labs with light boxes. Kids measure the light coming through and reflecting off an object compared with how well they can see it. At this point, a lot of the kids begin to understand that what we're seeing is the light being reflected off that object. Some kids still won't get that, so I find out why they don't get the idea that light must be coming from that object, focus on sources of light, compare mirrors to flat surfaces, and show how light goes back and forth. There are many ways to get kids to think about why it is that you see yourself in the mirror.

Would you prefer to have one computer for each student?

Not really. When I walk around during class, I see kids having really interesting conversations about what's going on, which indicates that they're really thinking about science. Many kids would lose out if they were by themselves. A real-life partner can ask questions of you and make you stop and think about what really is going on. The act of just explaining to your partner makes you realize what you understand and what your questions are.

What message do you have for teachers trying to use technology in the classroom?

Using technology is the right way to go because it helps kids learn the science, but it's going to take time. Technology will not completely free people from teaching, but it will change the way they teach. As a teacher, you need to be flexible, to have a willingness to change, and to be a lifelong learner yourself. Even if you have developed the perfect activity, you must be willing to say there are new materials and other ways to do things that can work well too.

It's also important to realize that there will be days of frustration and technology breakdowns in any classroom. But it's rewarding when the technology doesn't fail, when you designed activities for pedagogy and learning, and when kids do amazing things in class and afterward in high school.

POINTS TO PONDER

- Describe your fluency in information technology.
- Analyze the opportunities and obstacles you encountered in developing fluency in information technology.
- Analyze a science curriculum that incorporates technology. Describe both how technology constrains the curriculum and how technology improves the curriculum.
- Describe the model you use for evaluating uses of technology in education. Compare your model with those in the chapter.
- Select a technology plan for a local school or district (or find one on the Internet). Critique the plan on the basis of the pragmatic principles in this book.
- Create a technology plan for yourself, for the course you teach, for a school, or for a district.
- Describe an experience using technology in education that would help others and post it on the CLP web site.
- Watch the section of the CLP film called "The future of science instruction." Compare your views to those voiced by the participants.

RELATED READINGS

Kafai, Y., & Resnick, M. (Eds.). (1996) *Constructionism in practice: Designing, thinking, and learning in a digital world.* Mahwah, NJ: Lawrence Erlbaum Associates.

Linn, M. C. (1995). Designing computer learning environments for engineering and computer science: The scaffolded knowledge integration framework. *Journal of Science Education and Technology, 4*(2), 103–126.

President's Committee of Advisors on Science and Technology (PCAST) (1997). *Panel on educational technology: Report to the president on the use of technology to strengthen K-12 education in the United States.* Washington, DC.

Synder, L., Aho, A., Linn, M., et al. (1999). *Being fluent with information technology.* Washington, DC: National Academy Press.

9

Partnerships for Professional Development

Teachers, like all professionals, engage in a lifelong process of improving their classroom practice. Most schools allocate some time and resources to ongoing professional development. This chapter builds on the pragmatic pedagogical principles introduced in section II, Classroom Learning Partners, and introduces four pragmatic pedagogical principles designed to identify learning partners for professional development partnerships.

Individually and in partnerships such as the CLP group, classroom teachers developing a powerful pedagogical philosophy and designing effective classroom practices generally follow the same process of knowledge integration described in this volume for science students. Partnerships benefit from making thinking visible, reflecting on practice, adding new possibilities to the mix of ideas, and restructuring their views on teaching and learning to encompass a broader and more comprehensive range of instructional issues.

Teachers test and reformulate their ideas every day in the classroom. New technologies raise new issues about how to provide effective instruction. A partnership such as CLP, seeking a coherent pedagogical philosophy can test ideas across disciplines in many settings, and with learners differing in age, background, and motivation.

When policymakers reduce class size, fund technology in schools, approve standardized tests, or set standards for achievement, they follow an often implicit pedagogical philosophy. How can we assist policy designers in developing explicit, observable pedagogical philosophies that can be inspected, reformulated, and revised as their experience expands? A rich, coherent, articulated philosophy allows parents to analyze whether instructional decisions make sense, administrators to make curricular decisions, and policymakers to understand the implications of standards. Classroom teachers have a special opportunity to provide evidence from classroom experience to inform these debates.

An effective educational philosophy should connect to the intuitive, descriptive, and implicit models held by parents, political decision makers, citizens, and students. Ideally, instructional leaders can identify pivotal cases that motivate the community engaged in setting school policies to reflect on alternative models and make decisions informed by a powerful and coherent view of pedagogy. For example, when scientists questioned CLP's view that textbook principles were often inaccessible, we sought pivotal cases by interviewing expert scientists as discussed in chapter 2.

Communities often are disconnected: School districts select standards for achievement without determining whether they can be achieved by teachers and students. Similarly, states often decree standards without checking to determine students' entering capabilities and without allocating time responsibly given the gap between the standard and students' knowledge.

These gaps between decreed standards and evidence from classroom practice reflect differences in pedagogical philosophy. News articles regularly report descriptive pedagogical models held by policymakers, citizens, and reporters themselves. Often these articles espouse such views as "Set higher standards and students will meet them" or "I learned without computers, so why waste money on a fad?" or "Teach the basics and students will succeed in life." Educators need ways to engage these policymakers in discussions and offer alternatives for consideration in the same way that we engage students in science discussions and offer alternatives for explaining scientific phenomena.

Many policymakers, citizens, and concerned parents hold intuitive, descriptive models of pedagogy based primarily on perception of their own personal schooling experience. Students often articulate descriptive pedagogical theories such as "It's better to cram the night before than study regularly" or "Memorizing works better than understanding" or even "I can't learn science."

Educators sometimes despair at the slow progress of policymakers and citizens with regard to pedagogical philosophy. Similar desperation commonly is articulated when educators discuss the progress of students learning science. Rather than expressing frustration, however, we need to take action.

PRAGMATIC PEDAGOGICAL PRINCIPLES

The pragmatic pedagogical principles articulated in this chapter synthesize our experience with promoting knowledge integration in the CLP partnership. These principles describe ways to orchestrate the learning partners available to partnerships in developing pedagogical philosophies and classroom practices. The principles focus on three primary teaching partners: the classroom teacher as an autonomous learner, peers in the professional community, and rapidly expanding computer resources.

The first principle encourages partnerships to take advantage of technological resources and look for new technological opportunities as the pace of technological advance continues. It states: *Use technology as a teaching partner.* Technology should facilitate development of pedagogical philosophy and enhance effectiveness of classroom practice.

The second principle illustrates how partnerships can serve as their own learning partners. It states: *Use scaffolded knowledge integration as a partner for curriculum innovation.* Partnerships can build autonomously on the scaffolded knowledge integration framework to achieve a more coherent personal philosophy and more effective classroom practice.

The third principle illustrates how partnerships can, as a group, serve as learning partners for each other. It states: *Learn from other partnerships and from experts in related fields.* Following this principle, educators listen and learn from each other and improve each others' educational philosophies and practices.

The fourth principle calls for new professional development activities that combine the strengths of available learning partners and take advantage of new resources. It states: *Create new professional development partners.*

Use technology as a teaching partner

Our first pragmatic principle says that technology can serve as a teaching partner to facilitate development of a pedagogical philosophy and enhance effectiveness of classroom practice. Technology, however, frequently has been cast as an alternative to effective teaching. Early computer programs delivered drill and practice for mathematics, foreign languages, and other domains. They inspired some to claim that computers would replace teachers. Initial responses to technology not only included fear that drill programs would replace creative teachers, but also provided real evidence that technological tools increase instructional costs, often with little benefit.

Combining the strengths of technology and that of teachers becomes more and more important as technological solutions develop. Finding an effective partnership between teachers and technologies is an ongoing, never-ending undertaking because technologies change rapidly, making new solutions possible every year.

In the preceding chapter, we discussed planning for teaching with technology. In this chapter, we discuss how technology can form an effective, powerful, and useful teaching partner. Three main roles for technology partners are identified.

First, technology can effectively perform routine or repetitive activities, freeing teachers to do what they do best. Teachers make the most difference in learning by tutoring students, diagnosing weaknesses, planning lessons, responding to unforeseen circumstances, and redesigning courses on the basis of past feedback. In all of these areas, technology is quite deficient. However, technological tools can keep track of students, maintain grade books, perform routine calculations, provide online help, and in other ways enable teachers to spend more of their intellectual energies helping students to learn.

For example, our CLP instruction relies heavily on teachers diagnosing the models that students have and identifying pivotal cases for promoting knowledge integration. Successful teaching also involves localizing instruction to student interests and knowledge, supporting students as they reflect, and orchestrating social relationships in the classroom. When technology takes over the task of answering logistical questions, teachers have more time for these instructional tasks.

Second, many argue that technology can serve as a catalyst for educational change enabling schools, teachers, districts, and curriculum developers to rethink issues and address complex problems while planning for technology. The CLP project illustrates the benefits of technology as a catalyst for change. Graphing software as discussed in chapter 3 motivated educators to rethink instruction using graphs and enabled schools to revisit issues about depth of coverage of science topics.

Third, technological tools empower educators to speed up the cycle of design, classroom experimentation, and principled redesign of educational materials and classroom activities. In this chapter we encourage educators to engage jointly in this process of principled refinement while incorporating technological tools into the classroom.

Our CLP experience discussing technology in education with schools, teachers, policymakers, and others confirms that individuals bring a broad set of models to any discussion of teaching and learning with technology. Individuals view computers as productive tools, workplace tools, matchmaking tools, visualization tools, and learning partners. In this chapter we analyze the role of technology in promoting knowledge integration.

Focusing on the *productivity* model, some advocate that technology replace instructional activities. These advocates of technology expect drill and practice programs to replace mathematics instruction based on research with teaching machines, flashcards, and current software. To be sure, drill and practice proves highly effective for certain learning goals. For knowledge integration, however, drill and practice rarely helps. Drill might add models or ideas to the mix students have, but it neglects reorganizing, rethinking, and connecting ideas.

Computer technology also has been advocated as a replacement for the grade book, books, lectures, typewriters, calculators, dictionaries, encyclopedias, and whole topics such as algebra. Assessment of the impact and value of technology has revealed both effective and unsuccessful replacements. Replacing traditional approaches with technologically enhanced approaches can increase cost with little productivity benefit. In addition, unintended consequences such as repetitive stress syndrome actually may dramatically increase the costs of technology over traditional approaches. Research can help educators decide when spreadsheets, online drawing programs, video lectures, CD-ROM encyclopedias, and simulated experiments can replace traditional classroom activities.

Designing effective use of technology to replace existing practice involves iterative refinement of the new instruction, as our CLP experiences illustrate. New technologies can change the learning goals for students. Technologies such as computer-assisted design programs often raise new issues and require thoughtful curriculum redesign. In particular, adding computer-assisted design to courses necessitates a dramatic change to the curriculum because some exercises that are easy with paper and drafting board are more difficult, and other exercises that take many hours on the drafting board (e.g., adjusting a drawing to new specifications) can be performed in minutes with computer-assisted design tools.

Many developers created online grade books, tools for keeping track of attendance, and lesson plan templates. Teachers report, however, that early designs for such tools often copied the paper and pencil approach without new functionality. For example, instead of writing grades while circulating in the classroom, teachers had to log on to a computer to enter grades and other information. This decreased productivity and increased frustration for many. Even the best efforts to tailor the tool failed because the convenience of a physical grade book that can be carried easily from home to school were lost when a computer, often located at the school, took over this important task.

Personal digital assistants are only now gaining wide acceptance for calendars, address books, and record keeping. Ideally, these devices should enable educators productively to create schedules, record grades, and track student progress. These handheld devices might go beyond grade books in helping teachers to personalize instruction.

Many claim that word-processing, desktop-publishing, and computer-budgeting tools increase the efficiency and effectiveness of schools. Some argue, however, that these tools increase the costs and frustrations required to produce documents. Both groups can point to compelling examples. Still, materials produced in traditional ways often look shoddy and unprofessional compared with the simplest poster produced using desktop publishing. Of course, many productivity tools actually do take over dreary tasks that otherwise would consume time unnecessarily.

In assessing productivity tools, we ask about the functions that they replace, and the efficiency with which replacement occurs. In addition, unintended consequences, both negative and positive, deserve careful attention. For example, online encyclopedias may primarily increase the efficiency of plagiarism.

Following the *workplace* model, some advocate that schools primarily prepare students for jobs, introducing word processing, desktop publishing, spreadsheets, searching, and even computer programming. In promoting fluency in information technology (see chapter 8), these courses should include the ability to learn a new tool and focus on tools used in specific disciplines because students learning to use a workplace software program today are likely to encounter a completely different program by the time they take their first job. If students use productivity tools to carry out a science, art, mathematics, music, or English project, they also will learn to select the tools that make the most sense for the project, deal with unanticipated consequences, and become more autonomous.

Developing skill in learning to use new technological tools and selecting tools for a task also makes sense for the workplace. Businesses regularly upgrade software and computer platforms. Ideally, rather than devoting a separate course to the development of workplace skills, schools will incorporate the development of these skills into existing courses, select a suite of tools for the school, engage advanced students in school upgrade decisions, and encourage students to use these tools in new courses.

Following the *matchmaker* model, technology can scaffold new partnerships. For example, online discussion tools can augment meetings among teachers and connect isolated teachers to peers with similar concerns. Online tools can increase communication opportunities, transform discourse, increase equity, provide access to specialized experts, and enhance learning.

Designing effective online discussions for teachers has captured the attention of many research groups. These tools enable virtual partnerships that include virtual team teaching and online discussions among peers or with experts. These tools can be cumbersome to use, difficult to access, and far slower than conventional phone conversations. Therefore, listening and learning from each other can be enhanced when technological tools are deployed judiciously or hindered when these tools become frustrating.

Technological tools can synthesize results from other partnerships. For example, when science teachers jointly compile lists of the ideas students bring to science class, they can report these findings to others.

Online resources also can synthesize classroom experiences with new technologies. Many online forums permit teachers to comment on their experiences using technological tools

Following the *visualization* model, technology can enable new understanding. For example, visualizations already succeed for many scientists. They can enable learners to access previously unavailable information that is difficult to interpret. From visualizations, expert scientists gain insights into the dynamics of molecules and the nature of the cosmos. These tools may empower students who communicate better with computer drawing and animation tools than they do with paper and pencil. However, tools designed to support experts also can backfire, confuse, and frustrate students rather than provide effective instruction or communication.

Following the *learning partner* model of technology, schools can increase understanding of different topics, as the CLP project illustrates. For example, with the Electronic Laboratory Notebook, we guide students in conducting a complex experiment. With Cybercoaching, we combine technology and teachers to provide guidance. Designing computer tools as learning partners requires considerable refinement (longer than 10 years in our case) to succeed. Fortunately, others can benefit from our experience.

In summary, we have many opportunities to use technology as a teaching partner in the classroom. Partnerships benefit from carefully analyzing the various models for incorporating technology and finding the best solution for their situation.

Many stable uses of technology now exist in the workplace and the science laboratory. Some of these make sense in the classroom. However, simply borrowing workplace successes or expert tools without analyzing the specific valuable contributions technology might make to education sells the field short. We need to borrow tools developed for others and creatively build on these tools to create educational environments while encouraging the design of tools that address pedagogical issues and problems specific to education.

To illustrate the process of making technology a learning partner, we discuss how our CLP partnership evaluated expert tools, designed new trials, and created a unit on the science of sound. Graduate student Brian Foley, in collaboration with the CLP partnership, selected and created technological tools, tested them in the classroom, and improved them on the basis of feedback from student experiences.

Sound Curriculum: Using technology as a learning partner for the science of sound. The CLP partnership followed the learning partner model of technology to create the sound unit. The sound unit is found on the CD-ROM.

The Electronic Laboratory Notebook and the sound sensors that came with the classroom computer, enabled us to design sound experiments with the same scaffolding as that used for the heat and temperature experiments. Students could make predictions, carry out experiments, display their results in real-time graphs, and reflect on their findings. In addition, students could pool results of several investigations and jointly inspect them using the tools developed for comparing various insulators and conductors in heat and temperature units.

Selecting a visual representation for sounds challenged the group. Textbooks represent sound in waves (Fig. 9.1). Because waves include both frequency and amplitude information, they can confuse observers. Foley initially implemented sound waves, using sound probes and online tools. Distinguishing amplitude and frequency when observing this representation for sound challenges both experts and students.

Building on successes with heat probes, we hoped that using sound probes in real-time collection of sound information would help students to interpret results. We created the AudioDissector program (Fig. 9.2) to help students interpret sound waves. In doing so, we encountered an unanticipated consequence: The classroom background noise often resulted in a messy depiction of sound waves. In addition, the representation was confusing.

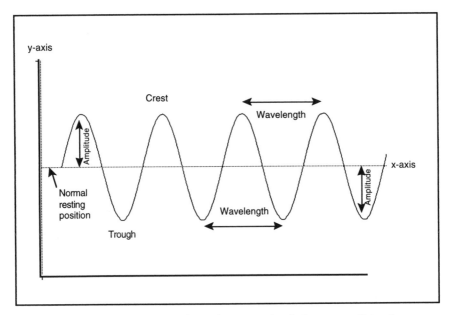

FIG. 9.1 This example drawn from a textbook shows a traditional representation of sound as an amplitude versus time graph. This representation is common in physics texts, but many students fail to understand what it represents. (Prentice Hall, 1993).

To represent the many components of a complex sound better, and to make amplitude and frequency more prominent in the representation, the group suggested representing sound using the Fourier transform as depicted in SoundSpace (Fig. 9.3). The SoundSpace representation captures the amplitude and frequency of multiple sounds as data points. This representation separates the two variables in a straightforward way. The SoundSpace representation also is more sophisticated than the wave representation typically found in the textbook, providing a foundation for later instruction. SoundSpace, however, does not collect information over time.

The sound wave and SoundSpace representations, offer two distinct visual depictions of the nature of sound. How do they support knowledge integration? Do they connect the models of sound we teach to students? The sound wave representation helps to teach sound as vibration in terms of a model. The sound wave representation also connects well to the sounds generated by, for example, drums or stringed instruments. In addition, sound waves can help individuals understand how the ear works as a detector, explaining why some vibrations can be detected but not others. Sound waves can illustrate how sound vibra-

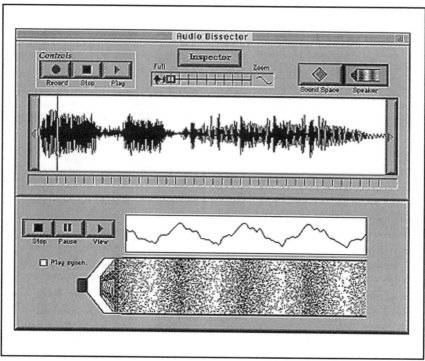

FIG. 9.2   The software program AudioDissector shows different
representations of sound. The top sound wave shows the kind of background
noise the classroom can generate when collecting data. The bottom shows a
speaker animation. The speaker moves back and forth creating ripples in the
dot density (representing air pressure).

tions interfere with each other or how sound mixing occurs for musical
productions.

The SoundSpace representation also has useful connections to personally relevant problems. For example, the talented individuals who
put together multitrack compact discs (CDs) can hear 16 or more
tracks when listening to a recording. These same individuals find a
slight glitch on a recording annoying. They can hear the parts of a complex sound. Personalizing and representing this ability to hear multiple, distinct tracks of sound can bring the science of sound to life for
students. Both the SoundSpace and the sound wave representations
help to explain the complexity of listening to a concert.

We concurrently designed activities and assessment involving complex sounds. We also investigated whether providing these multiple
representations would be helpful or confusing for students.

Were these representations successful? Foley evaluated the impact of the sound unit and found some students made substantial progress (Fig. 9.4). Others were confused by the multiple representations. Refining the unit to ensure that the many representations of sound were linked rather than ignored by students required more iterations, as discussed later in this chapter.

In summary, partnerships for professional development can integrate and refine their views of technology by considering the various roles technology plays in learning, and by designing uses for technology that reflect their pedagogical philosophies. In the first versions of the sound unit, the multiple representations of sound appealed to some students, but as a group these representations probably interfered with knowledge integration. Therefore, opportunities to use

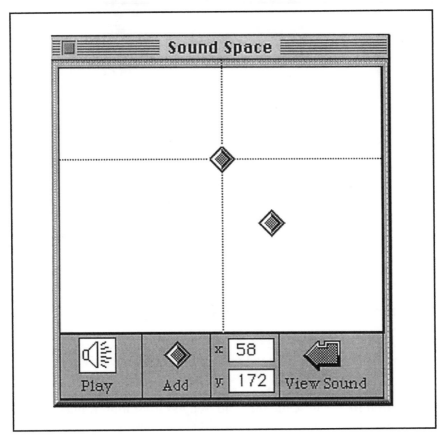

FIG. 9.3 SoundSpace: The space is a two-dimensional rectangle. The horizontal position controls the pitch of the sound whereas the vertical position controls the volume. Two sounds are shown in the space.

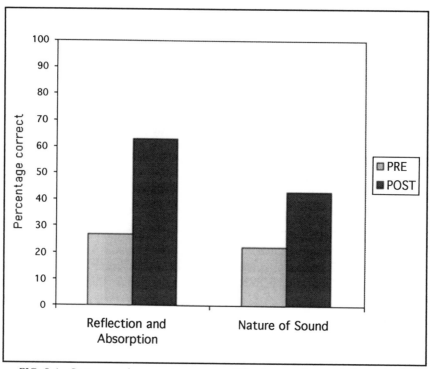

FIG. 9.4 Some sound concepts are more difficult to understand than others, such as how a drum works, but students make gains after instruction when they are provided with different representations of sound in various activities.

technology as a partner in the classroom clashed with the CLP pedagogical philosophy of knowledge integration. Later versions discussed in this chapter show how CLP resolved the conflicts between knowledge integration and multiple, available technology partners.

Use scaffolded knowledge integration as a teaching partner

Our second pragmatic pedagogical principle says that partnerships can use the pragmatic pedagogical principles in section II as teaching partners to create robust pedagogical philosophies. Partnerships can get a head start on developing a philosophy that promotes knowledge integration from the scaffolded knowledge integration framework.

Individuals and partnerships building a coherent pedagogical philosophy, in common with all other learners, build on what they know, add powerful ideas to their mix of views, and reflect. This approach is exemplified in teacher-researchers who regularly test their ideas and incorporate feedback from these tests into classroom practices. Crucial to an effective pedagogical philosophy is development of pedagogical content knowledge.

Pedagogical content knowledge refers to knowledge about a topic that enables improved teaching of that discipline. In science such knowledge involves an understanding of the ideas students bring to class, the context in which students apply their science knowledge, and the multiple models of the same topic used by students and experts in the various contexts of application. Teachers learn this pedagogical content knowledge by talking with peers, listening to students, asking questions, and reflecting. This knowledge leads to better teaching of the science topic. For example, for the science of sound, teachers need to build on an assortment of practical and sometimes incoherent ideas (Fig. 9.5).

As the CLP partnership found, to encourage knowledge integration and build on what students know, teachers must identify pivotal cases and models at a level of analysis that connects to student views. Pedagogical content knowledge goes beyond the science learned in courses that prepare experts.

The CLP pragmatic pedagogical principles describe ways to determine models for science courses. Students need models that clarify confusions and motivate more thinking. Knowing a range of potential models enables teachers to test alternatives and find those best suited for current students.

Many observers of science teaching complain that science teachers lack sufficient understanding of scientific models held by experts. The process of developing pedagogical content knowledge partly involves gaining deeper and more coherent understanding of models held by ex-

---

Sound can travel if it has something it can travel through.
Sound travels only through air.
Sound travels in straight lines, but can't go around corners.
Sound travels as particles through the air.
Sound travels by bouncing off objects into your ear.
Sound travels forever unless there is friction to slow it down.
High-pitched sounds travel faster than lower pitched sounds.
The speed of sound is always the same.
The speed of sound is different through different mediums.
Sound is blocked by water or solids.
Sound gets trapped by water or solids.
Sound travels until it becomes absorbed.
Sound dies away over distance and is harder to hear when it's far away.

FIG. 9.5   Models of sound: Students have multiple ideas about sound and the way sound travels.

perts and the intuitive and observational models held by students. Science teachers face the challenge of sorting through these various models and selecting alternatives to add to the mix of ideas for each of their students. Professional development programs can take on the task of collecting examples from the broad range of ideas that students

---

Fresh from my work with Jean Piaget and inspired by claims for the benefits of discovery learning, I agreed to teach science to a group of middle school students. I asked the students which topics they would like to investigate and amassed equipment for the 20 most popular topics.

I brought the materials to class and found that the students had no idea how to conduct investigations. I gave them more time, encouraging them to ask questions. Eventually, a few students in each class got started. In one class students began designing airplanes using paper and balsa wood and comparing their flight trajectories. In another class, a student began investigating burning matter, comparing candles of different thicknesses and placing some under jars and others on the table. Immediately most students emulated the leader.

I was disappointed and asked the research team for advice. The classroom teachers said students needed more structure to conduct investigations. The scientists said students needed more time to figure out how to experiment. I suspected Piaget would advise coaching students and encouraging them to reflect. In the next version of the curriculum, I worked closely with smaller groups of students, constantly asking them questions about their methods, procedures, and conclusions. The students I was able to engage were much more successful than those who worked independently.

I asked the research team how I could help more groups. We converted my questions and hints into a set of challenges for each of the 20 topics. Students carried out two challenges before designing their own investigations. Only some of the students moved on to investigations of their own, and most students recycled the procedures from the challenges instead of inventing new questions or methods..

Applying the scaffolded knowledge integration framework, I can critique my experience. I realize now that students might prefer to start by critiquing investigations and developing some criteria to apply to their own investigations. Students lacked the shared criteria we promote in the CLP program. I also realize that students may have preferred to investigate personally relevant problems but were inhibited by their beliefs about school science and by the challenges we designed. Important elements of autonomous learning were omitted in my classroom.

FIG. 9.6   Linn teaches middle school and reflects on knowledge integration.

Prepare a 10-minute lesson.
Divide participants into groups of four persons.
Present this lesson to the other members of the microteaching group. Other group members play the role of students. Videotape the sessions. After one member of the group presents a lesson, pick someone to facilitate a discussion. Ask the presenter the following questions:
- Did you feel the presentation went well?
- What were your goals?
- Why do you think it worked or didn't work?
- What are some suggestions the group can provide?

Repeat the process until all members of the group have a chance to present.

Use the video to further discussion. Have different groups critique each others' videotape. The group provides feedback to each presenter. Help one another to identify strengths in the lessons of each other and provide suggestions for areas in which they might improve.

FIG. 9.7 Microteaching: This is one variation of microteaching that permits groups to help critique and improve each others' teaching.

have, encouraging partnerships to post findings, and helping to build on the findings of others.

Articulating a pedagogical philosophy. To use the scaffolded knowledge integration framework as a teaching partner, educators need to distinguish their views of pedagogy from those in the framework. We find it helpful to start by writing a brief essay describing beliefs about teaching practices and the nature of learning (Fig. 9.6). Educators can practice elaborating on personal philosophies by responding to views reported in the news such as those stating that "standardized tests improve teaching" and that "technology costs too much for education."

Partnership members can test the congruence of philosophy and practice by observing their own teaching practice using videotape or audiotape. Videotaping of teaching, originally called MicroTeaching, has a long history. Figure 9.7 provides some suggestions about making a videotape and learning from it. Following the scaffolded knowledge integration framework we recommend making predictions about the lesson using the form described in Fig. 9.8 before videotaping a lesson. As seen in Fig. 9.8, the form asks for predictions about the kind of ideas the students will provide, the sorts of actions the teacher might take, and the likely outcomes of the lesson. To make this sort of lesson effective, a short, focused instructional topic is best. The lesson might in-

Name: Date:	My predictions about the microteaching topic:
What are your goals for the lesson?	(write your predictions here)
Will students have opportunities to try things out on their own?	
What kinds of social supports are provided in the lesson?	
Does the lesson involve using multiple models or multiple ways to representing information?	
What do you think will be the most successful part of the lesson?	
What will students find the most challenging to understand?	

FIG. 9.8   Prediction form filled out by individual teachers before the group meets to help promote reflection.

Videotape yourself teaching to your students.
Find a colleague or colleagues whose opinion you respect as a teacher
Show the videotape of your teaching. Solicit feedback using the following questions:

• How do you think it went?
• How would you characterize my teaching style?
• Did I demonstrate an understanding of the material?
• How did students respond to my teaching?
• What are some alternatives I could use to introduce the lesson?
• How might I motivate students to participate more?
• At this point, what do you think was giving students the most trouble?

FIG. 9.9   This is an example of a video watch and possible questions to ask a colleague when soliciting feedback and critique abut your teaching.

volve tutoring a student on a complex problem, leading a small group discussion, responding to student questions, or making one's own thinking about a topic visible.

Several strategies help to make watching a videotape or listening to an audiotape effective. Suggestions are found in Fig. 9.9. Many recom-

Problems with Current Teaching	New Goals
"I have a tendency to keep talking when I get interested in the topic, but forget to monitor my students' interest in what I am saying"	Design new ways to listen to students and encourage them to provide feedback during the lesson.
"I noticed that I look at students to the right half of the room because I face the board and turn around half way."	Try to address all the students and make better eye contact.
"I give out answers right away when students ask questions without giving them a chance to think.	Create a list of responses and prompts that ask more questions to get students to reflect."
(add more video observations here)	(add new goals here)

FIG. 9.10   This is a sample worksheet that can be used after a video watch to help analyze strengths and weaknesses in teaching.

mend watching the video with a peer and discussing interpretations. A checklist can help determine whether predictions are borne out. In following the scaffolded knowledge integration framework, individuals might watch the video, reflect on strengths, and identify places where improvement could be made. As the form suggests, this process should conclude with a list of goals for the next teaching of the topic (Fig. 9.10). By regularly reflecting on practice, reviewing ideas, and holding these ideas up to those suggested by others, educators can identify new ideas that may prove pivotal in the development of a personal philosophy.

To make pedagogical thinking visible, the teacher might keep a list of ideas that make sense, identify new ideas to add to the list, and select one or two ideas, at most, to work on at any given time. In Fig. 9.11, we show a possible format for keeping track of ideas and describing their application in context. In keeping with the principle of building on what you know, select new accessible ideas that build on what has been successful in the past.

The scaffolded knowledge integration framework recommends critiquing as another way to develop a pedagogical philosophy. Readers might start by critiquing the scaffolded knowledge integration framework, identifying gaps and questionable recommendations, and test-

Goal	Things I've tried	Reflections
Try to get more students to talk during class discussion.	Wait 10 seconds before calling on anyone. Start discussion that catches students' interest such as a prediction about something or a live experiment.	I was a little nervous because of the dead pauses. I noticed that more kids were raising their hands after these pauses.
Present multiple models of the same phenomena using mixed media.	When teaching about heat and temperature, I tried shaking a box of balls to demonstrate kinetic energy of molecules. I also had students use HeatBars.	Students didn't link these two models right away. I had to help students see the relationships between the two models.
Listen to ideas of students; find out what their ideas are about science.	Ask students probing questions during the work period and record them with a notebook. Ask students to explain and take notes using a tape recorder.	One student said he had never thought about this until I asked him!

FIG. 9.11   A table or checklist of ideas can help teachers reflect on their
practices while trying out new things in the classroom.

ing out alternatives. These and other activities enable educators to use the scaffolded knowledge integration framework as a partner in creating a coherent and useful pedagogical philosophy.

Sound Curriculum: Pedagogical content knowledge and pedagogical philosophy.

In developing the sound curriculum, CLP had the opportunity to apply the scaffolded knowledge integration framework when the science of sound, described earlier, did not succeed in promoting knowledge integration. We started by determining the kinds of ideas that students typically bring to science class about the nature of sound (see Fig. 9.5). Students come to science class with widely ranging ideas drawn from very different contexts of activities that include playing musical instruments, listening to music, seeking to keep their rooms quiet, using the telephone, and building listening devices, such as walkie-talkies. Understanding these ideas, a part of pedagogical content knowledge, enabled design of accessible instruction.

Foley, working with the CLP partnership, considered the sorts of questions and observations that students might wish to understand as a result of studying the science of sound. Students expressed interest in understanding how musical instruments work, distinguishing the sounds of different kinds of music (e.g., "creaking door" or classical music), understanding the process of sound recording, explaining why sound does not travel in outer space, explaining echoes, and designing a concert hall. Students also wondered about the ear as a detector of sound and wanted to explain why animals can hear sounds different from those humans are able to hear.

Foley generated a repertoire of promising models for sound. Experts describe sound as a vibration. This view, found in many textbooks, resonates with student ideas. It makes less sense as an explanation of how sound engineers mix various sounds to design a compact disc recording. A source detector model of sound, similar to the model we developed for the science of light, also helps to explain some of the problems that interest students. Both of these models apply to some problems that interest students. Neither completely explains the way orchestras sound in different halls.

After connecting these models to the sound representations, Foley tried the unit again. The sound curriculum was relatively unsuccessful. The technology was difficult to interpret. The vibration model was complex, built on only some of the ideas students brought to class, and connected to only some of the representations. Also, the problems students wanted to solve were difficult to explain using the available models and activities. Foley reflected on these experiences, discussed them with the CLP group, and redesigned the instruction as described later in the chapter.

In summary, the scaffolded knowledge integration framework can serve as a teaching partner by helping designers connect pedagogical philosophy and technology. The framework also can help partnerships analyze their own teaching practices and critique other innovations.

Learn from other partnerships and from experts in related fields

Our third pragmatic pedagogical principle encourages partnership study groups involving teachers at one or several schools. These groups can meet regularly, either in person or as discussed later, online, to discuss their practices. Ideally, experts from other disciplines contribute to these partnerships.

Study groups can critique pedagogical principles espoused by others, test personal pedagogical principles, debate pedagogical perspectives, critique videos of classroom practices, and design educational innovations. For example, groups can analyze videos of classroom instruction such as those developed by the Third International Mathematics and Science Study (TIMSS).

Teacher study groups have proved extremely successful for Japanese education. In Japanese schools, teachers have time to meet together and regularly observe demonstration lessons. Each year, teachers prepare one demonstration lesson and get feedback from peers specializing in their subject matter or grade level. Because Japan has a national curriculum, successful practices are shared widely.

We hope to encourage a similar process of building on each others' success. Partnership groups everywhere can conduct important educational research that others can use. Partnerships of concerned teachers at school sites (or virtually connected) can develop innovations or localize innovations in their schools and communicate with others. They have the opportunity to test educational innovations and philosophical perspectives in the contexts they understand. This provides a richer and more authentic test of pedagogical principles than is characteristic of university initiated research projects conducted in only a few schools. Furthermore, research conducted by study groups applies directly to their own classrooms and therefore can be readily implemented. Groups might ask: Where do lectures fit? How do texts fit? Why are some units more motivating than others? How can we connect science to students' personal concerns? How can instruction ensure that students will use the knowledge gained in future problem solving? When should small groups or collaborations be used in instruction?

In summary, educators have many ways of learning from each other. These include team teaching, virtual team teaching, observing each other's instruction, teaching lessons for each other, analyzing student work in joint sessions (see Ask Mr. K section), and forming study groups. By responding to questions, conundrums, and research issues raised by others, we build knowledge for the field of education.

Sound curriculum: Using peers as learning partners for the science of sound.

To illustrate how educators working in partnership can listen and learn from each other, we return to the sound unit. After Brian Foley completed the preliminary design for this unit, he presented it to the CLP partnership for further discussion and elaboration. The group responded in two primary ways. First the group refined the model of sound used in the unit and helped design a set of personally relevant problems that students might revisit during their lives. Second, the group helped improve the technological representations of sound.

The group contributed more personally relevant sound problems such as: When can everybody hear in the classroom? How do CDs sound? Why do CDs sound differently depending on where you stand in the room? The group reflected on terms to describe sound, asking how the term "sound" is used and about terms such as volume, "pitch," and the like. The group identified web resources on sound, suggesting ways to use online, peer-to-peer discussions about the nature of sound, and engaging students in the same classroom and distant peers. Students might describe the different musical instruments they play and discuss how these instruments transmit and produce sound. These discussions could enable students who do not play musical instruments to learn from others while engaging instrument experts in teaching peers. Enabling distant peers to conduct discussions about sound would ensure that individuals who play unusual instruments could be included.

These activities resulted in a list of what we call sound "facets" or pieces of sound knowledge that make sense to students, teachers, experts, and other citizens. Taken as a group, these form a repertoire of possible models that individuals might have. They are an excellent source of information for the design of assessments because students ultimately need to distinguish among these ideas and select those that are most productive and effective in explaining observable phenomena. These facets articulate the pedagogical content knowledge of sound.

The research group refined the curriculum and assessments for sound (Fig. 9.12). These efforts improved the sound unit and also raised some serious questions about teaching this material. The group initially allocated 2 weeks to the science of sound. This turned out to be woefully inadequate. Four weeks made much more sense. Including the science of sound along with heat, temperature, and light proved difficult in a one-semester course.

The CLP partnership found that adding sound to the energy curriculum reinforced ideas students had learned previously about energy, but it also added nuances and confusions. For example, sound could offer a source-receiver model similar to that used for light. However, we needed to distinguish the mechanisms governing how light and sound travel so that for students to adequately understand issues such as acoustics versus lighting for a room.

The partnership also noted that the unit needed to incorporate the tremendous advances in this field including advances in acoustics, sound recording, digitization of sound, sound systems design, concert hall design and more. Any unit on the science of sound would need regular reflection and updating to meet the needs of middle school students whose interests in music and sound recording are relatively well developed.

Much of this information is available on the Internet, suggesting the advantages of using the KIE to design classroom projects. Students could contrast approaches to sound-proofing a room, research the distinctions between various recording studios, or study methods for amplifying musical instruments in concert halls. All of these challenges and complexities in teaching about the science of sound also make it

- You are standing 50 yards away from a huge wall made of foam rubber.
  Would you hear an echo if you clapped your hands?
  What is the main reason for your answer?
  What would be different if the wall were made of concrete?
  Would you hear an echo if you clapped 3 feet away from the concrete wall?
  What is the main reason for your answer?

- Alicia and Ahmad can hear the radio playing in the next room. Alicia says that the sound must be traveling through the wall, but Ahmad disagrees saying that the sound goes through the cracks in the wall because sound cannot go through wood. Who do you think is right?

Alicia's view: Sound *can* go through the wall.
Ahnad's view: Sound goes through the cracks only.

Why is a sound quieter when there is a wall between you and the source?

- Bertha is crushing some ice in a blender. She tries all of the settings and notices that when the blender is on the "pulverize" (highest) setting it makes a higher pitched sound than when it is on "chop" (lowest). What does this tell you about the relative speed of the motor in the two settings? What is the main reason for your answer? Write a principle that you can use to justify your answer?

- Gunjan notices that when he shakes a piece of poster board, it makes an interesting sound. What could Gunjan do to make a higher pitched sound? What could he do to make a louder sound?

- In outer space there is no air at all. Two astronauts are outside of their ship. One of the astronauts hits a tuning fork against the side of the ship. How would the tuning fork sound to the other astronaut (ignore the space suits)? What is the main reason for your answer?

Miriam's mother calling her

Miriam under water

Miriam loves to swim under water in the pool. But she cannot hear her mother calling when it is time for dinner unless she is really loud. Her sister says it is because sound doesn't travel under water.
Does sound travel under water?

However, one time Miriam was wearing her watch under water and heard the alarm going off, so she thinks that sounds can travel under water.

How could she hear her watch alarm?

Why does Miriam have trouble hearing her mom?

FIG. 9.12   Assessment items used to test students' understanding of the nature of sound.

ideal for lifelong learning because students have reason to revisit their ideas when they upgrade their sound systems.

In summary, partnerships can learn from each other. As a group, the CLP partnership weighed alternative models for students on the basis of classroom experience as well as a scientific perspective. We were able to look at lifelong learning issues from the standpoint of building on what students know and considering what they might want or need to know in their personal lives. In addition, classroom studies with careful analysis of successes and failures shed light on, the design of the sound unit and can help future designs.

Create new professional development partners

All partnerships continuously engage in the knowledge integration process. Teachers improve both their pedagogical philosophy and their classroom practice. Our final pragmatic pedagogical principle says to design a professional development program to support this process of ongoing knowledge integration. Groups can orchestrate the contributions of all available learning partners and create new partners. For example, one of our advisory board members, Jim Minstrell, has established an online and mutually supportive group of physics teachers. Minstrell is encouraging teachers to develop a comprehensive facet list for the topics commonly taught in precollege science.

Keeping each other informed of research findings and new technological tools is another function of sustained professional development. Online communities may facilitate the sharing of this information. Currently, teachers learn about advances, new technologies, and research findings at professional meetings or in professional journals. However, only a small proportion can attend meetings, and journal articles may lack necessary details. Augmenting and enhancing communication using online resources offers promise.

Ongoing professional development programs can serve as matchmakers to unite teachers wishing to form online study groups. Much research demonstrates the advantages of team teaching. By team teaching a topic, each participant learns from the other teacher. Teams formed using online resources can take advantage of this opportunity and increase its use.

Professional development in the United States often is satirized as "glow and go," or "make and take." In the "glow and go" model, an inspirational speaker reminds educators of their many accomplishments. Individuals develop a confident glow and go out into the world. Such professional development programs may neglect reflection on strengths and limitations. In addition, glow and go approaches may not enable communities to become self-supportive because participants relate to the motivational speaker rather than help each other to learn.

In following the "make and take" model, educators at professional development workshops use materials provided by the workshop leaders to make a lesson and take it to use in their classrooms. Many find this approach rewarding because they can implement content or materials not typically available. Ideally, participants' innovations will build on what they already know and localize materials using their pedagogical philosophy. Our new partnerships offer a sustained process of borrowing ideas, building on them, testing them, and using results to improve one's personal pedagogical philosophy.

Professional development programs that orchestrate individuals, peers, and technology as learning partners can set teachers on a path toward lifelong learning. Establishing mechanisms that allow individuals to listen and learn from each other over long periods will ensure the kind of sustained professional development desired by most educational leaders.

For example, teacher professional development groups can jointly design units, such as the sound unit illustrated in this chapter. This unit was built initially by a single teacher. The partnership helped the developer assess and build technological tools to enhance the instruction. The group jointly revised the unit, looked at classroom results, and made suggestions for improvement. Finally, the group brainstormed ways to create new materials that take advantage of ever changing technological resources.

Ideally, professional development programs will support each educator undertaking the design and refinement of new curriculum materials such as the sound unit, or develop local adaptations of existing materials. We encourage readers of this book to create these kinds of professional development communities using resources at our web site.

REFLECTIONS

Finding teaching partners represents an ongoing task for educators, researchers, or administrators. Educational innovations develop rapidly, so creating technology-enhanced instructional materials is a never-ending process. Ideally, participants in this process will support each other. Partnerships can build on the pragmatic pedagogical principles of section II, refining these principles and the scaffolded knowledge integration framework they define.

American models for professional development often have neglected building partnerships among educators. Frequently, professional development implements an outmoded pedagogical philosophy in which lecturers or presenters provide information that they assume their audiences will absorb. Just as students build on what they know, so do all educators build on personal models and beliefs. Redesigning professional development opportunities so that every participant can build on their own knowledge and understanding makes sense, supports knowledge integration, and ultimately can transform science education.

ASK MR. K

Can teachers incorporate technology into their classes?

I think that partnerships are the key. If I could get any message across to teachers, it would be to get involved with other people doing these things. I look back on my career, and even before CLP, when I was part of the Northern California Committee on Problem Solving in Science group, I was in a partnership. The way that worked was that everybody had to present a lesson of some type to that group and get critiqued.

That partnership formed a lot of my early teaching habits. My partnership with CLP was a great thing. Most university research never filters down to the teachers, even at those science conferences. At those conferences, you usually get either publishers presenting their materials or teachers doing hands-on things that they've done. But you never really get, at least at the conferences I've attended, what's really current in research for learning or understanding.

What is your hope for new teachers?

My hope is that they find some partners early on their career that really can serve as colleagues. For me, fellow teachers who are now my longtime friends and partners in CLP have been good for introducing new ideas and serving as friendly critics to my own teaching.

Another thing I would say is that I hope young teachers don't get frustrated too early but keep giving things a try. The trial and refinement process is an important part of making something work, especially in a classroom full of energetic kids and lots of computers. Taking on the attitude that you and the kids will learn something in the end, even if things don't work out right away, is essential for lifelong learning.

Can all teachers use scaffolded knowledge integration?

I hope that the ideas or framework we use for scaffolded knowledge integration can be used by any teacher or any student. In science, there are lots of opportunities to show visualizations and give neat demos to help make things more explicit, but I would guess that in other fields teachers can do the same with things such as role playing and simulations such as a mock trial.

What guides your thinking about pedagogy?

Each school is its own pedagogical community, and, ideally school communities should consider each other's teaching approach while also recognizing that they will be held to state and national standards. You can try to align your curricula with those standards, but not to the point that you neglect your own principles and needs. School communities should interpret standards for their kids, families, and local concerns.

POINTS TO PONDER

- Write a short essay describing your pedagogical philosophy. Discuss how your philosophy applies to the use of computers in instruction.
- Videotape yourself teaching. Analyze the video using the pragmatic pedagogical principles in this volume. Compare your analysis with your pedagogical philosophy.
- Observe a colleague teaching or watch a video of another teacher. Identify some promising practices learned from the observation.
- Interview a few students you have taught about the learning partners in your course. Analyze their comments using the CLP framework.
- Locate state or national science standards. Discuss connections between your philosophy and the standards.

- Analyze your approach to encouraging gender equity in science courses.
- Watch the complete CLP film Computers, Teachers, Peers— Science Learning Partners again. Write down your impressions and reactions. Compare your reactions to those from the first viewing of the film.

RELATED READINGS

Darling-Hammond, L. (1997). *The right to learn: A blueprint for creating schools that work* (Jossey-Bass Education Series). San Francisco: Jossey-Bass Publishers.

diSessa, A. A., & Minstrell, J. (1998). Cultivating conceptual change with benchmark lessons. In J. G. Greeno & S. Goldman (Ed.), *Thinking practices*. Mahwah, NJ: Lawrence Erlbaum Associates.

Fensham, P. J., Gunstone, R. F., & White, R. T. (1994). *The content of science: A constructive approach to its teaching and learning*. Falmer Press.

Karlpus, R. (1967). *A new look at elementary school science*. Chicago, IL: Rand McNally.

Lewis, C. (1995). *Educating hearts and minds: reflections on Japanese preschool and elementary education*. New York: Cambridge University Press.

Shulman, L. S. (1986). Those who understand: Knowledge growth in teaching. *Educational Researcher, 15*(2), 4–14.

10

Outcomes and Opportunities

As we discovered, the Computer as Learning Partner (CLP) curriculum succeeded for a diverse set of learners and achieved a complex set of goals because it included a rich variety of features.

When we revisited the students we first had met in the eighth grade, we were pleased to find that CLP had provided a firm foundation for their future science learning. In their high school interviews, these students demonstrated that they had found new learning partners, including some they had encountered but not used in the eighth grade. Maturity combined with many role models for knowledge integration and some powerful scientific ideas had enabled CLP students to integrate their knowledge successfully after completing the CLP course.

How did the CLP students compare with students who had studied the typical curriculum?

Lawrence Muilenberg, a high school teacher and member of the CLP partnership, helped us compare high school seniors who had studied CLP in middle school with those who had studied the typical middle school curriculum. We found that the students who had participated in CLP were far more successful at understanding heat and temperature than their non-CLP counterparts (Fig. 10.1). Specifically, the under-

standing of the twelfth grade students who had studied the typical curriculum resembled that of the CLP students at the beginning of the
eighth grade.

How did CLP students perform on standardized tests?

Nancy Songer studied the response of CLP students to items from the
National Assessment of Educational Progress. Songer distinguished
multiple-choice items requiring recall from those requiring interpretation and analysis of energy concepts. She found that CLP had little effect on multiple-choice items that required recall. In contrast, on
items requiring interpretation, CLP students outperformed compara-
ble eighth graders and older students. The CLP students also performed better on some items requiring interpretation of graphs.

We also wanted to know whether the fewer topics "covered" in CLP
would affect the students' performance on standardized tests. Our col-
laborator, Douglas Kirkpatrick, found that CLP students were just as
successful as their counterparts on standardized tests at the end of the

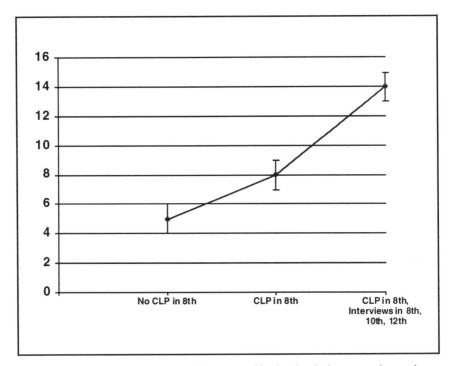

Fig. 10.1   The differences in performance of high school physics students who
have and have not had CLP instruction on a test of energy concepts.

eighth grade, even though they had studied fewer topics in CLP than they would have encountered in traditional classes.

Each time we revised the CLP curriculum, we conducted design studies to document that the new version improved knowledge integration. As described in chapters 2 through 5, we found that in the first eight versions of CLP we achieved a 400% increase in student performance on our most difficult outcome measure. We also found that boys and girls were equally successful on all our outcome measures.

How does CLP compare to instruction in other countries?

With the CLP curriculum, most of a semester is required to teach students about energy. Students study complex, personally relevant problems in depth, instead of being exposed to numerous, isolated examples. Cross-national comparisons support our depth approach. Sparked by findings from the Third International Mathematics and Science Study (TIMSS), U.S. educators are rethinking a science curriculum described as "an inch deep and a mile wide." The TIMSS results revealed that Japanese and American students diverge sharply in science performance between the fourth and seventh grades. Although students in the two countries perform similarly in fourth grade, by seventh grade Japanese students remain near the top of all countries studied, whereas American students score at about the middle of all countries studied, and about one grade level lower than Japanese students.

One important difference between the eighth-grade curriculum in the United States and Japan is the number of topics covered. Japanese students, like CLP students, cover eight topics, whereas typical American students cover 35 to 40 topics.

Our experience with the CLP partnership underscored our belief that a science curriculum is most successful when it is developed and regularly refined by people with diverse interests and different areas of expertise—classroom teachers, scientists, educational researchers, computer specialists *et alia*—who come together in a spirit of mutual respect to fulfill a common goal.

Debate was often heated in the course of designing CLP. For example, we debated key instructional issues such as what level of analysis would be both appropriate and accessible for introducing a new concept. Out of that debate came a curriculum that was strong, multifaceted, equitable, and appropriate for a wide variety of learners.

The design process at once drove and reflected what we were attempting to accomplish in the classroom. We integrated our knowledge, built on diverse ideas, made our thinking visible, learned from each other, and constantly reflected on the classroom experience.

This process, combined with clear goals, such as promoting knowledge integration, spurred our creativity at every step of the way. For example, rather than accept existing computer tools, our partnership revised and revised until we were convinced that we were using computers in a way that promoted knowledge integration. Accordingly, we started with real-time data collection but ended up with the Electronic Laboratory Notebook that included predictions, reflections, collaboration with other groups, connections to the heat flow simulation, and synthesis of findings.

We also found that our negotiations with each other about what pedagogical principles to emphasize made decision making easier and more effective as we progressed. In our subsequent work on the Knowledge Integration Environment (KIE) project, we successfully found ways to make the Internet a learning partner for knowledge integration because we already had in place a set of agreed-on criteria and powerful examples.

Our project made it clear that learning science is complex. By revealing that students follow complex paths to knowledge integration, our case studies helped to explain why the fleeting coverage in most middle school textbooks cannot succeed. Many students rebelled when asked to reflect about their scientific notions in the CLP classroom, but most eventually become engaged in integrating their ideas.

The case studies also explained why the many proposed quick fixes have failed. Innovations need iterative refinement to become effective for students. We need more than quick fixes. Partnerships and design studies are needed to create instruction that leads to lifelong learning.

We also need mechanisms to ensure that curricular materials build on the ideas that students find compelling. Our projects on house design illustrated the importance of adapting materials for local use. Students in the Southwest had ideas about adobe; those in the Northeast used their experience with bricks; and those in California worried about earthquakes.

As the examples in section II illustrate, the CLP partners have learned from mistakes and failures. Our first efforts to identify science principles for students were unsuccessful. Students did not engage in knowledge integration when we emphasized molecular kinetic theory, so we sought the more accessible heat flow model. Promoting autonomy proved extremely difficult. We regularly explored trade-offs between providing too much structure in projects and leaving projects too open-ended. We knew that peer interaction was important, but found it difficult to orchestrate. We found that online discussions could support small groups and increase the quality of student comments in a large class size (32 students). It remains a challenge for science instructors to reward collaborative work and to assess students individually when they work in a group.

The CLP project alerted us to other student needs beyond the scope of our project to address: Students were seeking more examples that tie science to their own interests. They needed more opportunities to critique accounts of scientific phenomena. They wanted broader connections across science topics and more opportunities to do projects and connect them to the work of scientists.

As discussed in chapters 8 and 9, we have responded to these needs by initiating three new partnerships that use the CLP pragmatic pedagogical principles and take advantage of the Internet to give students the support they need for carrying out complex projects: the Knowledge Integration Environment partnership (KIE) uses Web-based software tools to create student-centered science activities; the Web-based Integrated Science Environment (WISE) partnership, helps students explore interdisciplinary problems such as global ecology; and SCOPE, the Science Controversy On-line: Partnerships for Education (SCOPE), helps students understand how scientists debate current issues.

We invite everyone interested in knowledge integration and science learning to join these partnerships. We also hope that *Computers, Teachers, Peers—Science Learning Partners* will motivate readers to form new partnerships and report their experiences.

See you at our web-site: *www.clp.berkeley.edu*

POINTS TO PONDER

- Look at a version of a state or national test used in your area. Analyze how the items align with the topics you teach.
- Reflect on the role of state tests in the design of instruction. Do these tests encourage students to become lilfelong science learners?
- Discuss why American students might be less successful than students in Asia and Europe on international tests.
- Reflect on how the CLP film, this volume, and discussions with your peers contributed to your understanding of science learning.

RELATED READINGS

Linn, M. C., Shear, L., Bell, P., & Slotta, J. D. (1999). Connecting school science with real science: A knowledge integration model of partnerships between teachers, scientists, and educators. *Educational Technology Research and Development, Special Issue 47*, 61–84.

Shymansky, J. A., Kyle, W. C., Jr., & Alport, J. M. (1983). The effects of new science curricula on student performance. *Journal of Research in Science Teaching, 20*, 387–404.

Walker, D. F. & Schaffarzik, J. (1974). Comparing curricula. *Review of Educational Research, 44*, 83–111.

Glossary

Activity structures: Activity structures organize the interactions among participants in a classroom to enable learning. They include small-group discussion, large-group discussion, individual experimentation, teacher-led reflection, and other patterns of intellectual interactions. Multistep activity structures often implement a specific form of learning. For example, in the jigsaw activity structure small groups specialize in a topic such as heat flow. Then new groups formed by including experts from each of the specializations solve a complex problem.

Agreement bars: Agreement bars are a feature of the Electronic Laboratory Notebook software that encourages students to reach consensus. Each student working in a group indicates his or her level of agreement with a group-written conclusion. After more discussion or changes to the group note, members can alter their agreement.

Assessments: Assessments are any collection of methods used to elicit students' accomplishments and knowledge integration. These include pretests, posttests, surveys, interviews, homework assignments, project assignments, class presentations, small-group discussion captured on videotape, interviews captured on audiotape, problem solutions, laboratory reports, or standardized tests.

Autonomous learning: Autonomous learning refers to self-directed engagement in the practice of knowledge integration. Autonomous learners take responsibility for their own learning instead of relying on scaffolds or external demands. In the CLP curriculum, projects enable students gradually to conduct larger and larger autonomous investigations. Lifelong learners of science engage in autonomous knowledge integration.

Beliefs about science: Beliefs about science refers to the ideas, views, and perceptions that students have about the scientific inquiry process. The inquiry process is interpreted broadly to include the scientists, social interactions, experiments, conclusions, debates, conjectures, and reports that contribute to scientific research and development. The CLP partnership developed assessments of beliefs about science that asked students to explain the nature of scientific knowledge, the character of scientific disputes, the practice of science, and the interpretation of scientific findings. For example, students reported that "science is a collection of facts," "only adults can be scientists," and "scientists disagree because they distrust each other."

Computer as Learning Partner (CLP): The acronym CLP is an abbreviation for the Computer as Learning Partner project, an educational research project at the University of California supported by the National Science Foundation under the direction of Professor Marcia C. Linn.

Conceptual change: Conceptual change describes a process in which learners' adopt a new, coherent explanation for a scientific phenomena. Some research groups look for students to abandon one conception in favor of another and call this conceptual change. The CLP group views conceptual change as a form of knowledge integration. From the CLP perspective, conceptual change occurs when new concepts get added to the mix of ideas, are sorted out, and eventually lead to a restructured view. In the CLP view, ideas are not abandoned but instead are reorganized and reinterpreted. For example, students who believe that metals impart cold may reinterpret this view to explain that heat flows faster to metals than to other materials.

Concurrent design: In CLP, we design assessments concurrently with the instruction following the concurrent design methodology commonly used in engineering. Creating assessments aligned with the instruction is more likely when the designs are created at the same time. In addition, the designers often learn about their goals by comparing the designs for the assessment and the instruction. In CLP, we iteratively improved the assessments along with the instruction.

Continuum Line: The Continuum Line, designed by Nancy Songer, is both an assessment and a class activity about insulation and conduction. Students can either design and label their own continuum line or place materials such as Styrofoam, silver, cardboard, or Saran Wrap™ along a line labeled at the end points. The labels have varied. Two options are "good conductor" and "good insulator" or "poor insulator" and "good insulator."

Cybercoach: The Cybercoach, designed by Helen Clark, allows teachers quickly to compose coaching messages on student projects by using an electronic collection of hints and suggestions that have been relevant to the project for other students. A single human tutor can efficiently coach many students. In the CLP curriculum, we used the Cybercoach for the portfolio activities.

Design studies: Design studies are research investigations carried out in classrooms to investigate the effectiveness of all aspects of the instruction. Often these studies result in revisions of the instruction. For example, we might learn that a subset of the students participate in the online discussion and alter the environment to meet the needs of the other students. Or, we might learn that students have an intuitive idea that does not connect to the instruction and add an activity that addresses the intuition. These studies use a broad range of methodologies including observations, classroom tests, interviews, case studies, teacher diaries, and portfolios. Ideally design studies are carefully worked out by the partnership involved in creating the instruction.

Electronic discussion: Electronic discussion occurs in a computer environment in which students and teachers enter comments that are broadcast to other participants. In the CLP curriculum, students contribute to an online, asynchronous discussion using the Multimedia Forum Kiosk.

Electronic Laboratory Notebook: The Electronic Laboratory Notebook, designed by Judith Stern, scaffolded students to conduct scientific inquiry in the CLP curriculum. Using the Electronic Laboratory Notebook, teachers design prompts, help notes, real-time and simulated experiments. Students then carry out experiments with the help of Electronic Laboratory Notebook checklists, notes, principles, and prototypes.

Equity: Equity refers to the process of ensuring that each student has the same opportunity to learn, to use computers, or to engage in some other instructional activity. The CLP partnership sought to create equitable instruction for all students enrolled in school including students of both sexes, with learning disabilities, and from diverse racial and ethnic groups. Designing for equity involves research to understand the obstacles and subtle pressures that alter the learning environment for individuals. For example, we found that ensuring equitable access to class discussion meant including electronic discussion in the mix of activity structures.

Expert interviews: Expert interviews are question and answer sessions in which scientists respond to problems in their area of specialization. The CLP partnership interviewed experts to understand how specialists use their integrated understanding to respond to problems that students typically face.

Frames: Frames are topics for organizing scientific arguments. Students can frame their argument using boxes that enclose Internet links in the SenseMaker software.

HeatBars: HeatBars, software designed by Brian Foley and Eileen Lewis, simulates the rate of heat flow in two parallel bars of material. The simulation allows students to choose the material of the bar, the starting temperature, the temperature of the heat source, and the duration of the experiment. Students select from materials such as copper, wood, silver, aluminum, and glass. See the CD-ROM.

Holistic grading: Holistic grading refers to the process of rating student work on a single dimension such as knowledge integration. The CLP partnership developed criteria and methods for training raters to give reliable holistic scores to students' portfolio projects and design activities.

Kinetic model of heat: In the kinetic model, heat refers to the total kinetic energy in a substance. Temperature is a measure of the average speed or kinetic energy of the atoms or molecules.

Knowledge integration: Knowledge integration refers to the process of making sense of science that includes adding new ideas to the mix of views about a topic, linking and connecting new and existing ideas, sorting out the ideas available, reflecting on the ideas while solving problems, and restructuring views to achieve more coherence. In the CLP curriculum, students link and connect the ideas they bring to science class to CLP experiments, everyday examples, firsthand experiences, ideas of other students, prototypes, and principles. Students progress in knowledge integration by gaining more robust and coherent perspectives on a science topic.

Learning partners: Learning partners in CLP refers to aspects of instruction that help students with knowledge integration. Learning
partners can model effective reasoning patterns, encourage reflection, provide hints, introduce pivotal cases, and support sustained
reasoning. Teachers, peers, and computers all can serve as learning
partners.

Level of analysis: Level of analysis refers to the mechanism governing
an explanation of a scientific phenomenon in the CLP curriculum. In
science, many explanations occur at a microscopic level of analysis
in the sense that they depend on interactions among molecules, atoms, or subatomic particles that cannot be observed directly. Explanations at a macroscopic level of analysis often make more sense to
students because the factors influencing the outcome are observable. For example, students can observe heat flow when they stir hot
soup with a metal spoon. Scientists use models at many levels of
analysis, and part of understanding a scientific phenomena involves
linking explanations from one level to another.

Microcomputer-based laboratories (MBLs): Microcomputer-based laboratories (MBLs) designed for students by Bob Tinker and his collaborators, allow sensors or probes to be connected to an interface box
and a personal computer. The hardware for MBLs permits students
to measure physical phenomena such as the temperature of a cup of
hot chocolate and see the results graphed on the computer. The CLP
project first used MBLs with the Apple II computers. Currently,
many versions are available.

Molecular kinetic theory: Molecular kinetic theory states that temperature is a measure of the kinetic energy of molecules. In this model,
the molecular motion of atoms or molecules shows the relation between temperature and heat.

Multimedia evidence: Multimedia evidence refers to electronic material that combines several media such as text, digital video, images,
or sound. In the CLP curriculum, multimedia evidence is offered
over the Internet and used to construct a scientific argument. Students construct arguments using multimedia evidence in the software SenseMaker.

Multimedia Forum Kiosk: The Multimedia Forum Kiosk, designed by
Sherry Hsi and Christopher Hoadley, is a stand-alone discussion tool
that uses multimedia evidence to introduce a topic. The Multimedia
Forum Kiosk allows students to review the multimedia topic introduction, electronically post an opinion, read comments by others,

and contribute more comments to the discussion. Students can display their names and photos with their comments or they can choose to make anonymous contributions.

Normative models in science: Normative scientific models refers to accounts of scientific phenomena accepted by most scientists. Most scientists view normative scientific models as correct or likely to be correct. For example, molecular kinetic theory is a normative view of heat and temperature.

Pedagogical content knowledge: Pedagogical content knowledge, described by Professor Lee Shulman at Stanford University, refers to the knowledge and understanding of a discipline necessary to teach it effectively. Pedagogical content knowledge involves understanding the ideas students bring to class, the normative scientific models, and the pivotal cases that help students achieve knowledge integration.

Personally relevant problem: A personally relevant problem is a question faced by a typical individual. In the area of heat and temperature, individuals face problems such as keeping warm in cold climates, keeping food safe for picnics, or making sense of the wind-chill factor.

Pivotal cases: Pivotal cases motivate students to restructure their understanding and achieve a more robust and coherent view of a scientific phenomenon. Pivotal cases are naturally controlled experiments that add convincing evidence to the mix of ideas held by students. Pivotal cases, when introduced, enable many students to improve their knowledge integration.

Polyline: Polyline, a software program developed in Israel by Rafi Nachmias, allows students to explore the concept of a scientific variable. Students experiment to determine how a set of undefined variables influence the drawing of a polygon. They predict the influence of a variable and test their prediction by entering values and watching the polygon appear on the screen. The variables determine the size, number, shape, and other properties of the drawings. Polyline introduces both computers and the concept of controlling variables in experimentation.

Portfolios: Portfolios are collections of student work that capture their progress in knowledge integration. Students include drafts of their work, comments by teachers or parents, and their own reflections on their progress. In the CLP curriculum students put their small, medium, and large projects in their portfolios and also include comments from coaches and reflections on their progress.

Pragmatic pedagogical principles: Pragmatic pedagogical principles capture instructional phenomena at a level of analysis that enables easy connection to everyday teaching situations. Pragmatic refers to the usefulness of a principle for connecting to typical experiences and encouraging knowledge integration. Modeled after pragmatic scientific principles, these principles organize and structure this volume. For example, a pragmatic pedagogical principle says, "Encourage students to investigate personally relevant problems and revisit their science ideas regularly."

Pragmatic scientific principles: Pragmatic scientific principles capture scientific phenomena at a level of analysis that enables easy connection to personally relevant problems. By pragmatic we refer to the usefulness of these principles for fostering knowledge integration in everyday situations. For example, a pragmatic scientific principle related to heat and temperature says, "The more heat is added, the hotter an object gets." These principles are used in the CLP curriculum to help students to abstract, generalize, and connect their class and everyday experiences. These principles are designed to enable students to revisit their scientific ideas and enhance their knowledge integration after they finish a science class.

Probes: Probes are analog sensors or devices that monitor the environment. Through an interface box, the data gathered from probes are converted to digital information and communicated to a computer. Probes allow students to collect and measure physical phenomena and display it on the computer. The CLP curriculum uses temperature and light intensity probes for real-time data collection.

Productive thinking program: The productive thinking program, designed by Professor Martin Covington at the University of California, Berkeley, engaged students in reasoning about complex situations and using inductive and deductive logic to reach conclusions.

Prompts: Prompts in the CLP curriculum are sentence starters that students complete as they conduct scientific investigations. Prompts motivate students to reflect on their scientific work. The Electronic Laboratory Notebook provided various forms of prompts to encourage reflection and promote knowledge integration. For example, students respond to prompts such as: "We predict that ... " or "Something that helps explain our results is ... "

Prototypes: Prototypes are everyday examples that students understand and can connect to pragmatic scientific principles. Typically
students can predict the outcome in a prototypic situation, but cannot necessarily explain why the outcome occurs. For example, students can predict that a metal pole will get hot faster than a wooden
pole when they are roasting marshmallows, but may be unable to explain that metal is a better conductor than wood. Students link prototypes to experiments in the Electronic Laboratory Notebook.

Real-time data collection: Real-time data collection refers to the process of using probes to collect data and computers to display data
while an experiment is conducted. MBLs allow students to use
real-time data collection to display temperature changes in the
Electronic Laboratory Notebook.

Role models: Role models are individuals who depict career paths or
reasoning patterns that students can add to the mix of ideas they
have about science or another topic. For example, science courses
often feature the life stories of living or dead scientists to reinforce
the diversity of people involved in the practice of science. In the CLP
curriculum, students use computers named after a set of diverse and
interesting scientists. Students research the lives of these scientists, post their reports, and discuss the nature of science.

Scaffolding: Scaffolding, a term used by education philosopher Jerome
Bruner, refers to the help and guidance provided to enable students
to perform complex tasks. Scaffolding takes many forms including
help from peers, guidance from software, and coaching from teachers. In the CLP curriculum, our learning partners all provide scaffolding. Scaffolding can make a behavior or practice explicit by
using a role model or a prototype. As students become more autonomous they need less scaffolding to engage in knowledge integration.

Scientific inquiry: Scientific inquiry refers to the whole range of activities that lead to advances in scientific understanding. Scientists and
students engage in scientific inquiry to enhance their knowledge integration and to establish scientific ideas that others can use. The
inquiry process involves a broad range of scientific activities that include recognizing a problem, making an educated guess, formulat-
ing hypotheses, carrying out careful observations, critiquing
results, predicting the consequences of a hypothesis, performing experiments to test predictions, communicating results to others, negotiating understanding with others, abstracting findings into
principles, and planning additional investigations. In the CLP curriculum, we tried several approaches to teaching about scientific in-

quiry including the development of pragmatic scientific principles governing inquiry.

Scientific reasoning: Scientific reasoning refers to the normative models used to make inferences in scientific inquiry. In the CLP curriculum, students use scientific reasoning to construct arguments and make reports. They critique experiments by assessing the use of scientific reasoning by others.

Self-monitoring: Students engage in self-monitoring when they reflect on their understanding and progress in learning. Some students spontaneously monitor their activities whereas others seem surprised when asked to predict how well they will do on a test. Reflection activities can help students become more effective at self-monitoring. Lifelong learning involves skill in self-monitoring.

SenseMaker: SenseMaker, software designed by Philip Bell, scaffolds students to construct scientific arguments using Internet evidence. Students can sort evidence in the form of web links, organize the evidence in frames, and communicate their argument by arranging the frames. The SenseMaker was first used for the How Far Does Light Go? debate project.

Shared criteria: Shared criteria are standards that a group endorses for evaluating arguments or evidence. In the CLP curriculum, students negotiate shared criteria for their Electronic Laboratory Notebook reports. Educators develop shared criteria to evaluate teaching practices, curriculum materials, software, and assessments.

Simulated experiments: Simulated experiments are investigations in which students use software to carry out comparisons and reach conclusions. In CLP, experiments in the Electronic Laboratory Notebook that do not involve real-time data collection are simulated. Students design simulated experiments using the same format they followed for hands-on experiments.

Social roles: Social roles are the positions individuals hold in the community. For example, individuals might be expert scientists in one community and tone-deaf music enthusiasts in another. In the CLP curriculum, we encourage students to experiment with social roles such as science critic or science instructor to enable them to integrate their ideas about the social context of science.

Statistical Programs for the Social Sciences (SPSS): The acronym SPSS refers to software that allows users to analyze data using established procedures such as analysis of variance, regression, and chi-square.

Thermal Model Kit: The Thermal Model Kit, software designed by Mark Thomas, allows students to build two-dimensional models of everyday objects and simulate the flow of heat.

Transfer: Transfer refers to the ability of a student to apply understanding learned in one situation to a problem, topic, or issue encountered in another situation. Students can transfer understanding from one problem to another or from one science topic such as heat to another topic such as sound. To assess knowledge integration in the CLP curriculum, we look at students' ability to transfer their understanding to new personally relevant problems, to situations governed by the same pragmatic scientific principles, and to new scientific inquiry situations.

References

American Institutes for Research (1998). *Gender gaps: Where schools still fail our children*. Washington, DC: American Association of University Women Educational Foundation.

Ames, C. (1992). Classrooms: Goals, structures, and student motivation. *Journal of Educational Psychology, 84*(3), 261–71.

Bell, P. (1997). Using argument representations to make thinking visible. In R. Hall, N. Miyake, & N. Enyedy (Eds.), *Proceedings of CSCL '97: The Second International Conference on Computer Support for Collaborative Learning* (pp. 10–19). Toronto, Canada: University of Toronto Press.

Bell, P. (1998). *Designing for students' conceptual change in science using argumentation and classroom debate*. Unpublished doctoral dissertation, University of California, Berkeley, CA.

Bell, P., Davis, E. A., & Linn, M. C. (1995). The knowledge integration environment: Theory and design. In J. L. Schnase & E. L. Cunnius (Ed.), *Proceedings of the Computer Supported Collaborative Learning Conference, CSCL '95, Bloomington, IN* (pp. 14–21). Mahwah, NJ: Lawrence Erlbaum Associates.

Bell, J. E., Linn, M. C., & Clancy, M. J. (1994). Knowledge integration in introductory programming: CodeProbe and interactive case studies. *Interactive Learning Environments, 4*(1), 75–95.

Bell, P., & Linn, M. C. (in press). Scientific arguments as learning artifacts: Designing for learning from the web with KIE. *International Journal of Science Education, Special issue*.

Bell, P., & Stern, J. (1994). National Information Infrastructure: Access isn't enough. *Computer Professionals for Social Responsibility, 12*(2), 4–5.

Brown, A. L., & Campione, J. C. (1994). Guided discovery in a community of learners. In K. McGilly (Ed.), *Classroom lessons: Integrating cognitive theory and classroom practice* (pp. 229–270). Cambridge, MA: MIT Press/Bradford Books.

Bruer, J. T. (1993). *Schools for thought: A science of learning in the classroom.* Cambridge, MA: MIT Press.

Burbules, N. C., & Linn, M. C. (1988). Response to contradiction: Scientific reasoning during adolescence. *Journal of Educational Psychology, 80*(1), 67–75.

Burbules, N. C., & Linn, M. C. (1991). Science education and the philosophy of science: Congruence or contradiction? *International Journal of Science Education, 13*(3), 227–241.

Bruner, J. S. (1960). *The process of education.* Cambridge, MA: Harvard University Press.

Chi, M. T. H., Bassok, M., Lewis, M. W., Reimann, P., & Glaser, R. (1989). Self-explanations: How students study and use examples in learning to solve problems. *Cognitive Science, 13*, 145–182.

Clark, H. C. (1996). *Design of Performance-Based Assessments as Contributors to Student Knowledge Integration.* Unpublished doctoral dissertation, University of California, Berkeley, CA.

Clement, J. (1990). Genius is not immune to persistent misconceptions: Conceptual difficulties impeding Isaac Newton and contemporary students. *International Journal of Science Education, 12*(3), 265–273.

Clement, J. (1993). Using bridging analogies and anchoring intuitions to deal with students' preconceptions in physics. *Journal of Research in Science Teaching, 30*(10), 1241–1257.

Cohen, E. G. (1984). Talking and working together: Status, interaction, and learning. In P. L. Peterson, L. C. Wilkinson, & M. Hallinan (Eds.), *The social context of instruction: Group organization and group processes* (pp. 171–187). New York: Academic Press.

Collins, A., Brown, J. S., & Holum, A. (1991). Cognitive apprenticeship: Making thinking visible. *American Educator, 15*(3), 6–11, 38–39.

Covington, M. V. (1998). *The will to learn: A guide for motivating young people.* Cambridge, UK: Cambridge University Press.

Darling-Hammond, L. (1997). *The right to learn: A blueprint for creating schools that work.* San Francisco: Jossey-Bass.

Davis, E. A. (1998). *Scaffolding students' reflection for science learning.* Unpublished doctoral dissertation, University of California, Berkeley, CA.

Davis, E., & Linn, M. C. (in press). Scaffolding students' knowledge integration: Prompts for reflection in KIE. *International Journal of Science Education.*

Davis, E. A., Linn, M. C., Mann, L. M., & Clancy, M. J. (1993). Mind your Ps and Qs: Using parentheses and quotes in LISP. In C. R. Cook, J. C. Scholtz, & J. C. Spohrer (Eds.), *Empirical studies of programmers: Fifth workshop* (pp. 62–85). Paper presented at the Fifth Workshop on Empirical Studies of Programmers, Palo Alto, CA. Norwood, NJ: Ablex.

De Corte, E., Linn, M. C., Mandl, H., & Verschaffel, L. (Eds.). (1992). *Computer-based learning environments and problem solving,* (NATO ASI Series F: Computer and System Series). Berlin: Springer-Verlag.

Dewey, J. (1901). *Psychology and social practice (University of Chicago Contributions to education).* Chicago: University of Chicago Press.

Dewey, J. (1938). *Experience and education.* New York: Collier books/ Macmillan.

diSessa, A. (1988). Knowledge in pieces. In G. Forman & P. Pufall (Eds.), *Constructivism in the computer age* (pp. 49–70). Hillsdale, NJ: Lawrence Erlbaum Associates.

diSessa, A., & Minstrell, J. (1998). Cultivating conceptual change with bench-mark lessons. In J. G. Greeno & S. Goldman (Ed.), *Thinking practices*. Mahwah, NJ: Lawrence Erlbaum Associates.

Driver, R. (1983). *The pupil as scientist?* London, England: Open University Press.

Erickson, G. L. (1979). Children's conceptions of heat and temperature. *Science Education, 63*(2), 221–30.

Eylon, B. S., & Linn, M. C. (1988). Learning and instruction: An examination of four research perspectives in science education. *Review of Educational Research, 58*(3), 251–301.

Fensham, P. J., Gunstone, R. F., & White, R. T. (1994). *The Content of Science*: A Constructive Approach to its Teaching and Learning. Falmer Press.

Feynman, R. P., Leighton, R. B., & Sands, M. L. (1995). *Six easy pieces : essentials of physics, explained by its most brilliant teacher.* Reading, MA: Addison-Wesley.

Friedler, Y., Nachmias, R., & Linn, M. C. (1990). Learning scientific reasoning skills in microcomputer-based laboratories. *Journal of Research in Science Teaching, 27*(2), 173–191.

Friedler, Y., Nachmias, R., & Songer, N. B. (1989). Teaching scientific reasoning skills: A case study of a microcomputer-based curriculum. *School Science Education, 89*(1).

Gardner, H. (1987). *The mind's new science.* New York: Basic Books.

Gardner, H. (1993). *Multiple intelligences: The theory in practice.* New York: Basic Books.

Gardner, M., Greeno, J. G., Reif, F., Schoenfeld, A. H., diSessa, A., & Stage, E. (Eds.). (1990). *Toward a scientific practice of science education.* Hillsdale, NJ: Lawrence Erlbaum Associates.

Gelman, R., & Linn, M. C. (1987). On the use of hands-on materials in science class. *Continuum: Newsletter of PATHS and the Philadelphia Renaissance in Science and Mathematics* (May/June), p. 3.

Gordin, D. N., Polman, J. L., & Pea, R. D. (1994). The Climate Visualizer: Sense-making through scientific visualization. *Journal of Science Education and Technology, 3*(4), 203–226.

Hoadley, C. (In press). *Teaching science through on-line peer discussions: Speak easy in the knowledge integration enfironment.* International Journal of Science Education, special issue.

Hoadley, C. (1999). *Scaffolding scientific discussion using socially relevant representations in networked multimedia.* Unpublished doctoral dissertation, University of California, Berkeley, CA.

Hoadley, C., & Hsi, S. (1994). Multimedia: A chance for change. *Computer Professionals for Social Responsibility, 12*(2), 10, 12–13.

Hoadley, C. M., & Hsi, S. (1993). A multimedia interface for knowledge building and collaborative learning. In *The Adjunct Proceedings of InterCHI '93, (International Computer–Human Interaction Conference)* (pp. 103–104). Amsterdam, The Netherlands: Association for Computing Machinery.

Hoadley, C. M., Hsi, S., & Berman, B. P. (1995). Networked multimedia for communication and collaboration. Paper presented at the *Annual Meeting of the American Educational Research Association, April,* San Francisco, CA.

Hoadley, C. M., Mann, L. M., Linn, M. C., & Clancy, M. J. (1996). When, why, and how do novice programmers reuse code? In W. Gray & D. Boehm-Davis

(Eds.), *Empirical studies of programmers: Sixth workshop* (pp. 109–129). Norwood, NJ: Ablex.

Hsi, S. (1997). *Facilitating knowledge integration in science through electronic discussion: The Multimedia Forum Kiosk*. Unpublished doctoral dissertation, University of California, Berkeley, CA.

Hsi, S., & Hoadley, C. M. (1997). Productive discussion in science: Gender equity through electronic discourse. *Journal of Science Education and Technology, 6*(1), 23–36.

Hsi, S., Hoadley, C. M., & Linn, M. C. (1995). Lessons for the future of electronic collaboration from the Multimedia Forum Kiosk. *Speculations in Science and Technology, 18*, 265–277.

Hsi, S., Linn, M. C., & Bell, J. E. (1997). The role of spatial reasoning in engineering and the design of spatial instruction. *Journal of Engineering Education, 86*(2), 151–158.

Hsi, S. H., & Agogino, A. M. (1994). The impact and instructional benefit of using multimedia case studies to teach engineering design. *Journal of Educational Multimedia and Hypermedia.*

Hunt, J. M. (1961). *Intelligence and experience.* New York: Ronald Press Co.

Hutchins, E. (1996). *Cognition in the wild.* Cambridge, MA: MIT Press.

Hyde, J. S., & Linn, M. C. (Eds.). (1986). *The psychology of gender: Advances through meta-analysis.* Baltimore, MD: Johns Hopkins University Press.

Inhelder, B., & Piaget, J. (1958). *The growth of logical thinking from childhood to adolescence; an essay on the construction of formal operational structures.* New York: Basic Books.

Jasanoff, S., Colwell, R., Dresselhaus, M. S., Goldman, R. D., Linn, M. C., & others (1997). Conversations with the community: AAAS at the millenium. *Science, 278*(5356), 2066–2067.

Kafai, Y. B. (1995). *Minds in play: Computer game design as a context for children's learning.* In Computer-based learning environments and problem solving. Hillsdale, NJ: Lawrence Erlbaum Associates.

Kafai, Y., & Resnick, M. (Eds.). (1996). *Constructionism in practice: Designing, thinking, and learning in a digital world.* Mahwah, NJ: Lawrence Erlbaum Associates.

Karplus, R., & Thier, H. D. (1967). *A new look at elementary school science: Science Curriculum Improvement Study.* Chicago, IL: Rand McNally & Co.

Keller, E. F. (1983). *A feeling for the organism: The life and work of Barbara McClintock.* San Francisco, CA: W. H. Freeman.

Kessel, C., & Linn, M. C. (1996). Grades or scores: Predicting college mathematics performance. *Educational Measurement: Issues and Practices, 15*(4), 10–14, 38.

Kuhn, D., Amsel, E., O'Loughlin, M., & with the assistance of L. Schauble (1988). *The development of scientific thinking skills (developmental psychology series).* Orlando, FL: Academic Press.

Kyle Jr., W. C., Linn, M. C., Bitner, B. L., Mitchener, C. P., & Perry, B. (1991). The role of research in science teaching: An NSTA theme paper. *Science Education, 75*(4), 413–418.

Laws, P. W. (1997). *Workshop physics activity guide.* New York: Wiley.

Levine, D. I., & Linn, M. C. (1977). Scientific reasoning ability in adolescence: Theoretical viewpoints and educational implications. *Journal of Research in Science Teaching, 14*, 371–384.

Lewis, C. (1995). *Educating hearts and minds: Reflections on Japanese pre-school and elementary education.* New York: Cambridge University Press.

Lewis, C., Schaps, E., & Watson, M. (1995). Beyond the pendulum: Creating caring and challenging schools. *Phi Delta Kappan, 76,* 547–554.

Lewis, C., & Tsuchida, I. (1997). Planned educational change in Japan: The case of elementary science instruction. *Journal of Educational Policy, 12*(5), 313–331.

Lewis, E. L. (1991). *The process of scientific knowledge acquisition among middle school students learning thermodynamics.* Unpublished doctoral dissertation, University of California, Berkeley, CA.

Lewis, E. L. (1996). Conceptual change among middle school students studying elementary thermodynamics. *Journal of Science Education and Technology, 5*(1), 3–31.

Lewis, E. L., & Foley, B. (1987–1997). *HeatBars visualization* [software]. Berkeley, CA: University of California at Berkeley.

Lewis, E. L., & Linn, M. C. (1994). Heat energy and temperature concepts of adolescents, adults, and experts: Implications for curricular improvements. *Journal of Research in Science Teaching, 31*(6), 657–677.

Lewis, E. L., Stern, J., & Linn, M. C. (1993). The effect of computer simulations on introductory thermodynamics understanding. *Educational Technology, 33*(1), 45–58.

Lieberman, D. A., & Linn, M. C. (1991). Learning to learn revisited: Computers and the development of self-directed learning skills. *Journal of Research on Computing in Education, 23*(3), 373–395.

Linn, M. C. (1970). *Effects of a training procedure on matrix performance and on transfer tasks.* Unpublished doctoral dissertation, Stanford University, Stanford, CA.

Linn, M. C. (1972). An experiential science curriculum for the visually impaired. *Exceptional Children, 39,* 37–43.

Linn, M. C. (1978). Influence of cognitive style and training on tasks requiring the separation of variables schema. *Child Development, 49,* 874–877.

Linn, M. C. (1980). Free-choice experiences: How do they help children learn? *Science Education, 64*(2).

Linn, M. C. (1980). Teaching children to control variables: Some investigations using free choice experiences. In S. Modgil & C. Modgil (Eds.), *Toward a theory of psychological development within the Piagetian framework* (pp. 673–697). Windsor, Berkshire, England: National Foundation for Educational Research Publishing Company.

Linn, M. C. (1980). When do adolescents reason? *European Journal of Science Education, 2,* 429–440.

Linn, M. C. (1982). Theoretical and practical significance of formal reasoning. *Journal of Research in Science Teaching, 19,* 727–742.

Linn, M. C. (1983). Content, context, and process in adolescent reasoning. *Journal of Early Adolescence, 3,* 63–82.

Linn, M. C. (1984). Redesigning science education: What is the role of science education research? In R. Bybee (Ed.), *Redesigning science and technology education.* Washington, DC: National Science Teachers Association.

Linn, M. C. (1985). The cognitive consequences of computer environments for learning: Policy issues in computer education. In COGNITIVA 85. Paris.

Linn, M. C. (1985). Fostering equitable consequences from computer learning environments. *Sex Roles, 13,* 229–240.

Linn, M. C. (1985). Gender equity in computer learning environments. *Computers and the Social Sciences, 1*(1), 19–27.

Linn, M. C. (1986). Computer as laboratory partner. *Teaching, Thinking, and Problem Solving, 8*(3), 5, 12.

Linn, M. C. (1986). Meta-analysis of studies of gender differences: Implications and future directions. In J. S. Hyde & M. C. Linn (Ed.), *The psychology of gender: Advances through meta-analysis* (pp. 210–231). Baltimore, MD: Johns Hopkins University Press.

Linn, M. C. (1986). Science. In R. Dillon & R. J. Sternberg (Eds.), *Cognition and instruction* (pp. 155–204). New York: Academic Press.

Linn, M. C. (1987). An apple a day. *Science and Children, 25*(3), 15–18.

Linn, M. C. (1987). Cognitive consequences of technology in science education. *Journal of Research in Science Teaching, 24* (4/5), 285–506.

Linn, M. C. (1987). Establishing a research base for science education: Challenges, trends, and recommendations. *Journal of Research in Science Teaching, 24*(3), 191–216.

Linn, M. C. (1989). Perspectives for research in science teaching: Using the computer as lab partner. In H. Mandl, E. De Corte, N. Bennett, & H. F. Friedrich (Eds.), *Learning and instruction in an international context* (vol. II & II, pp. 443–460). Oxford: Pergamon Press.

Linn, M. C. (1989). Science education and the challenge of technology. In J. Ellis (Ed.), *Informal technologies and science education* (pp. 119–144). Association for the Education of Teachers in Science (AETS) Yearbook. Washington, DC: ERIC Clearinghouse for Science, Math, and Environmental Education.

Linn, M. C. (1990). Establishing a science and engineering base for science education. In M. Gardner, J. G. Greeno, F. Reif, A. H. Schoenfeld, A. diSessa, & E. Stage (Eds.), *Toward a scientific practice of science education* (pp. 323–341). Hillsdale, NJ: Lawrence Erlbaum Associates.

Linn, M. C. (1991). Adolescent scientific reasoning. In R. M. Lerner, A. C. Petersen, & J. Brooks-Gunn (Ed.), *Encyclopedia of adolescence* (vol. 2, pp. 981–983). New York: Garland Publishing.

Linn, M. C. (1992). The computer as learning partner: Can computer tools teach science? In K. Sheingold, L. G. Roberts, & S. M. Malcom (Eds.), *This year in school science 1991: Technology for teaching and learning* (pp. 31–69). Washington, DC: American Association for the Advancement of Science.

Linn, M. C. (1992). Encouraging knowledge construction. In E. De Corte, M. C. Linn, H. Mandl, & L. Verschaffel (Ed.), *Computer-based learning environments and problem solving.* Berlin: Springer-Verlag.

Linn, M. C. (1992). Gender differences in educational achievement. In J. Pfleiderer (Ed.), *Sex equity in educational opportunity, achievement, and testing: Proceedings of the 1991 Educational Testing Service Invitational Conference.* (pp. 11–50). Princeton, NJ: Educational Testing Service.

Linn, M. C. (1992). Science education reform: Building on the research base. *Journal of Research in Science Teaching, 29*(8), 511–551.

Linn, M. C. (1994). Gender and school science. In T. Husén & T. N. Postlethwaite (Ed.), *The international encyclopedia of education* (2nd ed., vol. 4, pp. 2436–2440). New York: Pergamon Press.

Linn, M. C. (1994). A research base for science education: Historical perspectives. In H. Behrendt (Ed.), *Zur Didaktik der Physik und Chemie-Probleme und Perspektiven* (pp. 26–59). Kiel, Germany: GDCP.

Linn, M. C. (1994). The tyranny of the mean: Gender and expectations. *Notices of the American Mathematical Society, 41*(7), 766–769.

Linn, M. C. (1995). Designing computer learning environments for engineering and computer science: The scaffolded knowledge integration framework. *Journal of Science Education and Technology, 4*(2), 103–126.

Linn, M. C. (1996). Cognition and distance learning. *Journal for the American Society for Information Science, 47*(11), 826–842.

Linn, M. C. (1996). From separation to partnership in science education: Students, laboratories, and the curriculum. In R. F. Tinker & T. Ellermeijer (Eds.), *Microcomputer based labs: Educational research and standards* (vol. 156, pp. 13–46). Berlin: Springer-Verlag.

Linn, M. C. (1996). Key to the information highway. *Communications of the Association of Computing Machinery, 39*(4), 34–35.

Linn, M. C. (1996). Microcomputer-based labs: Educational research and standards. In R. F. Tinker (Ed.), *NATO advanced workshop on microcomputer-based labs* (1st ed., vol. 156, pp. 13–49). Heidelberg, Germany: Springer-Verlag.

Linn, M. C. (1997). Finding patterns in international assessments. *Science, 277*(19 September), 1743.

Linn, M. C. (1997). The role of the laboratory in science learning. *Elementary School Journal, 97*(4), 401–417.

Linn, M. C. (1997, February 22). Scaffolded knowledge integration and assessment, R. Shavelson & P. Black (Chair). Paper presented at the *Science Education Standards: The Assessment of Science Meets the Science of Assessment*. Washington, DC: Board on Testing and Assessment: National Academy of Sciences/National Research Council.

Linn, M. C. (1998). Affirmative Action in the 1990s: Perspectives from Willystine Goodsell Award Winners. *Educational Researcher, 27*(9), 4–5.

Linn, M. C. (1998). Affirmative Action in the 1990s: Next Steps. *Educational Researcher, 27*(9), 20.

Linn, M. C. (1998). The impact of technology on science instruction: Historical trends and current opportunities. In K. G. Tobin & B. J. Fraser (Ed.), *International Handbook of Science Education* (vol. 1, pp. 265–294). The Netherlands: Kluwer.

Linn, M. C. (in press). Designing the Knowledge Integration Environment: The partnership inquiry process. *International Journal of Science Education.*

Linn, M. C. (in press). The Knowledge Integration Environment: Designing activities to promote lifelong learning. International *Journal of Science Education.*

Linn, M. C. (1998). When good intentions and subtle stereotypes clash: The complexity of selection decisions. *Educational Researcher, 27*(9), 15–17.

Linn, M. C., Bell, P., & Hsi, S. (1998). Using the Internet to enhance student understanding of science: The knowledge integration environment. *Interactive Learning Environments, 6*(1–2), 4–38.

Linn, M. C., & Burbules, N. C. (1993). Construction of knowledge and group learning. In K. Tobin (Ed.), *The practice of constructivism in science education* (pp. 91–119). Washington, DC: American Association for the Advancement of Science (AAAS).

Linn, M. C., Chen, B., & Thier, H. D. (1977). Teaching children to control variables: Investigation of a free-choice environment. *Journal of Research in Science Teaching, 14*, 249–255.

Linn, M. C., & Clancy, M. J. (1992). The case for case studies of programming problems. *Communications of the ACM, 35*(3), 121–132.

Linn, M. C., & Clark, H. C. (1995). How can assessment practices foster problem solving? In D. R. Lavoie (Ed.), *Towards a cognitive-science perspective for scientific problem solving* (vol. 6, pp. 142–180). Manhattan, KS: National Association for Research in Science Teaching (NARST).

Linn, M. C., & Clark, H. C. (1997). When are science projects learning opportunities? *Research Matters. http://science.coe.uwf.edu/narst/research/projects.html*

Linn, M. C., Clement, C., & Pulos, S. (1983). Is it formal if it's not physics? *Journal of Research in Science Teaching, 20*(8), 755–770.

Linn, M. C., Clement, C., Pulos, S., & Sullivan, T. (1989). Scientific reasoning during adolescence: The influence of instruction in science knowledge and reasoning strategies. *Journal of Research in Science Teaching, 26*(2), 171–187.

Linn, M. C., de Benedictis, T., & Delucchi, K. (1982). Adolescent reasoning about advertisements: Preliminary investigations. *Child Development, 53*, 1599–1613.

Linn, M. C., de Benedictis, T., Delucchi, K., Harris, A., & Stage, E. (1987). Gender differences in National Assessment of Educational Progress science items: What does "I don't know" really mean? *Journal of Research in Science Teaching, 24*(3), 267–278.

Linn, M. C., Delucchi, K., & de Benedictis, T. (1984). Adolescent reasoning about advertisements: Relevance of product claims. *Journal of Early Adolescence, 4*(4), 371–385.

Linn, M. C., diSessa, A., Pea, R. D., & Songer, N. B. (1994). Can research on science learning and instruction inform standards for science education? *Journal of Science Education and Technology, 3*(1), 7–15.

Linn, M. C., & Eylon, B. S. (1996). Lifelong science learning: A longitudinal case study. In *Proceedings of Cognitive Science Society, 1996* (pp. 597–602). Mahwah, NJ: Lawrence Erlbaum Associates.

Linn, M. C., & Eylon, B. S. (1994). Curriculum and the psychology of learning and instruction. In T. Husén & T. N. Postlethwaite (Eds.), *The International Encyclopedia of Education* (2nd ed., vol. 9, pp. 5338–5342). New York: Pergamon Press.

Linn, M. C., Hadary, D., Rosenburg, R., & Househalter, R. (1979). Science education for the deaf: Comparison of ideal, resource, and mainstream settings. *Journal of Research in Science Teaching, 16*, 305–316.

Linn, M. C., & Hyde, J. S. (1989). Gender, mathematics, and science. *Educational Researcher, 18*(8), 17–19, 22–27.

Linn, M. C., & Hyde, J. S. (1991). Trends in cognitive and psychosocial gender differences. In R. M. Lerner, A. C. Petersen, & J. Brooks-Gunn (Eds.), *Encyclopedia of Adolescence* (vol. 1, pp. 139–150). New York: Garland Publishing.

Linn, M. C., Katz, M., Clancy, M. J., & Recker, M. (1992). How do LISP programmers draw on previous experience to solve novel problems? In E. De Corte, M. C. Linn, H. Mandl, & L. Verschaffel (Ed.), *Computer-based learn-*

ing environments and problem solving (pp. 67–101). Berlin: Springer-Verlag.

Linn, M. C., & Kessel, C. (1996). Success in mathematics: Increasing talent and gender diversity among college majors. In J. Kaput, A. Schoenfeld, & E. Dubinsky (Ed.), *Research in Collegiate Mathematics Education* (vol. 2, pp. 101–144). Providence, RI: American Mathematical Society.

Linn, M. C., Layman, J., & Nachmias, R. (1987). The cognitive consequences of microcomputer-based laboratories: Graphing skills development. *Journal of Contemporary Educational Psychology*, *12*(3), 244–253.

Linn, M. C., & Levine, D. I. (1978). Adolescent reasoning: Influence of question format and type of variables on ability to control variables. *Science Education*, *62*, 377–388.

Linn, M. C., & Muilenburg, L. (1996). Creating lifelong science learners: What models form a firm foundation? *Educational Researcher*, *25*(5), 18–24.

Linn, M. C., & Petersen, A. C. (1985). Emergence and characterization of sex differences in spatial ability: A meta-analysis. *Child Development*, *56*, 1479–1498.

Linn, M. C., Sloane, K. D., & Clancy, M. J. (1987). Ideal and actual outcomes from precollege Pascal instruction. *Journal of Research in Science Teaching*, *25*(5), 467–490.

Linn, M. C., Shear, L., & Slotta, J. D., Bell, P. (in press). Organizing principles for science education partnerships: Case studies of students' learning about 'rats in space' and 'deformed frogs'. *Educational Technology Research and Development*, *47*(2), 61–85.

Linn, M. C., & Songer, N. B. (1991). Cognitive and conceptual change in adolescence. *American Journal of Education*, *99*(4), 379–417.

Linn, M. C., & Songer, N. B. (1993). How do students make sense of science? *Merrill-Palmer Quarterly*, *39*(1), 47–73.

Linn, M. C., Songer, N. B., & Eylon, B. S. (1996). Shifts and convergences in science learning and instruction. In R. Calfee & D. Berliner (Eds.), *Handbook of educational psychology* (pp. 438–490). Riverside, NJ: Macmillan.

Linn, M. C., Songer, N. B., & Lewis, E. L. (Eds.). (1991). Students' models and epistemologies of science. *Journal of Research in Science Teaching*, *28*(9).

Linn, M. C., Songer, N. B., Lewis, E. L., & Stern, J. (1993). Using technology to teach thermodynamics: Achieving integrated understanding. In D. L. Ferguson (Ed.), *Advanced educational technologies for mathematics and science* (vol. 107, pp. 5–60). Berlin: Springer-Verlag.

Linn, M. C., & Stein, J. (1985). Unfulfilled promise: School computing needs a booster shot. *Tech Trends*, *30*(2), 20–22.

Mandinach, E. B., & Linn, M. C. (1986). The cognitive effects of computer learning environments. *Journal of Educational Computing Research*, *2*(4), 411–427.

Mandinach, E. B., & Linn, M. C. (1987). Cognitive consequences of programming: Achievements of experienced and talented programmers. *Journal of Educational Computing Research*, *3*(1), 53–72.

Mann, L. M., Linn, M. C., & Clancy, M. J. (1994). Can tracing tools contribute to programming proficiency? The LISP Evaluation Modeler . (Special issue on computer programming environments). *Interactive Learning Environments*, *4*(1), 96–113.

Nachmias, R., Friedler, Y., & Linn, M. C. (1990). The role of programming environments in Pascal instruction. *Computer Education*, *14*(2), 145–158.

Nachmias, R., & Linn, M. C. (1987). Evaluation of science laboratory data: The role of computer-presented information. *Journal of Research in Science Teaching, 24*(5), 491–506.

Noddings, N. (1984). *Caring: A feminist approach to ethics and moral education.* Berkeley: University of California Press.

Papert, S. (1968). *Mindstorms.* New York: Basic Books.

Pea, R. D. (1985). Beyond Amplification: Using the computer to reorganize mental functioning. *Educational Psychologist, 20,* 167–182.

Pea, R., & Gomez, L. (1992). Distributed multimedia learning environments: Why and how? *Interactive Learning Environments, 2,* 73–109.

President's Committee of Advisors on Science and Technology. (1997). *Panel on educational technology: Report to the president on the use of technology to strengthen K–12 education in the United States.* Washington, DC.

Pulos, S., & Linn, M. C. (1981). Generality of the controlling variables scheme in early adolescence. *Journal of Early Adolescence, 1,* 26–37.

Rice, M., & Linn, M. C. (1978). Study of student behavior in a free choice environment. *Science Education, 62,* 365–376.

Riel, M. M., & Levin, J. A. (1990). Building global communities: Success and failure in computer networking. *Instructional Science* (19), 145–169.

Roschelle, J., & Kaput, J. (1996). Educational software architecture and systemic impact: The promise of component software. *Journal of Educational Computing Research, 14*(3), 217–228.

Rubin, A. (1992). *The Alaska QUILL network: Fostering a teacher community through telecommunication.* Hillsdale, NJ: Lawrence Erlbaum Associates.

Sadker, M., & Sadker, D. (1994). *Failing at fairness: How America's schools cheat girls.* New York: Maxwell Macmillan International.

Scardamalia, M., & Bereiter, C. (1992). A knowledge building architecture for computer supported learning. In E. De Corte, M. C. Linn, H. Mandl, & L. Verschaffel (Ed.), *Computer-based learning environments and problem solving.* Berlin: Springer-Verlag.

Schank, P. K., Linn, M. C., & Clancy, M. J. (1993). Supporting Pascal programming with an online template library and case studies. *International Journal of Man–Machine Studies, 38,* 1031–1048.

Schoenfeld, A. H. (1989). Explorations of students' mathematical beliefs and behavior. *Journal for Research in Mathematics Education, 20*(4), 338–355.

Schonfield, J. (1995). *Computers and classroom culture.* Cambridge, UK: Cambridge University Press.

Schwab, J. J. (1962). The teaching of science. Elements in a strategy for teaching science in the elementary school. Cambridge: Harvard University Press.

Shulman, L. S. (1986). Those who understand: Knowledge growth in teaching. *Educational Researcher, 15*(2), 4–14.

Shulman, L. (1987). Knowledge and teaching: Foundations of the new reform. *Harvard Educational Review, 57,* 1–22.

Shymansky, J. A., Kyle, W. C., Jr., & Alport, J. M. (1983). The effects of new science curricula on student performance. *Journal of Research in Science Teaching, 20,* 387–404.

Sloane, K., & Linn, M. C. (1988). Instructional conditions in Pascal programming classes. In R. E. Mayer (Ed.), *Teaching and learning computer programming: Multiple research perspectives* (pp. 207–235). Hillsdale, NJ: Lawrence Erlbaum Associates.

Slotta, J. D., & Linn, M. C. (in press). The Knowledge Integration Environment: Helping students use the Internet effectively. In *M*. J. Jacobson & R. Kozma (Eds.), *Learning the sciences of the 21st Century*. Hilldale, NJ: Lawrence Erlbaum Associates.

Soloway, E., Clancy, M., Linn, M., diSessa, A., Miller, P., Resnick, M., Papert, S. (1993). Should we teach students to program? *Communications of the ACM, 36*(10), 21–24.

Songer, N. B. (1989). *Promoting integration of instructed and natural world knowledge in thermodynamics*. Unpublished doctoral dissertation, University of California, Berkeley, CA.

Songer, N. B. (1989). Technological tools for scientific thinking and discovery. *Journal of Reading, Writing and Learning Disabilities, 5*, 23–41.

Songer, N. B. (1996). Exploring learning opportunities in coordinated network-enhanced classrooms–A case of kids as global scientists. *Journal of the Learning Sciences, 5*(4), 297–327.

Songer, N. B., & Linn, M. C. (1991). How do students' views of science influence knowledge integration? *Journal of Research in Science Teaching, 28*(9), 761–784.

Songer, N. B., & Linn, M. C. (1992). How do students' views of science influence knowledge integration? In M. K. Pearsall (Ed.), *Scope, sequence and coordination of secondary school science, Volume I: Relevant research* (pp. 197–219). Washington, DC: The National Science Teachers Association.

Stein, J. S., & Linn, M. C. (1985). Capitalizing on computer-based interactive feedback: An investigation of "Rocky's Boots". In M. Chen & W. Paisley (Ed.), *Children and microcomputers: Research on the newest medium* (pp. 213–227). Beverly Hills, CA: Sage Publications.

Stein, J. S., Nachmias, R., & Friedler, Y. (1990). An experimental comparison of two science laboratory environments: Traditional and microcomputer-based. *Journal of Educational Computing Research, 6*(2), 183–202.

Stern, J. L. (1990). *E-LabBook* [software]. Berkeley, CA: UC Regents, University of California at Berkeley.

Stern, J. L. (1994). Computers in Education: Everybody's business. *Computer Professionals for Social Responsibility, 12*(2), 1–2.

Stern, J. L. (1995). Digital video for educators. *Syllabus, 8*(4), 10–13.

Stern, J. S., & Kirkpatrick, D. H. (1991). Computer as lab partner project. *Chemunications Newsletter, VII*(2), 1, 14–15.

Sternberg, R. J. (1985). *Beyond IQ: The triarchic theory of human intelligence*. Cambridge, England: Cambridge University Press.

Synder, L., Aho, A., Linn, M. et al. (1999) *Being fluent with information technology*. Washington, DC: Committee on Information Technology Literacy.

Tinker, R., & Berenfeld, B. (1993). A global lab story: A moment of glory in San Antonio. Hands On!, 16(Fall), 3. *http://www.terc.edu/handson/handson.html*

Tinker, R., & Berenfeld, B. (1994). Patterns of U.S. global lab adaptations. Hands On!. *http://www.terc.edu/handson/f94/patterns.html*

Tinker, R. F. (Ed.),(1997) *Microcomputer based labs: Educational research and standards* (vol. 156). Berlin: Springer-Verlag.

Tinker, R. F. Scientific Affairs Division. (1996). *Microcomputer-based labs : educational research and standards*, (NATO ASI series. Series F, Computer and systems sciences; vol. 156). Berlin; New York: Springer.

Turkle, S. (1984). *The second self: Computers and the human spirit*. New York: Simon & Schuster, Inc.

Turkle, S. (1995). *Life on the screen: Identity in the age of the Internet*. New York: Simon & Schuster.

Tsuchida, I., & Lewis, C. (1996). Responsibility and learning: Some preliminary hypotheses about Japanese elementary classrooms. In T. P. Rohlen & G. K. LeTendre (Eds.), *Teaching and learning in Japan* (pp. 190–212). New York: Cambridge University Press.

Vygotsky, L. S. (1962). *Thought and language*. Cambridge, MA: MIT Press.

Walker, D. F., & Schaffarzik, J. (1974). Comparing curricula. *Review of Educational Research, 44*, 83–111.

Webb, N. M. (1989). Peer interaction and learning in small groups. *International Journal of Educational Research, 13*(1), 21–39.

Wellesley College Center for Research on Women (1992). *How schools shortchange girls*. Washington, DC: American Association of University Women Educational Foundation.

White, B. Y. (1993). ThinkerTools: Causal models, conceptual change, and science education. *Cognition and Instruction, 10*(1), 1–100.

Wiser, M. (1988). The differentiation of heat and temperature: History of science and novice-expert shift. In S. Strauss (Ed.), *Ontogeny, phylogeny, and historical development*. Norwood, NJ: Ablex.

Wiser, M., & Carey, S. (1983). When heat and temperature were one. In D. Gentner & A. L. Stevens (Ed.), *Mental models* (pp. 267–298). Hillsdale, NJ: Lawrence Erlbaum Associates.

Appendix A:
Student Interviews—Lee and Pat

Note: The questions asked during these interviews can be found on the CD-ROM.

LEE PRETEST INTERVIEW

Insulation and conduction

You'd put it [soda] in tin foil because, "it keeps it cold." Why?
> Uhm, I don't know. I guess because my mom   (observation)
> puts it in foil and so I think it keeps it cold....
> I've seen a lot of other people do it too.... I don't
> know, it keeps all the, it wraps all the coldness in
> it, the can.

You said "yes." "because putting something cold in a thermos keeps it cold."
> Because all of the air stays trapped in.... I don't   (air trapped;
> know. Something's that, like doesn't let any air   doesn't let
> in.   air in)

Why is wool good for keeping things hot, but bad for keeping things cold?
> Well, it kind of is making things hot because it's
> warm, and then, but then a lot of air can get

into it…. People wear wool in clothes to keep   (observation)
warm.   (air)

You think that Styrofoam is good at keeping
things cold, but poor at keeping things hot?
I've tried it with cold. 'Cause like there's   (experience)
Styrofoam coolers.

Thermal equilibrium

Metal and wood?
I don't know but, uhm, like if I leave something   (experience
metal in the sun and then I like touch it, it's   with sun)
like really hot.

So how do you think the metal gets hot?
Well, I was thinking 'cause the sun when it   (reflection/
shines on it, it kind of makes a reflection and   mirror and
it's a kind of a mirror.   sun)

You said all of them would be room temperature
except the cold coke. So after 8 hours you think a
cold coke would still be below room temperature?
Uhm … yeah a little.

So do you think that everything in this room is
the same temperature?
Uhm … No. Well like the … the computer's   (observation,
warm because it's running. And the … the water   computer
out of the faucet would be colder, cold water.   running)

Temperature and heat energy

Do you think if two things have the same temper-
ature, then they have the same heat energy?
I'm like not really sure what heat energy really is.   (uncertainty)

Nature of science

You said "No, they [scientists] could be wrong."
How?
Well, sometimes I just think something and
then like later on they find out a different
answer for it and so with the old books could
have the wrong answers. [Scientists] … they'll

all get different answers.... Well, they all, they
can all be different experiments and come out
with different answers, and some of them are
wrong ... well, because they all have different
ideas and they all do different experiments and
came up with their answers.

So you think that they agree on anything?
They agree on like, just little things like the
colors of something.

Evaluating experiments

Why don't you think it'll be accepted?
Well, like uhm ... do they mean that the mice
are smarter because they have bigger brains? ...
The ones that are all alone, they're from the
same litter, so it could be just the litter ... and I
don't know.

*Do you think science has to do with your life out-
side of school?*
Not really.

*You said you agree: "If it gets complicated, then I
don't enjoy it and it gets boring, then I daydream."*
Yeah. Then I get lost. [I prefer to memorize]
because complicated material, I never
understood it and I would take tests.

Do you think everybody can learn science?
I don't know like I don't think that some person
can just come and invent something because
you need to like know all the little wires and
stuff. I couldn't do it.

LEE INTERVIEW 2 AFTER THERMAL EQUILIBRIUM INSTRUCTION

Heat energy and temperature

*Do you think that one of them [large and small hot
cocoa] has more heat energy than the other? Or
do you think that they have the same heat energy?*
This one has more ... because it has more liquid   (class model)
in it.

*What if I had a big cup and a small cup of hot co-
coa and put them in this room. What would happen after awhile?*
    They'd cool to room temperature.   (class model)

Which one would lose more heat energy?
    Then the one with more in it will cool faster   (observation)

*Which one would lose more heat energy when it
cooled off?*
    I don't know.   (uncertainty)

Well which one has more heat energy?
    The big one.   (big = more)

*And if they both cool down, which one do you
think loses more heat energy?*
    The little one.

Why?
    I don't know. 'Cause there's less, less heat   (not
    energy.   connected)

*So if it has less heat energy, how does it lose
more than the big one?*
    I don't know.   (uncertainty)

Thermal equilibrium

*Did you always use to think that everything in
the room was the same temperature?*
    Well, almost everything except things that are   (class model,
    like run by electricity are warmer.   not quite)

*What would happen if you touched the metal
bowl in the cabin? How would it feel?*
    It would feel colder, but it's the same   (class model)
    temperature of the room, but your body
    temperature's hotter.

*What happens if you touch a piece of wood in
that room. How would it feel?*
    I think it would probably feel warmer ... than   (observation)
    metal.

Why does wood feel different than metal?

I don't know, 'cause like when you touch it, it's   (class model,
harder for this to go to the temperature of your   not quite
body and it's easier for wood because it's like   connected)
solid.... Because it's ... I don't know. It's going
slowly here, it goes—(no ... I don't know if it
goes slower or quicker.

So [metal strips in the trunk] you think the tem-
perature of the metal will be higher than the tem-
perature of the wood? Why is that?

Because uhm ... I don't know. Metal gets hotter.   (observation)

Because you think the metal strips in the trunk
would be higher than the temperature of the
wooden strips?

I don't know if they'll be the same.   (uncertainty)

Why would they be the same?

Because they're both in the same area.   (observation)

Which one feels hotter?

The metal.   (experience)

In a chemistry lab students were drying equip-
ment in an oven. The temperature of the oven
was 150°C. In the oven were metal spatulas,
glass beakers, and asbestos pads that had been
there overnight. What do you predict the temper-
ature of each is?

Uhm , probably 150°C.   (class model)

So they'll all be 150?

Well no uhm metal, the metal things will be   (experience)
hotter and the asbestos sponge will probably be
the coolest, and glass will be hot.

Why do you think the metal will be hotter?   (class model)
Probably, well they'll probably all be 150, but   (tries to
when you touch the metal it'll feel hotter.... The   connect
heat energy. Something about the heat energy.   class and
                                                        experience)

Heat and temperature distinction

*What do you think the temperature of the two
beakers are?*
   150.

*Which one do you think will have more heat en-
ergy?*
   The bigger one.... It's bigger.   (big = more)

Science learning

How are you doing in the class?
   I have a B.... Well I like it, it's easier to learn
   without the book because you're like explaining
   it, but uhm I don't know.... [The other science
   teacher] always used a book and it made it
   harder.

*What do you think is the most helpful in the class
for understanding things?*
   When he like uhm , when Mr. K's explaining   (experience)
   something and he demonstrates it with different   (accurate
   things.... Like when we touched the mouse pad   self-reflection)
   and then we touched the leg to the desk, the
   mouse pad seemed warmer but they were both
   the same temperature, ... but I don't really
   understand it.

*Which part of the experiment is most helpful to
you?*
   Probably the graph because the graph is easier   (visualization)
   to understand.

LEE INTERVIEW 3 AFTER RATE OF HEATING AND COOLING
INVESTIGATIONS

Thermal equilibrium

*What can you predict about the temperature of
objects in the room?*
   They'll probably be the same temperature as the   (class model)
   room in the air-conditioned. It depends how
   long the air conditioner has been on, ... 'cause
   uhm it cooled down to the surrounding of the

air conditioning and if it's been sitting there for awhile, then it'll just go to the same temperature.

If you could touch the different things, would they all feel the same?

No, they'd probably feel colder because—oh wait, some things will feel colder than others. It depends what you're touching.... Like metal than something like the pillow.

(observation)

Why?

I don't know.

(uncertain about reason)

Insulation and conduction

Place [each material] here on the Continuum Line: metal, Styrofoam, wood, glass, wool, ceramic floor tile, paper, and saran wrap.

Well I'm not really sure what the difference is because the person I'm working on the computer with, she like does everything.... Well, like sometimes I'll type, but if I have to write what she says if I don't, then she corrects it.

(defers to partner)

Out of those objects, which do you think would be a good insulator?

I don't know.

(uncertain)

Do you think metal's a good insulator or conductor?

I don't know. I don't know any. I don't even know what like an insulator is.

(uncertain and confused)

LEE INTERVIEW 4 AFTER INSULATION AND CONDUCTION INVESTIGATIONS

Thermal equilibrium/Insulation and conduction

Sean was making a pizza and put the dough in the oven with the light on to keep it warm while it was rising. The dough was in a metal bowl on a

*wooden board. The dough was forgotten, and
Shawn returned to it several hours later. What
can you say about the temperature of the metal
bowl, wooden board, and the metal rack in the
oven. How do the temperatures compare?*

> It would all be the same temperature, ...　　　　(class model)
> because it has been sitting in there, so they
> would be the same temperature as the
> surroundings.

*If you could touch the metal and the wood, how
would they feel?*

> The metal would be hotter.　　　　　　　　　(experience)

Why is that?

> I don't know.　　　　　　　　　　　　　　　(uncertain
> 　　　　　　　　　　　　　　　　　　　　　of link)

*What is the difference between the metal and
wood?*

> One is a good conductor, or the other is a good　　(class model)
> insulator.

Which is which?

> Metal is a conductor, and wood is a good
> insulator.

Can you think of a reason why that would be?

> I don't know.... I don't know. It [conductor]　　(uncertain,
> keeps things hot.　　　　　　　　　　　　conductor
> 　　　　　　　　　　　　　　　　　　　keeps things
> 　　　　　　　　　　　　　　　　　　　hot)

Insulation and conduction

*What would you use to wrap a drink to keep it
cold?*

> Saran wrap.... 'cause that's what I always use　　(experience)
> and it works.

How do you think it does that?

> I don't know. It traps all the cold air inside.　　(traps air)

*Do you think aluminum foil would be a good
wrap?*

Oh yeah, that's what I meant. Foil Yeah. I didn't mean saran wrap, I meant aluminum foil.

(accepts alternative)

Create a container to keep things hot and cold. What would you make it out of?
Uhm , maybe metal, ... because, I don't know.... I don't know. I don't know. It just seems better.... If it was outside, the metal would get hotter if the sun was on it, but it would feel hotter than plastic.... Yeah, like if metal was on the outside, and you had like cold stuff on the inside, then it would probably melt faster.

(uncertain)

Why would you use metal on the outside?
I don't know. On the experiment we did, metal was a good conductor.... The one with the [heat] bars.

(experience)

Why would you want to use a conductor to keep things hotter?
I don't know.

(uncertain of link)

What would happen if I put something cold in that container?
I guess it would keep it cold.

(uncertain)

How does it do that?
I don't know.

(uncertain)

Like what do you think is happening?
I don't know.

(uncertain)

What if I put something hot inside?
It would keep it hot.... 'cuz it holds the heat energy inside.

(class model interpreted: hold sheet energy)

You placed identical sized blocks of wood, metal, sugar, and glass on a warm hot plate. The top of each cube is covered with wax. Which wax will melt first?
The metal.... Cuz metal feels hotter.

(experience)

Uhm , so what makes the wax melt?
  The heat.   (observation)

*How does the heat get to the hot plate to the
wax?*
  I don't know.   (uncertain
                                                          about link)

*Did HeatBars help you understand insulators
and conductors a little bit?*
  Yeah, a little bit. Like which materials are better   (observation)
  insulators and conductors.

*Did it help you understand what makes a good
insulator and conductor?*
  No.   (no link)

Heat and temperature distinction

*You have stored a big block of ice in your freezer.
You want to compare the temperature of the big
block of ice to a small ice cube that was also in
the freezer. How do the temperatures compare?*
  The same temperature.

As what?
  The freezer ... because they are both in the   (observation)
  same place.

Which one has more heat energy?
  The big one.... Because it is bigger.   (big = more)

LEE INTERVIEW 5 AFTER HEATBARS AND FINAL EXAMINATION

Insulation and conduction

*You want to keep a soda cold for your school
lunch. You said, "Styrofoam. It's a good insulator." What does that mean?*
  Uhm , to keep the cold air in.... Uhm I don't   (uncertain
  know.   link)

Let's say this is a cold soda and we put Styro-
foam around it. What happens?
    It keeps the soda colder.   (observation)

How?
    Uhm ... I don't know. It just keeps the cold air in.   (mentions air)

Do containers or wraps that help keep hot ob-
jects hot also keep cold objects cold? You said
"no, because some wraps are only good insula-
tors and some are only good conductors." So
what does a good insulator do?
    It keeps the cold air inside.   (connects
                                                to air)

And a conductor does what?
    I'm not sure what a conductor does.   (uncertain)

So insulators would be good for keeping things
cold. Would they also be good for keeping things
hot?
    I think some of them.   (distinguishes
                                                heat and cold)

But not all of them?
    Yeah.

"To keep things hot, you would use something
like aluminum, and to keep thing cold you would
use something like Styrofoam." Is that okay?
    That was like a guess.... I don't know. It's just   (connects to
    'cause at home we always use like aluminum to   parental
    keep things hot.... Like if my mom made like   practice)
    uhm stuffing or something, she'd put ...
    aluminum foil.

You said aluminum was excellent for keeping
things hot. Is that okay?
    Yeah.... It keeps the heat energy in.   (uses
                                                    vocabulary)

So heat energy can't travel through aluminum?
    It can. I don't know....   (Uncertain)

Did you do any labs where you wrapped things in aluminum?

Yeah.... We wrapped a Coke in aluminum, but it didn't keep it any colder than a Coke wrapped in nothing.... Well I know it's bad for keeping things cold because of that one experiment we did. But I'm not sure why. (recalls class result)

So wool is excellent for keeping things hot and poor for keeping things cold. How does it keep things hot?

I don't know.... I don't know. I just wrote that it was excellent because people wear wool to get warm. (connects to personal practice)

Like what do you think is happening?

I don't know. (uncertain)

Say I'm cold and put on a wool sweater, what does it do?

Uhm ... keeps the cold air out. (connects to cold air)

Suppose you hold one end of a metal nail and put the other end on a piece of ice. You said, "Colder. Heat energy flows out of the nail and metal's a good conductor. If you hold a match at the end of the nail, you have the other end, it would get so hot you'd have to drop it and with something like glass you wouldn't." So heat energy is flowing out of the nail into what?

I don't know. Mr. K said it would happen.... But I don't know why. (recalls authority from class)

Give an example of a good conductor. You said, "aluminum because it keeps things hot". What do good conductors do?

I don't know. (uncertain)

How about insulators? You said, "Because it keeps things cool."

Because it uhm keeps the cold air in. (connects to cold air)

So will it keep the hot air in, or just cold air?
Uhm I don't know. (uncertainty)

Heat energy and temperature

*In general, are heat energy and temperature the
same or different? You said " Different. Temperature can be either hot or cold but heat energy is
the amount of heat in an object." Can you think
of an example?*
Uhm, I don't know. Uhm ... I don't know. (uncertain)

*Let's say I had a cup of boiling water and a pot
of boiling water.*
Oh yeah. It depends on the size. Like ... I don't (recalls class
know ... both can be the same temperature but result)
the amount of it can be different so one holds
more heat energy than the other one.

Can you give me an example?
Like ... with a pool, oh wait, with the ocean (big = more)
water and the bucket, uhm this boy he
measured the temperature of the bucket water
and the ocean water and they were the same,
but the ocean water has more heat energy
because it's larger than the bucket of water.

LEE LONGITUDINAL TENTH GRADE

Insulation and conduction

*If you were going to wrap a cold soda to take to
school for lunch, what is the best thing to wrap it
in?*
I don't know.... Usually, people wrap it in tin (class model—
foil, but we learned that it doesn't work, and I connected
don't remember what did work. I think it was better)
paper or something like that.... That's what Mr.
K told us last year.

Heat energy and temperature

Were the [big and small] milk shakes the same temperature when they were poured into the glasses?
  The same.

What about 0 minutes later or 15 minutes later, assuming you didn't drink them?
  That one would probably be colder. The half   (uncertain)
  one.

The half one would be colder. And why do you think that?
  Oh, I meant it'd probably be warmer, ... because   (big = more;
  it has less liquid, so it loses temperature faster.   connected to
    temperature
    loss)

And what would make it warm up? Where ...
  The air.... It warms the soda.   (air has more)

So you don't remember anything about heat energy?
  I, I remember, but I never understood what. I
  never understood what heat energy was.

Thermal equilibrium

You arrive at a ski cabin during the winter and no heat was left on. The room thermometer reads 5°C. What can you predict about the temperature of the objects in the cabin?
  Uhm, they would be the same, ... 'cause they'd   (class model)
  all be the same temperature of the room.

So did you remember something from Mr. K's class?
  I remember talking about it, but I don't   (class
  remember what the answer is.   observation)

Suppose you walked all around the room and touched them.
  Uhm, the metal would probably feel colder than   (observation)
  the wool.

*You can feel some difference. So why, why is it
that metal feels colder than wood say in a cool
environment?*
  Don't know.   (uncertainty)

*You and a friend are buying several materials for
a project and have purchased several long strips
of aluminum and several long strips of wood at
a hardware store.*
  I think they'd be the same temperature....   (uncertainty
  Don't know. Just 'cause of the area they're in.   —air)
  So you'd be the same temperature as the air.

What would you feel if you touched them?
  The wood wouldn't feel hot, but the metal   (observation)
  would.

So, what's going on? Any ideas?
  No, I don't know.   (uncertainty)

Light

*The power is out in your home, and you are
looking for a book to read with a flashlight. Explain everything that happens that allows (or
does not allow) you to see the book.*
  I don't know.

*You are playing games with two friends. You are
"it" and you walk into a dimly lit room. One of
your friends is wearing a white T-shirt, and the
other a black T-shirt. Which one will be easier to
see?*
  The white t-shirt, 'cause it shows up. It's like   (observation)
  brighter. Kind of glows more.... It's easier to
  see.

*At the ceiling [of the room with the candle] it'd
be what?*
  Most bright.... I don't know. It's just the way   (observation)
  the flame's pointing.

So direction of flame makes a difference.
  I don't think so, I don't know.   (uncertainty)

So how do you decide whether light will reach	
something or not?	
I don't know.	(uncertainty)

John is standing in a room with a window and a
room light in the middle of the room. If it was
daylight outside and the room light was off, could
the person see the car?

Yeah.... 'cause it's daylight out.... Makes it so   (observation)
you can see.

What if it were nighttime outside with no moon,
no streetlights, and the light in the room were on.
Could you see the car?

No.... I don't know. I never can at my house   (experience)
when I look out.

What seems necessary for you to see the car?

Light where the car is.   (light needed
                             to see)

Science learning

What do you remember from Mr. K's class about
the experiments that you did? Or did you do ex-
periments or simulations?

I think we did some. Most of them on the   (observation)
computer with ... Oh yeah, we did do some on
keeping things cold, but I didn't really
understand them.

LEE LONGITUDINAL TWELFTH GRADE

Insulation and conduction

If you were going to wrap a cold soda to take to
school for lunch, what would be the best thing to
wrap it in to keep it cold?

Uhm ... I've never really kind of figured it out,   (more
... but I guess it would be paper.... And I'm not   accurate
really sure why.   observation)

What if you took the, uhm , Coke, and took it out
of the refrigerator, put it on the table and just let
it sit there. What would happen to it?

Well, eventually over time it will drop down to   (more class
room temperature, ... just 'cause the   ideas better
surrounding temperature, the air around it, the   connected)
cold air would like go out of the soda, and the
room temperature air would go in, 'cause the
soda's a metal can. Metal ... absorbs different
temperatures really easily.

The air from the outside goes in?

Uhm , yeah, basically. Not the air, just like the   (grapples with
temperature.... Yeah like the heat ... 'cause if   connections of
it's a room temperature room compared to the   air, heat,
cold soda, then the, it's like turning warm air   temperature)
compared to the soda.

Okay, so, if you wrapped it in paper, that would
keep it colder longer, sitting on the table?

The uhm , paper would kind of be helping the   (distinguishes
cooler air in, and like keeping the, keeping the   paper and can)
warm air out. Uhm, paper ... uhm, paper's
different from like just the can, 'cause the can
absorbs the heat better than the paper.

Heat energy and temperature

Let's say you have those two blocks of ice, and
you have them in the freezer, and the freezer's set
at 0°C. And, you want to find out what the tem-
perature of the ice is. What would you guess that
the temperature of the little one would be, and
what would be the temperature of the big one?

Zero degrees.

Even though they're different sizes?

Uhm, yeah, but I was thinking maybe the bigger   (making
one ... not the whole thing, but parts of it, like   connections)
in the center might be ... be lower than zero, ...
Uhm, because it has more ice surrounding it,
the inside, than the smaller one, so it just gets
cooler.

What would happen if, uhm, you were to take
both of them out and put them on the table?

> Probably they would melt.... The smaller one   (connects
> would melt quicker and ... that's it ... I'm just   thermal
> confused.... I still think the little one would   equilibrium to
> melt sort of ... it would melt quicker, just   insulation/
> because there's less ice surrounding it, keeping   conduction
> it cold.   (more = melt
>   slower)

Put them both in a cooler freezer?

> Uhm , probably the smaller one would go down   (has to absorb
> quicker.... Or maybe the bigger one, just   cold air)
> because it's probably already colder, but then
> there's more of it ... and.... Because there's less
> of it to ... there's less to absorb the cold air. The
> bigger one is more, it's bigger, but if it's already
> colder, then (laughs) ...

Thermal equilibrium

Chemistry students were drying equipment in the
oven, the temperature of the oven was 150°C
and they put all these things in the oven over-
night.... Uhm, what do you predict the tempera-
ture of each of those things to be?

> I'd say ... just 'cause they're all in the same   (class model)
> temperature, they'd all have the same
> temperature. A 150 was the oven temperature.

What if you were to touch them, which you prob-
ably wouldn't do, but say if you imagined that
you touched them, touched this metal spatula,
touched this one ... what would ... ?

> Uhm, the metal would probably feel hotter than   (holds two
> the wood.... Uhm, 'cause the wood probably,   unresolved
> uhm ... I don't know, if the wood absorbs it   models)
> more, like, so ... . It absorbs the heat like, it
> doesn't, like the metal ... uhm, maybe the metal
> would be hotter because it's a good conductor
> of heat. Or ... just feel hotter.

Okay, so assuming they are the same tempera-
ture, why does the metal feel hotter?
    Uhm ... I don't know.   (uncertainty)

Insulation and conduction

This is a continuum line,
    Okay. Paper would be a good insulator.... Uhm,   (observation)
    and metal is a good conductor. Wool would be a
    good insulator too, because it, like, you use
    wool to wrap around you when you're cold, and
    it kind of keeps the warmth in.

Would that work if you wrapped the wool around
the cold Coke?
    Probably, yeah.   (connects hot
            and cold)

Say if you had a silver platter and a pottery plat-
ter, and you put them into an oven—they're both
about the same size—and you put them into an
oven 450°F with your gloves, and you brought
them out and put them on the table. Which of
those do you think would stay warm longer?
    Probably the silver. Uhm, 'cause silver's kind of   (links silver
    like a metal, so uhm, it'd probably hold a lot   to metal)
    more heat. And uhm, the other one, the other
    one's heat would be ... It's hard, because once
    you start thinking about it, it can like reverse
    what you're saying, 'cause the metal is a good
    conductor so it would absorb the full air, like to
    ... I think it would cool off quicker. If it was in
    the oven, and I touched them, the metal one
    would be hotter, and, 'cause it absorbs more heat
    than the dish would.

Okay, so you bring them out, and you put them
on the table, and ... which one gets, which one
stays warm?
    The metal one.... Uhm, the metal feels hotter   (Holds two unre-
    when you take it out, so I think that it will stay   solved models)
    hotter longer, but then I'd also think about,   (resolves by
    uhm, metal absorbs temperature quickly, so it   choosing links

would absorb the coolness. Mm ... probably I
think that the metal one would cool faster.

*Say if you're boiling noodles, and you need to
stir them. And you can use a wooden spoon or a
stainless steel spoon. Which one would you use?*
    Uhm , the wooden one. Because, uhm, after you   (reflecting on
stir it, the spoon will feel hot... if you use the   observations)
stainless steel?

What would be happening?
    I don't know.... It'd be that just steel is hotter   (both absorb)
... gets hotter.... So it's...it absorbs a bunch of
heat out of the noodles.... I don't know, the
heat ... it, the spoon just absorbs the heat from
the water, and when you take it out, it'll start to
cool down, but the wood absorbs the heat too,
but it just doesn't feel as hot.

*Okay, what's ... what similarities and differ-
ences are there between those two situations
with the hot noodles and the cold shovel?*
    Uhm , they're both absorbing the temperature.   (heat =
Hot temperature and cold temperature.   temperature)

Light

*Here's a question about light tell me what you
think, how you think it would be with, uhh, lighting up his face or lighting up his body.*
    Mm ... I think the mirror would be good for ...   (reflecting
lighting up his body, and ... the white panel   and linking)
would be good ... for lighting up his whole body
(laughs) too, and the black—if the black panel
was—if you had like a shiny black panel.. I don't
think it would light him up at all.... Maybe the
mirror panel would light up his face more than
his whole body.

*If it's a sunny day and you put on a pair of sun-
glasses, how would objects appear around you?
Would they appear lighter or darker without the
sunglasses?*

Uhm , I think it depends on what kind of
sunglasses you're wearing, but I think that
normal ones would just darken, black lens
glasses, they appear darker ... just 'cause it ...
the shade of the lens is darker. It would be, like,
blocking the light.

(reflecting on observations)

Can you tell me where the light is coming from?
It's the light from, up, like from the sun down,
just reflecting off of objects.

(more links)

How does seeing work?
Uhm, the light goes into your eyes.

Does the light go ... how far does light go?
It would fill the whole thing.... You just wouldn't
be able to see it.

(distinguishes light presence and light detection)

*How about if it was ... outside, and you had a
candle sitting on the ground. How far would it
go?*
Uhm, it depends on where, if it goes at all. It
would just run ... it ... wherever you can walk
and still see the candle, it goes.

(bases presence on detection)

Science learning

*Do you remember, uhm, doing an experiment like
this [insulating something] in Mr. K's class?*
I can't really remember. I'm trying to, uhm,
figure out the answer.

*Okay, uhm, let's go back to the cold Cokes ques-
tion, and let me ask you whether... what you ...
your answer today, do you think that you ... do
you think you have the same answer that you
gave at the end of the eighth grade? Do you think
you understand it about the same? Do you understand it better now?*
I think I just understand it about the same,
maybe, I think, but not more ... than Mr. K's class.

Have you used the things that you learned in Mr. K's class?

    I don't think so.

Describe for me your main memories of Mr. K's class.

    Uhm, I just remember the ... lot of stuff on computers, and, I was usually always last, and I was really confused with stuff.

Was it the computers that made it confusing for you?

    Uhm ... not really, no, it was just the work. And I was really stuck. I would try hard as ... as hard as I could, and I just couldn't ... sat around most of the time.... I just didn't want to do the schoolwork.

But how ... how about now?

    Uhm , I feel most of the time, it really depends on the kind of teacher you get. Say the teacher's just like ... the class is worthless, and we don't know anything, and then there's others that you really learn, you analyze everything.   (teacher important)

Have you used the ideas from Mr. K's class?

    Uhm , not really.

Do the computers help you understand the science?

    Kind of. It gives you something to look at ... Uhm, to look at all your data together, and it helps you, uhm , sort out percentages and stuff.

What did you like about your science classes in high school?

    Uhm ... well, I started paying attention more in biology my second semester when I took it when I was a sophomore.... First semester I didn't really work. Part of the second semester I started working really hard, 'cause I was ... I had transferred schools, ... and I understood a lot easier, and it started getting kind of interesting, the stuff we learned in it.   (changing the process)

*Do you think that had to do with the way it was
taught?*

> The way it was taught.... Uhm, instead of like,
> uhm , the teacher just jumping straight [in]
> she, uhm, would explain every vocabulary word
> she said along the way, and she would make sure
> you understood every step she took before she
> went on so that we would know what she was
> talking about.... Yeah, but this year it was a
> different kind of teacher. It depends on the
> teacher.

And how about experiments?

> Uhm, most of them were good. Some of them I
> find good, but most of them, I find myself ... are
> really pointless. They're things you can notice
> just by looking at a picture, or just reading
> about it.... And we should just do simple things.

*How about, uhm, memorizing. Does that help
you?*

> Well, whatever I ... all the stuff I've ever had to   (memorizing
> memorize I've just forgotten, so I don't know if   fails)
> memorizing works, I mean, I'm sure it would
> work on a test or something, but in the long
> term it doesn't do any good.... I know I
> understand it really when I can go over it, or
> like tell someone, explain it to someone. If I ...
> if I know enough to explain it to someone else,
> then I ...

Can you tell me how well you did on the test?

> Yeah. Except when I do, uhm, when I know most
> of them, sometimes I'm not too sure on some of
> them, I really don't have an idea, but if I have to
> guess a lot of them, I'd be in trouble.

Career plans

What are your plans for the future?

> Uhm , I'm still kind of undecided on that....
> Well, I know I want to do something with, like,
> that has to do with, like, I don't know what kind

of word to use, but like [lab technician] in hospitals.

What are your plans for college?
Well, uhm , I know I'm like, the one college I think I'll go to most is [state college], but I don't know what I want to major in and what classes I want to take yet. Probably I'll need a little experience.

Yeah. A little more. Are you planning to take science classes?
Uhm, probably, if I get into [hospital work] … have to take some kind of a science class.

PAT PRETEST INTERVIEW

Insulation and conduction

How is it that it [a can holder] keeps things [like a soda] cold?
Uh, I guess it [is] some kind of insulation foam stuff. (connects to experience)

What is it that foam stuff does?
Keeps it cold. I think it keeps it hot, too. Like if you put it on a cup, it keeps it hot. If we took a cold soda out of the fridge and wrapped wool around it and brought it to school. Would that help keep it cold? Probably keep it the same or it might get hotter. (insulation serves as a barrier) (wool might impart heat to object)

You said insulators work both ways. So what do you mean by that?
Well, like it just keeps the temperature in, so if you have an air conditioner on it keeps the air cold, and if you have your heater on it keeps it hot. (insulation is a temperature barrier)

What if you had to keep a drink cold or something. Would you rather have aluminum foil or wool [or Styrofoam]?
Well, I was thinking that wool keeps people hot. I don't know about wrapping a drink in it. (wool imports heat)

What is it that the wool does to keep something hot?
    The fibers. I don't know.

                                           (describes an observation, personal experience)

What do you think it [foil] is doing to keep it cold?
    It is a conductor so it keeps it cold. I think the Styrofoam is an insulator, and the wool would be, too. I don't know. And the metals are conductors and nonmetal things are insulators?

      (conductor as either barrier or imparting cold) (distinguishes insulators and conductors in terms of material)

What [is] a good insulator?
    Yeah. Like on the pipes.... it has fibers that I guess just keep the heat in.

      (describes fibers as a barrier, keeping heat in)

Heat and temperature

Are heat energy and temperature the same or different?
    I don't know what energy is.

      (describes limits of knowledge)

Why don't we start with temperature.
    Okay. It is uhm, the measure in degrees. Or the how hot it is, or how cold it is.... Is heat energy how long it stays hot? I don't know.

      (describes temperature as a measure, connects heat energy to colloquial sense of energy getting used up over time)

Thermal equilibrium

*Say we put a metal spoon and a wooden spoon
into an 80° C oven for 4 hours... and we asked
you what you predict the temperature would be
after 4 hours in the oven.*

I think the wooden spoon would be a little
warmer than room temperature than it was
because wood is not that ... it is not a
conductor. And... the metal spoon would be
hotter.

(conductors
can reach a
higher final
temperature
than
insulators)

*So why is it that you think that the metal spoon
would get so much hotter than the wooden
spoon?*

Because it would attract heat when you are
stirring noodles or something and you use a
wooden spoon so the metal doesn't get hot and
burn.

(metals can
attract heat)

*Let's say we had to predict the temperature of
these objects 8 hours after they are placed in the
room.*

Well, eventually after 8 hours, a Coke would
heat up and the hot chocolate will cool down.
So, ... unless they were heated or cooled ... will
... be at room temperature. ... The cold Coke
and hot chocolate, it will eventually get the
same because the heat or the cold goes out into
the air, and the temperature of the air would
just make it room temperature. If you just a
block of like ice in there, and it gets bigger, it is
more cold than the air, and the room would get
cold.

(objects come
to room
temperature,
reaching room
temperature is
a process)
(air transports
heat and cold;
temperature of
the air causes
room
temperature)

*So these things [metal and wood block] have
been here overnight about 12 hours. Now touch
both of them. Does one feel colder than the other?*

Yeah, the metal one.... Well, obviously it is. But
I don't know why. Maybe because it is in a draft.

(draft, air, can
influence
temperature)

Why do you say "Obviously it is?"

Well, because, you just proved it. This one is colder than this one.

(counts physical feel of the metal as "proof" that it has a lower temperature than the wood)

This one feels colder than this one, but say we measure their temperatures, put a thermometer here and here and they are both the same. Is that possible?

Well, yeah. A conductor, but I don't know how.

(entertains possibility that conductors behave differently)

You said that metal heats fast. Can you say a little more about that?

Well, I guess, you stuff a metal spoon into ... boiling water, the metal spoon would heat up really fast... I guess it attracts heat or something. I don't know. It just is.

(connects a description "heat up" with an explanation "attracts heat")

Suppose you put one end of a metal nail in your hand and the other end on a piece of ice. At the end of 5 minutes, how will the end of the nail in your hand feel? ... What do you think is going on here?

Because the nail is conducting the coldness from the ice. And the nail will then get cold. And it would be the same too if you put it in hot water. It would feel hot.

(objects can conduct heat or cold)

Thermal equilibrium

Say we put a metal spoon and a wooden spoon into an 80°C oven for 4 hours, ... and we asked you what you predict the temperature would be after 4 hours in the oven.

I think the wooden spoon would be a little warmer than room temperature, than it was, because wood is not that ... it is not a conductor. And ... the metal spoon would be hotter.

(conductors can reach a higher final temperature than insulators)

So why is it that you think that the metal spoon would get so much hotter than the wooden spoon?
Because it would attract heat when you are stirring noodles or something, and you use a wooden spoon so the metal doesn't get hot and burn.

(metals can attract heat)

Let's say we had to predict the temperature of these objects 8 hours after they are placed in the room.
Well, eventually after 8 hours, a Coke would heat up and the hot chocolate will cool down. So, ... unless they were heated or cooled ... will ... be at room temperature.
The cold Coke and hot chocolate, it will eventually get the same because the heat or the cold goes out into the air. And the temperature of the air would just make it room temperature. If you just [put] a block of ice in there, and it gets bigger, it is more cold than the air, and the room would get cold.

So these things [metal and wood block] have been here overnight for about 12 hours. Now touch both of them. Does one feel colder than the other?
Yeah, the metal one.... Well, obviously it is. But I don't know why. Maybe because it is in a draft.

Why do you say "Obviously it is"?
Well, because, you just proved it. This one [metal] is colder than this one [wood].

This one feels colder than this one, but say we measure their temperatures, put a thermometer here and here and they are both the same. Is that possible?

Well, yeah. A conductor.... But I don't know how.

You said that metal heats fast. Can you say a little more about that?

Well, I guess, you stuff a metal spoon into ... boiling water, the metal spoon would heat up really fast.... I guess it attracts heat or something. I don't know. It just is.

(connects a description 'heat up' with an explanation 'attracts heat'

Suppose you put one end of a metal nail in your hand and the other end on a piece of ice. At the end of 5 minutes, how will the end of the nail in your hand feel? ... What do you think is going on here?

Because the nail is conducting the coldness from the ice. And the nail will then get cold. And it would be the same too if you put it in hot water. It would feel hot.

(objects can conduct heat or cold)

PAT INTERVIEW 2 AFTER THERMAL EQUILIBRIUM INSTRUCTION

Thermal equilibrium

[Objects in a room] would all be the same temperature? Why do you think that?

Because [if] they're there for a week, they would heat up or cool down to the room temperature

Do you think they'd feel the same?

The [metal] stove would feel colder [than the wood chair], but they would still be the same.

(applying result from classroom experiment measuring temperatures of objects that feel different)

Why do you think that?

Well, it's because of, like, the heat energy in your hand. And that, uhm, because your hand is

hot, it [metal] feels colder at first and then your
hand warms it up, so that it doesn't feel as cold.

(connecting
information
from
classroom
investigation)

So the metal stove would feel colder at first.
Uhm, because it's a conductor.... Well, it's
taking the energy from the ... 'cause your
hand's hotter, it feels colder.

(continuing to
attempt
connections.)

Your hand's hotter than what?
Than the room temperature.... I don't know.

(limit of
connections,
uncertain)

What do you think might be going on there?
Uhm ... it's just, it just feels colder because it's
metal ... It's taking the heat energy from your
hand.

(metal actively
takes heat,
similar to
'attracts heat'
argument
made in the
first interview)

But what's happening with the wood?
Uhm it's not a conductor, so it just like stays
the same.

(similar to the
barrier view
expressed
earlier)

What stays the same?
The, how it feels.

So what is it that the conductor you think is do-ing?
Well, it takes the heat energy from your hand or
wherever and it makes it feel like it's colder.

('takes heat
energy' similar
to 'attracts
heat' of last
interview)

Is there such a thing as cold energy?
No.

So the heat would be going from ...
    Your hand to the metal.

(adds a class
connection)

And with the wood?
    It just, it feels the same because it's not a
    conductor.

(conductors
always feel the
same)

*And if it's not a conductor, what will happen
then?*

    It just is I guess.

(distinguishes
when heat
'goes' to
another object
based on
whether it is a
conductor)

*You are taking some wood and metal strips out
of a hot car trunk. So if you took the temperatures of the strips, which would be hotter?*
    They would be the same.... They would be the
    trunk temperature because they're, they go to
    the temperature of the trunk.

(describes
reaching the
same
temperature)

And what if you touched them?
    The metal would feel hotter ... because it's a
    conductor, and it conducts more heat so that it
    feels hotter.

(acknowledges
possibility of
relative rates
of conduction)

It conducts heat from where to where?
    Well, it's from the sun and the air ... to the
    metal, inside of it or something.

(reiterates the
idea that air
transports
from last
interview)

What exactly is going on there?
    Well I don't know. It's just, it takes more energy.
    Heat energy or something.

(trying out a
connection for
heat energy)

*So you think the metal has more heat energy than
the wood?*
    Yeah, but the temperatures are the same....   (uncertain,
    Well, is it [the metal] hotter than your hand?   asks the
                                                  interviewer to
                                                  clarify relative
                                                  temperature of
                                                  hand and
                                                  metal)

Yeah.
    Well, then the heat energy would be coming   (describes
    into your hand and so that it would feel hot and   metal cooling
    eventually you'd cool down.   to temperature
                                                  of hand)

With the wood, you touch the wood.
    It doesn't, I mean it feels like the room
    temperature of the room.

Why is that?
    Because it's not a conductor.... I don't know.   (distinguishes
                                                    feel of
                                                  conductors
                                                  and
                                                  nonconductors)

Say you touched, here's the metal strips.
    Well, if you held it [metal] in your hand long   (uncertain
    enough, it'd be the temperature of your hand.   about the view
    And I don't know ... the wood, I guess it would   that wood 'just
    just ... I just, I don't know.   is,' perhaps
                                                  uncertain
                                                  about the
                                                  barrier model)

Heat energy and temperature

*So you think there'd be more heat energy in your
friend's [larger milkshake]? Why'd you think
that?*
    Because it has more volume.   (larger things
                                                  have more
                                                  heat energy)

What do you think about the temperatures?
    Well, they were the same at the beginning but
then, uhm the one with less would heat up
quick. Wait ... milk shakes are cold, right? It
would heat up more ... faster than the friend's
because it's less.

(describes the rate of temperature change for large and small milkshake, realizes starting temperature is important)

    I don't really get heat energy.

(uncertain about how to connect these ideas)

*What do you think would happen if you put a
drop of boiling water in your hand?*
    It wouldn't really hurt.

What if you put a cup of boiling water?
    It would hurt.

Which do you think has more heat energy then?
    The cup. Because there's more.

(larger things have more heat energy)

PAT INTERVIEW 3 AFTER RATE OF HEATING AND COOLING INVESTIGATIONS

Thermal equilibrium and rate of change

*What would be the temperature of the objects left
in the oven at 150°?*
    They'd all be 150°C. Because they would all heat
up to that temperature if they were left
overnight.

(thermal equilibrium view)

Would they heat up at the same rate?
    Uh ... I'm not sure. Probably not all of them.

(unequal rates of heating)

*So which ones might heat up faster or slower
than others?*
> Probably the metal things would heat up faster.   (metals heat
> ...Because metal is a conductor.   up faster)

What does that mean to be a conductor?
> Uhm ... that it, heat energy comes into it faster   (comes to it
> and it would feel hotter.   faster,
>   refinement of
>   the 'attracts
>   heat'
>   argument
>   made earlier)

*So you were saying that these things were all the
same temperature but the metal objects would
feel hotter? ... Why would they feel hotter?*
> I have no idea.   (increased
>   uncertainty
>   over last time
>   question was
>   asked)

*And then maybe I touch the asbestos pad and
how would that feel?*
> It would feel warm, but not as hot as the metal.   (increased
>   distinctions
>   among
>   materials)

*So why do you think the metal feels hotter than
the other objects?*
> Because it's something like the heat energy   (reviewing
> flows into your hand differently, or something.   class ideas, not
> And then you'd feel different too.   fully
>   connected)

What do you mean by differently?
> I forgot which one. I forgot which way it goes,   (recalls idea
> but I don't remember. It's like the heat energy   but not sure
> goes into your hand and then it feels hotter and   how to
> then your hand would cool it down and   connect it)
> something.

What is the temperature of the objects in this
room?

    They're all the same. They're whatever
temperature the room is, ... because they're all
room temperature. It's just, they are.

(connects lack
of change in
temperature to
thermal
equilibrium,
reminiscent of
barrier idea
about
materials that
do not conduct
as discussed
earlier)

Would it make any difference, do some of those
objects come to room temperature faster than
others or slower than others, or do they all come
about the same time?

    I don't know. I guess ...

(uncertainty)

So do some things in the same environment cool
faster than others or not.

    I don't know.

(distinguishes
rate of heat
from rate of
cooling)

But if you went around the room and touched
them, do they feel the same?

    Well, the metal things would feel colder
probably than the wooden things. Uhm... I don't
know. Just like the metal conducts heat and like
wood and I guess plastic is just like, uhm, is
opposite of conductor. Like there's fewer of
them.

(categorizes
plastic and
wood as the
opposite of a
conductor)

So you say metals conduct heat ...

    Or cold.

(distinguishes
conduction of
heat and cold)

So I pick up this piece of metal and it feels cold
to me. Why?

It's because your hand is hotter than, uhm, at first it feels cold and then your hand will warm it up. It's like if you were outside and you walked into where it's cold, you'll feel colder than actually, you got all used to it.

(persists in interpreting class idea)

But when I touch the wood, it doesn't feel cold. What's going on there?

Uhm, I don't know. Maybe there's like fibers and there's like little tiny tiny holes in wood, and so maybe the heat energy goes through your hand, and it doesn't stay in it or something.

(fibers and holes in material allow heat energy to pass through without staying)

Doesn't stay in the wood or doesn't stay in my hand?

It wouldn't stay in the wood.

(wood "just is")

But it does leave my hand and go somewhere?

Yeah, it always goes somewhere.

(heat energy actively leaves the hand)

Conduction and insulation

What would you wrap a frozen candy bar in to keep it cold for your lunch?

The metal, ... because I think the metal would keep the cold in, uhm, better than something like, uhm, a napkin or something because there's little holes in the fiber, and the heat energy would come into the candy bar and then make it heat up.

(holes let heat out; metal keeps things cold)

So if I had a frozen candy bar sitting unwrapped here, how would you heat it up?

Heat energy would come into the candy bar and raise temperature.

What if I used something like Styrofoam? You know how it comes in sheets?

I think metal would be better because it's, uhm, the little holes. There's holes in the Styrofoam.

And wool?
Holes.

So the holes are a problem. Would anything that didn't have holes work as well as aluminum foil? For example if I used a plastic bag.
I guess it would.... Well, I don't know, I guess it would. But I think metal's better than plastic, I don't know why though.

So metal's a good conductor. What does it do?
They hold the temperature in, and they don't have little holes in it, and so the heat energy won't go out of, or go in at all.

(barrier model for a conductor when its keeping things cold)

So a good conductor would help keep things cold if they were cold already?
It's like thermoses are metal on the inside, or they have metal in them.

(connects to everyday experience)

What does an insulator do?
That's the word. It is ... well what do you call it, the pipes, they have insulation, and it's just like a big blanket around it ... I don't really know how it works.

Why do you think people would wrap them around ducts or pipes?
Because, uhm, well maybe it's so the hot water would stay hot from the heater to the bathroom and like it would save energy an stuff.... Good insulators would also be like wood, wool. Styrofoam would be somewhere in the middle I think, and same with saran wrap. And paper would be like three.

(in the middle)

So do we know what an insulator does yet?
Sort of. I don't know what it does, but actually I don't know. It just, on the pipe it keeps the

water warm the whole way so it doesn't ... I guess the metal like doesn't cool it down or something.

(uncertain about connections between metals that could 'cool it down' and insulators that 'keep it warm')

What about cold things? Do you think insulators would keep them cold?
I think, oh I don't know. I think I keep switching. I don't know.

(realizes that the connections among these ideas are not consistent)

Metal and wood spoons for stirring noodles?
They'd be the temperature of the water, but the metal would feel hotter than the wood.

(connects to answer for thermal equilibrium although this situation is more complicated)

These ends of the spoon that are sticking out of the water would be the same temperature as the water? ... And they would be the same temperature as each other you said?
Yeah, it would all be the same temperature.

But you were saying the metal one would feel hotter? ... How did these ends of the spoons get hot?
Well for one thing the steam would be blowing up and then just the heat energy would just flow up to the top because ...

Flow up to the top from where?
Uhm, probably through it, like the inside more. It would just start, I think it's like diffuse or

something. Anyway, goes up and pushes out the coldness and takes over because there, it's more concentrated here than the air.

(envisions heat and coldness)

You said something about diffusion and then you decided that wasn't right.
I don't know. I'm not sure. I mean I guess it would work, except diffusion was, I don't know. I'm not sure.

(weak connection to some notion of diffusion)

Wood and metal spoons in ice water?
I think the spoons would be definitely the same temperature as the water.

How do these spoons get cold?
Like the heat energy like leaves.

The heat energy from ... ?
Well, from the spoons. The heat energy would go back into the water I think, and then it would cool.

What would cool?
Actually, all of it would cool 'cause well, I mean the outside temperature wouldn't be cooling the water.... The ice water temperature would go up a little.

Heat energy and temperature

You were saying that the objects would all be 150°. So here I have a big beaker and a little beaker, so they would be the same temperature? Could you say anything about the heat energy of these two? Would that be the same? Would that be different?
I think it would be the same if they're the same temperature.

(heat energy and temperature are the same)

Is that a general rule?
I think so.

So if I had a cup of boiling water and a pot of boiling water, would they have the same heat energy?

Uhm, actually I guess they wouldn't. I don't know. I guess … Well, if there was a more amount of water then the one with more water would have more heat energy, … because there's more volume of water.

(heat energy varies with volume)

Does that apply here or not?

Uh … I don't know. I guess. I'm not sure.

(cannot resolve inconsistency, comfortable with waiting)

Learning in class

Are the class discussions useful or not?

I'd rather do an experiment.

(enjoys adding more ideas)

How do you like the experiments?

I like them.

What parts help you?

Writing the principle maybe…. It helps you like see it because it's all the information and you can understand it…. The principles because they just sum it up.

(acknowledges criteria in connecting ideas)

PAT INTERVIEW 4 AFTER INSULATION AND CONDUCTION INVESTIGATIONS

Thermal equilibrium

[The objects in the oven], would they get hotter than the oven do you think?

No. I don't think so…. The metal would feel hotter than the wood…. It's just cause metal's a conductor and wood's an insulator.

(uses class terms)

And how does that make a difference?
    I don't know. It's just like metal will feel hotter
or colder than wood does because, uhm, like it
attracts heat or cold, and like with your hand,
it'll feel different, but then the wood probably
wouldn't feel that hot but it would be warm.

(metals attract
heat; wood can
warm up)

So the metal attracts the heat from where?
    Uhm, the air I guess.

(air carries
heat)

*So when you touch it though, it feels hotter. Why
is that do you think?*
    Well Mr. K said it was something like if your
skin, when you touch it, it's like the heat energy
is going between your hand and the object then.
Well, actually, he said this about a cold thing. I
don't know about a hot thing, but I guess it
could be mostly the same. But it like, your hand
changes to the temperature really fast, so it
feels cold at first, and then it feels hotter, so it
... if you uhm ...

(connecting
class ideas to
more
situations)

If you touch a metal thing like this?
    If I touch like this side of it, then in like another
minute I have to move to this side to see if it
was still cold, you know because it would feel
hot. It wouldn't feel cold that long.

(accurate
observations)

And what about with the wood?
    Uhm, the wood would just it wouldn't. It would
feel warm if you held it, and uhm, yeah it would
feel warm but not really hot, I mean you could
hold it, and it'd be warm, but it wouldn't burn
you unless it was like in a really really really hot
oven. And then it would feel warm for like a
minute or two and then it would go back to
normal or to your hand.

(static nature
of feel of
wood)

*So why wouldn't it feel as warm as the metal?
They're in the same oven, right?*
    Yeah ... and I think they're the same
temperature, but it's just 'cause this one is, the
metal is a conductor. I'm not really sure what

(connects to
class
experiments;

that means, but that's what he said. And it's
like, I don't know, but when we did the potato
thing, the Styrofoam like held the heat in more,
so like the wood probably would too. But I
wouldn't really wrap a potato in wood, but I
don't know. It doesn't seem like the same thing.

still actively
considering
alternatives)

*So you said this is a good conductor, how do you
think that helps it feel hot?*
Well, I think it just like, attracts heat energy or
something, I don't know. But it just does.

(attracts heat
energy)

Attracts heat energy from where?
From the oven or like the air. Or if it's touching
like the coils.

(touching
makes it
attract heat
energy)

*How would you design a container to keep some-
thing hot?*
Well, now I would put Styrofoam I guess, but
before I would have put metal. Before the
potato. And I'm not really sure why but it just, it
is.

(linking to the
potato
experiment in
class)

*So the potato thing changed your mind. So what
is it you think the Styrofoam would do?*
Well it's like, uhm, they're little holes in it so it
like traps air and it's like, uhm, like a blanket
and all the little holes, and so it keeps it warm,
but before I thought it would let heat energy
out, with all the little holes, but I guess not. But
Mr. K said the aluminum and the air or were like
the same, if you just didn't wrap it in anything
and wrapped it in aluminum. So I think
Styrofoam or you could use wool but I don't
know if you would want it with food.

(rich set of
connections,
loosely tied
together, from
class and from
reflection)

*So what is it that the Styrofoam would do that
the metal couldn't do?*
Well it just like keeps the air in because ... all
the little holes. And so the air goes into the
little holes and stays there.

(building up
the holes idea,
making more
connections)

*Say you put a hot thing into your container, what
would happen after some time?*

Well it would probably cool down a little bit, but
it would stay warmer than if you did it, if you
just left it out, or if you put aluminum on it.

(adds slow
heat flow to
the barrier
view)

With aluminum, what would happen?

Oh, uhm, the heat energy would go out to the
air from the whatever you had in there.

But there's no holes in the aluminum.

I know. I don't get it. That's like the heat energy
would want to go to the aluminum because it
like takes the ... attracts the heat energy. And it
would just stay there and not be in whatever you
had in there.

(tries to sort
out holes and
attracting
heat)

PAT INTERVIEW 5 AFTER HEAT BARS AND FINAL EXAMINATION

Insulation and conduction

*[Styrofoam] You said it was a good insulator.
Can you say a little bit more about it?*

It has little holes in it.... Air goes into those
holes, and it is like ... uh ... its makes it cold. It
keeps it cold.... Well, it's like a blanket sort of.
And it just keeps the heat energy from coming
in.

*Are there some experiments that help you see it
that way?*

We wrapped our Cokes in different materials,
and the one with Styrofoam was the best.

*The Styrofoam,... you said, could keep it cold,
plus it will keep hot things hot.*

Because, well, it's like a barrier so that heat
energy won't come in or it won't go out.

Heat energy and temperature

*What is it that makes them different? What are
they?*

Well, temperature is like the measure of hot or
cold it is. And something could have high

temperature but low heat energy because it's small, like a drop doesn't have much heat energy, but it could be really really hot.... The Chili experiment. One was bigger, one was smaller. They both had the same temperature, and the bigger one had more heat energy because there was more space for it.... Heat energy will flow from the hot thing to the cold thing. But I guess it will still have heat energy in it, so I am not really sure.

How do you know it had more heat energy?
    I don't know. But it just stayed, so it was bigger.... Because it just is. It is big, so there's more.

    (distinguishes and describes gaps in knowledge)

So if you had, say, an ice cube and a big block of ice they were the same temperatures. Do they have any heat energy? ... Do cold things have heat energy?
    Well, heat energy is going into them all the time.... So, it would get to room temperature.... I am not sure.

Let's say we have a pot of boiling water and a cup out of the pot. Both are 100°. Which one has more heat energy?
    The big one, ... because it's big. So there is more. It has more mass.

Thermal equilibrium

The objects in the oven ...
    Because, the air, well not much of the air, will be coming in, and like heat energy will not being going out that much? It would be whatever the temperature is of the surround. And so, they would just be ... it's just like another 'room' in the oven, so then their room temperature would be 80.

    (surround, class principle)

*You said all of them would be at room tempera-
ture. I see. Can you say a little bit more about
that?*

Well, originally everything would get to room   (class
temperature, so in 8 hours, I think the hot   principle)
chocolate would cool by 8 hours, and the
wooden table, the bowl, the spoon, and the
plate are already at room temperature, unless
someone stuck them in the freezer.

Can you give me an example of a good conductor?
Copper.... Well, because it doesn't have all these   (holes model)
little holes like the insulators do. And heat energy
goes right into it very easily without the air.

How do you think the metal one would feel hotter?
Because we are colder. So, like if it was in like   (temperature
boiling water, and then we held on to it, all the   difference)
heat energy would go into our hand real fast.
And it would feel real hot at first, and then it
would just feel like your hand.

And what if it were just a wooden spoon?
It would just feel warm. It would probably stay
warm. It wouldn't burn you.

*But if they are the same temperature, why do
they feel different?*

Because the wood has those little holes of air in   (knowledge
it. And they just ... it feels different. It's not a   integration
conductor. [holes] ... They keep air ... I'm not   around still
really sure. The air does something. Makes it   air)
like not go in. Makes heat energy not go.

Why does the nail in the ice feel cold?
Well, there's not really cold energy. I am not
sure how that works, but if there was cold
energy, it would be like the cold energy was
going into the nail and then make it cooler, but
I think it is like the heat energy is coming up
from your hand into the ice and it feels cooler
because the heat energy is going away. And then
it feels cool because there is not much heat
energy.

So, you said the heat energy. Is going from where to where?

> Because it ... the heat energy is going away from the nail and so it feels colder, because there is less heat energy in the nail.... Probably heat energy is going into the nail. Not that much.

(direction has two interpretations)

Visualization

What about the heat bars experiment that ... the evidence you used there in your answer. Do you remember? ... Why did that help you see?

> Because it's the same thing. There was a thermometer on the end of a bar and the heat was coming from the other end. And then the heat ... from the heat source and the heat energy flowed through whatever it's flowing through, the bar, I guess, and then it measured the temperature.... Copper was the best.

Foil, you said, would be poor for keeping things hot and poor for keeping things cold. Can you say a little bit more about it?

> Well, it's conducting, not an insulator. It doesn't have those little air pocket things, so, and it's a conductor, so, it would like ... for something hot, all the heat energy would conduct to the metal, and it would just go away.

Go away to where?

> The air. And like the wool and the Styrofoam they have the little air things, so it would be something good.

PAT LONGITUDINAL TENTH GRADE

Insulation and conduction

If you were going to wrap a cold soda to take to school for lunch, what is the best thing to wrap it in?

> Well, we found out last year that it's not aluminum. It would be like plastic wrap or

[Note to Reader: Add annotations to this interview. See Ch. 8 Points to Ponder.]

bubble wrap I think was the best.... I just remember that it was pretty much anything but foil would work okay.

And why is that?

Because, uhm, I forget what he called it. I'm trying to remember.... There were little heat currents or something that would. They were called ... oh I'm confusing myself.

The word may come if you can describe what happened.

Okay. The metal would kind of, like aluminum foil, would kind of pull the cold out of the soda into the air because ... the cold like, it just moved right out onto the metal because metal is the conductor, and then it would be released into the air. I forget if it happened that way or if the heat in the air, like the metal pulled the heat in from the air into the soda. I forget if the cold left or if the heat came in, but it's probably both.

Does that make sense that there could be both?

But it could also be just one. The heat could come in or the heat would leave depending on whether it was hot or cold.... I really never kind of understood whether there was both or not.

There's such a thing as cold energy and heat energy?

That's what it's called, heat energy.... I'm not sure if there's cold energy or not. I guess there could be, but I think it was maybe just heat energy.... The more I think about it, I think there was only heat energy, but I'm not sure.

What would make a cold soda warm up?

The heat in the air. If the air was hotter than the soda.

Which we presume it will be.

Yeah. Then the metal, like the foil, or I guess on the can maybe I'm not sure.... So whatever is in the little metal particles attract heat and so they would, the heat energy would kind of be

sucked on to the can and would go into the
soda and warm it.

*But if you wrapped it in you were saying plastic
wrap or bubble wrap, what would be different
about that?*
Because of the air pocket.... There's something
with how the air is an insulator. If you have like,
uhm, let's say the Styrofoam wrap, that's really
porous. So then the air kind of holds in the
little holes and then it insulates against heat
energy coming in.

I just wondered what insulates mean.
Well it's the opposite of conducting and ...

So what's conducting?
I don't know. I know what it is, but I can't
describe it. Conducting is like, uhm, it attracts
the heat and holds the heat right there and lets
it go. Like a metal wall I guess if this makes
sense. Hot on this side and cold on this side,
then the metal wall would pull all the heat
energy into it and it would like leave and go into
the cold.

*So if that's a conductor, what's an insulator
now?*
Uhm, well I know that air is an insulator. Let's
see I'm trying to describe it. I guess if you had
the same situation, but the wall was Styrofoam
sheeting or something like that. The air would
kind of get stuck in the pockets, and that
doesn't let the heat energy ... or doesn't. The
air is not metal, so it doesn't pull the heat as
fast, but eventually the little heat particles
would diffuse through the wall, but it doesn't
have the initial pull on all of it.

So is heat matter? You said heat particles.
No, ... I guess heat energy.

*What would happen with that Styrofoam wall
there?*
I think it's like neither will keep, neither
Styrofoam nor metal would keep it cold forever,

but Styrofoam is better because the particles would eventually diffuse through because everything's always moving and stuff. The metal just adds to it. It just sucks all the little energies into the wall ... I'm trying to think. I know how I want to say it, but it's not coming out right.

Heat and temperature distinction

You and your friend are sharing a milk shake. Because you aren't very hungry, you and your friend divide it up as you see here. What can you say about the heat energy present in each of your glasses of milk shake?
Well, I think initially they'd be the same into the same situation, but I think, oh gosh, uhm, ... I think the smaller one would warm up faster because there's less matter for the heat in the outside to fill up.... I think it would take longer for the heat to diffuse through all of the friend's because there's more of it than to mine which is half its size.

What do they have to do to cool down?
Well the heat energy. Everything has some amount of heat energy. Even the coldest thing. But, uhm, the heat energy in it would leave into the freezer because if heat energy had a brain it would want to make everything isotonic. I think that's right. Well, equal. And with the environments and what's in it, that's why like a soda would heat up on the outside so that everything's the same.

Would these two end up losing the same amount of heat?
Well, I think the smaller one would cool down faster because it had less heat energy in it. You know I said before that the thing with more matter would have more heat energy like. Heat energy and temperature, that's the same thing, right?

What do you think?
    I didn't think so. But they could have the same
temperature, but not the same amount of heat
energy. I wasn't sure.

*Well, let's take another example. Suppose you
had a cup of water in a pot and.... In this pot
you have 10 cups of water.... We put them on the
stove on identical burners and we want to heat
them both to boiling.*
    I think you'd have to put less heat energy in
where there's less water.... .I don't know. I want
heat energy to be a particle.... I don't think it
would be the same. I think there'd be more heat
energy where's there's more matter.

Thermal equilibrium; insulation and conduction

*You arrive at a ski cabin during the winter and
no heat was left on. The room thermometer
reads 5°C. What can you predict about the temperature of the objects in the cabin?*
    I think if the house was absolutely shut, no
drafts or anything like that, then they should all
be the same temperature.... I guess if it was
long enough, it would be the same temperature
eventually, given no outside things.

*What if all the windows and things were open
and the thermometer still registered 5°C?*
    Well there might be something. Like if there   (draft
was one window and a lot of breeze came in, ...   influences
                                                                         temperature)

*What would happen if you went around and
touched all the objects in the room. Would they
feel the same?*
    Not if they were metal things.... Metal things
would feel colder because metal's a conductor
and the wood things are not.... Oh. I just
remember like when we had to touch the table,
it felt cold, and the wood parts didn't. I think
it's because your hand is warmer, and so it feels
colder on the metal.

So why would it feel colder?
> Well, I mean if it's, if the degree measure is colder than your hand, then it would feel cold.

But you were saying ... the wood doesn't feel cold.
> Uh. Uhm, I guess it has to do with the air that's inside of it, ... inside the wood, ... because well, it's porous. I mean it's like the soda question, but.... I'm really not sure. I've heard this before.

You and a friend are buying materials for a project and have purchased several long strips of aluminum and several long strips of wood at a hardware store. You place the strips in the trunk of the car. It is a hot day and ... you left the strips of metal and wood sitting in the trunk of their car. When you returned several hours later, you and your friend have different predictions about the temperature of the strips of metal and wood in the trunk.... What would happen if you touched the metal strips?
> Well, if everything was equal inside the trunk, no sun, ... if it was all equal, I think they'd be equal temperatures.

Would they feel the same?
> The metal would feel hotter, ... because it's a conductor.

What does it conduct?
> Heat energy.... The heat energy went from the air to the metal to your hand and so you're feeling it from the metal, but I guess it came from the sun.

So what would happen when I touched the wooden strips?
> They wouldn't feel as hot.... Little air pockets? It has something too with little air pockets. Why can't I remember? ... Because the air insulates it.

Insulation and conduction

*Suppose you hold one end of a metal nail and
put the other end on a piece of ice.*
    Well, I'm not sure about the time exactly, but I
think it would be. Like the heat energy would go
from my hand to the nail, but it would also get
like cold. If the nail is kind of, oh gee, this is a
hard one. Wouldn't the heat energy go from my
hand into the top of the nail, but what's it like?
Is it hotter outside, or am I in a freezer?

*I'd say in a room like this. You got a big block of
ice here. A nail which you're holding one end of
and the other end is resting on the ice.*
    I think the heat or the coldness sort of, should
come up. Then the heat from the nail should go
into the ice. And then it should make the nail
cold. Then if my hand is hotter than the nail, it
should warm up to. So, ... the heat would go
from my hand to the nail? ... I guess it would go
up to the ice.... But I'm not sure.

Light

*The power is out in your home, and you are
looking for a book to read with a flashlight.
a)You shine the light toward the ceiling while
looking toward your desk. Explain everything
that happens which allows (or does not allow)
you to see the book:*
    Let's see. The light would go up and hit the
ceiling. This is in a house right?... It would um,
hit the ceiling. I'm assuming the ceiling would
be white because most are. It would reflect
down. I mean if you had a black ceiling, it would
probably be absorbed.... I think would depend
on the flashlight, how big the flashlight was....
If the beam was big enough, then the light
would go up and kind of break and come down
in an arc, and I'm not sure with this flashlight if
she could see 'cause the light would kind of be
like that. Do you know what I mean? But if it

was a big enough flashlight and the arc went like that, then she would see.

So you showed the arc actually not reaching the table in one case, and then passing the table in another.

Well it depends. If you had like a pen light, it wouldn't reach. But if you had a giant lantern, it would go.

So what would have to happen for her to see that book?

Uhm, the light beam. The original beam of light would have to be big enough that when it shines up, it would break into an arc and the arc would be big enough to reach the book.

Does light have to do anything after it shines on the book or is that enough?

I guess it might have to reflect. I think kind of what it does is it reflects off of things and that lights them up.... I'm not really sure about the reflecting, but I suppose if it reflected, it would reflect into the air sort of, or maybe onto the ceiling again if it was strong enough and at the right angle and everything.

You shine the light towards the ceiling while looking towards your desk. Explain everything that happens which allows (or does not allow) you to see the book:

Well, I guess the beam would be narrower because it wouldn't have that arcing kind of thing. So she'd probably have to move the light around to hit the book and then I suppose the light would hit the book and reflect off.... Well, if the light reflected off the paper towel thing and hits the paper. If the paper had eyes, it could see it, but that was blocking the reflection of the light to my face, to my eyes.

Your family decides to eat dinner without the lights, instead lighting a candle in the middle of the table. How far does the light from the candle go?

Well the light from the candle would probably
be able to come from all directions, not like a
flashlight where it's directed. If it came out of
the bottom of the flame, I guess it could bounce
off the table, bounce to me, and off the ceiling.
I think it could go anywhere. I mean it would
have to go to the wall to the floor to go under
the table, but I think under the table would be
the hardest.... It'd be darker under the table, I
think.

But there'd still be some light under that table.
Uh-huh, but there's no way you can really test
that is there?... Do you have like a light meter
or something?

You are playing games with two other friends.
You are 'it' and you walk into a dimly lit room.
One of your friends is wearing a white T-shirt,
and the other a black T-shirt.
Okay, you could see the white T-shirt better
than the black,... because light reflects off of
white, but it's absorbed into black. That's why
you want to wear a white T-shirt on a hot day.
I'm not sure where the light was coming
from.... Well, if equal light was shining on them
and everything like that, then the light would
bounce off the white T-shirt and come back to
your face.

It is a very sunny day and you decide to put on
a pair of sunglasses. How do objects now ap-
pear to you?
Well depending on the color of your glasses,
they'd look more the shade of the glasses. If you
had brown lenses, they'd look brown. If you had
rose lenses, they'd look pinkish because you
have something in front of your eyes, kind of
colors it a little.

So do things look the same degree of brightness,
just a different color?
Oh well, like. I think it depends on the
sunglasses. Cause like if you had UV protection,
it would be a little altered.

*So what do sunglasses do that change the way
things look?*
　I think the lenses kind of distort the light rays
　that are coming straight into your eyes. If
　they're darker, I guess it absorbs the light a
　little so it doesn't come right into your eyes,
　but it's not like solid, thick black. So the light
　still comes through so you can see.... Kind of
　changes the amount of light, I think.

Learning science

What do you remember about Mr. K's class?
　Well, we did the study with the Cokes.

Did it seem like science was okay?
　I'd rather do like, uhm, life science. I don't
　really care too much about chemistry and that
　sort of stuff, but, uhm, I don't know I think he
　made it more interesting than I thought it was
　going to be.

What worked in that class?
　There was a little bit of lecturing, but not much,
　mostly, uhm, just working on the computers.

Science career

*What do you plan on doing as a career or do you
know?*
　Um, well I want to be a doctor ... medical
　doctor.

Men and women in science

*Why do you think there are more women going
into medicine or science in general?*
　It's more allowed by society, and women realize
　that they can actually do things.

Learning

When you take science classes, how hard do you generally have to work?

Well, I have a good teacher, which I have mostly, I don't have to work very hard. I study. I don't really study every day, but I always do the homework and I prepare usually 2 days before a test.

What does a good teacher do for you that a bad teacher doesn't?

Take the time to explain things ... like if you have a question. That they're willing to help and, uhm, just like, uh, mostly that I could go up to my teacher after class and say, "Well, I was thinking if it's like this, would it still be the same?" Most of my teachers have been good teachers.

Do you like classes with lectures or do you like classes with discussions or classes with hands-on experiments?

I like experiments. I like dissections. I don't know, I might be a surgeon. I just think they're a lot of fun, more fun to get into it. Uhm, I like lectures. I mean, they're not my favorite thing in the whole wide world, but like taking notes I don't mind really, but I don't like watching videos and taking notes off the videos. They put me to sleep most of the time.... I did most of my sleeping through biology this year, but I still learned it. From the labs and the lectures and stuff.

Say the teacher presented something and you didn't understand it real well. What would you do?

Well, after, it'd probably be a lecture or something, discussion. Then if I still didn't understand it, I'd probably go look it up in the textbook. Then, uhm, take some notes down from the textbook and find ... pinpoint what I don't understand specifically and then I'd probably ask friends or if my teacher was a good teacher, I would ask him before class or something. It's like, "I don't understand what happens to the ATP."

How did the day go today?
I thought it was good because we got to actually, I learned stuff ... About like, oh how my sunglasses work. 'Cause I didn't understand how like light worked and I think it was kind of cool that I got the right answer or very close.... Uhm, I think you asked the questions well, and I'm sure you have to keep asking me if it makes sense to me, but that kind of was annoying. I wouldn't be saying it, but I guess I said things I don't understand. I liked having Mr. K here.... He's really sweet. He's one of my favorite teachers, I think. I had another question. When I was doing my first test, it said, uhm, like men or women are better at these things, and I realized that I'd never had a woman science teacher.

Wow.
I was really surprised ... that all my teachers were men. I think schools should think about that.

PAT LONGITUDINAL TWELFTH GRADE

Insulation and conduction

If you were going to wrap a cold soda for lunch, what is the best thing to wrap it in to keep it cold?
I think the best thing was wool, I know it wasn't aluminum. We talked about air being a cushion and metal being a conductor so even air is better than aluminum ... practically, I wouldn't choose wool. I would choose saran wrap, because wrapping it in a sweater would be a little awkward.

[Note to **Reader**: Add annotations to this interview. See Ch. 8 Points to Ponder.]

What is a conductor?

   ... Okay, you can't say a conductor conducts....
   It attracts the heat energy.

*So if you had your aluminum can wrapped in
foil what would happen?*

   It takes the heat energy from the air, the
   surroundings, and transfers it into the can, into
   the soda.

*And if you had wool, what would happen? Or sa-
ran wrap, either one?*

   It doesn't attract heat energy, so it doesn't pull
   it into the can and the air provides a cushion,
   but the air that's trapped in the fibers, probably
   in the folds, provides a cushion, and that keeps
   it insulated.

So would it get warm eventually?

   Eventually I think so.... Eventually, the heat
   energy from the air would flow into the can and
   warm the soda until it's room temperature.

*And once it was room temperature, would it get
warm?*

   No. Once it is at equilibrium.

Heat energy and temperature

*We have a freezer here set to -40° and they have
both [large and small ice blocks] been in there
for a week. What temperature would each piece
of ice have?*

   They would both be at -40° if they had been
   there for a week.

*And if you take it from that freezer and put them
at 0° ... ?*

   I think the smaller one will warm up faster....
   The smaller one will reach 0° faster than the
   larger one.... If you were measuring from the
   center ... it would take the heat energy longer
   to reach the center of the larger one 'cause it

has to pass through all that extra ice than if it went straight to the center of the smaller one.

So the larger one would take longer. What would happen to the heat energy? Do they have heat energy since they are cold? What happens to heat energy during this process?

It gets from the 0° environment into the ice.... When they were in -40, they were 40°, and then they were moved up to 0°. Then the heat energy from the surroundings moved into the ice and mirrored the content of heat energy in the ice cubes.

What is the difference between heat energy and temperature?

Temperature is the measure of how much heat energy there is? Is that close? (laughs) It was something like that, wasn't it? Umm, heat energy is like a physical thing and temperature is just a recording. I think.

(cannot give a clear definition but can describe the process)

So you were saying that the two blocks of ice are at the same temperature. Is their heat energy the same?

I think when it moved from -40° to 0°, the big block of ice had to gain more heat energy to get up to 0° because there is more mass. So, because it has more mass, and is generally bigger, I think the larger one would have more heat energy.

Science learning

Do you remember when you did this in Mr. K's class?

Yes.... I remember it was really hard, and I wasn't sure what I was doing. I remember learning it and having trouble with the concept because it was before I ever talked about things you couldn't see or heat energy kind of existing. I couldn't understand the difference between temperature and heat energy and then I thought I did, but now I can see that I don't.

*When you answered this question in the eighth
grade, do you think you answered it similar to
how you did today?*

I think I probably understood it better then
because it was fresh. I wasn't exactly sure, but
I'd probably remember what he said and I just
put that down…. I think I forgot about it, 'cause
I'm really fuzzy on it…. I think I remembered it
better in eighth grade than I do now just
because of the progression of time.

*Do you think that, when you think about it, you
understand it better now?*

I think I understand it about the same. It was
fresher in my mind then. I think I understood
the concepts of insulation and conduction then
and I think I still do to some extent.

Do you ever think about it?

It's probably there because I learned it but I
don't sit down and say, "Oh, I have these two
cakes. Which one has more heat energy?" Not in
those terms exactly, but I am sure its in my
subconscious.

*When you took chemistry, did you use anything
you learned in Mr. K's class?*

Oh yeah. When we started talking about
conductivity and things like that. We talked
about light, which we didn't learn in Mr. K's
class but we did learn in an interview a few years
ago with mirrors and that kind of thing. And I
remember some of the details from that.

Thermal equilibrium

*In the chemistry lab students were drying equip-
ment in the oven at 150°C, and in the oven were
a spatula, glass tubes, ceramic dishes, asbestos
pads…. They put the stuff in the oven and then
they came back the next day. What temperature
would the things be?*

They are all the same temperature but they all
feel different…. I think it was one of those

equilibrium things when, if they're left long
enough, they'll approach the same temperature.
If you had something at 100° and something at
200° and you put them in a environment that
was 150°, they would both reach the same
temperature, 150° ... because some are
conductors.... Metal feels hot, wood doesn't.
Glass doesn't feel as hot at the metal. Ceramic I
am not sure about.... I don't think it's very hot.

Why?

Because the heat energy flows from the metal to
my hand better than it does from the wood....
But because metal is a conductor, it's more
noticeable.

Insulation and conduction

*This is a continuum of conductors and insula-
tors. Would you put those items were they belong?*

I put metal at the conductor end. I would put
wool as an insulator, but I don't really know the
degrees of whether wool's better than wood. I
would put Styrofoam as an insulator because it
has a lot of air. Anything porous is a good
insulator, ... because it has a lot of air and air
insulates well.... That's why you put that pink
stuff in houses 'cause it is cushiony ... and it
holds the air in the walls.

*You place a silver platter and a ceramic platter,
both the same size, into an oven at 450°F for 3
hours, and then you take them out and you put
them on the counter. Which one will stay warmer
longer?*

Terra-cotta, I think,... because the metal will
release the heat energy into the air. Do you want
to know why, do you want to hear my thought
process? ... These terra-cotta plates and you put
them in the bottom of your bread basket to keep
the rolls warm.... It holds the heat in and the
heat rises through the buns. I've seen them. I
think those are pottery and not metal because I

think once you take the metal out, the heat will just go. If you have a cookie sheet when you are baking cookies you can touch the cookie sheet in like a minute and you can use it again in a couple of minutes. But I don't think you can with a terra-cotta thing. It wouldn't feel as hot as the metal, but it would hold the heat longer. It wouldn't dissipate as fast.

Does it matter how ... if you put the platters on a metal surface what would that do?
I think it would probably speed up the metal platter. It would probably speed them both up because the metal table would attract the heat energy towards it faster than, say, a wood table or whatever else you had it on. I think it would probably speed it up.

How does it attract heat?
It's one of those things that just happens (said jokingly) You see, they've got me chemically screwed-up, like "Oh, there's excess," and "It lacks equilibrium." Chemistry is so in my brain, 'cause they're similar things, similar topics, but it doesn't matter 'cause they're different.

What was different about it?
It was about more physical things. Chemistry. Like these are atoms and these are like heat energy waves transferring, and so even so, you want an equilibrium and energy, but it's different from saying you want your carbon atoms to be balanced.... I think so. I mean, I guess you could say the metal table atoms are lacking in heat energy, and therefore it would want to take the heat energy away from the platters, so I guess they are the same. They just seem different.

Do you think the model of the atoms versus the model of heat flow are consistent with each other? Do you think they contradict each other?
They're consistent. Okay.

Conduction

If you are stirring boiling noodles, which one is safer, a wooden spoon or a metal spoon?
　　A wooden spoon 'cause mommy always says that if you used a wooden spoon, you won't get your hands burnt, because, metal is a conductor and the heat would flow from the water to the spoon and from the spoon to your hand and it would hurt, but since wood doesn't conduct as well, it doesn't have the heat feeling. It doesn't have the temperature rise as a metal spoon, even if it has the same heat energy.

Say that you are shoveling snow and you take this metal shovel with you outside and you start shoveling. Five minutes later, how does the shovel feel. You're not wearing gloves, by the way.
　　The heat energy from your hands is flowing into that part of the metal, and then you have an equilibrium.... But there's not enough heat in just your hands to heat up the whole shovel. So when your hands aren't, the heat energy's leaving from the shovel into the air, and if you touch it again, there's a big difference between the heat energy in your hand and the amount of heat energy in that part of the shovel.

What if you put on gloves?
　　Well, the shovel would have the same thing happen, but you probably wouldn't notice with the gloves on. Where your hands were would be the same temperature as your hand. You just wouldn't notice it and if you moved your hand to another part of the shovel, you probably wouldn't notice it either, unless you were wearing really cheap gloves.

These objects have been in the room for 8 hours, and the room has been at the same temperature. After 8 hours you come back and you tell me what temperature each of these things is going to be.
　　They should all be at room temperature. But they're not going to feel like it.... A child ... if

you stuck it in a child, it would be 98°,
hopefully. No matter how long you leave a child
at room temperature, it's not going to be 60° or
whatever because a child has its own source of
heat energy. Its skin might be 60°, or maybe if
you touched his clothes, they would feel at room
temperature. A metal plate would probably feel
colder because if the heat you bring with you in
your hand there is a big difference because of
the conducting. The hot chocolate, the liquid
would be at room temperature and the cup too,
but it wouldn't necessarily feel that way
depending on whether it was metal or
something else. The table would be a room
temperature. Styrofoam would be at room
temperature. I think the cold Coke would be at
room temperature, but if you touched the can,
it would feel colder because of the conductivity.

Light

*Okay, these people are playing a game with a
flashlight, and she gets points every time she can
flash the light on his face and all over his whole
body. So, which of the three materials, mirrored
panel, white panel, or black panel, would be best
to light just his face? How about for his entire
body?*

This isn't fair! We only had to learn about this
for about 2 hours, 2 years ago! (laughs) Black
panel was bad for anything because it just
absorbs everything. And then the mirrored
panel and the white panel, one diffracts, the
light. Maybe the mirrored panel diffracts and it
would be good for his whole body, and then the
white panel focuses it? and would be good for
his face, but I might have those backwards.... I
know we worked on it, and we said that the
mirror panel would be the best to reflect
directly because it is what you use, but it turned

out to be the opposite. I think the white panel would go straight to his face.

What has to happen for Helen to see John?
There has to be light behind Helen, or even in front of her if she had a flashlight or something, and the light has to bounce off of John and back into Helen's eyes for her to be able to see him.

Let's say it's a sunny day and you have sunglasses on. How do objects appear to you? Darker? Lighter? The same?
Are they black sunglasses? Not like purple ones or anything?... I think generally things would look darker because ... light is just sort of absorbed, and it doesn't penetrate into your eye as well, and so if it doesn't go into your eye, then what you see is darker because you need light to see clearly and to see bright colors.

So light comes to your eye.
The light goes through the sunglasses first, and some of it is absorbed. A lot of it goes through, or you wouldn't be able to see at all. Anyways, a little bit is absorbed by the black, and the rest goes into your eye. So I guess what happens is that a little bit of light doesn't go into your eye, your retina, or whatever.

How far does the light go out?
How far? Depends on how good the candle is. If you can see the candle and not just the flame, I guess it must go at least to you.

What if you can just see the flame and not the candle?
Some must go to you or you wouldn't be able to see it. I mean it depends on the size of the candle. I know in order for you to see it, the light has to reach you, but you could be on the very periphery just far enough that it wouldn't go past you, it wouldn't get to you, but if you can see it pretty clearly, it will probably go past you.

What about if the lights are on. Would it be the same?

I don't see why not if the light's still there just because there is more light. I mean, it doesn't say that there is less light from the candle.

How about if it were outside and you were standing the same distance away?

Well, in the gymnasium was it reaching to the walls? To bounce off the walls? And make more light?... Well, if the light were strong enough, and if you weren't standing too far away from the wall, and it the walls aren't black, then it could reflect the light of the candle off of the wall and it would sort of go all over the place, bouncing off of things, and it would just go all over the place. If it was outside and it wasn't bouncing off of anything, it would just go on. It's hard to say how far it would go.

Science learning

About Mr. K's class, what is the first thing you think about?

Computers. I tried to get used to them, but I didn't have much success. I remember them being really hard. Computers aren't my strong point. I thought it was interesting. I was a bit challenged, and I never felt really comfortable with the computers.

Once you got used to them, do you think they helped you learn?

Yeah. I remember there was something we had to do. It was like the conclusion of it and we had to match up statements, I did that wrong so many times! I remember doing it over and over, and I felt like the computer and I didn't work well together.... It made me frustrated but I think when I eliminated what was wrong, I understood it better.

How about the labs in Mr. K's class. Do you remember those?

I remember the can and that box. It's like a box that is totally sealed, and there's something inside it, and there are little prongs, and you can move around things. It was like the first thing we did in the class.... It was tricky.

Since middle school have you studied heat and temperature again?

Not as much as in Mr. K's class, but we kind of touched upon it in chemistry when we talked about metal substances, and ionic substances and bonds, and that some are conductors and that kind of thing. Not in the same way, though, not as physical as "what do you want to wrap your soda can in?" ... I took biology and physiology, and we didn't talk about it.

What did you like about high school science?

I liked it all. (laughs) I liked my life sciences classes better than chem, a lot better than I liked chemistry. I always have an easier time because it seems more real and chemistry just seems too abstract. I don't like physical science. I like "the lung does this and the heart does this," but not "these little atoms come together because of electronegativity"... (laughs) It's just really not my thing.

So you liked the biology and the physiology?

We didn't do a lot of labs in biology. I don't really remember doing any at all. In physiology we did a lot. Dissections, we did five dissections: brain, heart, fetal pig, liver, enzymes, diffusion lab.

Did the labs help you understand?

Yeah. I liked the ones that are kind of open ended, but guided, and you have to figure things out but there is some guidance. But this is what the diffusion lab was. They said show this somehow, but they should have given us a little more guidance. I mean, I'm kind of cautious, and I don't want to just start mixing chemicals, but we had a couple in chemistry where it was like, "Okay, just do the lab" and I didn't want to do it. I didn't want to make an explosion. But I like trying to figure it out for myself. I don't want to just read about it.

So if you are trying to learn something new for science class, how do you do it?

I like to see it, I like to do labs, and I don't like rote memorization. I think it helps because you need to have the facts ready and clear, not to memorize, but just so you know. I like to have things told to me and then sort of memorize them and make the connections myself. I don't really like to jump into something and have to find. I like to prove rather than find. Like, we did this lab with indicators in physiology. You had all these solutions and indicators and you are supposed to drop it and see what happens but you could do it by research first. So, I'd have much rather researched it first and figured it out and then tried it and it turned out as I'd predicted. You know, find the facts and then prove it for myself.... Rather than just doing it.... I want to know what I am looking for.

Read the right answer in textbooks.

Well, not just that. I mean I would read the right answers in a textbook, but I wouldn't want to just read the textbook and then take a test.... I wouldn't want to just figure it out by myself.... If they just said "here's this big old trig problem, now figure it out and then see how it relates," I'd say forget that!

Did you ever use principles and prototypes in Mr. K's class?

(interviewer shows pictures)

I don't remember.... Oh, wait, yeah! I think they help. Sometimes they make me more confused because they give you an idea [like this one] because you need to know more than what they tell you.

How about details?

They are useful to me. I like to know everything about the experiment even if it is not relevant to the experiment and then figure out by myself what is relevant and what isn't.

Did learning science in Mr. K's class change the way that you thought about learning science before his class?

It was a different way to learn science. I mean, he didn't have much of lectures. It was more of an individual "go at it" kind of thing. It was really different because the teacher before liked to just lecture, lecture, lecture. It was okay, really, 'cause I like to take notes. I mean, there is no way I don't like to learn except when they say, "Here is a book. Read it and learn it."

Career

What do you want to study in college?

I want to major in biology.... Medical school, probably. I didn't want to go premed because I want to have the option if I wanted to become a botanist or something else along the way, I could have a choice. I will probably end up in medical school and everything, but I may end up going in a completely different direction after 4 years of college. I mean, I changed a lot of things after 4 years in high school, and I don't want to study next year what I am going to be doing for the rest of my life.... I'll be in science.

Ummm. I wanted to ask you about the way males and females are treated in your high school classes. Did you ever notice a difference?

No, I never have.... I think there are smart men and smart women and ... I mean, most of my science teachers are male, you could say that.

Do you think that makes a difference?

No. I guess you could think "Oh, only men are science teachers," but there's no reason for it.

They're probably just men that like science. It just sort of happened that way.

What did you think of the activities today?
I thought they were interesting. They were hard but you could figure them out, maybe. I wish I'd understood them more.

Appendix B—Table of Contents From CD-ROM

The Book

- Authors
- Overview
- Acknowledgements
- Features
- Ask Mr. K
- Reviews

Framework

- Accessible science
- Visible science
- Learning from others
- Lifelong learning

Resources

- Curriculum
- Case studies
- Software
- Images
- Assessments
- Annotated Bibliography

Participate

Order

Author Index